PIONEERING SEBASTIAN AND ROSELAND

PIONEERING SEBASTIAN AND ROSELAND

Bringing Alive the Past

ELLEN E. STANLEY

America Through Time®
ADDING COLOR TO AMERICAN HISTORY

America Through Time® is an imprint of Fonthill Media LLC
www.through-time.com
office@through-time.com

Published by Arcadia Publishing by arrangement with Fonthill Media LLC
For all general information, please contact Arcadia Publishing:
Telephone: 843-853-2070
Fax: 843-853-0044
E-mail: sales@arcadiapublishing.com
For customer service and orders:
Toll-Free 1-888-313-2665
Visit us on the internet at www.arcadiapublishing.com

First published 2017
Reprinted 2020

ISBN 978-1-63499-016-5

Typeset in 10.5pt on 13pt Minion Pro
Printed and bound in England

This book is dedicated to Pam Cooper for all of her assistance and advice, and to all of my friends and family that encouraged and supported me.

Ellen E. Stanley

Preface

Every area has a unique history with a story to tell. How did the early history of the Sebastian and Roseland area affect its growth? Why was Florida so far behind in the colonizing race, considering the fact that it was discovered well before the rest of the U.S.? Florida was an English colony at the time of the Revolutionary War; why didn't it join the other thirteen colonies to the north? The Sebastian/Roseland area has always been a beautiful, fertile place; why was it so late in getting settled? An exploration of the national, state, and local influences throughout the area's history provides answers to these questions while presenting a wonderful story for all to enjoy.

Background helps explain what brought firstcomers to Sebastian and Roseland. There were a large number of negatives that took quite a bit of time for settlers to overcome. First and foremost, Florida was a hostile environment for anyone who was not an Ais Indian. Second, individual choice trumped government control. Individuals, not governments or corporations, created the area. The Revolutionary War passed Florida by for the most part because Florida was only a colony of the U.S. for twelve years versus 150 years of settlement for colonies in the north, and it was still in a primitive condition.

Later, the Sebastian/Roseland area experienced late settlement compared to the rest of Florida due to several negative factors: it did not have a fort, and it did not have a port. The area did not even have enough Native Americans to bring in soldiers once it belonged to the U.S., hence few trails were created. Tropical vegetation in the area was practically impenetrable. Animals and insects were vigorously ferocious. The features of the coastline accounted for many shipwrecks and made it dangerous to stop. It was extremely difficult to get people and supplies in an out of the area before steamboats and trains. Until transportation improved, the area had primarily adventurous passers-through: frontiersmen, sportsmen, and explorers, not settlers. Those individuals did spread the word, however. The negatives discouraged developers as well, until transportation improved. Transportation changes figure largely in all explanations. Steamboats, trains, and roads brought civilization; natural abundance formed the basis for successful commerce. Moreover, the over-promoted mystique and the lure of primitive wilderness prompted individuals to keep coming.

Florida has always been different from the other states. It had a patchwork of allegiances as a colony that set it apart. From 1513 to 1718, it was held by Spain; from

1719 to 1721, Pensacola was a French territory; from 1763 to 1821, Florida was a British holding; and finally, in 1821, it became a territory of the United States, and became a state of the United States in 1845. Spain retained possession for 283 years; England for 20 years; France held Pensacola for three years. Florida was a U.S. territory for 24 years.

Similarly, the Sebastian/Roseland area has been under several jurisdictions. Since Spanish occupation, it has been part of the territory of East Florida, St. John's County, Mosquito County, Santa Lucia County, Brevard County, St. Lucie County, and finally, Indian River County. Although now Sebastian and Roseland are confined to the area south of the St. Sebastian River, this was not always the case, and therefore places and people outside of the current boundaries are included in this history.

As well as many jurisdictions, the area has had a confusion of names. The federal census has been rather cavalier in bestowing names. Census takers were not adventuresome enough to find some of the early settlers. In the 1870s census, Brevard County had only Fort Capron Post Office residents enumerated, and the Park and Baird families were not included at all. For the 1880 census, the census takers finally found the Sebastian and Roseland pioneers, in what was named The District East of St. John's River Precincts 4 & 5. By 1900, the post office names of Sebastian and Roseland existed, but were merely Precinct 8 in the 1900 census, ignoring the post offices. In the 1910 census, the area was Election Precinct No. 1. By 1920, the towns were finally acknowledged in the census enumeration as Roseland and Sebastian Precincts.

Newspapers followed the varied local usage of names. The area was Barker's Bluff in reported voting records in 1883. One 1885 newspaper stated that St. Sebastian Bay residents changed the name of their town to Sebastian after it was New Haven, but in 1888 the name was "Sebastian, formerly known as Barker's Bluff." U.S. Post Office names were "New Haven," applied for by Thomas New in 1882-1884, "Sebastian" post office, started by Sylvanus Kitching in 1884, and "Roseland" post office, named by Dempsey Cain in 1892. Likewise, the St. Sebastian River has not been immune to name change, although it kept Sebastian at its core. It has rather fluidly appeared as Sebastian River, Sebastian Creek, Saint Sebastian River, San Sebastian River, or St. Sebastian River, at varying times. The U.S. Board of Geographic Names in Reston, Virginia, officially approved the name "Saint Sebastian River" in 1988. Saint may be spelled out or abbreviated. Indian River was "Rio de Ais". Barker's Bluff vanished when it was torn down to become paving for local roads. No attempt has been made in this work to standardize the names; Sebastian River or St. Sebastian River is the same river.

This preface has been a roundabout explanation for the choice of subject matter, and a clarification of the setting. This work is an attempt to explore the reasons for the growth of the area and provide glimpses into the interesting surroundings, and the circumstances and lives of the people who formed Sebastian and Roseland. Perhaps the following chapters will enlarge your understanding of the wonderful place we call home.

Ellen E. Stanley, 2016

Sebastian the Gem on the River

Where ebbs and flows the lazy tide
Of Indian River in its pride,
Where stately palm trees, tall and rank
O'er shadow all the river's bank
Where glittering sands and waters meet
Beneath the happy children's feet
There on the slope Sebastian lies,
Beneath the balmy southern skies,
Sebastian the Gem on the river.

As long the river's bank we ride
We view its scenes with conscious pride.
Through palms and oaks we catch the gleam
Of Indian River's silvery sheen
Amidst grapefruit and orange trees
Whose fruit sways gently in the breeze.
Sebastian lies there on the slope
The city of great future hope;
Sebastian the Gem on the river.

Composed by A. M. Saunders, reprinted January 7, 1926, *Vero Beach Press*

Acknowledgements

AC: Sketches by Annie Cox, Naples, FL artist

BLM: Courtesy of US Bureau of Land Management Government Land Office. BLM GLO www.glorecords.blm.org.

DPC: Courtesy of Library of Congress, Prints & Photographs Division, Detroit Publishing Company Collection, Reproduction Number:
LC-DIG-det-4a23616, *Off for the Indian River*

EES: Photographs by author

GB: Courtesy of Library of Congress, Prints & Photographs Division, George Barker, photographer. Reproduction Number:
LC-USZ62-97272, *Hammock by Indian River with Lane*

OBH: Ocean Breeze Heights, Indian River County Plat map, courtesy of Archive Center, Indian River County Main Library, Vero Beach, FL

RK: Rodney Kroegel Collection—Courtesy of Brevard County Historical Commission Archives, Central Brevard Library, Melbourne; Archive Center of Indian River County Main Library, Vero Beach; and Sebastian Area Historical Society, Inc., Sebastian, FL

WHJ: Courtesy of Library of Congress, Prints & Photographs Division, Detroit Publishing Company Collection, William Henry Jackson, photographer. Reproduction Numbers:
Palmettos LC-DIG-det-4a03564
Sebastian Creek and Steamboat Cleo, LC-DIG-det-4a03566
Pelican Island, LC-D4-3645
Duck Shooting on the Cleo, LC-D418-7099
S.V. White on the Indian River, LC-D418-7997

Contents

1

Land of the Ais: 1400s-1600s

Long before Sebastian or Roseland had a name, the area had defining features that set it apart from the rest of the Florida east coast. This locale in the very early days was far different than its current appearance. Some but not all of the major landmarks still remain, but other significant ones have been added. All wildlife, including mosquitoes, has much diminished, and much of the landscape has been dried out and tamed. The land was home to Native Americans, the Ais Indians—not the Seminoles, as they came much later. Then the Spanish came to north Florida, and came to visit the Sebastian-Roseland area for fishing, as have sportsmen and commercial fishermen ever since. However, it took a very long time for anyone other than Native Americans to settle in the area.

Sebastian and Roseland are found below Cape Canaveral, Grant, and Micco, bordered on the east by the Indian River, and on the north and west, roughly defined by the St. Sebastian River. Roseland is tucked into that topmost part of the St. Sebastian River. Sebastian's southern boundary ends below Pelican Island approximately where the Narrows of the Indian River begin, a little north of Wabasso. In early times, the most notable landmark of this area was the St. Sebastian River in the north part of Sebastian with its high banks at the inlet and freshwater spring. A mile further to the south was the remnant of a prehistoric river bed that still had fresh water oozing out of the sand at low tide. A high ridge runs parallel to the Indian River, the Atlantic Coastal Ridge, a relic barrier island from ancient times, and there were marshes, hammocks, pinelands, some Native American footpaths, and dense undergrowth throughout the area.

A mammoth Ais Indian shell mound known later as Barker's Bluff formerly overlooked the western shore of the Indian River in the southern part of Sebastian, opposite Pelican Island, just north of the Narrows, where the Indian River broadened. Covering approximately a quarter-acre of land, Barker's Bluff was one of the most visible landmarks of the area until the 1900s, when it was removed to pave roads.

The Indian River is a shallow brackish body of water along the eastern coastline, fed both by inland rivers and inlets to the ocean. The Indian River is actually a lagoon, with many shifting inlets from the ocean. It is separated from the Atlantic Ocean by several barrier islands and is the most extensive barrier island/tidal inlet system in the country. Originally called the River Ays, after the first inhabitants of the area, the Ais tribe, the name was later changed to the Indian River. The river flows approximately 156 miles and is up to five miles wide.

There have been several inlets to the ocean along the Indian River over time. Sebastian

Inlet has only been open in modern times and in very early antiquity. Fort Pierce, Indian, Indian River, Gilbert's Bar, St. Lucie, Jupiter, and Hillaboro/Hillsborough Inlets are all names that have appeared on maps or been mentioned in reports over the years. None of them were permanent. Water pressure from the rivers flowing into the Indian River and storms and hurricanes have caused the opening and closing of inlets over the years. The inlet opposite St. Lucie Village might be the only one that was consistently open through the years, although it closed permanently in 1911. This impermanence of the inlets has caused much confusion in the placement and descriptions of the east coast of Florida in its early years.

This unique setting produced an explosion of flora and fauna unimaginable today. It is much diminished today, but the many descriptions in the following pages render some notion of what used to be—a rich, dangerous, varied canopy of life.

Native Americans

Florida was inhabited by many tribes of Native Americans that arrived 10,000 to 20,000 years ago, part of the great migration from Northeastern Asia. Several major groups were at home in Florida, with many subgroups. The major groups were the Timucuans, Tocobaga, Calusa, the Apalachee, the Tequesta, the Ais, and the Jeaga. They were primarily hunter-gatherers, some of whom also practiced agriculture. Due to the many shipwrecks on the East Coast, they also became rather sophisticated in the art of salvaging from the wrecks and incorporating their finds into their everyday lives, making jewelry from iron, silver, gold, and copper.

The present-day Sebastian and Roseland area was home to the Ais. Their main village may have been in the Fort Pierce area, although there was archeological discussion that might place it as far north as Vero Beach or Sebastian. The Ais left behind shell middens, mounds containing large numbers of oyster shells and village refuse. The most noted of these in the Sebastian area was the mound later known as Barker's Bluff. Middens have been found all through the area.

By 1500, the various tribes occupied the entire Florida peninsula and Florida Keys and had reached an estimated population of 100,000. The human population of Florida would not be this great again for another 300 years. With the advent of Europeans, this population dwindled. European diseases of bubonic plague, chicken pox, dysentery, diphtheria, influenza, malaria, measles, scarlet fever, smallpox, typhoid, typhus, and yellow fever decimated the native population in the northern missions and the rest of the state in the epidemics of 1595, 1612-1617, 1649-1650, and 1655-1656. Wars and slavery aided their demise. In 1704, when Ais leaders visited Havana, they brought home disease that added to the deaths. By 1743, the remnants of the natives left were around Biscayne Bay, weakened by disease and alcoholism. They were effectively gone by 1777.

1492

Pastoral, primitive Florida was forever changed with the intrusion of world events in 1492, and forever after would continue to be altered by happenings of events on a greater stage, at world, country, state, and county levels. Looking for the Far East in 1492, a new continent was found. The desire for new trade routes and Christopher Columbus' discovery of the New World was the commencement of Europe's interest in the Americas. In 1497 and 1498, John and Sebastian Cabot explored as far south as Cuba along the eastern coastal area of America.

1500s

The 1500s in Florida's history was marked by little more than its discovery. Europe eyed this newly located land for possible profit. Florida got a slow start in the European race to colonize and exploit the Americas. It was a difficult land in which to survive. Treacherous coastline, hurricanes, savage natives, hostile environment, and little of obvious value all slowed the momentum. There were many failures.

Maps including Florida were created in 1502, 1508, and 1511. Ponce de 's discovery of Florida on Easter Day (Pascua Florida) in 1513 is the accepted first discovery, as it was officially sanctioned and recognized by Spain. De León had received a royal contract to sail northwards through the Bahamas to search for a large island rumored to be in that direction, and found Florida. He first sighted the Florida coast near Mosquito Inlet at the southeast end of Timucan territory. He then sailed southwards past the land of the Ais, where native huts were sighted, perhaps fishing camps or small villages. Men were sent ashore and two Spaniards were wounded by fishbone-tipped arrows. One Native American was kidnapped and taken for a guide. Ponce De León continued south, mapping and naming places. The Rio de Canoas (River of Canoes) was marked, probably either the Indian River or Mosquito Lagoon. His map may be the earliest details of Florida. He named the state La Florida for the holiday, and for the flowers observed there.

More voyages followed by Columbus, Ponce de León , and others to Honduras, Mexico, and most of the West Indies. Towns sprang up on Hispanola, Jamaica and Cuba, and Puerto Rico. Soon Spain began exploiting the wealth of its new possessions; individuals were mining, trading in slaves, and growing many commodities such as grain, sugar cane, and cotton. Fortunes were being made. More expeditions included Florida in their discoveries. In the 1500s, both France and England became interested in the wealth pouring out of the New World.

In 1521, Ponce de León led a failed expedition to plant a colony, probably at Charlotte Harbor. Pánfilo de Narváez received a patent in 1526 to settle Florida. He left Spain with 600 colonists and soldiers. This attempt failed due to desertions, ship wrecks, and poor planning. Hernando de Soto made an expedition in 1538 with 550 armed men and

200 horses into the interior to Apalachee and Pensacola Bay in Florida, and continued on to Arkansas, Missouri, Kansas, and Oklahoma. They successfully made the return to Spain, but with severe losses. Three major expeditions failed, in a large part due to Native American hostilities. In 1558, Tristán de Luna y Arellano was chosen to lead an expedition of 1,500 individuals to Florida to plant a colony. He failed, as did his successor Ángel de Villafañe , at Pensacola.

France attempted and failed to start two settlements in Florida. One venture to plant a colony in Florida was headed by Jean Ribault with three French ships and 150 individuals that arrived at the St. Johns River in 1562. This effort to establish Charles Fort met with many disasters, causing it to fail. In 1563, the French erected Fort Caroline.

At that point, Spain stepped in and sent Pedro Menéndez de Avilés to destroy Fort Caroline and drive out the French. He was tasked to found a settlement in La Florida and Christianize the local natives. He sailed with nineteen ships and 1,504 colonists, soldiers, and sailors, some of which were lost at sea. Menendez founded St. Augustine in 1565, so named for the festival of San Augustine, establishing a mission to convert the Indians.

In the fall of 1565, Pedro Menéndez proceeded south from St. Augustine and destroyed the French fort at Cape Canaveral, taking prisoners. He then headed south 20 leagues, marching on the west side of the Indian River, also named Rio de Ais/Ays, Rio Indrio de Ais, or Ais River. He arrived south of the St. Sebastian River in November 1565, perhaps at an Ais village named Pentoya, and met with Ais leaders. Menéndez planned to set up a small fort near the Ais where he could garrison his men while he went to Havana for more supplies and to receive ransom for the French prisoners from Canaveral. He negotiated a treaty with the Ais and constructed a fort. There are varying opinions as to the placement of this fort. One source places it at Sebastian, and another in the vicinity of the Narrows, north of Vero Beach.

Captain Juan Velez de Medrano was placed in charge with fifteen days' supplies, and Menéndez sailed on to Havana with his prisoners from Canaveral. The fort ran low on supplies, and repeated native attacks made foraging for food impossible. One hundred of the 150 men at the fort mutinied and began marching south to the St. Lucie Inlet. Velez went after the men and convinced them to go with him, heading out for Havana. On the way, they intercepted the ship bringing their supplies and the company continued south. Menendez erected block houses all along the south Florida coast from 1566-1567. Most of these block houses lasted only until the spring of 1568, destroyed by native attacks.

Twenty years later, by 1585, St. Augustine had a population of 300. Native hostilities doomed other attempts at settlement. In 1586, an English expedition of 23 ships and 2,000 men, led by Sir Francis Drake, happened upon St. Augustine and completely destroyed it before continuing on. In 1598, the population of St. Augustine was 225 soldiers and 400 others.

1600s

In the 1600s, the only real foothold in Florida's development was by the Spanish in St. Augustine and across the Panhandle. St. Augustine was rebuilt, but it was clearly little more than a military outpost and center for missionaries. Reported populations in 1602 were 56 slaves, 57 married men, and 107 children. By 1674, Franciscan missions had spread across the Florida panhandle, to convert, civilize, and exploit the native population. There were 52 missionaries by 1680. The native population largely refused to become Christian and remained hostile. Below the panhandle, Florida, including the Indian River area, was mostly ignored by all, except for fishing expeditions once or twice each year. The St. Sebastian River undoubtedly received its name from the Spanish. Concluding that there was no gold and little else of worth in La Florida, Spain concentrated on exploiting its other possessions. By contrast, the thirteen English colonies to the north of La Florida were experiencing settlement in the 1630s all along the eastern coast.

Jonathan Dickinson

The most extensive and earliest English first-hand account of the Indian River area of Florida was provided by Jonathan Dickinson. Dickinson was an English Quaker, born in Jamaica in 1663. He and his family and some others left Jamaica August 23, 1696, on a commercial venture to Philadelphia on the *Reformation*, to open a branch of the family mercantile business there. The ship had 25 passengers and crew, and a cargo worth £1500. The *Reformation* was part of a convoy of twelve or thirteen ships out of Jamaica. On September 24, 1696, Dickinson and his group were shipwrecked in a storm on Hobe Sound Beach on Jupiter Island off the eastern coast of Florida. Two other ships of that convoy also wrecked. The *Burrough* or *Smith* foundered north of Jupiter Inlet on September 23, and the *Nantwitch* went down south of Indian River Inlet near Fort Pierce.

The *Reformation* shipwrecked group with Jonathan Dickinson made their way northwards along the coast of Spanish Florida, seeking to reach St. Augustine. They started out with some items from the shipwreck. They endured hostility, physical abuse, and theft of all possessions from the native tribes they encountered, which nonetheless allowed them to continue their trek north, partly on shore, and partly by boat. Five of the group died from the exposure and starvation they suffered. These people were not equipped to live off of their surroundings, and received very little food or support on their journey. They spent some time in Jece, the Ais town, which was thought to be in the Vero Beach area. With the help of Spanish soldiers, the castaways left Jece on November 3 and traveled north by boat on the Indian River. They met up with some others from one of the other wrecks on their way, and ended their journey to St. Augustine on November 15, 1696. They finally arrived in Philadelphia on April 1, 1697.

Jonathan Dickinson kept a diary which preserved the details of this journey northward up the coast; the diary described the unfolding events and native tribes encountered. This tale of suffering and heroism of the survivors excited great interest, and it was seen as an instance of divine intervention. His diary was published, and went into sixteen printings in England and America, along with three printings each in German and Dutch. This was only one of hundreds of wrecks off the east Florida coast over the centuries, but it is probably the one most famously documented by a survivor.

Waning Spanish Influence

While the thirteen English colonies to the north were growing and prospering, gaining new colonists, the Spanish suffered a continually diminishing sphere of influence in Florida until only St. Augustine, the garrison at St. Marks, and Pensacola remained, along with Native Americans, and English and French traders. Florida remained in Spanish hands with minimal settlement until 1763, when it became a British territory.

2

Florida—Spain and England's Bargaining Chip: 1700s

The 1700s was a time of tremendous growth, change, and upheaval throughout the century in the Americas. Some activity and attention filtered down to the Indian River and St. Sebastian River in this century. There were explorations, naval battles, and shipwrecks, but no settlers yet. On a global scale, scientific advancement in the 1700s was providing more knowledgeable and therefore safer and faster ocean travel, with such disparate subjects as longitude and the Gulf Stream bringing America closer to Europe.

Florida underwent massive change. Ownership of this land vacillated from Spain to England, and then back to Spain once more. Spain left little impact on the lower part of the state. France held Pensacola for three years. Once England added Florida to its colonies, however, England had tremendous interest in its value. Expeditions were sent out to explore. When the thirteen northern colonies broke away from England there were repercussions in Florida, bringing wartime activities to the Indian River.

In the 1760s, the discovery of longitudes greatly affected mapping and sailing, making it no longer necessary to sail by latitude alone—that is, direct east-west sailing. The lunar distance method to calculate longitude was initially labor intensive and prone to error because of the time-consuming complexity of the calculations for the Moon's position. However, in 1767, the Nautical Almanac was first published, providing tables of pre-calculated distances of the Moon from various celestial objects at three-hour intervals for every day of the year, making the process much less complex. Lunar calculations were widely used for navigation at sea from 1767 to about 1850.

Another boon to sea travel began in 1512 when Juan Ponce de León discovered the Gulf Stream, the warm, rapid current of water that flows northward from the southern tip of Florida up the coast of North America, turning east at Newfoundland and heading across the Atlantic. In an endeavor to explain the differential sailing time between America to England versus England to America, Benjamin Franklin began the mapping of the Gulf Stream, working with various ships' captains. He measured temperature, speed, and direction, producing a map of the Stream in 1770. Eventually, this information was put to use in trans-Atlantic and coastal sailing.

Early 1700s, Spanish Florida

The early 1700s saw raids on Spanish Florida by the English, and many of the natives went over to the English, lured by better trade relations. The Spanish never had a strong hold on the native population. Pirate raids further destabilized the situation. In 1702, Governor James Moore of Carolina attempted to take St. Augustine. He succeeded in destroying much of it, but was unable to destroy the great stone fort, Castillo de San Marcos. Moore returned in 1704 to destroy more of the string of missions which was part of the Spanish defense system, taking prisoners. By 1708, all of the missions outside of St. Augustine had been destroyed. Hostilities continued in Florida, and Spain could not hold its frontier posts. The 1763 Spanish census reported populations of 3,046 in St. Augustine and 800 in Pensacola.

Spanish Plate Fleet, 1715

In 1715, treasure came to the East Coast of Florida and was left behind, forming a lure to gold seekers for the next 300 years. A fleet of eleven Spanish galleons and a hired Dutch ship heavily laden with treasure foundered, driven on the reefs and shoals of the Atlantic Ocean from the Sebastian area southward to Fort Pierce along the coast, due to strong northeast winds from a hurricane. These ships carried specie and plate, and the gold, silver, platinum, pearls, and jewels accumulated from the New World. One ship in the flotilla, *El Grifon,* escaped. There were hundreds of survivors who made it to shore on the morning of July 31, 1715. A campsite for the survivors and a base camp for salvagers were set up on the barrier island across from the St. Sebastian River Inlet. Some survivors marched north to St. Augustine to report the disaster, and rescue parties and supplies were sent. Pirate Henry Jennings attempted take the gold from the Spanish as they worked to salvage it from the wrecks in a running gun battle. Beachcombers over the centuries have been finding bits of the wreckage and treasure on the beaches after stormy weather. Many divers have searched and found sunken treasure, hence the well-earned name, "Treasure Coast." The McLarty Museum that opened in 1970 near the site houses historical exhibits. It was built by the state on land donated by Robert P. McLarty.

The War of the Quadruple Alliance 1719-1721

Austria, Holland, France, and England warred against Spain in the War of the Quadruple Alliance from 1719 to 1721. In Florida, the desirable Pensacola area became a target of France. Jean-Baptiste Le Moyne, Sieur de Bienville, organized an expedition and captured Pensacola. The Spanish recaptured it. Pensacola was retaken by the French and the Fort San Carlos was destroyed. Peace was declared in 1720, but the fate of Pensacola was not decided until March 27, 1921, when a treaty formally returned Pensacola to Spain.

Florida English Territory 1763-1784

The Seven Years' War ended in the Treaty of Paris of 1763, bringing a close to years of hostility between Spain and England. In the treaty, France ceded Canada to England, and ceded Louisiana to Spain. Spain gave Florida to the English, and the English returned Havana to Spain. At that time, the few remaining natives on the Atlantic coast left with the Spaniards for Cuba. Florida was almost completely unpopulated when that occurred. On October 7, 1763, the British reorganized the possession into East Florida and West Florida. West Florida ran from the Apalachicola River to the Mississippi River; the rest was East Florida. England began investigating what it had obtained. Agriculture was encouraged by bounties, especially on the cultivation of indigo and sugar cane and in production of the naval stores, such as rosin, tar, and turpentine. Veterans of the Seven Years' War were given Florida land grants in 1763, but not many were accepted or settled. Instead, this sparked the interest of land speculators and promoters such as those of the East Florida Society in London, which exerted a strong influence on the course of Florida history from 1764 through 1770. Instead of undertaking serious colonization, these land barons held land grants for speculation instead of settlement. However, during the 20 years of British rule, more improvements were noted than in the 250 years of previous Spanish rule. Prosperity was lost when it went back under Spanish rule.

In contrast, by 1763 in the northern American colonies, the population was expanding, economies were prospering, and trade was flourishing. Cities were growing, manufacturing was increasing, and the whole of the eastern seaboard was becoming more civilized. Events caused the colonists to become restless under British rule, and they looked toward western expansion. Colonial relations with England were worsening, slowly edging towards revolution.

Seminole Indians

Another change for Florida arose when the flood of white settlers advanced south along the Carolina frontier into Georgia, causing several of the southeastern Indian tribes to begin moving into Florida. Concurrently, Lower Creek Indians in Georgia and Alabama desired independence from the Upper Creeks, also spurring Indian migration into Florida. Yuchi and Yamassee Indians also became part of the exodus to Florida. By the 1760s, the Florida Indians began to separate from the tribes in the land to the north, taking on a new identity and way of life suited to the vastly different Florida surroundings, and they became known as Seminoles. The word Seminole is thought to be a corruption of the Spanish word cimarron meaning "wild people" or "runaway," or the Muskogee word sim-in-oli which means "runaway" or "wild." Runaway slaves who escaped to Florida seeking freedom were given refuge by the Seminoles.

The first Creeks settled at Chocuchattee (Red House) near present-day Brooksville, Florida, around 1760. They were cattlemen. By 1763, the Alachua and Oconee Indians were relocated in central Florida in the area of Gainesville and Payne's Prairie, and became part of the Seminole Indian identity. Relations with the Indians were poor, with the exception of the trading policies of companies such as the Panton Leslie Company. The native east coast tribes had dwindled. Of the ones who remained, some succumbed to raids by the Yuchi and Creek Indians from northern Florida and Georgia and others were killed by Spaniards or died from disease. The Seminole population in Florida at this time was small, perhaps only 1,200. The Sebastian and Roseland area was entirely unpopulated, except for occasional fishing boats. It was the turn of the century before the first Seminoles began appearing there.

Promoters and Explorers

Promoters, such as Dr. William Stork in 1766, flooded England and Europe with pamphlets extolling the virtues of Florida's rich soil and mild climate. This brought immigrants from the British Isles and colonies, and from Greece, Italy, and Minorca, primarily to the St. Augustine area, and to New Smyrna. Indigo, a crop that was grown successfully in South Carolina, had been recommended to be grown in East Florida. It was in demand not only as a dye, but also for its medicinal properties. It was used as an emetic, cathartic, and sub-astringent antiseptic, as well as for scarlet fever, typhus fever, and in cases of mortification and gangrene. It could be used both topically and internally. Some varieties of indigo were grown from Georgia to North Carolina. Although it successfully cultivated much sought after indigo of superior quality and profitability, the New Smyrna colony did not survive due to the harsh conditions there. It was abandoned in 1777, with survivors relocating to St. Augustine.

England began to examine its new possession. It needed accurate maps of its regions and its boundary lines. Indian populations needed to be charted. Botanists and biologists searched the territory's flora and fauna for commercial possibilities of new medicinal and agricultural plants, new species of animals, and new sources for needed and desired commodities.

Advertisements appeared in London's *Gazette* and other newspapers and magazines promoting Florida. In 1762, the king's geographer, Thomas Jefferys, published a promotional book of Florida, but it contained little data, a few of his maps, and was mostly inaccurate.

William Roberts

William Roberts' 1763 *Account of the First Discovery and Natural History of Florida* was the most reliable source of information then available on the recently acquired province of Florida at the time it was printed. Roberts never visited Florida; he was a professional writer who depended on the works of others. His work was a compilation of all the known facts and information available in England after the Seven Years' War. Florida was an empty land about which little was known. Roberts' book was the first with accurate information.

However, he was also a propagandist and presented Florida as a land with a climate that was "pure and wholesome" with soil "rich and fruitful." Roberts described twelve European settlements, and 27 Indian settlements. He did note that the coast was flat, sandy, full of shoals, and difficult to navigate because of trade winds, shallow winding channels, and sea currents. He praised the fine bays, harbors, inlets, and wide shallow rivers. The Indian River area was mentioned in his account as the Rio de Ays three leagues north of Rio Santa Cruz, and he noted the five fathoms of water at the entrance leading into a fine harbor. The Florida map by T. Jefferys, Geographer to His Majesty, in Roberts' work includes the Rio de Ays. Some opposing views were presented as well. In his introduction, he stated that map maker John Mitchell denounced East Florida as being a land of "pestiferous sea coasts, swamps and sunken lagunes."

When the Spanish left, they left little behind except immovable property and real estate. They took everything else with them. All that was left was unfriendly Indians, and the residential, municipal, and military buildings, along with the uncultivated and unpopulated land of the peninsula. It had virtually no population, except for Indians. Land grants were offered, promoting the cultivation of grapes, silk, cotton, cochineal, and indigo. Promotional ads were placed in *Scots Magazine* and *Gentleman's Magazine* in 1763 by the British government. Denys Rolle was an enthusiastic supporter who wrote articles in *Gentleman's Magazine* and others.

William De Brahm

William De Brahm was commissioned in 1764 by the king and appointed Surveyor for the Southern District of North America, ordered to make General Surveys of this newly acquired territory. He began the general surveys in 1772. He provided a wealth of information about the state, including detailed tide information and the latitude and longitude of many rivers, shifting inlets, and other features. He compiled a list of the inhabitants of Florida by name and occupation. His census stated that there were 188 men, women, and children, 1,400 indentured servants, and 900 Negroes. The tenth inlet south of Cape Canaveral was called Hillsborough, alias Indian, alias Ays Inlet. That inlet was at that time frequented by Spanish fishing schooners bound for Cuba. The Ays Stream was considered famous for mullet and bass. The men would fish from boats, leaving their schooner in the harbor. He created many maps for his surveys, but none included details of the future Sebastian/Roseland area.

Bernard Romans

Bernard Romans, well known as a surveyor, cartographer, botanist, and navigator, was one of the individuals sent to Florida to explore and report. At a young age, he emigrated from the Netherlands to the United Kingdom, and obtained education in engineering. He immigrated to America around 1757 during the Seven Years' War and entered the King's service in 1761. He was a surveyor and was appointed Deputy Surveyor of Georgia in 1766. He was promoted to Deputy Surveyor for the Southern District. From 1769 through 1775, Bernard Romans traveled extensively through East and West Florida as a surveyor and cartographer.

The results of his travels were published in his book in 1775, *A Concise Natural History of East and West Florida,* with the intent to encourage other residents in the British colonies to relocate to Florida. The book also contained detailed sailing instructions and charts intended as an aid for navigators and shippers. After the book was published, Romans left Florida and fought in the Revolutionary War.

In the schooner *Betsy*, he performed East Florida coastal surveys in 1769. The settlement of Captain Rogers at Cape Canaveral was the most southerly settlement that he found. He traveled through the Indian River area, including future Sebastian/Roseland. He wrote that the water commonly called the Indian River was known as Southhillsborough by De Braham, Aisa Hatcha (Deer River) or Hysweelake by the Indians, and Reo d'Ais by the Spaniards. The only important river in its northern area was the St. Sebastian, according to Romans. A discovery directly opposite the mouth of the St. Sebastian in the Atlantic was the site of some of the wreck of the Spanish Plate Fleet of 1715. Surveyors in his crew found coins washed up in the surf after stormy weather. His writings advised ships to avoid Cape Canaveral and the shoals of the curve of the land north of Rio d'Ais; the coast north of the Rio d'Ais inlet to the sea was flat, treacherous, and remarkable due to the Palmar de Ais, or Palm Grove of the Ais.

Spanish fishermen from Havana regularly visited the coast and the Rio d'Ais to fish one or two times a year, mainly for bass. Their huts could be found on the coast. Romans wrote that the Rio d'Ais abounded with so much fish in various kinds that it was possible to sit on the bank and stick the fish with a knife or sharp stick as they swam by. Of the future Vero Beach area, he reported that the area at the beginning of the tropics had a salubrious climate, fertile soil, and many opportunities for settlers. There were no hard freezes to destroy southern crops, nor was it too hot to grow northern produce. However, he did believe the area was excessively hot in July through September. Florida was the healthiest spot on the continent, in his view.

An interesting inclusion in the book was a description of the dress of Floridians. They were clad very plainly with a slight waistcoat and trousers of striped cotton, often without a coat. If there was a coat it was short and of light material. In winter, a coat was made of a blanket, worn with Indian boots. Women's dress was light and not very expensive. He had much advice for potential colonists, including what to bring with them and what to expect. One section specified a long list of ailments common to Florida, with remedies. The chronic illnesses listed were dropsies, consumptions, hemorrhoidal and habitual fluxes, relaxed and bilious habits of body, ruptures, worm fevers, leprosy, elephantiasis, and body yaws. In his navigational instructions, he observed that between Cape Canaveral and the Indian River inlet to the south, the coast was flat and not to be trusted.

Dr. Herbert Kale

According to Dr. Herbert Kale in 1976, ornithologist of the Florida Audubon Society, rats, house sparrows, mocking birds, and cardinals were unknown in the Indian River area in 1776, and arrived with the settlers. Otters and birds were much more plentiful then, due to the marshy nature of the land at the time.

William Bartram

William Bartram also wrote of his trips through Florida, taken first with his father John Bartram, Royal botanist to King George in 1765, and again in 1774. This noted ornithologist embarked upon a four-year journey through eight southern colonies. Bartram collected specimens and made many drawings and took notes on the native flora and fauna and the Native American Indians. He was a naturalist, known for the quality of his drawings of birds and plants, many of which appeared in his popular book *Travels*, first published in 1791. It has been published many times since then. His travels are documented with historical trail markers in many states. There is controversy and disagreement as to whether he actually was in Sebastian. However, on May 28, 1985, a William Bartram Trail marker was dedicated by the Pelican Island Garden Club. It stands in Riverview Park, Sebastian.

James Adair

James Adair was not impressed with Florida. He wrote of Florida in the 1700s in his *History of American Indians*. He did consider East Florida more situated for trade than West Florida. East and West Florida were considerably superior to the West Indies, but he stated that Florida was a large peninsula consisting of sandy barrens, level foreground consisting of tussocks and mixed land, and a number of low swamps with very unwholesome water and noxious vapors, a "dreary place." Inhabitants anywhere outside the sea air would be liable to fevers and agues.

Revolutionary War

British Florida did not have the same background or experiences as the thirteen British colonies to the north. It was in a more primitive and undeveloped condition. There were no difficulties over taxes, little trade, and it had a small population. As the thirteen American colonies to the north of Florida began undergoing the throes of the American Revolution, the loyalist British colonies of East Florida, West Florida, Bermuda, Jamaica, Nova Scotia, and St. Johns (Prince Edward Island) did not join with those thirteen colonies in their break from England. Florida became a center for Loyalists. The pro-British Florida colonists enjoyed a war-time boom, supplying the British armies and ships.

Dr. Wilbur H. Siebert's paper, *East Florida as a Refuge of Southern Loyalists 1774-1785,* presented before the American Antiquarian Society, provided an insight into East Florida at the time of the Revolutionary War. By autumn of 1775, ships from New England, Virginia, and South Carolina traveled to the Loyalist colonies to seize munitions, and the South Carolina ship *Commerce* seized the British *Betsy* carrying ordnance to the East Florida garrison at Fort St. Mark, bringing it to General Washington. In late 1775, because of the unsettled conditions in New England, migration into Florida virtually halted. By 1776, Britain took measures to defend East Florida, organizing troops, including those known as the East Florida Rangers. St. Augustine and Pensacola became centers for increased trade with the Indians of the southern colonies, supplanting Augusta, Georgia, and Charleston, South Carolina. As a consequence, Florida's population centered in Pensacola and St. Augustine. From July 1776 to September 1778, three campaigns against East Florida were undertaken from Georgia, and more skirmishes in East Florida followed during the war.

In 1777-1778, Georgia, North Carolina, and South Carolina issued acts against Loyalists forcing them out of the colonies or imprisoning them, confiscating their estates. By royal order, Florida accepted Loyalists fleeing the northern colonies. Those individuals were to be given free land grants in East Florida. Seventeen seventy-eight saw a flood of individuals fleeing the war into East Florida, nearly 7,000 from Georgia and Carolina, including 350 South Carolinians going into St. Augustine in April 1778. Seven hundred or 1,500 more were expected at that time. In 1782, about 4,000 troops and Loyalists were transported out of Savannah and brought to East Florida, and more thousands kept coming. Seventeen thousand, three hundred seventy-five is one total given of those arriving, added to the resident population of around 5,000. Some of the newcomers erected crude huts around St. Augustine, and others spread out into the surrounding countryside and St. Johns River area.

In the period around the Revolutionary War, as a contrast to this activity, the Indian River area had the least population of any time in its history, according to historian Gene Lyon of Vero Beach. The Ais had vanished, there were no Spanish, and the British had not yet settled there, nor had the Seminoles.

Florida Spanish Territory 1784-1821

Florida again became a Spanish Territory from 1784 to 1821. Eventually, due to the Spanish capture of the Bahamas and the Spanish victory at Pensacola, the English returned East Florida and West Florida to Spain with the Treaty of Paris in 1783. Nine thousand, nine hundred thirty-eight English evacuated Florida, and the last shiploads departed in 1785. Their destinations were varied: England, Nova Scotia, the Bahamas, Jamaica, Dominica, West Indies, or elsewhere. Some departed into western North America. Some few remained with the Spaniards.

However, the Spanish influence was weaker than it had been prior to 20 years of English occupation. Companies such as Panton Leslie were allowed to continue to trade in Spanish Florida. Not all American colonists and Loyalists left Florida. Many had created homes. Those settlers remaining in Florida were confident that Florida would eventually become part of the United States. Revolution and disorder in other Spanish possessions divided Spain's attention.

Vincente Manuel de Zespedes became the governor of East Florida. He had hoped to restrict the residents of East Florida to Spaniards and Catholics, but this proved to be unrealistic. Moreover, Spanish authorities were unable to control the flow of new immigrants from the north. Foreign settlers began to be allowed in Florida, including Americans, in 1790. Hundreds of parcels of land were granted to Americans between 1790 and 1804 in exchange for a modified oath of allegiance to Spain. Soon the population between the St. Marys and St. Johns Rivers was primarily American. More and more of East Florida trade was with Americans. In 1795, with the Treaty of San Lorenzo, the northern boundary was reduced to the 31st parallel. In 1800, the Louisiana Territory was transferred to France. When the United States purchased Louisiana in 1803, Spain realized it was not able to retain its hold on Florida.

3

Florida in Turmoil and War, Fleming Grant: 1800s-1830s

In the early 1800s, Florida was again in a state of flux. After a failed attempt to break from Spain, it passed again from Spain to England, and then to the United States. An outside event, however, was to have strong repercussions in civilizing Florida: the invention of the steamboat. The War of 1812 was followed by the First Seminole War, and the nation's first depression occurred. However, Sebastian/Roseland received a printed description of the area in the topographical reports and achieved its first landowner, if not its first settler, George Fleming. Its population remained at zero.

Robert Fulton first installed a steam engine in *North River Steamboat* to drive paddlewheels in 1807, and travel was never the same again. Steamboats were not dependent on tides or winds, and could travel any waterway. They had large capacity for both cargo and passengers. This was a forerunner of a major change for Florida.

Spain Was Losing Florida

In the early 1800s, Spain's hold on Florida had weakened, and much had changed in the 20 years of English rule. Spanish authorities attempted to close the border in 1804 to encroachments from northern settlers, but this was ineffective. In 1812, there was an unsuccessful attempt to separate East Florida from Spanish rule. The inhabitants staged a revolution and declared the area an independent state, which failed. Spain, however, was losing control of Florida.

War of 1812

During the War of 1812, General Andrew Jackson fought the Alabama Creek Indians. The surviving Creeks fled to Florida, joining the Mikasukis around Tallahassee. Many skirmishes followed. The last major movement of Indians into Florida came after the Creek War in Alabama Territory in 1813-1814, which started as a war between the Upper and Lower Creeks. Some white settlers at Fort Mims were killed, causing General Jackson to retaliate, crushing the Red Stick faction of the Upper Creeks who had led the fighting. Some 1,000 Red Stick Upper Creeks migrated into Florida at that time.

In 1816, Jose Coppinger became the Governor of East Florida. He made several large land grants that had previously been contrary to Spanish law, and other grants were made on the eve of ceding Florida to the United States, including that to George Fleming. It became clear that Spain could not effectively govern and utilize Florida. However, Spain held the Florida territories until 1821.

George Fleming and the Fleming Grant

Irish-born George Fleming came to Florida sometime in the late 1700s. He worked for a mercantile company in Charleston that sent him to St. Augustine to handle their affairs. He married Dona Sophia Fatio, the daughter of an influential Swiss businessman, Don Francisco Fatio, in 1791, and settled at "Hibernia," his large estate on the west bank of the St. Johns River. He attained the rank of Captain in the Royal Spanish Colonial Army.

A grant of land was awarded to George Fleming August 8, 1816, for distinguished and extraordinary services rendered, both personally and in a pecuniary manner, in the defense of the province of East Florida. The grant was made by Governor Kindelin and approved by the King of Spain. The Royal Title was issued by Governor Coppinger. It was the first land in the Sebastian and Roseland area to be owned by an individual. He was originally awarded 980 acres, but it was increased 20,000 acres after the governor was apprised by Fleming of his rank and services to the crown.

George Fleming petitioned for a survey of his land grant in the area of Sebastian. This survey was certified February 3, 1820, which was less than a year before the state of Florida was ceded to the United States. The survey reduced the red tape involved in receiving confirmation of the grant. However, the validity of the grant was questioned by the United States, and it went to court. On May 15, 1832, the Superior court of East Florida decreed that the grant was valid. However, George Fleming had died by that date, causing further complications for his heirs, his wife Sophia, and their children. Sophia Fleming and his children sold the land in 1837 to Charles Downing. The survey and plat of the grant were approved and certified on March 1, 1845. Sophia died in 1849. It was not until the legalities were untangled that Fleming's heirs were able to sell the land. The Second Seminole War complicated settlement even further. The Flemings never lived on this land or cultivated it. However, this was the first official ownership of land in Sebastian. Echoes of this land grant followed for nearly 100 years. Title complications followed ownership through the years until put to rest by President Hoover in the 1930s.

War of 1812 Aftermath

In the post-war climate of the War of 1812, many natural history societies sprang up that encouraged scientific study of the flora and fauna of the west. Florida became caught up in this enthusiasm, even prior to becoming a U.S. possession. One like-minded group of scientists, headed by geologist William McClure of Philadelphia, spent the winter of 1817 exploring north Florida and traveling south on the St. Johns River, shooting and procuring specimens. This was apparently achieved without running afoul of either soldiers or Seminoles.

First Seminole War, 1817-1818

All of the 1812-1814 turmoil was the basis for the First Seminole War, waged 1817-1818 by General Jackson. The war was a highly irregular military intrusion by Americans into another country's territory, Spanish-held Florida. He and his troops harried Indians and captured and executed two Spanish citizens, but this incursion did little to remove the Indians or lessen their strength. Of benefit to Florida, however, during the Seminole Wars the United States military cut the first American-made roads into the Florida interior, although they were impermanent, rough-cut dirt roads, only wide enough for a wagon. The American support of General Jackson's actions, the French occupation of Spain's territories, and the onset of a revolution in Spain encouraged the ceding of Florida to the United States.

Adams-Onis Treaty of 1819

The Adams-Onis Treaty, signed February 22, 1819, settled boundary disputes between Spain and the United States, banishing many tensions between the two nations. It also ceded Florida to the United States. Actual ratification of the treaty was delayed for two years. Part of the Adams-Onis Treaty of 1819 stated that only Spanish grants dated prior to 1818 would be recognized by the United States. Accordingly, Spain hastened to award a number of Spanish land grants, including the Fleming Grant of 1816. The issue of the legitimacy of these grants tied them up in courts for decades.

Panic of 1819-1821

The War of 1812 was a triggering event for the panic of 1819, the first major American depression. Mainly in the south and west, there was a collapse in cotton prices, together with a tightening of credit that caused banks to call in loans. Farms went into foreclosure and banks failed, adversely affecting the U.S. economy. The shock over these events brought home the role played by the government, and helped elevate Andrew Jackson to the presidency.

1820 Sale of Public Lands Act

The United States government enacted a federal law April 20, 1820, that replaced the earlier credit system of payment for public lands, and lowered the price. Under the 1820 act, land would be sold for a minimum of $1.25 per acre of tracts as small as 80 acres. Public lands that were to be offered for sale by District Land Offices would be by public auction. Any land that remained unsold after the auction would be available at the minimum price to any person that was a citizen, or intending to become a citizen, over 21 years of age and head of a household. The lower price was an attractive inducement to settlers and land speculators. Sebastianites later purchased land under this act.

1820s

Spain's occupation of Florida ended in 1921. Spain's legacy was a military outpost with very little cultivation, civilization, or population. It was not self-sustaining. The original native population of 25,000 was nearly eradicated. Approximately 5,000 Seminoles had taken up residence in northern Florida. A few English settlers remained from the earlier 20-year British occupation. Some Spanish settlers remained. Runaway slaves from Alabama and Georgia added to the population, as well as some white settlers, some with slaves who moved into northeastern Florida. Some runaways settled in the Apalachicola area. Florida was the least populated that it had been since it was discovered in 1513. The Spanish census of Pensacola enumerated 713 inhabitants. Along the Escambia River were 380 white Americans with 73 slaves.

Florida U.S. Territory 1821

Eighteen twenty-one was a year of momentous change for Florida. On January 24, 1821, the governorship of the Florida Territory was offered to General Andrew Jackson by President James Monroe, and he accepted. On February 22, 1821, Florida was ceded to the United States by ratification of the Adams-Onis Treaty. The transitional period from Spanish territory to United States territory was a troubled one, marked by the new territorial governor, Andrew Jackson, jailing the outgoing Spanish governor. On July 21, 1821, Florida became a United States territory. This new government was finalized in 1822. The federal government ordered topographical reports to discover more about its new acquisition.

Transportation

Major concerns in territorial Florida were transportation and sparse population. As an incentive to settlement, Florida's legislative council chartered many internal improvements such as canals, roads, and railroads. Railroads seemed like a promising choice. The first "railway" mentioned in Florida was when the Legislative council of the Florida Territory chartered the Chipola Canal Company to construct a railway between the Chipola River and the eastern arm of St. Andrews Bay in 1828. This was never built.

Florida railroads were all the result of individual entrepreneurs rather than overall planning. All of these needed promoters to encourage investors. The earliest promotional article appeared in 1836 in a New York newspaper on a proposed railway in the Florida Territory.

Early railroads all had strap rails, which were wood timbers with nailed iron strap tops. These had a tendency to have the ends become loose and curl up under the weight of the trains. These were named snakeheads that could break through the floor of a passing coach. Solid iron rails were not produced until the 1850s in the U.S. These could become brittle with age and wore out rapidly. The first steel rails were imported in 1863 and did not have these problems. In 1880, the American steel industry began producing steel rails from the Bessimer process. At first the gauge of tracks varied, which necessitated offloading passengers and cargo from one train and reloading to another when moving from one railroad company to another. However, by 1886, railroaders understood the advantages of a uniform gauge and all switched to standard gauge rails. Then whole cars could be switched from one carrier to another. Some early trains were powered by horses or mules, walking on wooden planks laid down in the middle of the tracks. Florida entrepreneurs bought their steam engines from domestic builders such as Mathias Baldwin in Philadelphia.

As early as 1829, steamboats began plying Florida waterways on the St. Johns and Oklawaha Rivers. The economics of some towns like Palatka changed from agriculture to tourism when steamboats came into common use carrying passengers. The first steamboat to travel the Apalachicola was the *Fanny*, built in New York and brought to Florida through the coastal waterways in 1827. On January 28, 1828, the first steam-powered vessel arrived in Columbus, Georgia, through the Apalachicola and Chattahoochee River systems. Soon after that, schooners were arriving in Apalachicola to transport cotton and other goods brought downriver by steamboat. This was also the beginning of passenger service from Florida all along the Apalachicola, Chattahoochee, and Flint River waterways.

Most early steamers were designed for the deeper eastern rivers and had difficulty with the shallow southern waterways, so they were replaced by boats following the design of Henry Miller Shreve of Ohio. His boats were equipped with more powerful high-pressure engines and were built with double decks to accommodate passengers and cargo. Ohio River boat builders produced most of the boats used on the Apalachicola. In 1834, the *Hyperion* was built specifically for the Apalachicola River and it was delivered through New Orleans to Captain Adam Leonard of Apalachicola.

St. Johns County, July 21, 1821

One of the first acts of Governor Jackson was to divide the state into two counties, Escambia and St. Johns. St. Johns County included the entire Florida peninsula. The lengthy problem of the Spanish land grants was overseen by Richard Keith Call. Tallahassee was chosen as the seat of the territorial government due to its central location. This decision was decidedly unpopular with the Red Stick Creeks that had settled in the Tallahassee area and the neighboring Mikasukis. They, along with Lower Creeks in Apalachicola River Valley, and Alachuas and Oconees in the peninsula, were all becoming Seminoles whose common bond was hatred and fear of the encroaching white settlers and a lack of trust in government promises.

1822 Topographical Reports

An August 10, 1822, report of a topographical study of East Florida reported in *Independent Chronicle & Boston Patriot* provided a description of East Florida that was not very flattering: "The cursory examination argues against large quantities being capable of cultivation. The coast area is protected by a ridge and by easterly winds from the 'miasma of the interior' of the state." Moreover, the east coast is protected from the "inconveniences attendant on a direct exposure to the ocean by a narrow strip of land between the ocean and long lagoons. The Pinelands indicate fertile land. The west coast not so well protected, is low and covered with mangroves from Cape Sable to Punta Larga."

A continuation report dated August 17, 1822, described what may be the first English printed description of the Sebastian area:

> Pelican Island is a small mangrove key, eight miles south from Turkey Creek, nearest the west shore. Below Merritt's Island is the mouth of St. Sebastian's River, eighteen miles from the south end of Merrit's Island, and distinguished by a high red sand bluff, on the south point of entrance. This stream has pine lands along on its banks which in general are very high bluffs of light colored sand. It comes from the southeast and has a very serpentine course. The whole western shore past St. Sebastian is imposing.

The land around the St. Sebastian River area was described as a healthful place with hammocks and pinelands mixed with oak and hickory scrub. Note that Pelican Island was mentioned by name and known as a point of interest by 1822 in the new East Florida Territory.

Treaty of Moultrie Creek, 1823

Florida had become a haven for Creek Indians and related tribes, as well as runaway slaves. There were many differing opinions of how the problem of Indian relations should be settled. Finally, in 1823 after the Red Stick War, the commissioners met with a number of Seminole chiefs and completed the Treaty of Moultrie Creek, which provided that the Seminoles move to a four-million-acre reservation in the middle of the southern Florida peninsula. This migration began in 1824, but not all went, and not all remained once they arrived there. Bands of Indians continued to roam amongst the settlers. Not all encounters were friendly. A rough-cut military trail was created in 1825 by Colonel James Gadsden and his troops along the east coast of Florida.

Mosquito County, 1824

In 1824, the Legislative Council in Tallahassee created Mosquito County from St. Johns County, and Sebastian/ Roseland changed its county once more. Also in 1824, statewide ordered land surveys began by Colonel Robert Butler, surveyor general, enabling sales of public lands, which began in 1825.

1830s

Seminoles vs. settlers occupied much Florida thinking during this period. However, in the 1830s, Sebastian was in the limelight. Even though only Seminoles laid claim to the area, the title to the Fleming Grant was cleared, so that title could pass to settlers. However, the Seminole concerns undoubtedly hindered any settlement there. Sebastian had no inhabitants. The U.S. 1830 census of Florida enumerated approximately 1,000 individuals total.

By 1829, when Andrew Jackson became president, Florida settlers were demanding that the Florida Indians be removed to the territory set aside for them west of the Mississippi. In the 1830s at Fort Gibson, chiefs signed an agreement to move west. Upon their return to Florida, their decision was denounced by younger Seminoles, led by Osceola and Coacoochee. Most recanted and agreed not to go. The lone holdout that stuck by his agreement to go west was assassinated on his trip to Fort Brooke at Tampa with his band.

At Fort King, eight chiefs agreed to go west. General Wiley Thompson, the agent in charge of the removal, handled the relationship with these Indian chiefs so poorly that he was ambushed and shot by Osceola and a small band. Major Francis Dade and a column of troops traveling from Fort Broke to Fort King were massacred that same day by chiefs Micanopy, Alligator, Coacoochee, and their warriors.

Despite the dangers and difficulty of travel, individuals were drawn to explore the wilds of Florida. Into this setting came John James Audubon, one of many who succumbed to the lure of a new frontier. In November of 1831, John James Audubon arrived in Florida and spent the next six months on the east coast of Florida exploring, sketching, and obtaining specimens of water birds for the third volume of his book of bird illustrations, *Birds of America*. He traveled by pony or on foot, and in all manner of boats. His work served to fuel greater interest in Florida.

Travel

Prior to the 1840s, travel in the U.S. from the north to Florida was hazardous and had no certain schedules. It took four to eight days sailing by ship from New York to Charleston or Savannah, or one could travel by stage coach over poor roads. The faster coastal steamers did not come into use until the 1840s. Travel south from those points was similarly difficult.

Railroads and Steamers

To spur settlement, Florida's legislative council chartered many internal improvements such as canals, roads, and railroads. Railroads provided the easiest and cheapest solution to transportation problems in Florida, and between 1830 and 1860, Florida governments chartered as many as 20 railroad building projects. Four rail lines were built in the territorial period. There was one from St. Joseph to the Apalachicola River, and a short line in Escambia County. In 1831, the charter was given for Leon Rail-Way Co. It failed, and new promoters reformed the company as the Tallahassee Railroad Company, which ran from Tallahassee to St. Marks. It opened in 1837 with mule-drawn wooden cars pulled over wooden rails covered with iron. It carried both passengers and freight. In 1836, another ran between St. Joseph and Lake Wimico. Many of these early railroads in Florida were created by individuals for purely local business ventures.

Steamboat companies saw the possibility of profit in Florida. Regular steamboat service started on the St. Johns River, running in part in the Atlantic to Savannah, in the early 1830s. Suwannee River steamboat traffic began in winter of 1836 when supplies were brought to the fort at Suwannee Springs five miles below White Springs. When Fort Fannon was built, there was regular steamboat service between Fannon Springs and Cedar Key. The fort was crowded with soldiers and families fleeing Indians.

2nd Seminole War 1835-1842

December 1835 and January 1836 saw massacres on 22 plantations. These actions marked the commencement of the Second Seminole War. Frightened settlers fled, and Mosquito County was virtually emptied. It had enjoyed a modest growth until 1835, when a severe freeze occurred, further compelling settlers to leave. There was so little activity that the records for Mosquito County were kept by the clerk of St. Johns County. In the 1840 elections, only three votes were recorded.

The Second Seminole War was the most expensive and lost the most men. It lasted seven years, and damaged the reputations of commanding officers. It also contributed to the rising abolitionist movement, as another objective of the war was the retrieval of runaway slaves and elimination of the safe haven they found in Seminole Florida. The war did remove the majority of the Seminoles.

The federal government attempted to move the Florida Indians to reservations west of the Mississippi River. This was only somewhat successful. General Jesup began an extensive campaign with 4,000 men in the fall of 1837, at which time he estimated there were no more than 200 Indians remaining north of Lake Monroe. During that campaign, Colonel Zachary Taylor built Fort Gardner and Fort Bassinger in the Kissimmee Valley. Taylor fought and won the most extensive battle of the Second War on December 25, 1837, the Battle of Lake Okeechobee. Fort Christmas was built the same day 80 miles to the north of that battle by General Jessup. Fort Ann was built at the haulover between the Mosquito Lagoon and the Indian River, that narrow strip of land between the two that necessitated the hauling of boats over that area to travel between the two bodies of water.

Lieutenant Levin M. Powell's force was given orders to explore the Indian River on its way to the Everglades in 1837. His group spotted a band of Indians and gave chase. Powell's force made camp on a high oak bluff on the north bank of the St. Sebastian River, and then scouted the river to its headwaters without discovering the Indians. The next day they continued south. The St. Sebastian River area was reported to have timber, a much sought-after commodity.

Forces under General Joseph Marion Hernandez moved down the Indian River from the haulover December 31, 1837, to erect Fort Pierce in 1838. During the building of Fort Pierce, from December 30, 1837, through January 2, 1838, Dr. Jacob Motte exclaimed on the vast size and variety of flora and fauna. Shelled oysters were described as six to seven inches by two inches in size, and bonitas, redfish, grouper, sheepshead, bass, and trout were caught that were 2 to 3 feet long. General Hernandez was directed to improve and clear the trail created in 1825 by Colonel James Gadsden. Along the eastern coast, this trail ran down the Atlantic Coastal Ridge from St. Augustine to Fort Capron, near Fort Pierce. This trail that General Hernandez's troops cut on its way from the haulover to the St. Lucie area came to be known as the Hernandez Trail. Fort Taylor was built on Lake Winder and Fort Floyd was erected approximately 30 miles west of Fort Pierce. Fort Floyd completed a line of forts across the peninsula from Tampa Bay to Fort Pierce, intended to contain the remaining Seminoles in Florida south of any settlers. The 1839 Mackay map of the Brevard County area was compiled by order of Brigadier General Zachary Taylor and indicated the locations of Seminole War forts.

Over many battles and skirmishes, Seminoles were reduced in number and in poor condition. Although greatly decreased in number, Seminoles still remained. Approximately 3,000 of them were removed by one or another means. On May 10, 1842, President John Tyler announced the termination of military action against those 240 Seminoles. An order issued August 11, 1842, created a reservation for those remaining, running from Pease Creek to Lake Istokpoga down the left bank of the Kissimmee River to Lake Okeechobee through the lake and the Everglades to the Shark River and then west to the Gulf of Mexico. This laid the groundwork for the subsequent Armed Occupation Act of 1842.

The ineffectiveness of the Seminole Wars to remove the Seminoles from Florida was a disaster for the many settlers in the central portion of the state who were growing cotton and sugar cane, and this war effectively depopulated Mosquito County. Statehood was still being promoted, in spite of the many problems, including the issue of whether to make it one state or two. A constitutional convention was held at St. Joseph in 1838, during which a constitution was completed and ratified by territorial voters, calling for one state. Florida did not actually attain statehood until 1845, as it had to await the admission of Iowa to statehood, to maintain the balance of free and slave states.

Panic of 1837-1843

The United States in 1837 entered a ruinous and long-lasting depression which sent the beginning banking system and territorial government of Florida into debt and bank failures. This was triggered by failures in wheat crops and cotton prices, factored in with land speculation, currency problems, and Britain's economic problems. This ruinous depression caused real estate and food prices to collapse, ruining farmers. Martin Van Buren failed to secure a second presidential term in the election of 1840, as he and Andrew Jackson were blamed for this disaster.

4

The Armed Occupation Act and the Indian River Colony: 1840s

In the 1840s, Florida was becoming settled and to some extent civilized through turbulent times. Travel was becoming easier. Individuals were using the land in Sebastian, but not yet purchasing any, except for the Fleming Grant, which was uninhabited. Wreckers and smugglers found the Indian River useful. By the time of the 1840 U.S. Census of Florida, the population had risen to 2,300 individuals, from 1,000 in 1830. In 1845, it was 70,000. The Armed Occupation Act was enacted in 1842, and by 1844, settlers were populating the Indian River Colony. Santa Lucia County was formed, and Florida became a state.

Travel

Common travel to Florida began by sailing ship from New York to Savannah or Charleston. Travel by train was possible in much of the North. By the 1840s, coastal side wheel steamers were in use, carrying passengers from the North into Florida, a faster and easier mode of travel than the old method of travel by sailing ship. In November 1842, the steamer *St. Matthews* started weekly service between Savannah and Palatka, the last link in the travel from New York to Florida via Savannah. This mode of travel was so successful that in 1845, the *William Gadsden* was added to the route. However, the cost of travel by steamer was approximately double that of by sailing ship. This easier mode of travel increased tourism, and a route was added in 1848 from Palatka to Enterprise.

Tourism had not reached the Indian River area, and not all increases in travel were due to tourism. A. W. Walker, the Collector in Fort Pierce, reported in the Territorial Papers in 1842 that there were smugglers importing illegal cigars and wreckers who plied the inlets of Indian River and waters of the eastern coast of the Florida Territory unhindered. One such visitor was Don Pedro Gilbert, a pirate and slaver who traveled those waters. Periodically he brought his ship *Panda* across the bar/inlet and up the St. Lucie River, which he used as a refuge to escape pursuers. That inlet became known as Gilbert's Bar Inlet.

Added to the problem were the hostile Indians that remained in the area. The government's answer to these issues was the Armed Occupation Act, which was only partially successful.

Armed Occupation Act August 4, 1842

Unable to completely eradicate the Indians in Florida or police the uninhabited parts of Florida, the state government determined that the burden should fall on the settlers. An Act of Congress was approved on August 4, 1842, titled, "An act to provide for the armed occupation and settlement of the unsettled part of the Peninsula of East Florida." Applicants were required to give formal notice of application for a permit to settle upon 160 acres of unappropriated public land that was not within two miles of a military post. The land could not be closer to a military post under the assumption that the settlers would protect themselves. The recipient of the land had to be the head of a family, over eighteen years of age, able to bear arms, and be a resident of Florida. To be entitled to the land, the settlers were required to hold the land against the Indians for seven years.

The act was created to encourage settlement in central Florida, as a buffer zone between Indians in the south and the populated areas of North Florida. The individuals were required to be ready, willing, and able to bear arms against Indians. Two colonies were created, one on the southern west coast on the Manatee River near Bradenton, and one on the east coast, the Indian River Colony, mainly along the Indian River. St. Augustine was the hub for all Indian River Colony land applications, permissions, and grants.

Word began to filter into the newspapers of settlers in the Indian River Colony just a year after the end of the Third Seminole War. A *Savannah Republican* article, published in the Charleston *Southern Patriot* September 8, 1843, reported that the schooner *Ellen* from Nassau traveled via the Indian River and brought 20 immigrants to Jacksonville, who said that the Indian River area had a great climate and fertile soil. There was an abundance of corn and vegetables, deer, fish, and oysters. They planted fruit trees that would mature in a year or two, and they expected a good harvest. The first photographer to visit Florida, Alfred A. Lansing, arrived in 1842.

In 1844, Edward C. Anderson, son of an old distinguished Savannah, Georgia, family, was assigned duty on the USS *General Taylor,* a coastal steamer surveying the waters and harbors of the Florida Territory, to prevent thieves from stealing live oak timber and protect the population from attacks by the Seminole Indians. In his diary, he told of his service, from March 16 to December 31, 1844, on the 152-ton *General Taylor* on the Indian River, among many others. He had little to say about the Indian River area, although his comments were extensive about other areas: "Saturday July 6th. Left the harbour of St. Augustine & proceeded to sea, touched at Indian River & landed a live oak agent, two horses & sundry dogs. At 6:30 pm continued on our course."

An article in the *Southern Patriot* newspaper May 24, 1844, reported that a surveying party at the St. Sebastian River came across a corn field of one-eighth acre or less. They saw tracks of a man, woman, and child which they supposed to be a family of Indians who had located there for fishing. The area was very dry from lack of rain.

The Indian River Colony

One hundred twelve patents on the Indian River from Merritt Island to Lake Worth were granted. The Armed Occupation Act was in effect for one year. One thousand, three hundred twelve patents were issued at Newnansville and St. Augustine. Settlers came mainly from Alabama, Georgia, Florida, and South Carolina. The largest concentration of settlers was around Fort Pierce, but the exact number of settlers is not known. John Barker held land north of St. Lucie Village; William F. Russell's and David H. Gattis' land was at St. Lucie Village; Douglas Dummett's was at Merritt Island; Ossian B. Hart's was near Fort Pierce; Mills O. Burnham was eight miles from Fort Pierce; Captain Reuben Pinkham's land was at Blue Hole Creek.

Fort Pierce remained manned until Aug 25, 1842, and was decommissioned at the end of the Third Seminole War. This abandoned fort provided temporary living quarters for arriving colony settlers until they could erect their own dwellings. Early houses were of pine saplings with palmetto roofs and sides, erected from what the people had cleared off of their land. Windows were covered with oiled paper. Settlers had candles, lightwood, and some whale-oil lamps. The only exception was Samuel Peck, who had a house framed out in Savannah and transported by schooner to his homestead. Peck left in 1845 and sold his house to Captain Mills Burnham. By 1845, the outlook for the colony had soured a little. The schooner *Caroline* carried settlers from the Indian River area who were leaving.

Settlers experimented with a wide variety of crops, which may have explained some of the failures. Crops of the settlers included arrowroot, tobacco, figs, rice, grapes, pumpkins, sweet potatoes, beans, corn, bananas, sugar cane, pineapple, Indigo, ginger, citrus, guava, custard apple, avocado, and tamarind trees.

In the 1840s, there were three routes to the Indian River region. Sailing down the Atlantic past Cape Canaveral was dangerous on the open sea around the Cape. The 1839 Mackay map indicated that there were three inlets from the ocean to the Indian River, the Indian River Inlet, Gilbert's Bar, and Jupiter Inlet below the Jupiter Narrows. These inlets were often shallow, and not always open. Another route was up the St. Johns River from Jacksonville to Enterprise on Lake Monroe to Salt Lake or one of the other lakes, then crossing overland to the Indian River. This method was extremely difficult due to land too marshy for wagons and water too shallow for boats. The third method was by way of the Mosquito Lagoon, hauling the boats over the intervening strip of marshy land, into the Indian River. It had numerous marshes and mangrove islands and there were several haulovers utilized. This route was favored by Indians and the army.

None of these routes were satisfactory. Many suggestions were made by the Florida territorial council, military, and settlers to improve transportation. A six or seven-mile canal between the St. Johns and Indian Rivers had been proposed by the territorial government, but was never accomplished. Settlers of the Indian River Colony requested a road south from St Augustine. The army requested a canal at Fort Ann between the Mosquito Lagoon and the Indian River.

Fort Pierce was the geographic center of the colony. The settlers depended on the Indian River for their livelihood and lived off of the land. The group included carpenters, musicians, a doctor, a cobbler, a lawyer, a gunsmith, and several sailors. Men engaged in hunting and fishing. Game and fish were their most dependable food supplies, including mullet, Spanish mackerel, and other fishes, along with oysters, turtles, wild hogs, venison, turkeys, and cattle. All partook in some sort of agriculture. There was not much commercial production, as markets were too far away and transportation was too difficult. However, some settlers had their own schooners and traded with the Bahamas, Cuba, and the Florida Keyes. Captain Burnham took turtles north to sell. Some supplies, such as coffee and sugar, were brought in by vessels engaged in coastal trade.

Their social life consisted of fishing trips, hunting, house-raisings, helping each other with field work, and tending the sick. Some had musical talent. A common project was to cut a better access through a narrow spit of land across from the mouth of the St. Lucie River, the Gilbert's Bar Inlet. This improved the water and fishing in the Indian River, but after a few years it closed up again, and was still closed in 1855. On occasion, the pressure of water from the St. Lucie River had forced it open over the years. Storms and hurricanes also affected whether it was open or closed. Another article in the *Southern Patriot* from November 16, 1844, reported that a party of settlers opened a trench at the Jupiter Inlet which had been closed for many years. They were partly done when a torrent of water went through and 30 feet of earth was swept away all at once, leaving an opening of 100 yards, 10 to 12 feet deep.

Santa Lucia County, March 14, 1844

By February 1844, the colonists had attended to the basics of clearing the land and building their homes, and were able to consider civic matters. Santa Lucia County was carved from Mosquito County, consisting of roughly the eastern half of Florida from Brevard to Palm Beach Counties. By July 1844, the settlers elected the first board of county commissioners to Santa Lucia County. William Russell was Inspector of Customs. The new county seat was at St. Lucie, but the clerk was permitted to keep the public records at home except when courts were in session. They set up a basic legal system with arbitration to handle any disputes and a volunteer company was organized to defend against Indians. However, there were still many hardships attendant to life at the colony. Living conditions were primitive and harsh; business was conducted in St. Augustine which involved difficult travel. By 1848, many had abandoned the colony.

1845 Florida Statehood

Meanwhile, in 1845, Florida finally attained statehood, with a population of less than 1,000. The Missouri Compromise of 1820 dictated that a balance be maintained between free and slave states. Florida joined as a slave state, and Iowa joined as a free state the same year. The new Florida state government began the process of transforming from a territory to a state, and reorganized counties to reflect the growing population. Mosquito County was renamed Orange County in 1844 and was reduced in size by the creation of Santa Lucia County. The 1847 legislature combined the offices of Clerk of Court for Santa Lucia and Orange Counties. J. C. Hemming was appointed clerk of the combined counties and served until 1850. However, the Santa Lucia County records were kept in the home of D. H. Gattis and were destroyed during the 1849 attack on the Indian River Colony. The first county commissioners were William B. Davis, John Barker, and Ossian B. Hart. In 1847, the county commissioners were Levy M. Crawford, William F. Russell, James S. Grant, W. D. Ward, and Jasper J. Papy. There were no elections in 1849 due to Indian troubles.

While steam locomotives were becoming common to the north, only one railroad existed in 1845 in Florida, the Tallahassee Railroad between Tallahassee and St. Marks, with mule-hauled trains. The U.S. Government gave Florida 500,000 acres of land which could be sold, parcels to be used for transportation projects.

In this new county, timber was considered a valuable commodity. As with all items of value, there were timber poachers. Surveys for timber were conducted. There was some smuggling undertaken of contraband articles from the West Indies into the United States. The revenue inspector's office at Charlotte Harbor was relocated to the Indian River in mid-1844 in response. Fishing and citrus industries had not yet become commercially viable along the Indian River.

The Crisis of 1849—The End of the Colony

Indian River Colony was a stable settlement until July 12, 1849. There are numerous versions of what happened to cause the end of the colony. There was panic and confusion at the time, and the tale was told over and over again by many people. Moreover, embellishments crept in. It was a newsworthy, catastrophic event. The bare account is that Indians killed John Barker, wounded William J. Russell, looted homes, and burned one house. The rest of the colonists all up and down the east coast panicked and fled to St. Augustine, abandoning their property and claim to the land. Some of them later returned to their land. Troops were sent to investigate. The Indian River Colony lasted just six or seven years, from 1843 to 1849. The same Indians killed and wounded settlers at Payne's Creek on the 17th. To avert war, Chief Billy Bowlegs turned in three of the culprits and the hand of a fourth who was killed. One escaped and was captured later. Various differing accounts of this massacre have been printed from diaries, biographies, oral histories that appeared in pamphlets, books, and newspaper articles over the years. The following are some credible accounts of this massacre.

Joseph Cushman

Joseph Cushman's article in *Florida Historical Quarterly* is based in part on a series of articles in the *Florida Star* 40 years later by William Peck, who was a fourteen-year-old colonist present at the time of the attack. It relates that a storekeeper by the name of Barker who resided near the Sebastian River was killed and badly mutilated by Indians who attacked in considerable numbers, plundering houses and firing on the colonists. William F. Russell, deputy collector of the settlement, was shot in the arm and his family was reported missing, as were a number of other persons, whom they feared were taken by Indians. Settlers left their homes, took to the river, and rendezvoused with a small schooner. They sailed up the coast to St. Augustine, where a volunteer force was organized to pursue the Indians.

Captain Mills Burnham

The Captain Mills Burnham version, published 77 years later and told by his grandson by marriage, Robert Ranson, is a coherent version. While Captain Burnham was away from the colony, four or five Indians killed John Barker, who had a store at Barker's Bluff. He was killed, it was said, because he cheated them in their trade on several occasions. Both Barker and Russell were disliked by the Indians. Word spread up and down the coast that an Indian uprising was beginning; they feared a massacre of all colonists. Major Russell convinced the other colonists that they should leave. However, it was felt that if Captain Burnham had been present, he would have convinced them not to flee and the majority would have stayed. Instead, they all fled to Captain Reuben Pinkham's ship. On the ship as they departed, Russell was struck in the arm by a bullet. Administering first aid to himself in the dark, he mistakenly poured ink on his arm instead of salve. In the morning, he saw the black arm, and feared that gangrene had set in. When they reached St. Augustine, he had Dr. Peck amputate his arm. The colonists met Captain Burnham in St. Augustine.

Caleb Brayton

Resident Caleb Brayton's letter to his wife Marian Brayton in Augusta, Georgia, on July 25, 1849, published in *Florida Historical Quarterly*, related a slightly different version. He stated the colonists were busy fortifying for an expected Indian attack, due to the events of July 12. On the 12th, four Indians went to Russell's house in the morning and were friendly. They stayed around for the day talking with others and idling. Later on, the four Indians approached Barker and Russell and shot at them. Russell was shot in the arm. The Indians chased after Barker and overtook and stabbed him, killing him. Russell ran to Gattis' house where Brayton was speaking with him. Brayton dressed Russell's arm and Gattis found that his guns were not in working order. Brayton, Gattis,

Russell, and another man ran to the shore to the boats and were fired upon by eight Indians. They took off and went to Brayton's for his guns, but the Indians were gone and everything was in ruins. Houses were ransacked and set ablaze, and cattle were killed. Thirty people left in a little schooner. Thomas Morrison and Brayton took arms and a boat looking for the other colonists. Two days later they found a boat ahead with Mrs. Russell, Mrs. Barker, and some others. Stopping at New Smyrna, they found that several others had walked from the colony to New Smyrna, 130 miles in four days.

Andrew Canova

Andrew Canova's telling of the tale is also different in his *Life and Adventures in South Florida.* Canova lived in the Sebastian area just nine years after the attack. In his version, Major Russell was a trader who had a poor reputation with the Indians. He and his brother-in-law Barker were working in Russell's garden when two Indians who wanted revenge against Russell fired at them. Barker was killed, and Russell was wounded. Mrs. Barker and Mrs. Russell seized the children and headed for the boat on the river. Russell joined them. They rowed across the Indian River and walked up the beach 40 miles in three days to Cape Canaveral, where they reached Captain Burnham and a detachment of troops under his command. Captain Burnham conveyed them to St. Augustine. Lieutenant Ripley, who was stationed at St. Augustine, was ordered to go to Fort Capron to protect the remaining settlers.

There are many versions and embellishments. In one telling, Both Barker and Russell were disliked by the Indians because of shady business dealings. Watered whiskey was one claim; defective gun powder was another. In another, Barker was hit by accident; the shot was intended for Russell. Yet another version: Barker and Russell were both wounded and ran for Russell's boat, and the Indians caught up to Barker, stabbing and scalping him. Russell escaped and sounded the alarm. In one account, it happened on Barker's Bluff, instead of Fort Pierce. An oral history states that Barker lived on Barker's Bluff, was good friends with the Indians, and was not killed by them. In another version, Captain Pinkham carried all of them to safety; in a different telling, his boat rendezvoused with another and they headed north together; in another, some of them met in New Smyrna and headed north. The number of Indians was variously four, five, eight, or a band.

Some of the settlers who remained or returned to the area were Captain Reuben Pinkham, Captain Mills Burnham, Major William F. Russell, Caleb L. Brayton, and D. H. Gattis. Their names appear in later records.

Captain Reuben Pinkham

One of the early trade boat captains was Captain Reuben Pinkham from Maine. He was an English pilot who settled in St. Augustine and later joined the Indian River Colony.

Captain Pinkham sailed his trading boat up and down the river and piloted other vessels through the inlet. He was the main means of transport for the colony. He had permit no. 19, dated January 27, 1843, on Orchid Island, 158 acres at Blue Hole Creek. After the Indian River Colony attack, the colonists left for St. Augustine in his boat. His grove was abandoned. His patent on his Armed Occupation Act land was received posthumously by his heirs June 18, 1890.

According to an article by Daniel McConville of Washington D.C., printed in 1915, Indian River Citrus is due to Reuben Pinkham of Maine. He moved to a place about five miles south of Vero on the north side of the Indian River inlet around the time of the Seminole Wars. He acted as a pilot for vessels entering the inlet at Fort Capron. Some crates of seeds washed overboard from a ship; their place of origin and destination was unknown. He planted these seeds and tended them until he was driven out by hostile Indians in 1843. The trees remained untended until the arrival of a scientist from Germany by the name of Hermann who settled in that locale in 1848. He relocated some of the plants to his property and cultivated them. His grove became very well known. However, he eventually abandoned it and returned to Germany. Trees were taken from this spot by others passing through, and became the nucleus for Indian River groves, per this article.

John Barker

In 1815, John Barker received a Spanish grant for land near St. Augustine, where Barker lived until 1822. He appeared in the 1840 census of St. Johns County. After settling near present St. Lucie Village in 1842, where he farmed, it is plausible that Barker built a second cabin upriver at Barker's Bluff, where he operated an Indian trading post. According to Alfred Michael, there were orange trees on Barker's Bluff, planted by Barker. Barker was granted Armed Occupation permit no. 69, issued April 19, 1843, for land that was south of the George W. Sprague's patented homestead, near present St. Lucie Village. On May 26, 1845, Barker was named an election clerk and inspector. Around 1846, he married Martha Russell, sister of William F. Russell. Barker applied for approval of his land patent November 30, 1848, with proof of homestead. His patent was received posthumously by his widow Martha on April 19, 1850. Martha Barker received certificate no. 27 for granted land in the Indian River Colony.

Major William F. Russell

William F. Russell held 51 acres of land near Fort Pierce with Thomas Hite. He also had land in St. Lucie Village. He came from North Carolina to settle on the Indian River in 1842. Russell was married to Susan Walker and had six children. He held the office of Customs Inspector for Indian River Colony, and later was appointed commissioner. The family left the area during the subsequent wars, and later returned.

5

The First Settlers: 1850s

The 1850s were a turning point for the Sebastian and Roseland area. At long last, it had settlers in the form of two men. Andrew P. Canova and Ed Marr were the first to settle in the area. Otherwise, the county was slowly growing, and some of its major problems were beginning to be addressed. The Haulover Canal improved access to the area. In 1855, Sebastian's county changed yet again from Santa Lucia to Brevard County. From 1855 to 1858, growth was interrupted by the Third Seminole War. Another economic depression occurred from 1857 to 1859, but fledgling industries began to emerge. Railroads and steamboats were becoming recognized modes of travel. By the late 1850s, the area began to attract sportsmen, and Pelican Island was gaining national attention as well.

In 1850, according to the U.S. Census, the population of Florida was 87,445, while in Santa Lucia County it was 139, which included 54 soldiers at Fort Capron, 53 free whites, 1 free black and 27 black slaves. There were 20 heads of families. Some of these had been part of the original Indian River Colony. None of these individuals were living in the Sebastian area. Total valuation for the whole county of real estate was $277,000, and $41,300 of personal property. The December 9, 1850, census enumeration relates: "The inhabitants of the County were driven from it on account of the Indian hostilities and only a few of them have, as yet, returned." Mills Burnham was St. Lucie County's first sheriff. In 1855, the population had risen to 163.

In the late 1850s, the cattle industry was introduced into Brevard County, primarily by settlers from Georgia who drove herds through Georgia and Florida down into the western part of the county. Numerous herds, both large and small, prospered there. By the mid-1850s, large herds were driven over the Capron Trail to Tampa to be sold. This growing industry was an event that would change the character of the county, and dominate much of the 1860s and 1870s.

Indian River Citrus

The fledgling Indian River citrus industry was created from the mating of several events. The Spanish brought sweet orange trees with them and planted groves when Florida was under Spanish control. John D. Sheldon later discovered one of those Spanish groves in Turnbull Hammock in Volusia County. He transplanted approximately 6,000 of those trees to Packwood Place near Oak Hill in Volusia County.

Douglas Dummett had an important influence on the growth of the Indian River citrus industry. He was the son of Thomas Henry Dummett who came to Volusia County in 1825 from Barbados, by way of Connecticut, and then to Tomoka, Florida, where he had sugar cane plantations. After financial problems, Thomas moved to St. Augustine, leaving his plantations to Douglas. In Tomoka, Douglas ran the sugar cane plantations and was postmaster. He was also an officer in the Mosquito County Militia prior to the Second Seminole War, and was promoted to captain.

Douglas Dummett began experimenting with citrus cultivation when he was living in Volusia County, planting wild sour-orange trees which had gone native and adapted to Florida's growing conditions. To these trees he grafted sweet orange tree cuttings from either the Sheldon trees, or the Turnbull groves at New Smyrna, according to differing versions. In 1928, he transplanted some of his orange trees to Merritt Island. His groves proved very successful, even surviving the 1835 freeze. By 1859, his crop was most likely 60,000 oranges. He shared his success with other growers, selling them budwood from his trees. Most of Indian River citrus came from these events.

Steamboats

The steamboat run from Charleston to the St. Johns River was a major route to and from Florida in the 1850s. It required a ship that was built strong enough to run in the Atlantic Ocean for a short period of time, yet had a shallow enough draft to get over the entrance to the St. Johns River. Moreover, it had to be able to make the difficult turns and stop at the landings en route to Palatka. Steamboat service was offered from Savannah to Palatka in 1850. Commercial barge service ran in the 1850s from Palatka to somewhere on the Oklawaha. The exact destination depended on river depth, which varied, and where the goods were going. These barges were moved by large groups of men polling.

Jacob Brock was an innovator who opened up a new area to the steamboat. He was from Hartford, Connecticut, and in 1840 he went to South Carolina where he constructed the side wheeler *Darlington*. He also added the title captain to his name. He first used the *Darlington* on the Pee Dee River, hauling cotton and other goods. After three years, he moved his business to Jacksonville, already established as a commercial and passenger seaport. Steamboat trade was common at that time between Jacksonville and Palatka, but was not common south of there. He decided to open steamboat traffic to Enterprise on Lake Monroe. In furtherance of this, he purchased land west of Enterprise and named it New Enterprise, laid out streets and lots, and built a steamboat wharf. By 1853, regular traffic ran to Enterprise by the *Darlington*. Before that, the unknown depths and possible problems had deterred others from advancing there, and he was the first to make the runs. Brock also started a shipyard in Jacksonville that became Merrill Stevens, and he built a tugboat that was used to free stranded steamers.

Railroads

The United States had a tremendous increase in railroad lines in the 1850s. The steam engines were the most important part of the assets of a railroad, eventually replacing horses and mules used to pull the trains. The northern states had far more railroads in use than the South, where there were many problems of costs of supplies for trains.

Florida, on the other hand, received incentives for railroading, but at this time was slow to acquire steam engines. The U.S. government ceded to Florida all of its million acres of swamp and overflowed land for drainage and reclamation and railroad incentives in 1850. In 1851, Florida organized the Florida Improvement Board to handle this land. A report was issued by it in 1854 showing how land could be used to finance a system of railroads from Jacksonville to Pensacola, and from Amelia Island to Tampa Bay. Railroading received a considerable boost in 1855; the Internal Improvement Fund gave land grants to qualified railroad companies. That year the "Central" (The Florida Atlantic and Gulf Central Railroad) surveys began on a route from Jacksonville to Alligator (Lake City), finishing in 1860. At Jacksonville, the railroads connected to other state railroads. Other connections were made to travel on the St. Johns River south. In 1858, the St. Johns Railroad was fifteen miles long. It ran from Tocoi Landing on the St. Johns River to New Augustine on the San Sebastian River, with horse-drawn trains. This had some drawbacks, however, as horses were apt to lie down to rest when they became tired. Mules were less likely to do so. There were other difficulties, such as alligators sleeping on the tracks. Early tracks were still of wood, and iron laid over wood.

Trails

Fort Capron was constructed in March 1850, and in that same year, the Capron-Hernandez Trail was completed from Fort Capron across to Fort Brooke, near Tampa. It became the dividing line intended to contain the Indian population to the south. Indians still strayed north of the Trail, however. Along the eastern coast, the Trail ran along the Atlantic Coastal Ridge from St. Augustine to Fort Capron, near Fort Pierce. Governor Brown continued to receive complaints from settlers about Indian depredations, and in early 1852, he ordered General B. Hopkins to organize a militia force to control the situation. Captain Aaron Jernigan's company was given this detail. Dempsey Cain, who later became a Roseland settler, was a member of Jernigan's company from May to September of that year. Fort Capron was garrisoned until June 14, 1858, at the end of the Third Seminole War.

William F. Russell

William Russell was one of the Indian River Colony individuals who returned to the area. He became inspector of customs, and operated a store and trading post at Fort Capron. Russell's grocery store supplied necessary items for settlers for many miles around. In 1850, William F. Russell was re-elected as a commissioner, and he remained one until 1855. Russell became a state legislator and Speaker of the House in 1854. He was present in the 1860 census in Brevard County, 1870 in Volusia County, and 1880 in Orange County. Russell died in Orlando at an old age.

Caleb L. Brayton

Caleb L. Brayton was another member of the Indian River Colony who returned. C. L. Brayton appeared in the 1840 census for Richmond County, Georgia. Consumptive Brayton went to the Indian River Colony in the hopes of improving his health, leaving his wife in Georgia. Brayton was a tax collector there, signing the 1848 report for Santa Lucia County's collected taxes. By January 1850, Brayton had returned to the colony but was staying near the fort, as he did not feel his house was safe yet. That year Brayton was elected sheriff, tax assessor, and collector. His address was given as Russell's Landing. He obtained the contract to carry mail from New Smyrna to Miami. His health continued to worsen, however, and Caleb Brayton died of tuberculosis June 9, 1854. His wife Marian arrived shortly before he died, returning thereafter to Fall River.

Civic Matters

Mail in Brevard County was intended to be delivered twice monthly, but this was often difficult to achieve. The route was by boat from New Smyrna to Indian River, and by horseback southward along the beach. It was often difficult to find water for the horse and feed had to be carried along. This was an arduous journey for horses. In 1854, John Hermans wrote that the Tallahassee post office often sent Indian River mail to Key West, and then to Miami, taking as much as three months to arrive, whereas if it were delivered by way of the St. Johns River, it would only take three weeks.

One of the biggest improvements in access to the Indian River area occurred in 1854. Plans begun many years before finally reached fruition. The requested canal was created at the haulover at Fort Ann over the 720-yard distance between the Mosquito Lagoon and the Indian River, as proposed by Colonel Worth. Ultimately it was decided that the Haulover Canal would be a cheaper alternative to other suggested improvements. Dr. George E. Hawes was awarded the contract and created the 3-foot deep canal with slave labor. This provided for open access from Ponce de Leon Inlet south to Jupiter Inlet, 156 miles of comparatively easy travel by water. There were many other surveys and proposals to improve transportation and land for settlement in Brevard County and the rest of the state, but little else was done until considerably after the Civil War.

At the Florida State House of Representatives General Assembly Meeting on November 27, 1854, in the roll call by counties, W. F. Russell was present for St. Lucie County. Russell was voted in as Speaker of the House. On December 21, 1854, Russell introduced a bill, "An Act to change the name and establish the County Site of St. Lucie County."

On January 6, 1855, the name of Santa Lucia County was changed to Brevard County, in honor of Theodore Washington Brevard, and the county seat was changed to Susannah. "County Site permanently established and located at a place known and designated as Fort Pierce and the name of said County Site shall be Susannah." State legislator Major William F. Russell had a wife and daughter both named Susan, which may have been an influencing factor. Susannah was a small town south of Fort Pierce. This name was apparently little used, as both the post office and the county seat were usually referred to as Indian River.

Florida Land Office

The General Land Office was created in 1812 by Congress. It was responsible for the issuing of land warrants and grants, collecting payments, preparing land patents and deeds, and maintaining records. Newnansville Courthouse in Alachua County was the site of one of the earliest land grant centers, and continued to be until after the Civil War. The county grew, the Florida Southern Railroad bypassed Newnansville, and in 1854, the county seat was moved from Newnansville to Gainesville. Newnansville suffered a slow decline thereafter. In Gainesville, a new courthouse was built, a frame building completed in 1856. In 1857, the Land Grant Office was removed to Gainesville to the new courthouse. In 1886, the original courthouse was replaced with a red brick courthouse, and the Land Offices and their records were housed there.

Third Seminole War 1855-1858

The Second Seminole War never really accomplished its aims. As a result, a third Seminole War erupted in 1855. It was said to begin through careless actions by some soldiers, followed by an attack by Indians. Some soldiers of an exploring party of Second Artillery personnel, led by First Lieutenant George L. Hartsuff, entered the village of Billy Bowlegs when it was deserted. When the men left, they took with them bananas from Bowleg's prized plants, and it is alleged that the men maliciously destroyed the banana plants. The next morning a party of 30 Seminoles attacked the military party, killing and wounding some of the men. This was the start of the third war.

The war was fought with less than 200 Seminole warriors against the U.S. Army and Militia force of more than 2,000 men. The mission of this body was to capture and remove the remaining Indians in Florida to western territory. The Indians did not want to be removed to the west, and spent much of the three-year war evading the troops. There were relatively few skirmishes between the two sides; it was mainly a war of attrition. Almost the entire war was fought in the Everglades and Big Cypress Swamp. The militia fared better under these conditions than the regular Army soldiers, as they had woodsmen's knowledge and abilities that the soldiers lacked. They managed to drive many of the more northern Indians southward into the Everglades. The war finally ground to a halt. It was impossible to supply the forts in the interior during the rainy season due to the poor transportation conditions, and in January 1858, the Indians sued for peace. On May 4, 1858, Billy Bowlegs surrendered, and he and most of his band prepared for the trip west.

Forts

Many Florida cities began as forts. Eighty-one were built; most were created to support troops during the Seminole Wars. None of them were in present-day Indian River County. Four forts were erected from 1835 to 1854 to stop blockade runners and the importation of arms and ammunition for the Indians during the Indian wars: Forts Dallas, Lauderdale, Jupiter, and Pierce.

Panic of 1857

In 1857, the U.S. suffered a nation-wide financial failure due to reckless speculation in railroads. This led to a literal panic in the financial district, causing stocks to tumble and 900 businesses in New York to close. The rest of the U.S. economy, including Florida, was hit by a severe depression that lasted until early 1859.

Andrew P. Canova and Ed Marr

The first actual non-Indian settlers in the Sebastian area were Andrew P. Canova and Ed Marr. Their stay was brief, but thanks to the writings of Andrew Canova, they had a major impact. He began writing a series of sketches on his experiences during the Indian Wars in Florida that were published in the *Southern Sun* newspaper of Palatka, Florida. Through his writings, Canova introduced Americans to the danger, adventure, thrills, beauty, and richness of frontier Florida that he had personally lived through. His articles proved so popular that he was persuaded to have them published in book form in 1885. His book was reprinted in 1906.

Canova was a native Floridian who could live off of the land, a woodsman supremely equipped to survive the Indian Wars. He enlisted January 3, 1856, as a private in William Hooker's Company, in the Seminole War of 1856. In July of 1857 he and Ed

Marr were mustered in under the command of Captain Jacob Mickler at Fort Brooke, Tampa, to enter the Everglades to capture Indians. His tales of their journey south down the Kissimmee River through Lake Okeechobee River to the Everglades and on to the Florida Keys described the physical drudgery of traveling through swamp, and of rowing down the clear, pure Miami River.

His descriptions brought to life the majesty of the variety of flora and fauna encountered along the way. Soldiers dined on pork, beans, hard-tack, and coffee, supplemented with the help of Canova with cooter, soft-shell turtle, deer, bear, hogs, turkey, cormorants, oysters, clams, bass, mullet, pompano, honey, custard apples, grapes, blueberries, huckleberries, swamp cabbage, comptie, papaws, rubber-tree fruit, Indian-grown corn, melons, bananas, and pumpkins. He described encounters with hostile and friendly Indians, frontiersmen, bears, panthers, snakes, bees, and alligators, and commented on the places where there were no mosquitoes. At Pavilion Key the water was so clear they could see millions of clams, which they feasted upon.

Of the Indian River region, he commented on looking into the clear water of the river and seeing horse-shoe crabs, sea-porcupines, tarpons, saw-fish, sharks, bishops, whiparees, and stingarees below. Roseate spoonbills, snowy egrets, blue herons, several kinds of ducks, teals, widgeons, water turkeys, purple gallinules, blue herons, Johnnie gogglin, black-winged curlew, mullet, pompano, drum, grouper, red snapper, saw-fish, alligators, and turtles were also found, although hunting had made some of them scarcer. Phelps was one of the frontiersmen he encountered.

Canova wrote a section on his life in Sebastian with Ed Marr. In November 1858, after they had mustered out, the two men left their lodgings at Tampa Bay to go to Honey Branch, St. Sebastian River, which Canova remembered from previous travels. They settled on land near the mouth of the St. Sebastian River, close to a cove with a spring. When they arrived, they immediately began to build a 14-foot square house, of poles and palmetto thatch, which took two days. It was watertight and built to last ten years. They made an unsuccessful attempt to create a citrus grove. These two men existed quite well on the abundance of deer, bear, turtles, fish, and fowl they found. Supplies were obtained by rowing by boat 30 miles south to Fort Capron, to Major William Russell's grocery store. Their nearest neighbor was Captain John Houston, fifteen miles to the north on Elbow Creek, Eau Gallie. In the 1860 Florida agricultural census for Brevard County, the only individuals enumerated in the Sebastian area were Andrew Canova, with eight acres of improved land and 35 acres unimproved, and Edward Marr, with eight acres improved, and 32 unimproved acres. Ed Marr remained at the property on the St. Sebastian River, and died there in 1864. Canova left to enlist in the Confederate Army for the Civil War on May 24, 1861, at St. Augustine.

In 1863, while enlisted, Canova stole food from a farmer in Tennessee, along with Isadore Papy and Herbert Pacetty. Canova was sentenced to six months of hard labor. He went AWOL in September of 1863, and was dropped from the muster rolls as a deserter. He spent years in Key West where he acted as a guide and pilot. He also tried his hand at sponge-gathering; the sponges could be seen 12 feet down in the crystal-clear water. He witnessed, even in the mid-1800s, algae blooms in the ocean that killed fish and other sea life. Around 1865, he took a job as an assistant at the Key West Lighthouse and then transferred to the Sand Key Lighthouse. He remained there until January 30, 1866, when he left to settle somewhere on the Indian River.

Phelps

Andrew Canova wrote of an encounter with another Indian River resident, Phelps. Phelps was one of the frontiersmen who lived in the Indian River region circa 1854 with a rifle named "Ruin" and five ferocious hunting dogs that were part bloodhound, obtained from Captain Douglas Dummett. The rifle was purchased from Captain Mills Burnham, for whom it had been custom made. Phelps' preferred diet was bear meat. In the 1840s, he had traveled with John C. Fremont over the Rocky Mountains where he was an avid huntsman and an excellent shot, hunting grizzly bears and eagles. In Florida, he hunted bears and alligators. Phelps was famous along the Indian River for his hunting prowess and storytelling.

Others

It is possible that there were some other settlers on the banks of the St. Sebastian River in the 1850s and 1960s, although there are no firm records of this and Canova does not mention any in his published works. Crumbling foundations upstream on the banks of the Sebastian River were later found, with basements similar to those in northern homes; also cherry, black walnut, and mahogany woods were found, along with wood paneling ruins. This lends credence to the idea that there were several families who came to the St. Sebastian River from New England during the 1850s and 60s, and later left. Marr and Canova built only from local materials, and Phelps had no such residence.

Pelican Island

Once the threat of Indian hostilities died down, sportsmen and naturalists began to be attracted to the Indian River area. Naturalist Dr. Henry Bryant presented a paper before the Boston Society of Natural History on January 19, 1859, of his observations at Pelican Island and headwaters of the Sebastian River on March 15 and April 20 of a prior year. He stated that Pelican Island was the most extensive breeding place he had seen for pelicans and he related details of bird movements and habits. Some sportsmen came from as far away as Europe to hunt and fish along the Indian River.

6

Civil War, Reconstruction, and First Permanent Settlers: 1860s

National events dominated Florida's history in the 1960s, as it did the rest of the country, with the Civil War and Reconstruction Era. This divisive period in U.S. history created tumultuous change in many ways, with many reversals of fortune for businesses as well as individuals. People were on the move as never before in its aftermath. Florida profited more than it lost. The Florida population in 1860 was 140,424; for the first time, the population of the state was as large as it had been with the native Indian population before the Spanish arrived in the 1500s. By the end of the decade, it swelled by another 47,000. Post-war prosperity gave some the ability to relocate or travel and ruined others, forcing relocation. Post-war, uprooted soldiers migrated west or to Florida. Later in their lives, several Civil War soldiers made their homes in Sebastian. The Civil War put an end to the railroad growth of the 1850s, and by 1865, railroads were going bankrupt. However, steamboats were on the rise. The Homestead Act provided cheap land.

Some early Florida state plans excited interest but still were not acted upon. The Internal Improvement Act that passed in 1850 with a design for an inland waterway along the east coast was one such plan. In the late 1860s and early 1870s William Henry Gleason organized the Southern Inland Waterway and Navigation Company, created to open an inland waterway from Jacksonville to Biscayne Bay, and to dig a canal to connect the upper St. Johns at Lake Washington with the Indian River at Elbow Creek. These projects were not completed in those years, but interest still remained to accomplish them.

1862 Homestead Act

As a spur to growth, on May 20, 1862, President Lincoln signed into law the 1862 Homestead Act, permitting settlement of public lands. To qualify, settlers had to never have taken up arms against the United States government, be 21 years of age or head of a family, and be a US citizen or citizenship applicant. Freed slaves and women were also permitted to acquire land under this act. It required five years of residence and improvements or cultivation of the land, acquired for a $15.00 fee, for 160 acres. In the

1880s, the application of Gottlob Kroegel is an instance of just how complicated this process could be.

Brevard County

The population of Brevard County in 1860, 246 individuals, was twice what Santa Lucia had been in 1850. By 1867, it remained the same. None of those enumerated were the soldiers present in the 1850 census, as those soldiers had been removed when Fort Capron closed in 1858. Only two of the listed inhabitants, Andrew Canova and Ed Marr, were at Sebastian. The 1860 Florida agricultural census of Brevard County listed 32 individuals, including Canova and Marr. Canova was gone by 1861, and Marr died in 1864. Dempsey Cain at that time was living in Lake City, Columbia County. According to the 1860 census taker William B. Watson, there were no individuals or firms in Brevard County producing any manufactured product valued $500 or over per year. The main production of the county in the 1860s was cattle, with 39 cattle owners, some with very large herds. Individuals primarily grew food for their own use. There were two merchants, Thomas Autman and Herman W. Ross, one mechanic, four carpenters, one physician, one mail carrier, and one gentleman. Thirty-one slaves were owned by four different individuals. In 1869, the State of Florida enacted its first school law, making Brevard County a school district. Schools could be opened when there were at least seven children who would attend. The county continued a slow growth in the 1860s.

Steamboats were prospering. One of the early ships was the *Madison*, operated by Captain James Tucker before the Civil War, bringing goods to sell to the settlers along the Suwannee River. It carried cowhides, beef, tallow for candles, chickens, eggs, hogs, venison, beeswax, and more.

Civil War

After the 1860 election of Abraham Lincoln to the presidency, Florida was the third state to secede to join the Confederacy in the Civil War in early 1861. The United States proclaimed a blockade of the Confederate coastline from Virginia to Texas, enforced by the Navy, to prevent the export of cotton and timber, and the import of weapons, ammunition, food, and medicine. This blockade was difficult because of the 1,400 miles of coastline. Moreover, navigation was hazardous as there were no operational navigation aids; the lighthouses were not lit, and the coast was thinly populated. The South Atlantic Blockade Squadron was responsible for the area from South Carolina to Key West. Although requested, no troops were sent by the Confederacy to protect the Indian River Inlet at Fort Pierce from the U.S. Navy.

There was considerable action on the Indian River. Some Floridians took advantage of the situation to erect salt works and to become blockade runners, smuggling goods and war materials. Tremendous profits could be made by these smugglers. The Indian River was broad, shallow, and isolated. It ran from 3 to 4 feet deep, requiring the use of small, extremely shallow draft boats that could run close to shore, each carrying small loads. Local fishermen had the advantage of knowing the waters extremely well. The Indian River gave access inland at the St. Johns River, as well as providing access to the inlet at Jupiter into the Atlantic. This inlet was faster and easier to use, being wider and deeper, and closer to the Bahamas. It was patrolled by Navy boats, however. The north part was accessible through the Haulover into the Mosquito Lagoon, but this was extremely shallow, only 1 to 3 feet deep, and boats usually had to be dragged through. This route received less use. In March 1863, the federal schooner *Norfolk Packet* chased the British schooner *Linda* up the Indian River Inlet. The *Linda* surrendered after shots were fired. In April 1863, the USS *Gem of the Sea* captured the *Maggie Fulton* in the Indian River, and later the *Ann*, the *Petie*, and the *Inez*. The *Rebel* was captured in the Indian River by the *Roebuck* in 1864, and the *Nina* was taken. The last blockade runner captured in the Indian River was the *Mary* in 1865.

Steamboats on the St. Johns River were used to transport goods and troops. One was the *Maple Leaf*. It was built in 1851 in Canada for carrying passengers. It was sold in Boston and chartered to the U.S. Army for use as a transport in 1862. It was sunk by a mine April 1, 1864, on the St. Johns River, carrying three infantry regiments.

Brevard County was becoming dominated by its cattle industry in the western part of the county. This cattle culture primarily flourished on the plains west of the St. Johns River. These cattle fed Confederate Civil War soldiers. This market created even more expansive herds. With the increasing herds came cattle rustling, branding of the wrong cattle, and property disputes. In 1864, the Brevard County Seat was relocated to Bassville in the western part of the county, reflecting the strength of the cattle industry's influence.

Reconstruction Era 1865-1877

Andrew Johnson succeeded Abraham Lincoln as president in 1865. His policy was to permit former Confederate states to rejoin the Union if they renounced slavery. The new Florida constitution was written to put this into effect in July 1868. Republicans took all statewide elections. Harrison Reed was Florida's governor from 1868 to 1872, during the turbulent Reconstruction period.

Post-War Travel

Florida travel was complex post-war. Commercial steamboat navigation between Florida and Charleston, South Carolina, resumed. Travel was also eased by the fact that vessels built for use during the Civil War were considered surplus afterward and were sold by the government to private interests. Two such steamboats were the *City Point* that went into service on the ocean and St. Johns River in 1865, and the *Dictator* in 1866, plying their trade between Charleston and Palatka.

A number of propeller-driven coastal steamers ran between New York, Philadelphia, or Boston to Savannah, a preferred method of travel over railroads, which had not improved. Shortly after the end of the Civil War, fierce competition in the north between rival steamboat companies drove some of these owners to seek new routes in Florida. The *St. Marys* and *St. Johns* were two of the coastal steamers running between Savanna and Palatka. The Civil War had stopped settlers and tourism, but by the winter of 1869-1870, the Savannah to Palatka water route flourished again with the luxury steamers *Lizzie Baker* and *Nick King.* The *Sylvan Shore*, a New York commuter, was sent south for the season to run between Savannah and Fernandina.

An 1869 guide book suggested travel by rail to Charleston, and then by steamer. Savannah was the most popular stopover to change vessels; however, many preferred the Charleston route, with a direct steamer *Dictator* or *City Point* from there to Palatka. Steamboats became numerous on the Suwannee after the Civil War.

In 1865-66, settlers could travel other routes from Jacksonville by a combination of river and lake travel by boat and rough roads cut into the wilderness. Travel down the Florida Atlantic coastline was still considered extremely treacherous. Commonly, travel was down the St. Johns River, or from Palatka to Enterprise or Lake Harney. From there, individuals traveled a rough wagon road to the coast, or by shallow draft boat up the St. Johns to Salt Lake, and then overland for about six miles.

The Civil War was the first American conflict to involve railroads, carrying supplies and men. The war crippled or destroyed nearly half of Southern railroad companies. Little maintenance or repair was carried out during the war years, as companies lacked funds. Florida had the fewest, weakest, and poorest railroads in the decade after the war, which were briefly controlled by the U.S. Army. Some received repairs, and all were returned to their rightful owners, but Florida railroads remained in bad shape financially. Most went bankrupt, including the Florida & Alabama Railroad. The systems remained rather primitive and it took sixteen hours to travel from Savannah to Jacksonville.

The Florida, Atlantic & Gulf Central restored its Jacksonville terminal after the war, reopened service between Jacksonville and Baldwin, and rebuilt the wrecked junction at Baldwin. However, it still defaulted on payments and was sold in 1868. The Pensacola and Georgia Railroad in the middle of the state survived undamaged but also suffered financially, was unable to make payments, and was sold in 1869. The Florida Railroad suffered the most damage and was auctioned off in 1866. By late 1860, the St. Johns Railroad resumed operations but still suffered financially. In 1870, it was sold and rebuilt, but it had not modernized; its trains were still being hauled by both steam engines and horses.

Politicking and fraud dogged the railroads, slowing recovery. State aid was eventually extended to the railroads in the form of a railroad bill allowing the Jacksonville,

Pensacola & Mobile Railroad Company to issue bonds; it was formed June 24, 1869, but it too folded through greed and fraud.

After the Civil War, experienced sailor James Paine Jr. was commissioned by the Post Office Department as a mail carrier for the small settlements along the river from Titusville south on the east coast of Florida. Mail arrived from Jacksonville by steamboat on the St. Johns River to Salt Lake Landing, and then by a trolley pulled by mules to Titusville. Paine delivered the mail by sailboat to the docks along the river.

In this confusing and turbulent period of Florida history, Dr. John Milton Hawks, in the interest of promoting land speculation, traveled along the Florida East Coast from St. Augustine to Biscayne Bay, prior to 1870. Along the way he observed "a few scattered dwellings, here and there an orange grove, and occasionally a farm." There were no inns or hotels, and any travelers, at best, could stay at the homesteads, as noted by the Hannas in *Golden Sands.*

Henry Titus

Henry T. Titus was a blockade runner during the Civil War, a famous and dashing figure who was a self-titled Colonel, born in Oklahoma in 1815. He was a filibusterer in Nicaragua and Costa Rica, and was arrested in San Juan del Norte by British officers for using vile language regarding Queen Victoria. In Kansas, he was involved in the pro-slavery riots in 1854, when Kansas became a territory and readied for statehood. Col. Titus and some 1,000 other Floridians and Georgians went to Kansas to support the pro-slavery cause. Col. Titus was taken prisoner by John Brown, but escaped. He was arrested for another escapade on the Indian River during the Civil War, transporting men trying to escape the Confederate Conscription Act, and he later became a successful blockade runner, becoming wealthy smuggling pricy goods for sale to the Confederate Government.

In 1867, Titus arrived at the camp at Sandy Point which was already filling up with criminals hiding out. Other settlers came back to Sandy Point immediately after the war, and by 1870, there were a few houses and stores. As with many stories of this sort, there are several versions. In one telling, Titus, the postmaster of Sandy Point, made his own decision to name the town Titusville in 1873. In other versions, Titus played a game of either checkers or dominoes with Captain Rice of Texas to see who would get to name the town. Titus won, and the town became Titusville. He built a hotel there, the Titus House, and he was a moving force behind having Titusville named the county seat.

Soldiers Who Came to Sebastian and Roseland

The Civil War brought about a political and social upheaval for Confederate states in the post-war period. It caused many people to uproot themselves and seek new homes.

The trauma of war caused many soldiers to feel unable to fit back into their former homes and occupations, and so they sought the wilderness frontiers of the West and Florida. Thus, the population in Brevard County began to grow. Desertion became not uncommon, as soldiers became disheartened by the death and suffering of the war. One in three Florida Confederate soldiers died, and many survivors were disabled. In some places in Florida there were bands of deserters.

There were ten Civil War soldiers who lived in Sebastian or Roseland for a time. Four of them joined Florida regiments, and the rest came from all over the United States to eventually find homes in Sebastian and Roseland.

William C. Braddock was a private in the 2nd Florida Cavalry of the Confederate forces from 1861 to1864. Around 1891, he and his family settled in Sebastian.

Andrew Canova enlisted in the Confederate Army as a Private, 3rd Florida Infantry, where he served from 1861 to1863. He was the only one to be in Sebastian before the war.

Dempsey Cain enlisted in the Confederate Army on May 11, 1861. Like Canova, he also served in F Company, 3rd Florida Infantry, where he became a Sergeant. He and his family moved to the St. Sebastian River in 1877.

James Raulerson served as a Private in the 9th Florida Infantry of the Confederate Army from 1863 to 1865. He moved to Sebastian circa 1903-1916 with his wife Welthean.

Charles Dukeshier was a Private in the 110th Ohio Infantry of the Union Army from 1862-1865. He was in the Roseland area circa 1912.

Robert A. Hardee attained the rank of Captain in the 9th Georgia Infantry of the Confederate Army under Robert E. Lee, and served from 1861 to 1863. The Hardees moved to Sebastian in 1889.

Benjamin F. Hardesty became a Sergeant in the 1st Special Louisiana Battalion of the Confederate Army from 1861 to 1865. In the 1890s he was living in Sebastian with his wife Ella.

William Wilson Layport was a Private in the 28th Regiment of Iowa of the Union Army from 1862 to 1865 and lived in Sebastian circa 1917.

Nathan E. Perrine was a Private in the 34th Illinois Infantry of the Union Army from 1861 to 1865 and lived in Roseland circa 1927.

Henry Ruffner attained the rank of Lt. Colonel of the 26th Virginia Cavalry of the Confederate Army, serving from 1862 to 1865. Around 1896, he moved with his wife to the Ercildoune area.

Once Canova and Marr were gone, the Sebastian area's population went back to zero, until at last, in this turbulent post-war period, two permanent settlers made their home in the Sebastian area: August Park and John Baird, around 1869. They came from very different circumstances and backgrounds, but both homesteaded and had families there.

August Park

There are several versions of August Park's origins before settling in Sebastian. He may have been born December 21, 1833, in Brussels, Belgium, and immigrated to the United States from Danzig, Germany. According to descendants Mildred and Lenore Park, he was born in Danzig, Germany, in 1833. He may have immigrated to the United States around 1865. Mildred and Lenore stated that he arrived first in New York and later came to Fort Pierce, settling in Sebastian in 1865. In one telling Park was a German sailor who had been to many countries, including Chili, on a ship with a cargo of Peruvian guano. Later he worked for the Florida Canning Company of New York, relocating from New York to Fort Pierce in 1868. He also briefly worked in City Point. In 1868, he married Polly Ann Gore, whose parents migrated to Florida from Washington, North Carolina.

After he arrived in Sebastian, he settled first on Barker's Bluff and built a home. At one point, he opened a store. August and Polly's son Charles Park was born on Barker's Bluff on August 21, 1869. August Park ran a trade boat from Titusville to Fort Pierce. Park also claimed land at Blue Hole Creek, north of the Indian River Inlet, about 2.5 miles north of present Fort Pierce Inlet, where he caught turtles and shipped them to New York.

John Baird

John Baird was born circa 1811 in New Jersey, as were both of his parents. In 1850, John, a farmer age 40, resided in Holmes County, Ohio, with his wife Sarah and seven children. All were born in New Jersey, except for the last two, who were born in Ohio. Sometime between 1854 and 1857, he moved to Ohio. The 1860 census shows John as a 48-year-old farmer living in Worthington, Richland County, Ohio, with his wife Cornelia, age 32, along with Sarah, age 23, Louise, age 17, Alilla, age 15, Ellen, age 12, and John, age 11. All were born in New Jersey, except Ellen and John, who were born in Ohio. Baird moved to Florida from Ohio sometime prior to 1869 when he settled in Sebastian to homestead.

In Sebastian, Baird built a small-frame house and started a citrus grove. He lived there alone for approximately ten years, until sometime after the June 4, 1880, census enumeration. The census related that he had a medical condition, anasarca, a form of dropsy. (Dropsy causes extreme fluid accumulation in the tissues due to cardiac problems, and can cause death. Foxglove, or digitalis, is the remedy.) Cornelia and two sons joined him in Sebastian after that date, and according to his homestead affidavit, may have been there with him some of the time before that. Baird operated the trade boat *Cornelia* for a while, and ran pineapples over to the Bahamas.

The Homestead Testimony of Claimant John Baird was dated Nov 21, 1881. In it he stated that he was 70 years of age, native born, and that the post office for his residence was Melbourne. He had established residency twelve years previously, or 1869. He had ten acres cleared and cultivated, raised crops every year, and had an orange grove, for a total value $1,000, on land not valuable for anything other than agriculture. His house burned, and five years prior to the affidavit, in 1876, he built another house. His family consisted of his wife and two children. He was consistently present on his homesteaded property, absent only for a few days at time during the twelve-year period. His family was absent a part of the time. He never made any other homestead entry and did not sell or convey any part of the land, according to his statement.

7
Discovering Florida and More Families: 1870s

Florida's Recovery

To the north, the post-Civil War period produced a booming economy that created a rising middle class and gave to many people leisure time and money for travel. For others, the war sent individuals looking for a new life, westward or to Florida. The 1870s in Florida was a restless time of recovery, and all manner of people were beginning to find Florida's east coast. The 1870 Florida population was 187,748, and growing. Florida was undergoing change.

To the people of the Victorian Era, the frontiers of the United States were uniquely appealing. Florida, in particular, was the embodiment of romanticism, with terror and tropical beauty. Victorian senses thrilled to its uncharted wilderness, dangerous, untamed nature, and menacing Indians. Wealthy tourists began coming to experience this wilderness from a safe distance, and often with a comfortable bed. They wanted to see natural Florida with its unspoiled springs, rivers, sunsets, palm trees, and alligators. The study of natural history became a popular American hobby, and many amateurs came to indulge this desire to study seashells, orchids, and other flora and fauna unique to Florida. People impoverished by the war saw it as a new start in a new land.

The Florida recovery included recognition of the need for better transportation to bring these people and commerce into the state. Its waterways were the solution; most railroads at this point were bankrupt from the war, and roads were practically non-existent. On February 10, 1871, the Internal Improvement Fund undertook a project to create an inland waterway by widening and deepening the channel from the St. Johns River to Biscayne Bay to create the only practical means of transportation for eastern Florida. Unfortunately, the Indian River section proved to be the most difficult and was not completed. Only dredging would allow the passage of large boats. Until the advent of the railroads, the rivers were the only viable means of travel.

Another bout of over-speculation in railroads was the cause of another severe depression from 1873 to 1878. The stock market plunged, again causing many failed businesses and lost jobs. Food prices collapsed, and rural America dropped into poverty. This was felt in Florida's fledgling commerce and tourism.

Florida had another sort of upheaval this decade as well. An earthquake shook the state January 12, 1879, the largest earthquake ever recorded in Florida. It struck about 11:45 P.M., possibly centered in the Palatka area, and was felt over a large part of north Florida. News accounts of the quake included Cedar Key, Gainesville, Jacksonville, St. Augustine, and Tallahassee, among other cities.

Brevard County

Brevard County was going through changes and growth as well. Its population had skyrocketed from around 250 in the 1860s to 1,216 in this decade. The predominance of this expansion was along the Indian River. However, this still-sparse population and the problems of travel and slow communications made it difficult to govern the county and fill government positions.

Cattle Wars

County boundaries were redefined in the 1870s, in part because of the cattle range wars that were still raging in the 1870s in western Brevard and Orange Counties. The free-range laws were in effect, and numerous battles were centered around brand altering, cattle rustling, and boundary disputes. A reign of terror and mob mentality gripped the area, with ranchers taking the law into their own hands. The Brevard County Clerk of Courts was kidnapped and held captive over these issues. The cattle economy still dominated Brevard County in the 1870s, even as the population was growing along the east coast. Dempsey Cain was the Brevard County Sheriff at that time, and he resigned in early 1870 when the range war was at its most violent. Severe flooding in 1878 was so extreme between the Kissimmee and St. Johns Rivers that it thinned cattle herds; alligators left the rivers and began attacking cattle on the prairies. Gunfights erupted between families in Orange and Baker County, resulting in the death of one of the Sheriffs.

In 1874, Eau Gallie on the east coast was voted as the seat of Brevard County government, emphasizing the population shift. When in 1879 southern Volusia County and Titusville were annexed to Brevard County, Colonel Henry Titus was vocal in his support of making Titusville the county seat of Brevard. The majority vote went to Titusville, over that of Rockledge and Eau Gallie, shifting the seat of government further north, but remaining on the east coast. Col. Titus donated the land for the county buildings. Titusville grew rapidly during the 1870s, and by 1880, it may have had as many as 200 residents. This freewheeling city had election problems in the 1870s that caused several local officials to be sent to prison. Some planned improvements in the county did not succeed. In 1879, a company was formed to widen the Haulover Canal, but was unable to obtain funding, and a proposed tram from Mosquito Lagoon to the Indian River never was realized, either.

Indian River Area

The lure of Florida resonated in the mindset of the Victorian Era, knowing nothing and caring nothing of cattle wars. It was the start of the Yankee Invasion and the beginning of permanent settlement of the area. Individuals to the north began to recognize the Indian River area as a destination for settling, vacationing, scientific study, hunting, and fishing, all lured by the exotic, lush scenery, and abundant and varied wildlife and fish. Many came for its touted healthful air. Some came to escape their pasts. Commerce began to expand along the Indian River. By the mid-1870s, these settlers had turned the area into a recognized trading center and a regular stop for commercial boats. Fish and turtles were important products sent north to St. Augustine for sale.

Brevard County had an outlook governed by the Indian River, the focal point for travel, commerce, and tourism. At this point in their history Sebastian and Roseland still were an unnamed part of the Indian River area, situated roughly between the Sebastian River at the north end, and to the south, Pelican Island and Barker's Bluff. These were the known parts of this river-dominated area. The population doubled there in this decade; two families were still in residence, the August Park and John Baird families, and the Dempsey Cain and David Peter Gibson families took up residence and became permanent settlers there as well, bringing the total to four families. Lang and Priest stopped, then passed on.

August Park

The Parks wintered in Sebastian and spent the summers at Blue Hole, according to Simeon Park. Their son Simeon was born in 1877 at Blue Hole. Mildred and Lenore Park said that early settlers stayed in August Park's home when they first arrived, and he allowed people to use his property for burial, the start of the current Sebastian Cemetery. Simeon Park related that many people at a time stayed with the Parks.

August Park continued on in the Sebastian area, and made an application under the 1820 Land Act for land located on the Indian River, just south of the St. Sebastian River, not on the Barker's Bluff property. August Park's Homestead Affidavit for this land was dated April 4, 1877, and the Homestead Application Form No. 5406 was dated July 11, 1877, for 43.5 acres. In order for the application to be approved, Park was required to be a United States citizen, which he set out to accomplish.

John Baird

John Baird also belonged to that class of individuals who came to Florida, stayed, thrived, and made their home there. He continued his residence in Sebastian, homesteading his land. On September 24, 1872, John Baird filed his application for land through the 1862 Homestead Act for 168 5/6 acres in the downtown Sebastian area around Main Street on the Indian River. He built his home near the east end of what became Main Street.

The Allure

The North was fascinated with Florida. Post-Civil War, Americans clamored for information about the country's other frontier. Moreover, recovering railroads and hotel entrepreneurs wanted to encourage tourism in Florida. This sparked a flood of books, brochures, and pamphlets about Florida. Settlers, ex-soldiers, outlaws, drifters, sportsmen, naturalists, vacationers, and speculators all started finding their way down the Indian River, some finding what they were seeking, and others failing. Travel to the Indian River area remained difficult, although 1877 was a banner year; two steamboats started plying the Indian River. However, it was not until the 1880s that steamboats and railroads finally made travel into the area more feasible.

The Others

There were those who passed through eastern Florida in the 1870s that were in sharp contrast to the settlers or leisure class of visitor. Florida had also attracted those who sought the anonymity and freedom of frontier life or a new start, and were leaving a past behind somewhere else.

Augustus Oswald "George" Lang

Barker's Bluff was a highly visible and attractive landmark along the Indian River that lured settlers and wayfarers. Augustus Oswald "George" Lang was one of those people who camped briefly on Barker's Bluff around 1870, at the same time as Dugald Priest and his family. As there is no mention of the Park family, it is possible that while Lang and Priest were there, the Parks were down at Park's Blue Hole property, or his other Sebastian property. Lang was born around 1831 in Germany and was an educated man. He served in the Confederate Army in the Civil War, but was listed as a deserter in 1863. In 1867, he was living on Lake Worth, and had built a snug little cabin surrounded by fruit trees and a vegetable garden. He lived in many places in Florida both before and after his short sojourn at Barker's Bluff, where he met Susan Carolina Priest, daughter of Dugald Priest, whom he married when she was only fourteen.

Augustus and Susan moved up the St. Lucie River twelve miles from Stuart, where he created a nice home. He was murdered by visitors to this home in January 1874, outlaws that he had known previously. It was most likely due to an unpaid debt. Susan was seven months pregnant at the time. The outlaws had asked him to take them up and across the river, then shot him when they got to shore. His body was never found, but his boat was found with blood and a bullet hole. When Susan went for help, the men went back and robbed the house. Two of the men were caught, tried, and sent to prison, and one was killed. Lang's son, Walker Augustus Lang, was born about a month after Lang's death. Susan remarried to John Smith of Fort Pierce in 1880.

Dugald Priest

Dugald Priest was a good example of someone who moved from his home state for a new start in Florida after the Civil War, but did not adapt or thrive in pioneering life, nor did he return home. He did not stay in any area for any length of time, never finding agreeable surroundings or work that suited him. His family traveled with him. He spent several months on Barker's Bluff with his family around 1870, with no mention of the August Park family in his tale.

Dugald Priest appeared in the 1860 Georgia U.S. Census at Waynesville, a 38-year-old railroad overseer born in North Carolina. His wife was Sarah C. Priest, age 28, born in South Carolina. They had two daughters at that time: Susan C. and Ida Isabella, age four and two, born in Georgia. In the 1850s, they may have lived at Jesup. According to a later son Joseph, his mother was Sarah Robinson, a Cherokee Indian. During the Civil War, Dugald worked for the railroad, and after the war in 1866, he and his family moved to Jasper, Florida.

Friends there talked about the Indian River area and the Priests decided to move there. He sold his crop and packed their household belongings with a horse team and an ox team and headed north over rough trails; there were no roads, and they slept in a makeshift tent. Their destination was Sand Point at Titusville, and they remained there for two weeks. The lack of neighbors was not appealing. No one was there except for Col. Titus and his family.

Priest and his family packed up yet again and traveled south to Grant by boat and there they eked out a living for a while. Apparently, their longest stay at this point was in Fort Pierce, where for about a year Priest was able to find work. After Fort Pierce, Dugald, Sarah, and their children Susan, Ida, Joseph, William, Raiford, and Frances went back up river to Barker's Bluff. A man by the name of Baskin had also lived there, and for a short time it was known as Baskin's Bluff. In residence when they arrived was Augustus Lang. The Priests stayed there for a few months, but had no way to make a living. This was around 1870, according to son Joseph's account.

They went back to Titusville where Dugald got a job working for Col. Titus, leaving behind their daughter Susan Carolina to marry Augustus Lang. Priest and his family went to Ormond in 1877, where they at last settled. Sarah Priest was the first teacher there. Dugald Priest died in Ormond around 1889, and Sarah died there in May 1918.

Dempsey Cain

A very different sort of family, that of Dempsey Cain's, joined the Bairds and Parks in the Sebastian/Roseland area and settled in 1877. Dempsey was born in Georgia on February 7, 1832, of Irish descent. At age 20, he enlisted in the Florida Troops during the Indian Wars on May 3, 1852, serving in Captain Aaron Jernigan's Company, General Hopkins' Division. Captain Jernigan's Company was tasked with protecting the Florida frontier settlers and their stock from the Indian depredations. Cain mustered out September 6, 1852. By the time of the 1860 census, Cain had relocated to Lake City, Columbia County, Florida. He was single, a carpenter, and lived in a rooming house.

When the Civil War broke out, he enlisted in the Confederate Army on May 11, 1861. It appears that he left service prior to the end of the war, as he became assistant keeper of the Sand Key Lighthouse on May 5, 1864, where he stayed until November 1864. Two years later, he became Assistant keeper of Jupiter Lighthouse from 1866 to 1868. From there he moved to Brevard County, where he became Sheriff from 1868 to 1870. The range wars were at their peak at the time he resigned as Sheriff. There he met and married Celia Padgett Bowler, a pregnant widow with two children. The marriage license of Celia Padgett Bowler to Dempsey Cain Sr. was dated December 15, 1870, and certified April 12, 1871, in Brevard County. They honeymooned in the St. Sebastian River area.

Dempsey, Celia, and family had been living in Olney, Florida, in 1877, when they moved to the St. Sebastian River, to the spot where they had honeymooned. Traveling down the old military trail, they brought their possessions with them in an ox-drawn wagon with their children, chickens, horses, and cattle. They settled on the northwest bank of the St. Sebastian River, claiming 20 acres through settler's rights, and erected a makeshift home. This land was west of where the railroad tracks were later laid. Constructing their permanent house involved some ingenuity. Their nearest neighbors were the D. P. Gibson family, and after their arrival, son Ralph Gibson assisted Dempsey Cain in cutting pine timbers for the frame of Cain's first real home. For siding, they used boards salvaged from wrecks. Roof shingles were cut from cypress. Cain homesteaded 20 acres and then 20 more farther east on the north side of the river. The Cains had seven daughters. Cain was a popular and generous man, liked by the Indians. Celia worked as a nurse.

Cracker Houses

Cain's home was most likely some variation of a Cracker House. On their arrival in Florida, pioneer settlers were faced with the problem of housing. Their first shelter might be a palmetto hut, but their first homes were often erected from native materials. If they could afford it, they could later on consider purchasing building materials from the north, to be sent down by ship or train. But to begin with, they needed protection from the elements, animals, and the voracious insect population. This style evolved to meet the problems of their environment. These houses were constructed of cedar, cypress, or other native trees, raised on pilings of rocks or bricks made of oyster shell and lime. Raising the houses on posts provided coolness, and discouraged snakes, etc. from entering. The simplest ones were one room with a plank floor and windows set to catch cross breezes. A fireplace and chimney was set on one side wall. A roofed porch provided a somewhat cooler, shady place to sit, and might wrap around the whole exterior. Windows had mosquito netting or shutters. A steeply pitched roof shed rain. Houses with more than one room could have a main hall running the length of the house; these were called "Shotgun Houses." Plumbing was exterior. Kitchens were also exterior, to minimize the risk of fires and to keep the rest of the house cool. There are many houses of this sort in the area. Any local wood house you see that has that raised floor was most likely built before the 1920s.

Lowndes County, Georgia

Sebastian gained population due to the Civil War. Several of the most influential Sebastian pioneers came from an area of Georgia close to the Florida border, that of Lowndes County, and also Brooks County which split from Lowndes County in 1858. When the Lowndes County area was settled in 1821 by four pioneers, it was a fertile, heavily wooded area inhabited by hostile Creek Indians. The rigors of surviving Indian hostilities and successful pioneering created a prosperous cotton, tobacco, and agricultural economy. However, Civil War privations brought it to a standstill, bringing ruin and forcing many to leave. The Sebastian area proved to be a promising haven for some. Captain David Peter Gibson was first; several other Sebastian families came later, like the Hardees, Lawsons, Vickers, and Ryalls. Trade boat captain William G. Abbott was also from Lowndes County.

Captain David Peter Gibson

Captain David Peter Gibson was one of those who left behind a questionable past, and he lived a colorful life when he arrived to settle in the Sebastian area around 1879, joining the Park, Baird, and Cain families. Captain David Peter Gibson was born circa 1832 in Georgia. He married Sarah Ann Aphire West sometime around August 31, 1853. From 1861 to 1862, Gibson, a farmer from Georgia, age 30, served in the Georgia Militia Company District 662.

The description of a murder case in the court records of Lowndes County, Georgia, in the racial incidents section, related the case of the murder of Grandison, a colored person, on July 7, 1866. The suspected murderer was D. P. Gibson, a white male. At the time of the report, no evidence was found against Gibson, and he was held over on bail until next term of the Superior Court for Lowndes County. Apparently he was not convicted and he remained in Lowndes County for several more years, for in the *Macon Weekly Telegraph* from October 15, 1869, was an article in the "From Lowndes County" section stating that D. P. Gibson had extensive vineyards for making wine.

While Gibson was in Valdosta, Lowndes County, Georgia, in 1876, he arranged the purchase of 158.9 acres of land on the St. Sebastian River. The Gibsons arrived about two years after the Dempsey Cain family, circa 1879, and settled on that property on a hammock near a spring on the south shore of the St. Sebastian River. With Gibson were his wife Sarah Ann and some of his six sons and two daughters. Gibson appreciated the finer things in life. This Georgia vintner brought with him a renowned hunting horse, Nimrod. Gibson brought pure-bred hogs as well, but they did not thrive in the Florida wilderness. His land was located in the Roseland area, between future Wauregon and the Indian River. Gibson planted pineapples and a large citrus grove there. He also maintained a small trading post in the area of the Sebastian Inlet for a time.

The spring on his property came to be known as Gibson Springs. This was located on the east bank of the South Prong of the Sebastian Creek near the bottom of a 20-foot bluff. It produced a steady flow of cool pure sulfur water. At that time and for many years after, it became a refreshing place for obtaining drinking water and swimming. It also became a popular spot for picnicking on the small island opposite the springs. Many years later, some Sebastianites discovered that the well had been plugged up, by what seemed to be a barrel, according to Jimmie Matthews. The spring seems to have vanished, now.

The Visitors

The viewpoint of the casual visitors to the Sebastian River and Indian River areas was a sharp contrast to that of the settlers. The 1870s had several noted descriptions published of the area, catering to the fascination and demand for even more information on the part of tourists and sportsmen about this mysterious land. These accounts tended to emphasize the positive aspects. Brochures and books of illustrations and photographs were popular, as were stereoscopes. The Indian River, Sebastian River, and Pelican Island became noteworthy, blossoming under this scrutiny. The area was lush, mysterious, and bountiful.

Stereoscopes

Stereoscopes were the hand-held viewers invented by Oliver Wendell Holmes in 1859. A three-dimensional image could be viewed looking into the eyepieces when paired identical photographs were inserted. This inexpensive entertainment became an overnight craze, and sales of the viewers and photographs were brisk. Railroads, hotels, and resorts took advantage of this interest as a promotional tool with images of Florida and elsewhere, fueling even more interest in the area.

Travelogues

Travelogues sold well, stimulating the interest in all things Florida. Forest and Stream Publishing Company commissioned two trips to explore Florida, a Lake Okeechobee trip in the winter of 1873-74, and another in 1874-75 on the Gulf Coast. The results were compiled in a book *Camp Life in Florida a Handbook for Sportsmen and Settlers*. The 1873-74 expedition was headed by Fred Ober, a Massachusetts naturalist, who wrote under the pen name of Fred Beverly for that book. He enumerated 62 species of birds, and reported finding abundant game and fish, naming the types of game fish found. A chapter by Thomas Jordan was devoted to the Indian River. In it he praised the quality of its fish and the healthful climate. He felt it would be an unequalled sanitarium for pulmonary subjects and a fine winter residence for invalids.

The book's chapter *Cruising Along Shore* by Fred Beverly described the Sebastian area. The men spent two days and nights wind-bound at St. Sebastian Creek. They visited the coast near the place where the 1715 fleet of Spanish galleons was driven ashore and lost. He described the high sand ridge, separating the river from ocean less than 300 yards across, thickly covered with scrub palmetto and gaily-colored flowers. He wrote that the high bluffs near St. Sebastian River had been selected as the site for a hotel, but felt the spot not well suited for such purpose. He related that Barker's Bluff was nearby, named after the man who lost his life there, killed by Indians at the same time Barker's friend Major Russell lost an arm.

"That's Pelican Island," Beverly's captain said, across from Barker's Bluff. Beverly described Pelican Island as "draped in white, its trees seemingly covered with snow, a circling flight of birds hovering over it, the water around dotted with hundreds of dusky objects, and the same dusky forms coming and going with no cessation in their flight." The island was covered with birds on the dead mangroves, hovering birds, nests, and fledglings; eagles and vultures were feeding on them. Two months later, the young birds had flown and the nests were full of eggs. Beyond Pelican Island to the south was the approach to the Narrows, guarded by two walls of living green, leaving but a narrow gateway.

More sportsmen traveled to the Indian River area, as it became known as a marvelous destination for outdoor recreation of hunting, fishing and birdwatching. A hunting trip was chronicled in *Appleton's Journal*, published in 1875, in a paper titled "An English Sportsman in Florida." A group of sportsmen traveled from Key West to the Indian River, first aboard the *Ida McKay* with Captain Merritt, a "conch" who was a professional wrecker (shipwreck salvager). Among sights they described in detail along the trip was the extensive turtle industry at St. Lucie.

Further on, north of the Narrows, the sportsmen came to the "Rookery," now known as Pelican Island. It was described as the greatest curiosity of the Indian River, a sportsman's paradise, due to the tremendous number of birds nesting there, of which they all shot a good many. North of Pelican Island they saw a man (unnamed) standing in the water gesturing and waving at them. The captain related that he was a half-crazy hunter who for years had lived on the bank of the Indian River in a log hut he had built. He had cultivated a small garden there. The previous October, a hurricane had carried away his house, garden, and possessions, and ever since the man hailed every passing boat and asked for supplies and news of the outside world. The boatload of sportsmen did not stop, and shortly after arrived at Sand Point, continuing on.

An account of the F. Trench Townsend expedition published in 1875 mentioned their viewing of the Rookery on the Indian River north of the Narrows, a pelicanry of tens of thousands of birds, the biggest congregation of pelicans in Florida. This group made camp at the St. Sebastian River and continued on north the next day.

Florida was publicized in photographs. In 1875, famous western photographer Benjamin Franklin Upton moved to St. Augustine to become the pioneer landscape photographer in Florida. Artists began coming to Florida to paint in the late 1880s as well. In March of 1876, the first Florida State Fair was held in Jacksonville, a boon to tourism there.

One of the most factual and enduring accounts of Florida was written by Sidney Lanier, a noted writer, poet, flutist, and public speaker. *Florida: Its Scenery, Climate, and History*, was written in 1875, and published by J. B. Lippincott. Lanier was a Confederate soldier who was captured and contracted tuberculosis while in a Union prison. As his poetry and music generated little income, he reluctantly accepted the assignment to write a commercial guidebook for Atlantic Coast Railway. He traveled in Florida for a few months, and fleshed out his impressions with factual, detailed research and conversations with others. This illustrated book became extremely popular, with a second edition published in 1876, and re-issues in 1877 and 1881. It contained a chapter on the St. Johns and Indian Rivers and included chapters on the history, climate, and benefits for those with consumption. The appendix detailed numerous travel routes to Florida.

Lanier's description of the Indian River: "Along this Indian River country is a marvelously bland air, and I have been told of many overworked men and incipient consumptives who have here found new life. The waters are full of fish in great variety; the woods abound in deer and other game; and the whole land amounts to a perpetual invitation to the overworked, the invalid, the air-poisoned, the nervously prostrate people, to come down with yacht and tent, with rod and gun, and rebuild brain, muscle and nerve." (Who could resist?)

Consumption

Consumption was the earlier name for tuberculosis, a widespread and deadly infectious disease of the nineteenth and early twentieth centuries, with no cure, and most common in a crowded urban environment. Fresh air and sunlight, and visiting or living in a climate with milder, purer air was thought to improve the consumptive's health, causing many of them to seek life in Florida. Milk pasteurization in the 1920s, streptomycin in the 1940s, and other later drugs finally proved to be successful against this disease.

Travel

Travel accommodations remained a maze of routes and types of conveyance in the 1870s. According to Sidney Lanier's account, there were several ways to reach the Indian River. One was travel by schooner from New York into Mosquito Inlet. The appendix to Lanier's book listed 24 schedules of routes by train from New York to Jacksonville. From Enterprise on the St. Johns by stage was popular, or one could travel by small steamer from Enterprise to Salt Lake, then by wheels to Sand Point or Titusville. A planned future route was to be from St. Augustine by the steamer *Mayflower* down the Matanzas, then by stage or tram road along the shore to Halifax River, then by small steamer along the Halifax and Indian Rivers. The little steamboat *Pioneer* ran the entire length of the Indian River. W. H. Churchill operated a tram road from Salt Lake to LaGrange from the mid-1870s.

The primary transportation route in and out of the Indian River area continued to be up the St. Johns River to Enterprise or Lake Harney and then either overland by wagon, or by way of the river to Salt Lake or Lake Poinsett. Some ships still made the difficult water voyage: the *Darlington, Wekiva, Fox, Volusia, Marion, Osceola, Astatula,* and *Waunita.*

Not all railroads failed in Florida after the war; some survived. The Pensacola and Mobile Railroad & Manufacturing Company flourished, opening in 1870. Also the Pensacola and Barrancas Railroad running from Pensacola to Barrancas opened that year, as did the St. Johns Railroad. However, the St. Johns was in a state of extreme disrepair. It was later sold and rebuilt, but hazards remained, such as alligators and bear cubs sleeping on the tracks. In 1874, the Pensacola and Perdido Railroad began hauling lumber. Slowly, other railroads began running in Florida.

In early 1875, George W. Parsons and his brother were New Yorkers who had traveled to Key West and Miami, spending several months. On their return trip they traveled the Atlantic north to Jupiter and proceeded up the Indian River from there. They were informed that plans were underway for a small steamer to make runs from Sand Point to the Indian River Inlet, commencing in 1876, and of a tram road from Titusville to Lake Harney. This was never built. They rode out a storm at Barker's Bluff, which was uninhabited at that time.

By the 1870s, there was sufficient concern over the fate of passengers from wrecked ships off of the coast of Florida that Houses of Refuge were planned at places where shipwrecked passengers could rest and recuperate. In later days, they became Coast

Guard Stations. Albert Blaisdell received the contract to build five houses of refuge. The ones at Malabar and Gilbert's Bar were the ones closest to the Sebastian/Roseland area. The Gilbert's Bar House of Refuge was built March 10, 1876, two miles north of the Gilbert's Bar Inlet. It is the only one of the buildings that exists in present day.

Before the trade boats and steamboats, settlers who homesteaded the Indian River area during the 1860s and 1870s depended on sailboats for supplies and outside contacts. During the early days of settlement along the Indian River, there were few stores, and it was a lengthy process to travel to them. Most travel was on the river, as a more convenient and faster method than land travel. Nearly everyone owned a boat of some sort. Individuals on the Indian River had to travel days or weeks to obtain even the most basic supplies. From Titusville, the closest store in any direction was at Fort Pierce. Travel by small watercraft took five to ten days for that full distance, and steamboats were infrequent as yet. A unique solution to the problem of shopping arose, that of the trade boats, which flourished during the late 1870s and 1880s, until driven out of business by the steamboats, trains, and civilization.

Trade Boats

Trade boats traveled the river from Titusville to Jupiter, with side trips up the St. Lucie to Pottsdam, later named Stuart. Some doctors and dentists also plied their trade on the river by boat. The skipper of the boat blew on a conch shell to let people know they were coming, or advertised their schedules ahead of time. Those who lived along the river had long piers extending out into the river for the convenience of the various boats.

Floating stores, as many as five at one time, provided early settlers along the Indian River a place to shop. Groceries, canned goods, clothing, and building materials formed the majority of the stock on these boats. They dealt in a little of everything else, such as cooking utensils, toilet articles, candy, liquor, and drugs. Mail was also carried before regular federal routes were established. Outside and local news was also brought along on these boats, welcomed by the settlers. Most of these traders bought their stock at Jacksonville, Daytona, or Titusville.

William G. Abbott

William Abbott was probably the first individual to come up with the idea of a floating store and put it into operation. John S. Abbott, his wife Rachel, and sons John and William were settlers from Lowndes County, Georgia, who lived at Enterprise, Florida, by 1870. In Georgia, John was a merchant. By the late 1870s, they had moved to New Smyrna. According to the 1880 census, John was then married to Martha J. Abbott, and was listed as a farmer, age 47; his two oldest sons worked the farm. He also had four other children.

In 1878, Abbott built a large two-masted schooner to use as a trade boat. On the first trip, the Abbots and Emily Lagow sailed from Mosquito Lagoon through the Haulover into the Indian River the first day. According to Emily's account, they reached Titusville the next day, and continued south, blowing a conch shell to attract attention, stopping and selling and trading all the way to Jupiter, and then returned. One of the stops was at Gilbert's Bar House of Refuge, and another was the lighthouse at Jupiter. They took on oranges from the groves. Individuals at stops along the Indian River were Enoch Hall, tax assessor at City Point, Mrs. Faber, Charles Creech, James Bell, and Judge Pain and family at St. Lucie. Captain Armour and family were at the Jupiter lighthouse. It is not known how long the Abbots continued to operate the trade boat.

Captain Benjamin Hogg

Benjamin Hogg was one of the earliest trade boat captains on the Indian River. He began around 1879, with his family aboard, making the run from Titusville to Jupiter. He began transporting all sorts of goods along the eastern coast, and he specialized in delivering live green sea turtles from the Indian River area and the Bahamas to Savannah or Jacksonville. He and his family also had an Indian trading post and store in Fort Pierce. Many other trade boats followed after William Abbott and Benjamin Hogg.

Steamboats

The coming of the steamboats revolutionized travel and commerce on the Indian River. They were large, and had a great capacity for carrying goods and people. Yet they were shallow draft craft that could navigate the shallow Indian River. They were fast, and not dependent on wind or currents for power. They had either side-wheel or stern-wheel propulsion, with steam engines that ran on wood in the beginning. A new industry started on the river, cutting wood for the steamboats, and later for the trains. At first, steamboat profitability was questionable because of the low population along the river, but with this easier transportation method came more people.

Pioneer

The *Pioneer* was indeed a pioneer. She was the first steamboat ever seen on the Indian River. The *Pioneer* was a small steamer of 44 tons, brought to the Indian River in 1876. Unfortunately, she only lasted a short time. Captain Thomas J. Lund brought the *Pioneer* through the shallow Haulover Canal from Mosquito Lagoon. He opened the way to future commerce along the river with this feat. However, there were only 250 people along the rivers between Eau Gallie and Key West in the late 1870s. Most of them were along the Indian River and had their own watercraft. Shortly after the *Pioneer* began service, she struck a submerged object and was laid up for repairs, and only a few months after that she burned to the waterline on April 19, 1877, while at anchor at Titusville. She had made regular trips between Titusville and Sebastian, twice weekly while she was in operation. Lund continued service on the river with other steamboats after the *Pioneer* burned.

Border City

The *Border City* was another early steamer carrying her first load of passengers on the Indian River on November 5, 1877, after having run from Jacksonville to New Smyrna. She made two or three trips to Titusville each year. These two steamers were the vanguard of what would become a glorious steamboat era in the 1880s.

8

The Creation of Sebastian: 1880s

Florida was growing; its population was 269,493 in 1880. Some events of a wider scope were felt in Florida during this time. In 1886, an earthquake in Charleston, South Carolina, was felt from New York to Key West. It was considered to be a seaward shift of the Continental Shelf. Sylvanus Kitching said in a letter that they felt the quake in Sebastian, but it was just a slight shake. In 1887-1888, a yellow fever epidemic spread across Florida. Jacksonville was hit particularly hard; however, the Indian River area had no loss of lives due to yellow fever, one considerable advantage of a small population and few visitors. Prohibition was upon them. In the 1887 election, Brevard County was voted dry. Many "blind tigers" or "blind pigs" (speakeasies) sprang up as a consequence, and liquor was also sold on the trade boats, which would have been difficult to check and regulate. As far back as 1857 or 1867, a sign on a building announcing that a blind tiger could be seen for ten cents meant that a drink of whiskey could be had upon payment of the ten cents. It was a method of avoiding paying taxes on liquor at that time. The name carried over into prohibition. Liquor sale became legal again in the early 1890s. Communication went modern; in 1887, the International Ocean Telegraph Company with the United States Signal Service strung telegraph lines between Jupiter and Titusville. Florida triumphed on the waterways; the 1880s decade was the era of the steamboat in Florida.

Brevard County

Brevard County was prospering. In the 1880s, the character of the county changed. Whereas in the 1870s it had been dominated by the cattle industry in the west part of the county, by 1880, it centered on the string of small towns along the Indian River and river commerce. Nine hundred thirty-two of the 1,497 population of Brevard County in 1880 lived east of the St. Johns River and only 565 on the west. In 1879, Titusville and the southern part of Volusia County were annexed by Brevard County, and in 1880, Titusville was voted as the county seat of Brevard County. At that time, the county officials consisted of a clerk of the court, assessor, collector, the circuit judge from

Orange County, the state attorney, county judge, treasurer, sheriff, superintendent of schools, a three-member school board, and five county commissioners. Tax collection began on a regular basis. The county jail was built in Titusville in 1880, and in 1882 the county courthouse was built. By 1880, there were seven schools in Brevard County with 130 pupils. Drs. D. Cowie and B. R. Wilson were early doctors in Titusville.

A survey by the U.S. Army Corps of Engineers in 1881 estimated a population of 1,600 individuals between the Haulover Canal and Lake Worth, with thirteen stores and eight post offices in that area. In 1887, telegraph lines were strung from St. Augustine to Fort Pierce, and many individuals and general stores had telegraph keys. That same year the cattle land west of the St. Johns River became part of the new Osceola County, emphasizing Brevard's shift from cattle culture to an agricultural culture, revolving around the growers of citrus, pineapples, and vegetables on the east side of the St. Johns River. During this decade, there was also a trend toward small farms. No matter what profession individuals engaged in, they each had a small farm on the side, of vegetables, pineapples, sugar cane, or a citrus grove.

Two newspapers covered the area. The *Star Advocate* was the East Coast's oldest newspaper, beginning as *The Star* in New Smyrna in 1877 and moving to Titusville in 1880. *Indian River Advocate* began in 1882, a newspaper based in Titusville that served as a local source of news, with its columns for both Sebastian and Roseland.

Post Offices and Towns

In the 1880s, with the advent of greater population and better services for mail delivery, little post offices began springing up, and around them, little towns evolved. Sebastian was the first in the area, in 1882, as New Haven. Roseland did not officially become a town until 1892. In the surrounding area on the Indian River was Micco to the north, and post offices were at Narrows, Orchid, and Enos on the barrier island. Sebastian was developing, focusing not on just a few families, but taking on the character of a small town. Several attempts at towns failed. Wauregon was planned and platted in 1889 but did not succeed, nor did Enos.

Barker's Bluff Voting District

The 1880s must have been a fascinating time in Sebastian and Roseland. Civilization was advancing in that decade. Sebastian took shape as a town; people were visiting and settling. Commerce blossomed under the advances in transportation.

Before it was a town or had a post office, the area of Sebastian in the 1880 U.S. Census was officially known as the District East of the St. Johns River; penciled in at the top of the page was Prct. 5&4. It was commonly known as Barker's Bluff, named for the highly noticeable Indian shell mound south of the downtown area on the Indian River; it must have been the unofficial hub of the area. Robert Spratt voted at Barker's Bluff, according to his 1883 land patent application.

In the year 1880, the Park family with guests Gottlob and Paul Kroegel, and the Baird, Cain, and Gibson families were the only inhabitants in the Sebastian/Roseland area. Park and Gibson may have had small stores, but there was no town. Sailboats were their primary means of travel; roads were little more than footpaths. Some trade boats and some steamboats plied the Indian River, but infrequently. The emphasis was more on fishing than on agriculture at this point, but getting their fish, oysters, turtles, and agricultural products to market was not consistent. These self-sufficient people caught or grew their own food and had to go to Titusville or Fort Pierce for anything they could not provide for themselves. They had no church, and did not have enough children for a school, until the Kitchings arrived.

August Park

August Park and his family were enumerated June 3-4, 1880, in the U.S. Census in Brevard County, District east of St. Johns River. The census stated that August Park, a 46-year-old fisherman from Prussia, was with 30-year-old wife Mary Ann (Polly Ann) from North Carolina. They also resided with children Charles, age ten, Henry, age eight, Susan, age six, Simeon, age four, and Katie, age two, all born in Florida. The household had three German boarders, Ernest Stypman and Charles Kroel (Charles F. Gottlob Kroegel) and his son. This was most likely at the Barker's Bluff property. A William Gore and family are on the same census page, almost certainly related to Mrs. Park.

Dr. James Henshall visited the Parks on his second trip down the Indian River in the winter of 1881-82. In his narrative, he described the residents of the area. At the mouth of the St. Sebastian he passed the property of David Gibson, and a few miles below, he arrived at Barker's Bluff and the cabin of August Park. Pelican Island was opposite it in the Indian River, only a few acres in size and the first of a series of islands forming the Narrows. About ten miles below the Narrows, nearly opposite Fort Capron, Henshall and his group entered Gardiner's cut, at the entrance to which was the turtling camp of Arthur (August) Park and Jim Russell.

Sometime after Henshall's visit, Park moved with his family to his tract of land on the Indian River that he was in the process of acquiring. Park became a United States citizen in 1882, when he signed his Citizenship Application renouncing allegiance to Germany, dated September 5, 1882, before the Circuit Court Clerk of Brevard County. On March 21, 1883, he paid his Homestead Application fee of $6.00.

On June 30, 1884, he became owner of the piece of land a little south of the St. Sebastian River on the Indian River with Certificate No. 4497. According to the 1886-87 directory, Park grew bananas, pineapples, and vegetables. From 1884-1889, August Park acquired more than 300 acres of land in Sebastian, Hutchinson Island, and Indrio, through the 1820 Sale of Public Lands Act and the Florida Internal Improvement Fund.

Some of his holdings later became the Estate of August Park Subdivision and the Park Cemetery. He was a commercial fisherman, and had several fish houses.

Charles Friedrich Gottlob Kroegel

Charles Friedrich Gottlob Krogel was 41 years old, and his son, Paul, was sixteen years old when they stayed with the Parks at Barker's Bluff. Gottlob Kroegel was a china maker who emigrated from Chemnitz, Germany, with his sons Paul, age six, and Arthur, age two, after the death of his wife on Christmas Day in 1870. They arrived in the U.S. in New York, then moved on to Chicago. He came to Florida in 1877, leaving his younger son Arthur in Chicago with relatives. In St. Augustine and Fernandina, Kroegel worked as a chef for a time. Kroegel and his son bought a small sailboat in Jacksonville and traveled south on the St. Johns River to Salt Lake, where they loaded the sailboat on a mule-pulled tram over to Sand Point. From there they headed south on the Indian River, amazed by the overabundance of tropical flora and fauna. South of the St. Sebastian River, they arrived at the voting district known as Barker's Bluff, with its highly visible namesake, which was described as taller than the tallest cabbage palm and as large as a football field. Directly opposite it was Pelican Island.

Kroegel was so impressed with Barker's Bluff with its view of Pelican Island and its nesting bird population that after much talk, he persuaded August Park to sell him his interest in the property, which Park had not yet formally acquired. Gottlob and Paul lived first in a thatched hut, and in 1882 built a more substantial house of lumber from St. Augustine when the hut was blown away by a gale in August of 1881.

Park had never actually filed for ownership of the Barker's Bluff property, and Kroegel determined that he would file for a homestead patent for it. This was a complicated procedure, due to the fact that he was still a German citizen. In order to obtain a homestead, he had to renounce his German citizenship, become an American citizen, live on the property, and improve it for five years. On August 1, 1882, he began this process and filed his Homestead Affidavit. In that affidavit he stated that he had two houses on the property, and five acres of cleared land. He also stated that due to the distance and want of necessary funds, he was unable to appear at the District land Office to make the affidavit. It was signed in front of the Clerk of the Court of Brevard County. Rather than endure the expense and complicated travel to Gainesville to the land office, he was permitted to file all of the paperwork through the Brevard County Courts. On August 9, 1882, Gottlob Kroegel paid the $13.60 receiver's fee. His entry onto the homestead property was noted as of that date, but his residence was dated as of 1880. In 1884, he filed his intention to become a citizen and resident, as attested to by the Brevard County Judge's Affidavit dated March 19, 1884, ordering that Charles Frederick Gottlob Kroegel be admitted as a citizen. The rest of the paperwork stretched out over several years. Included in the *Brevard County Naturalizations* list for 1865-1903 are sons Arthur K. Kroegel and Paul Kroegel.

By the time of the printing of the 1886-87 directory, the Kroegels had citrus groves on Barker's Bluff, and grew pineapples, beans, and other vegetables. The paperwork continued for Gottlob Kroegel's homestead application. On August 19, 1887, he filed a Notice of Intention to Make Final Proof. His land patent information forms provided first-hand details about his residence at Barker's Bluff. His improvements to the land were the building of a frame house, clearing and fencing the land, and planting orange groves. He had a framed one-story house 20 x 24 feet built five years prior; the first one burned down. Three acres were broken, and three were planted in crops, with six seasons of vegetables. He had been in residence seven years, ten months, and fifteen days. He had been voting at Barker's Bluff for three years, since being granted citizenship. Affidavits dated October 15, 1887, attesting to Kroegel's continuous residence, were filed by witnesses Valentine Gailer and Edward DeCourcey of Titusville, and Fritz Ulrich and Thomas J. DeSteuben of Narrows, Florida. October 15, 1887, was the date confirming that proof had been received, and that notice was published in the newspapers. Homestead Final Certificate was dated December 14, 1887, as was the paper filing the balance due payment of $3.58. On June 21, 1889, Charles F. G. Kroegel acquired the Barker's Bluff land through the May 20, 1862, Homestead Act, U.S. Certificate No. 6387, containing 143.18 acres. All told, his formal Homestead file contained 34 pages. Eventually, his other son Arthur joined Gottlob and Paul, and lived with them until he married. Kroegel prospered with extensive groves. He built the first fruit-packing house and kept bees. From 1908 to 1919, he was County Commissioner.

The Kroegel family sold the shell midden that was Barker's Bluff to pave local roads in the 1910s. Gottlob Kroegel moved into a new home on the property on New Year's Day in 1910, not too long before the last remaining section of Barker's Bluff, containing his old house, was removed. His obituary appeared in the *Vero Press* on October 18, 1923. Gottlob Kroegel was born October 24, 1837, and died October 10, 1923, nearly 86 years old, after an illness of more than a year. He was buried in Sebastian Cemetery.

John Baird

In 1881, John Baird filed his homestead application, but by 1883, pioneer John Baird had died. In 1883, Widow Cornelia Baird filed an affidavit that John Baird's homestead receipt was lost by fire, and being old and infirm Baird did not remember the date of that homestead receipt, but he made the final proof after the five-year period of required homesteading. In November of 1883, Cornelia, widow of John, sold three acres to Sylvanus Kitching. John's son, John V. Baird, took over operation of the *Cornelia* after his death. John Baird's certificate of ownership of the 168.56 Sebastian acres was issued posthumously January 30, 1884 as Certificate No. 3028.

Will Scott related working for the Bairds as a cabin boy learning to cook and sail on the *Cornelia*, which was a small, flat-bottomed boat of the "sharpie" design. Cornelia and her two sons lived aboard for a time. An 85-foot Oyster Bay schooner brought in goods from Jacksonville down the coast to the Indian River Inlet where the *Cornelia* picked up supplies for delivery and trade on the Indian River. All sorts of items were carried, from lumber to fabrics, hides, alcohol, spices, household items, and more. This was profitable until the Jacksonville Titusville & Key West railroad put in a branch from Enterprise to Titusville in 1885. This put the large schooner out of business. The *Cornelia* took over that route for a while, but it proved to be unprofitable due to too much competition. Afterward, Cornelia and her sons John and DuBois lived with the August Park family, per the 1885 Florida census. Cornelia died when she was washed overboard from the *Cornelia* during a storm, and her body was lost. The former Baird home was at one time used for church services, and was also the first schoolhouse.

Dempsey Cain

The Cains continued to do well on their property on the other side of the Sebastian River. The friendly Dempsey Cain family had a houseguest at the time of the 1885 Florida census, Frank Forster, who was born in Georgia, and later settled in Sanford.

David Peter Gibson

At the time of 1880 U.S. Census, Gibson's sons Ralph and Walter were enumerated, but neither David Gibson nor the rest of the family appeared in the census. However, by the time of the 1885 state census, the rest of the family had joined the Gibson household, along with a servant-cook F. B. Kennedy, and R. Hamilton, a servant-laborer. Gibson put his hand to many different ventures, including a trading post.

Over the ages, there had been several natural cuts in this area that formed and then closed again. One of Gibson's projects was to open an inlet to the ocean to improve access to the area; he is credited as the first who tried. He made several attempts to open an inlet. The first appears to have been in 1880, as Gibson's Cut is indicated on geodetic survey charts as early as 1880-1881. The inlet soon closed up again. In 1886, Gibson again tried to dredge an inlet through the peninsula across from Roseland and Sebastian, entering the Atlantic Ocean 2.5 miles north of New's Cut. This was no more successful than the first try, or New's attempt. There were no successful attempts to open an inlet until 1949.

From 1883 to 1885, Gibson acquired several plots of land through the 1820 Public Land Sale Act from the Register of the Land Office at Gainesville, Florida, bringing his holdings between the St. Sebastian River and the Indian River to nearly 300 acres. On Orchid Island he obtained another 116 acres. One parcel he acquired was 38 acres on June 20, 1883, on the peninsula separating the St. Sebastian River from the Indian River, and 97 acres February 13, 1884, at the same location. On February 13, 1884, he acquired 36.18 acres, on the north end of Orchid Island, and on May 9, 1885, 79.90 acres on the north end of Orchid Island were purchased. Gibson's house was two stories, 33 x 24 feet, built prior to 1889, overlooking the Indian River. It was later owned by Tom Hicks, and was located on North Indian River Drive near Roseland Road. It was constructed of unpainted cypress and had wide verandas across the front of the house on both floors. Steamboats may have stopped at Gibson's long wharf. Gibson's house was a well-known tavern in the early days

By 1885, he was the owner of groves and grew pineapples, and by 1886-87, he was a grower of bananas, coconuts, oranges, pineapples, and vegetables. Sarah Ann Aphire West Gibson died before 1885. His second wife, Ellen A. Gibson, was born circa 1834 in Georgia and married Gibson sometime before June of 1885.

Gibson seems to have considered himself above the law. As related in different accounts, he made no attempt to hide a polygamous relationship with a third wife/mistress Rose Kennedy, for whom he built the Octagon House at the end of his wharf as her abode. It resembled a large turret. Per Don R. Beaujean and Freida Thompson, this relationship was common knowledge. Also, he was apparently armed and resisted many arrest attempts.

Newspaper articles in 1888 in the *Florida Star* related a telling incident about Gibson's temperament. It took place at Sebastian, "formerly Barker's Bluff." D. P. Gibson was elected to the local Democratic Executive Committee to choose individuals to be nominated for office. His nominee was defeated by ballot and Gibson created a scene, saying his nominee should be declared the winner, despite the election results. This controversy continued for several months, with continuing newspaper coverage of Gibson's letters to the editor and Arthur C. Ford's replies, along with letters from a few others.

Population Growth

Soon, these families were no longer the only inhabitants of the area. Growth from 1880 to 1885 in the Sebastian/Roseland area steadily increased; from that point on, population began to swell dramatically. Promotional ventures attracted visitors and settlers from every state, including many from Georgia and South Carolina. Individuals arrived from England and Germany to settle along the Indian River. Just a few years made a difference, and a town was officially created.

New Haven

The Sebastian area became a named town when it was brought to life as New Haven by Thomas New, who filed an application for a post office and became its postmaster in 1882. Apparently he achieved this by fraudulent means, exaggerating the population. During the existence of New Haven there were merely six families there, Thomas

New, and the Gibsons, Cains, Bairds, Parks, and Kroegels. New was arrested in 1884. Many conflicting accounts swirl around this town's creation by the man who lived in the area just four or five years before he died. The Roseland area at that time was the northern boundary of the New Haven settlement. The *Star Advocate* newspaper's 75th anniversary edition published an article by Wanton S. Wegg from his *History of Florida*. His description included New Haven "settled in March 1882 by Thomas New, Esq. On Indian River 25 miles from Lake Washington. Population about 200 (sic). Good common school. Postmaster, Mr. Thomas New. Every inducement offered to desirable settlers. There is no frost." New obviously inflated the population to the newspaper as well.

Thomas New

Thomas New was born circa 1810 in England, and moved to the Sebastian area sometime after the U.S. Census of June 1880, or around 1881. New envisioned a great city on the banks of the St. Sebastian River. He strongly promoted the area. In order to make it more attractive to settlers, he attempted to open an inlet to the ocean with a shovel in 1881 near the river, New's Cut. It was very shallow and soon sanded over completely.

On April 14, 1882, Thomas New became Postmaster of New Haven and settled in. In 1883, he had a visitor from back home, F. R. Stebbins, who chronicled this event. Stebbins was a friend from Adrian College. "He (New) had a very pretty location, under the shadow of a fine group of palmettos and about half an acre set out with pine-apple plants. He keeps also a little stock of goods, and is starting another house." On February 13, 1884, New acquired a U.S. land patent under the 1820 Public Lands Act for 59.4 acres south of the Sebastian, and New also purchased 15.97 acres from August Park on March 6, 1884, in the general area of the Park Cemetery.

Accounts differ as to the outcome of New's position of postmaster. According to newspaper accounts, in 1882, he established a post office, claiming that about 150 individuals would use the postal facilities. He named the post office New Haven. In 1884, U.S. authorities accused New of abusing his authority, and he fled the area. Per a postal record, H. R. Olmstead stated that he believed that there were not more than 50 individuals in the postal area. In a further newspaper article in 1884, U.S. and state authorities were involved when Postmaster Thomas New of New Haven was arrested for the state crime of selling liquor without a license and what the *Tallahassee Floridian* newspaper called post office crookedness.

On June 23, 1885, New made his will. Eventually New's health worsened and he died on October 8, 1885. His obituary appeared in the *Florida Star* newspaper on October 14, 1885, stating that he died after a short illness at an advanced age, that he worked to open an inlet to the ocean, and that he resigned as postmaster over a year prior to his death. His will was probated in January of 1886, to settle a debt with the Pittsburgh

Book Directory of the Methodist Protestant Church Company. It was awarded title to the properties, and it then sold the land to James A. Hudson in 1889.

A *Vero Beach Press* article stated that Thomas New was a Texan who came to the area seeking relief from rheumatism, and attributed his cure to the delightful climate. Local residents told another version. According to Simeon Park, son of August Park, as told in Anna Newman's book, Thomas New came from Connecticut.

According to Lenora Park, granddaughter of August Park, as told in *Tales of Sebastian*, Reverend Thomas New was a retired Methodist preacher from Detroit who took up a homestead southeast of the Sebastian River around 1881. After he arrived, Reverend New lived with the August Park family until he homesteaded his own place. On April 14, 1882, Reverend New established the post office and operated a store on what is now North Indian River Drive. August Park was his assistant. When Reverend New's health began to fail in 1884, he moved in with the August Park family. He was sick there for a long while. August Park took over as postmaster unofficially until Sylvanus Kitching became postmaster. Park purchased the store from Reverend New. As requested, New was buried on his own property. According to Lenora, when the Dixie Highway later went through, it passed directly over his grave.

Sebastian

Sebastian arose as a town from the removal of Thomas New as postmaster and the dissolution of New Haven two years after it began, when Sylvanus Kitching became postmaster on November 13, 1884, and the New Haven Post Office was officially changed to the Sebastian Post Office, per document number 1,200 of the U.S. Post Office Department. Kitching transferred its location to Kitching's Store on Main Street at the Indian River, about a mile south of New's location. Thanks to Kitching's arrival, Sebastian now had a new name, two stores, Kitching's and Park's, a post office, and a dock, and would soon have a school and hotel.

Sylvanus Kitching

In the 1800s, there was a considerable tide of settlers from England arriving in Florida, and the Kitchings were part of that number. Sylvanus Kitching was from Warrington, England, born there in 1848. His three brothers Broster, Pennington, and Walter left England in 1867 and settled in Stuart, Florida. Both Broster and Pennington were in the Sebastian area for a brief period of time. Sylvanus was encouraged by his brother Walter to move to the United States, and in early 1883, he sold the family clothing store and headed to Florida with his wife Martha Maskery Kitching and five children, Stanley, Amy, Edith, Mary, and Clarissa. A sixth child, Alice, died in England. Sylvanus arrived in Florida in 1883, around 35 years old.

They traveled by the ship *Wyoming*, taking eleven days for the crossing to New York. From New York they traveled to Jacksonville on the Atlantic Coast Line Railroad. The next leg of the journey was by river steamboat from Jacksonville to Sanford, changing to another steamer from Sanford to Lake Poinset at Rockledge, and then to a sailing sloop from Rockledge to Sebastian. As related in a *Press Journal* article February 19, 1998, a trunk that the Kitchings used on their trip to Florida was filled with linens and fine dishes when they brought it over from England. That trunk with the Kitching name on it was loaned by a descendant of the Kitchings, Gwenda DeBarry, along with many other items of early local history, to the Sebastian Area Historical Society; they now reside in the Sebastian Area Historical Society Museum.

Rather than join his brothers in Stuart, Sylvanus chose instead to live in Sebastian. He settled south of the St. Sebastian River on a three-acre parcel he purchased from widowed Cornelia Baird in November of 1883. He built a frame house there and established an Indian trading post and general store. He later built a larger store that included a hotel on the second floor, mentioned in the 1886-87 Directory. He operated this establishment until 1925. The building consisted of two stories, containing the general store, his family's living quarters, and accommodations for visitors, which was a large upstairs room with cots. The premises were lit with lamps and candles. He also built a 1,100-foot dock on the Indian River for steamboats, to accommodate the relatively deep draft vessels. It was said to be the first one on the Indian River.

In 1844, Sylvanus and Martha's seventh child, their first child born in Florida, was named Florida and delivered in a makeshift tent in a rainstorm, before they had a house. Martha had five more children who were born in Cocoa, Florida, where the nearest doctor, Dr. W. L. Hughlett, resided. Sylvanus acquired a U.S. land patent for 27 acres in Wabasso on March 20, 1885, next to his brother Walter's property, acquired in 1884. Langley Kitching's property adjoined Walter's to the south. In an 1887 letter to a friend, Sylvanus related that his grove had rare kinds of lemon, lime and orange trees, and tomatoes. He also told that the Railroad Company informed him that they intended to build a bulkhead and warehouse at the end of his wharf, as the company had received the contract for running mail by steamboats, which would start July 1, 1887. He wrote that he might need to add more guest accommodations. He also informed his friend that a school was opened that year, and that it had enough funds for four months. With the Kitchings' children, there were enough children in the area for a school. The Kitchings eventually had eleven children living, including eight daughters, which attracted young men from all up and down the Indian River.

1885 Florida State Census—Sebastian

By the time of the 1885 Florida State census, the Knight brothers and Walter Kitching were added to the Baird, Cain, Gibson, Park, Kroegel, and Sylvanus Kitching households. The 1885 Florida State Census enumerated 43 individuals in six households in Sebastian: the D. P. Gibson house with seven members, which included cook-servant F. B. Kennedy and laborer R. Hamilton; fruit growers T. H. and Walter Knight; eight in the Sylvanus Kitching family; the Walter Kitching household with A. H. Mackey, James and William Mackey; seven with August Park's family, together with Cornelia, Jno and DuBois Baird; and twelve in Dempsey Cain's household, which included the two Bowler children, Robert and Mary, and Frank Forster and L. V. Ralston. Gottlob and Paul Kroegel were not included in the census. Walter Kitching resided primarily in Wabasso.

T. Howard Knight and Walter J. Knight

The Knight brothers were in the Sebastian area from approximately 1884 to 1889-1892. T. Howard Knight, age 27, appeared in the 1885 census of Sebastian as a fruit grower. Living with him was his brother Walter, age 21, who was disabled. Both were born in Pennsylvania, as were their parents. T. Howard Knight appeared in the 1886-87 directory of Sebastian as well, as a grower of bananas and oranges. He had fourteen acres of pineapples and peaches. Eventually, Mr. Knight built an expensive bungalow, farm buildings, and fences in the Ercildoune area, east of Wauregon.

A strange and lengthy article appeared in the *Indian River Advocate* on October 28, 1892, regarding the progression of a possible land swindle or theft of purchase money for the Sebastian property owned by T. Howard Knight of Philadelphia and Sebastian. Otis Greye of New York was either lost overboard from a steamer or faked his own death and absconded with the money entrusted to him for the purchase of Knight's property. Another man by the name of Henry H. Finley was also involved and disappeared. Apparently Knight's money was gone.

Florida State Gazetteer and Business Directory 1886-1887

By 1886, the Sebastian population more than doubled in one year. The tremendous impetus of growth could be observed in the *Florida State Gazetteer and Business Directory 1886-1887*, which included Sebastian for the first time. Sebastian went from a population of 43 in 1885 to a population of 91 a year later. Sebastian had fifteen businesses, according to the directory. Walter Kitching was Justice of the Peace and a banana and coconut grower. Sebastian consisted of Sylvester Kitching's Store that contained the post office and sold general merchandise, Kitching's hotel, the Sebastian House, and a saw and planning mill run by W. J. MacMillan. Dr. H. C. Sill was the local physician and was an orange grower. Mail was delivered twice weekly, Wednesday and Saturday, by steamer from Titusville. Steamers brought passengers leaving Titusville Tuesday and Friday. The nearest bank was Lyman Bank at Sanford. A blacksmith and a boat builder were needed in Sebastian, according to the directory.

Sebastian United Methodist Church

The year 1886 marked growth of another sort. That year the United Methodist Church was started in Sebastian, the oldest church in Indian River County. At the beginning, meetings were held in the Kitchings' home and the former Baird home, until a church was built. Prior to that, a Methodist pineapple farmer, Mr. Hickock, came by sailboat from Micco once a month to hold services. Other preachers also came through.

A church charter was granted in 1887, and in 1889, Henry B. and Emma J. Howard donated some of their homestead land for the site of the church. Funds to build the church were obtained by subscription, and these funds purchased lumber brought in by sailboat. From the boat, the lumber was floated ashore and carried by mule team to the building site. Paul Kroegel built the pulpit and the Groves donated a bell. Reverend T. A. Jordan obtained an organ. Women of the community raised money for the church by having suppers for the crews of ships stopping at Kitching's Dock, the only boat stop between Titusville and Fort Pierce at that time. These meals were also popular with local residents, who took advantage of the impromptu restaurant. Early church members who helped organize the church were Cassie Lawson, Mrs. Sylvanus Kitching, Mrs. James A. Groves, Mrs. Emma Hardee, and Mrs. George B. Hall.

Undoubtedly, prior to the church's formation, the area's residents had heard sermons by the Methodist circuit riders, preachers who traveled by boat or horseback to conduct worship services, perform baptisms and marriages, visit members of the church, and aid parishioners in establishing new churches in rural areas. Sebastianites may have requested that a minister be sent. These circuit riders were assigned districts that might take them many weeks to cover. The first such preacher in Florida was John Tripp, who was admitted to the South Carolina Conference in January of 1821 and was assigned a new, ill-defined circuit of South Georgia, which in the Minutes of the Conference was called Lappahee. It is supposed that his journeys extended into Florida. In 1822-1823, he rode circuit in eastern Alabama, western Georgia, and western Florida. In January of 1822, the first appointment was made in East Florida at Amelia Island. Florida had just become a U.S. territory, permitting Protestantism. It was wholly Catholic when held by Spain. Methodist ministers generally spent two years at a post, and then were rotated to another posting.

James A. Groves

Methodist Church member James A. Groves and family moved from Opelousas, Louisiana, to Sebastian sometime after June of 1885. He was a fruit grower. They built a frame house in Sebastian and named the sand trail that ran in front of their house Louisiana Avenue in memory of their home state. They were charter members of

Sebastian United Methodist Church; the bell they donated for the steeple had been used on a Louisiana plantation. After the railroad arrived in 1893, they built the successful Groves Apartment House on the south side of Louisiana Avenue, four stories high, with no plumbing or electricity. On February 3, 1935, fire swept through the groves of Dr. Rose and J. A. Groves. The Groves couple remained in Sebastian and were buried at Sebastian Cemetery.

Henry B. Howard

The Howards' were in Sebastian, Florida, by 1889 and were charter members of Sebastian United Methodist Church. Henry B. Howard acquired 120 acres of land through the 1820 Land Act on January 30, 1896, some of which was donated for the site of the original church. His land was just north of future Route 512, west of the railroad tracks. His home may have been on Louisiana Avenue, as they lived very close to the Groves' home in the 1900 census. From June 29, 1893, to August 10, 1896, he was the second Sebastian postmaster, after Sylvanus Kitching's tenure. Howard was a member of the salvage crew of the *Mary E. Morse* in September of 1900. In January of 1909 he moved, occupying the Riggs place, which was formerly the Holt place in Wabasso, and in September of 1909, he worked shelling the road north of Wabasso. In May of 1910, unpaid tax notices were published in the *St. Lucie Tribune* for the Sebastian property of the estate of H. B. Howard.

Street Names

It was in the 1880s that some of Sebastian's streets acquired names. The first was undoubtedly Louisiana Avenue, named by the Groves family, and the second was Main Street. In 1887, Sebastian had its first school, a one-story wooden structure on Louisiana Avenue near the depot site. It was also a social center for the town, hosting community plays, box socials, and public meetings. Kitching's Store became the official voting place for "Barker's Bluff" in Precinct No. 7, with inspectors Dempsey Cain, B. W. Jerome, Walter Knight, and clerk Walter Kitching, as reported in the October 11, 1888, *Florida Star*. The boundaries to the precinct were on the north Township Line 29/30, on the east the Indian River, on the south Township Line 31/32, and on the west the Brevard/Osceola County line. For many years, it was the only place to vote between Melbourne and St. Lucie. The October 6, 1888, primary was held at Sebastian, "formerly Barker's Bluff." Dempsey Cain was nominated for Justice of the Peace with thirteen votes cast, and won by a majority of one. Mercia Gibson was nominated for Constable, and won by a majority of two in twelve votes cast, as reported in the *Florida Star*. It was for that election that Gibson created such a scene.

Captain Robert Augustus Hardee

One of the last settlers in Sebastian in the 1880s was Robert Augustus Hardee, who was born in Quitman, Lowndes County (later Brooks County), Georgia, in 1833. Quitman had been the home of Ivey and Cassey Lawson for a time as well. It is about 20 miles from Hahira, Georgia, the home of the Lawsons, Vickers, and Ryalls.

The Brooks County Hardees were an illustrious family. Some of the children of Thomas E. Hardee and his first wife Gracy Ann Jones were Captain Robert A. Hardee of Sebastian and Gardner S. Hardee, who settled in Rockledge before 1869, and served in the Florida State Senate from 1888 to 1892. Son Thomas J. Hardee of Dade County, Florida, was a one-legged, confederate hero. His remains were buried at Sharpes, Georgia, in the family burial ground. Son James Blackshear Hardee was the father of Cary A. Hardee, Florida's governor from 1921-1925.

In the 1860 census of Tallokas, Brooks County, Georgia, Robert A. Hardee, a 27-year-old farmer, was living with wife Melissa V., age 18, son Thomas S., age 6, and son Robert, age 4, all born in Georgia. Living with them were Robert's brother Thomas J. Hardee, age 23, and A. W. Hardee, age 21, who was a superintendent of a railroad contract. Robert had two sons and one daughter by his first wife.

Robert A. Hardee attained the rank of Captain of the 9th Georgia Infantry in the Confederate Army under Robert E. Lee, and served in the Civil War from 1861 to 1863. He mustered out of the Civil War in February of 1863, unfit for duty because of rheumatism. He and his brothers returned to their Georgia home after the Civil War and found their property gone. They farmed cotton for a few years, and then the brothers Robert A., Gardner S. and Allen W. settled on the Indian River in 1868, at Rockledge. At the time of the 1870 census, Robert, age 47, had no family with him and was living at Sand Point, Volusia County, Florida. George S. Hardee, age 27, was living in the same area with his wife Emma, age 19, and a one-month old baby.

Robert's second marriage was to Emma Provida Willard of Madison, Florida, sometime after the 1870 census. Emma was born in 1850 in Madison, Florida. The 1880 census for Precinct 3 of the District East of the St. Johns River, Brevard County, enumerated R. A. Hardee, a 46-year-old farmer born in Georgia with 30-year-old wife E. P., born in Florida, 19-year-old daughter Leillis, born in Georgia, and 8-year-old son Robert, born in Florida. In the mid-1880s, Hardee founded the town of Hardeeville south of Titusville, at Jones Point on the Indian River, and offered free land to settlers there. He advertised in the *Florida Star* in 1886, "A Perfect Place for A Healthy Home on Indian River." Moreover, he established a lumber business at Hardeeville, which he also advertised in the *Florida Star* in 1887.

In 1889, Robert and his family moved from Hardeeville to Sebastian and built a large house on the north side of Main Street, east of future US Hwy 1, and planted two groves. He added later a store, dock, and an extensive fishing business. The Hardee Oak Tree was planted in 1891 by nineteen-year-old Bob Hardee and tended by his mother Emma, who protected it when Main Street was widened. It is still protected and still exists in the City parking lot at Indian River Drive and Main Street. In the shade of the tree, the Hardee Service Station was a popular gathering spot, sometimes hosting poker games in the back room. In 1890, Robert was the engineer of the steamboat *Sweeney*. At one point, he and Simeon Park had a fishing business together. Successful catches were gutted, packed in barrels with ice, and shipped to New York.

Robert A. died in 1909, and Emma moved in with son Robert G. and his family. The *Florida Star* from December 3, 1909, carried a Card of Thanks from the widow of R. A. Hardee of Sebastian to all of those who helped during his illness and death. The *Fort Pierce News* carried his obituary December 3, 1909. He died November 9, 1909. *Vero Press* carried the obituary of Mrs. Emma Hardee on July 17, 1924, who died at home on the riverfront. Both Emma and Robert were buried in Sebastian Cemetery.

Henry Benson

There are some mysteries that arise during research that are not easy to resolve. Henry Benson is one such puzzle. There are very few records of a Henry Benson in Sebastian in the 1880s, and they do not present a clear picture. According to the Bureau of Land Management records, Henry Benson of Warrington, England, acquired four separate parcels of land in Indian River County, 120 acres in March and May of 1885, in three locations: in southern Sebastian; on Orchid Island; and south of Wabasso. The Brevard County Will Book contains the will of Henry Benson of Sebastian, Brevard County, Florida and Chester County, Pennsylvania, dated September 18, 1886, with bequests to wife Martha Mary and others. Henry died January 26, 1897, at the Asylum for Insane at Chattahoochee. Henry Benson, with a wife Sophia, both born in England, were in Philadelphia, Pennsylvania, in the 1880 U.S. Census. These records do not agree, and no other records seem to apply.

Benjamin Jerome

The as yet unnamed Roseland area gained a new resident later in the decade. Connecticut bachelor Benjamin Jerome purchased land in 1887 and 1888, and built a home west of the Cains.

Gone

Some individuals stayed; others were gone. The 1880 U.S. Census contained five households that were no longer present in the 1885 Florida State Census, and little is known about these individuals. In the 1880 census, the next property to the north of August Park was occupied by Frank Smith, age 56, born in Georgia, living with his daughter Sarah Katie, age 18, born in New York. On June 3, 1885, he obtained a land patent for 40 acres in Brevard County. R. W. Pannamore, age 23, was a farmer from Georgia, his wife, M, age 26, was born in Florida. With them were two sons. T. E. Milgard, age 56, was a farmer from Massachusetts living alone. Fanny Canada from Georgia, age 28, was keeping house, not farming, with her two children. Edith Sellers was a 40-year-old woman, born in Florida and living alone, with no occupation listed. Anthony Deisner of Kentucky died not long after he obtained a land patent on June 30, 1884, for a lot of land roughly in the area of the eastern part of future Route 512 in Sebastian. His will was recorded May 17, 1886, and provided that Brother Deisner of Lexington, Kentucky, was entitled to rights under a Certificate for $2,000 that was issued by Ancient Order of United Workmen of Kentucky, and that $200 would be paid to his wife Dora Deisner and their children.

9

The Others—Communities, Neighbors, and Visitors: 1880s

Wauregan and the Indian River Land and Improvement Company

Wauregan did not claim the distinction of being named by a post office; it was a planned and platted town. The 18,000 acres of land for Wauregon was acquired by James W. Todd in September of 1888 from Herbert Linnel's holdings in the Fleming Grant. He organized the Indian River Land and Improvement Company with other New Rochelle, New York, investors for this purpose. This company was registered July 12, 1889, by seven New York City developers. It continued into the 1930s when it was dissolved by proclamation on September 13, 1936. Its principle address was Hardeeville, Florida, and had an office building in Sebastian that also housed some early school classes. The plat map was created by S. B. Carter, surveyor, and filed June 6, 1889, with the Brevard County Clerk.

The town of Wauregan was created from part of the Fleming Grant near future Roseland in the peninsula between the St. Sebastian River and the Indian River. It consisted of 90 blocks, L-shaped, bounded by Sylvanus Kitching's store and dock immediately south of the development, and by the properties of David P. Gibson, W. J. Knight, and August Park to the east. Land owners in Wauregan were W. W. Bissell, T. S. Drake, A. P. Hudson, H. H. Todd, and H. J. Zelm, the land speculators from New Rochelle who created Wauregan. Wauregan boasted of a major commercial development, the East Coast Turpentine Company, which owned most of the land in the Fleming Grant, where it harvested the pine forests for naval stores and timber, major commercial products. In 1893, the company was reorganized into the Sebastian River Land and Improvement Company upon the death of James W. Todd, with plans to include a hotel. Henry Flagler was approached to participate in this venture, but the individuals never agreed on terms. Flagler built his next hotel farther south instead, and Wauregon went into a decline, never really developing as a separate town. Roseland eventually encompassed part of the Wauregan area. During the 1890s, these same gentlemen were involved in the development of more Fleming land, the Trilby Plantation.

The Neighbors

The long barrier island on east of the Indian River on the Atlantic Ocean, running down the entire east coast of the area in question, was a prized location from very early times, due to its fertile soil and very mild climate. It was superb land for agriculture. The whole stretch of land has had several names, but was known primarily as Orchid. Across from Micco, it was called Micco in the 1880s, although the Micco post office was on the mainland. To the south, on the barrier island, were the post offices of Narrows, Enos, and Orchid. Due to the fact that early travel was mostly by way of the rivers, these were all near neighbors to Roseland and Sebastian, and friends were on both sides of the St. Sebastian River and the Indian River Lagoon. Some individuals had land on both sides of the rivers.

Micco

Several little towns came into being in the area during the 1800s. The Micco post office was opened in 1884 with John Bowie as postmaster. The well-known Oak Lodge, run by C. F. Latham, was just across the river from the post office. Micco, on the mainland, consisted of two houses; one house held the post office and the other one was the office of the Telegraph Office and Signal Service man. The nearest stores were ten miles away. However, Mr. Latham owned a good sloop and could bring in the necessary supplies.

Oak Lodge

Oak Lodge was a hotel for many years on the barrier island across from Micco. Weona Cleveland provided an intriguing history of the individuals, Charles and Frances Latham, who were responsible for Oak Lodge, which was an extremely popular lodging site on the Indian River from the late 1800s until 1910. Charles Latham was a laborer from Rhode Island who enlisted in the Union Army at Providence, Rhode Island in 1865, and served for six months. Four years after his discharge, in 1869, he married Mary Beatrice Erskine. In the following four years they had children Franklin Clare, Grace Maria, and Gardner Brown. Sometime in 1874 or 1875, the Lathams separated. While in Rhode Island, Charles Latham became acquainted with a widow, Frances E. Williams Betts, with her children Clara and Eva.

Charles Latham and Frances Betts came to Florida, perhaps as early as 1881, and built a small hotel or boarding house that they named Oak Lodge on the sand ridge across from Micco. It had an attractively landscaped slope down to the Indian River, and a flowing deep well brought fresh water to the lodge. The actual builder was Joseph McGruder of Rockledge. In 1883, Frances' and Charles' daughter Queenie was born. Latham's daughter Grace and son Franklin were living at Oak Lodge with Latham in the mid-1880s. In either August 1886 or 1887, Latham divorced his first wife Mary in Polk County and married Frances E. Betts September 28, 1887, at Enterprise in Volusia County.

Travel to Oak Lodge was by means of several conveyances. In 1889, Frank Chapman traveled from Gainesville to Titusville on the East Coast Railway, and from Titusville to Jupiter Inlet on a stern-wheel steamship on the Indian River to get to Oak Lodge. A group photograph, dated 1887 and believed to be of the first Oak Lodge, included Professor Jenks, Ma Latham, and a girl thought to be Queenie in the foreground. The building was two-story, large, and raised, and had paned windows and wood siding.

Frances Latham was the proprietress. She was deeply interested in the work of the scientists, naturalists, and botanists who stayed at Oak Lodge, collecting and shipping plants and animals for her learned guests. Oak Lodge not only housed visiting naturalists and sportsmen, it also served wealthy recluses and those who wanted to live in a tropical wilderness, but remain well fed. Frances was known for her cooking and her patience. She raised her grandchildren, daughters of Queenie and Lon Wells. In the 1880s, Oak lodge was also home to Frances' mother, Clarissa Burch, who died at Oak Lodge August 24, 1890.

On July 23, 1891, Charles Franklin Latham obtained 164.17 acres of land, through a patent granted to Civil War veterans; it was comprised of four lots located on the barrier island. The land was situated below Mullet Creek, north of Sebastian Inlet.

In September 1893, Oak Lodge burned, but Charles and Frances rebuilt it on a grander scale, perhaps some time after February 6, 1894, when naturalist Dr. Morris Gibbs described Oak Lodge as a palmetto hut or "cabbage house," a single room 15 x 30 feet. There were few nails used, and no windows or glass. Instead of windows, there was an open space 2 feet high which ran the full length of this low structure on either side, which was never covered, except for cheesecloth. There were no carpets. There were four beds. All guests slept in this room, which also held a table and sewing machine, along with trunks, guns, various tools, and boating, fishing, and hunting equipment. There were bird skins and all manner of other items for decoration on the walls. It also may have contained artifacts found from the 1715 Spanish Plate Fleet wrecks. Perhaps this was an interim structure erected after the fire, before they rebuilt. In 1894, the area had grown. When Dr. Gibbs arrived at Micco by steamer, it was a little station of four houses.

A local resident related that Oak Lodge had a widow's walk on top of the two-story building that Mrs. Latham liked to use. The laborers lived in another house and worked in the garden. Several hundred crates of early vegetables at a time were filled by them to go to northern markets.

To the south, there was not a house for more than ten miles on the other side of the river. There were 10 to 20 people at the lodge consistently in the winter months. In 1894, zoologist William Temple Hornaday stayed at Oak Lodge when visiting Pelican Island. John Baird, captain of a small schooner, made his headquarters at the Oak Lodge. Professor Jenks, a naturalist of Brown University, was an annual visitor.

Frank Chapman was a frequent guest. In 1898, Frank and Fannie Chapman spent their honeymoon at Oak Lodge. Herbert K. Job was another visitor in 1903.

Around 1900, Charles Latham left Oak Lodge and deserted his family. He made a pension application in 1903 at New York. By 1909, Frances faced serious hardships. Queenie died and Frances was taking care of five of Queenie's daughters; her crops failed, and she was in debt. Lou Wells, Queenie's husband, had the children adopted out and housed with several other families.

Oak Lodge burned to the ground on the night Halley's Comet was visible in the southern sky, May 19, 1910, and was not rebuilt. Halley's Comet is a continual visitor to the solar system, appearing every 75 to 76 years. It is the only short-period comet that is clearly visible to the naked eye from Earth and the only one that might be seen twice in a lifetime. When it appeared in 1910, it was the first comet to be photographed.

In 1915, Charles Latham filed additional pension papers from Stratford, Connecticut. He was in a veteran's home around 1915-1920, and went to Providence, Rhode Island, when he was discharged, living with the Dyson family. He died in Providence on March 25, 1925. In the 1920 U.S. Census, Frances Latham was 83 years old and living with her 45-year-old daughter Eva Betts in Oneida, New York. In 1995, the Oak Lodge site became part of a golf course.

Dr. William Miller Fee

Another near neighbor was Dr. William Miller Fee, a medical doctor who arrived in the Indian River area in the early 1880s and began medical practice at Melbourne. On March 31, 1884, he purchased 99.78 acres of land on the barrier island near Sebastian Inlet through the 1820 Land Act. When the railroads came through around 1892, he was called upon to treat the railroad crews. Their camps were exceedingly primitive and unsanitary, breeding grounds for such contagious diseases as typhoid. Some medications were sent by mail to the ailing men. Apparently, William M. Fee and his wife Mary died in 1900, together or within a short period of time of each other. Both wills were dated in 1889, and both were recorded in 1900.

Their grandson, William Irwin Fee, became the first funeral director in Fort Pierce and was the undertaker for the Ashley Gang bodies. He also owned the Fee & Steward Hardware Store and was active in many civic matters. He purchased 160.6 acres of land west of Wabasso in 1913. A pioneer in mosquito control, his methods reduced the mosquito population, and in 1927 he got legislation enacted to start St. Lucie County Sanitary District, which later was changed to the Mosquito Control District.

At that time, there were no screens for windows, and glass was rare. Mosquitoes were numerous. They were battled with hand-made palmetto whisks. People covered completely and wore hats draped with netting. Smudge pots were used to smoke them away. Where the pots were used was an indication if the person was a native or a northerner. If a northerner, then the pot was outside and there was netting on the windows. If the individual was a native, then the pot was inside, and there were no window coverings.

James T. Small

Land speculators from as far away as Androscoggin County, Maine, dabbled in desirable land in Florida. Realtor James T. Small of Androscoggin purchased land in Indian River County through the 1820 Land Act, 25.33 acres on May 9, 1885, Certificate No. 8183, on Orchid, at the northern tip of the county. There is no indication that he ever lived there.

Narrows

In 1896, the Titusville newspaper carried an explanation that "geographically, the Narrows extends from Barker's Bluff to the north line of Township 33, but for postal purposes the name includes only that portion ... which receives its mail from the Narrows post office on Gem Island." Narrows was created as a precinct in 1883, and the post office at the Narrows was opened in 1884 with Lewis B. Dawson as postmaster. The Narrows had a school and library by the early 1890s.

A July 16, 1885 *Florida Star Narrows* column is quoted partially here: "They are coming—Letters to parties here from the Northwest indicate a heavy increase to the population of the Narrows this winter, a general probing of Squatters Sovereign Homestead claims will be in order. A Two Dollar Palmetto Shanty with nothing to back it will not avail you now in Washington."

Apparently the government realized that it could tighten up on land purchase regulations, now that people actually wanted to move to Florida.

Robert B. Spratt

Robert B. Spratt appeared in the census records of 1870 and 1880 in Texas with his family. His Florida land grant application under the 1862 Homestead Act provided some of the details of his life along the Indian River. He filed his application for 124.76 acres, dated May 28, 1883, signed Robert B. Spratt of New Haven. His improvements to the land were made as of June 15, 1883, a two-story box frame house that he built with four rooms, 16 x 36 feet, and a good shingle roof. He cleared 10 acres and had 10 acres in cultivation, of which 3 acres were bananas and the remaining land was in fruits and vegetables. He voted at Barkers Bluff. He received his land patent Certificate No. 7100, dated April 29 1890, for the 124.76 acres. His land was on Orchid, one mile north of Dr. Sill's, facing Pelican Island at Spratt Point, and named for him. Sometime before 1910, he moved to his son-in-law's house in Duval County. He died there in 1941. His wife Sallie may have died between 1900 and 1910.

Dr. H. C. Sill

Dr. H. C. Sill was considered a leading citizen of Sebastian, according to the *Florida State Gazetteer*. With a residence at Sills Landing, Wabasso, he was an orange grower as well as a doctor. His property was one mile below that of Robert B. Spratt. He homesteaded 113 acres on Orchid on February 13, 1891. When this retired physician arrived on the Indian River some time prior to 1885, he built a small log cabin with a thatched roof and planted a garden and a small, unsuccessful orange grove. He was originally from Ohio.

Jack Spratt

Robert's brother Jack Spratt lived nearby. Jack Spratt and Frank Forster wrote some of the *Narrows* columns for the local newspapers, the *St. Lucie County Tribune, Florida Star, Indian River Advocate,* and *Fort Pierce News* in the mid-1880s to early 1900s.

In one of Jack Spratt's *Narrows* columns of September 6, 1888, he related a kitchen fire he had during the previous week that took out half of his roof before it was put out with the help of concerned neighbors, who came running when he yelled, "Fire!"

The Spratt lineage was Scotch-Irish Protestant, from South Carolina. One of the first settlers to the Fort Mill, South Carolina, area was Thomas Spratt, who arrived there around 1750. He was a Lieutenant from South Carolina in the Revolutionary War.

Enos

The town of Enos was created by Dr. James L. Enos around 1885. The Enos post office was created in 1888, between the Narrows Post Office and the Orchid Post Office, with James L. Enos as postmaster. According to the *Florida Star* from May 7, 1885, the land was procured and the site plat was filed June 27, 1889. The town size was one mile, stretching from the Atlantic Ocean to the Indian River. It was planned with several parks, and South, Central, and North Avenues, each 80 feet wide, extending from the Atlantic Ocean to the Indian River. It was planned to be landscaped with coconut, orange, lemon, and other fruit and ornamental trees. Two circular sections of lots were included. It was planned to have an academy with courses and lectures delivered in the winter months, and would have a large library connected and an elementary school. A hotel was planned. Unfortunately, this town faded when the railroad went through on the mainland, and not on the barrier island, as was rumored. The hurricane of 1893 also had a negative effect on sales. In 1897, Enos was re-named Stanwood by the new postmaster James E. Dodge.

The creator of Enos, James L. Enos, MD, was born in 1825 in New York, and was a graduate of State Normal College at Albany. He tried his hand at many things in many places, and was an editor, teacher, and publisher in New York, Illinois, and Iowa. He moved to Florida in 1884 and purchased the tract of land that became Enos. According to the *Florida Star*, he engaged in the culture of tropical fruits, and had orange and lemon groves, bananas, rare fruits, and an experimental garden. He was the postmaster and notary public.

Orchid

The town of Orchid was created on Frank Forster's homestead. It was named for the profusion of wild orchids growing in the area. In 1887, Lewis B. Dawson was the first postmaster. In 1888, Mrs. M. C. (Susan) Mohr was the postmistress. Frank Forster followed as postmaster. To the south of Orchid was the homestead of S. K. Michael and the Wigfields. North of and adjoining Orchid was the property of George W. King of Ohio. John H. Stuff of Illinois moved his family to Orchid around 1888. By 1888, Orchid had a schoolhouse with Mrs. Holonquist as headmistress. Other early landowners were T. R. Brownell, A. B. Goodnow, N. B. Hamilton, Langley and Susan Kitching, W. H. Martin and L. Swab. G. W. King's bee-keeping business produced eight tons of honey in 1894. The post office operated for 34 years and was discontinued when the area's service was assigned to Vero in 1921. According to the *Vero Beach Press Journal*, the Town of Orchid was re-activated in 1966.

Milton Card

The Card family was one of the more interesting and original families to own land in this area. Milton Card was unique. Originally from New York, he was a hunter, inventor, and a writer. He invented the trap that Annie Oakley used to launch her glass ball targets into the air. Under the pen name "Friar Tuck," he wrote for the Cazenovia *Republican Journal* in New York State. For several years he visited and wrote about the Indian River, usually spending his winters at James Paine's Inn at St. Lucie. Sometime around 1882, he finally decided to move to Florida.

On August 1, 1883, he acquired a U.S. land patent of 127 acres located southeast of Pelican Island on Orchid. Another was purchased south of Eldred across from Hutchinson Island, from Armed Occupation settler William Davis. According to local lore, this lot was purchased for a shotgun, a rifle, and two plugs of tobacco. On this piece of land, Milton and his wife Flora erected a large two-story brick home on the bluffs overlooking the Indian River.

Their daughter Lucia Zora married Fred Alispaugh and joined the circus, working with lions and tigers. The couple later moved in with her parents and bought an elephant. The house became known as the "Elephant House." Apparently the elephant was very friendly and would wander into the neighbors' yards, requiring it to be fenced in, as related in Zora's memoir *Sawdust and Solitude*.

The Germans

The Indian River area attracted several German immigrants. According to U.S. Census records, German-born August Park's home was host to three of them in June of 1880, when Ernest Stypman, Gottlob Kroegel, and Paul Kroegel were present in Park's household. Frank Forster, Baron Captain Thomas Jefferson DeSteuben, and Fritz Ulrich were other German settlers along the Indian River.

Frank Forster

Frank Forster was born about 1857 in Germany and arrived at the Indian River sometime in the early 1880s, possibly with Thomas DeSteuben, and homesteaded on Orchid. In the period of 1885-1886, he acquired several pieces of property in the Narrows, Wabasso, and around Winter Beach. By 1886, he had five acres of orange groves at the Narrows. Per the March 22, 1888, *Florida Star* newspaper, the Orchid Post Office was still located on the Frank Forster homestead. According to an article in the *East Coast Advocate*, by 1891, he had lemon as well as orange trees, but none were bearing yet. By 1905, Forster had 20-30 acres of citrus groves. Later, he was said to have the largest and finest orange groves in the county, and had his own packing house. On July 5, 1894, he married Mary Albertina Enos, daughter of a Kankakee, Illinois family. She died shortly after childbirth in 1903, and was buried in Kankakee, Illinois. He remarried to Dena sometime between 1909 and 1912. Frank and Dena Forster are listed in the 1920 U.S. Census as living in Wabasso. Dena Forster died May 21, 1924, in Baltimore, Maryland. He died October 24, 1933, at Kankakee, Illinois.

Baron Colonel Thomas Jefferson DeSteuben

Baron Colonel Thomas Jefferson DeSteuben, who was born in Virginia of German descent, visited the Thomas Richards family in Ancona, Florida, in 1880-81. Two years later, he settled permanently in Rio. He was the attorney who represented Ernest Stypman in his dispute with Flagler over railroad land compensation. He married Mary Jane Stypmann, daughter of Ernest's brother Albert. At the time that DeSteuben filed a Homestead Notice of Witnesses for the homestead application of Gottlob Kroegel in 1887, his home was on land at Narrows, sixteen miles south of the Kroegels. In 1900, he was living with his wife Mary and son in Brevard County, Precinct 10. By 1920, he was 80 years old, living in Jensen, St. Lucie County, with wife Mary, age 50. Thomas Jefferson DeSteuben Jr. is listed on the Fort Pierce Memorial, erected February 20, 1920, of soldiers from St. Lucie County who died in WWI.

Ernest Stypman

Ernest Stypman was born February 3, 1840, in Falkenberg, Germany. He immigrated in 1872 with his father and a brother, joining two other brothers in New York. Four years later, in 1876, he moved to Florida, where he filed homestead claim for 160 acres of land at Duck Point near Sebastian and built a home. Around that time, he married Frances Hunter, and a year later, became employed as a carpenter with the U.S. Coastal and Geodetic Survey crew, surveying and mapping coastal Florida. The crew lived and traveled down the Indian River aboard the *Steadfast*, a steam-powered survey vessel. Perhaps it was during these travels that he stayed with August Park.

Stypman discovered the St. Lucie River and wrote to brothers in New York and Germany about the promising area. Otto arrived in 1882, and he and Ernest sailed down the Indian River to investigate. Both decided to move to the St. Lucie and settle on the south shore. Ernest built a large house and planted a pineapple plantation and pines. He also went turtling with August Hars and carried their catch to Titusville aboard their schooner, *Dora*. In 1885, Ernest Stypman obtained land patents for 154.22 acres of land on either side of future US Hwy 1 between Sebastian and Wabasso, and 33 acres in downtown Stuart. Stypman also was a major stockholder and organizer of the East Coast Fish Company, and in 1886 donated land for the first school on the St. Lucie. By 1891, he was a judge. When Flagler was bringing his railroad through downtown Stuart in 1893, Ernest had rather heated and extensive negotiations with Flagler over compensation for the land. Baron Captain DeSteuben was his attorney during these negotiations. Ernest and Otto owned a considerable portion of downtown Stuart.

Fritz Ulrich

Fritz Ulrich was a civil engineer born about 1844 in East Prussia. He arrived on the Indian River before 1885 and settled on Fritz Island, located just north of the Merrill Barber Bridge in Vero Beach. On July 23, 1891, he acquired a U.S. 1820 Land Act patent of 159.02 acres located at Winter Beach, west of the railroad, south of Quay Dock Road. According to the 1910 and 1920 U.S. Censuses of Georgiana for Precinct 10 of Brevard County, Fritz was an East Prussian citrus grower with his own grove, living with wife Alice M., born about 1860, who was Irish.

Fritz Light

Another German who came to the area in the 1880s was Fritz Light. He worked in Sylvanus Kitching's store and as a handyman for over ten years. He was on the list of registered voters in Sebastian in 1902 and 1909.

Captain Walter Kitching

Walter Kitching was well-known in Sebastian and all up and down the Indian River as a trade boat owner and captain, and although he appeared in the 1885 Florida Census in Sebastian with his brother Sylvanus Kitching, he resided primarily in the Wabasso area. The Kitching brothers were the sons of an international stock broker ruined in the crash following President Lincoln's death. At age 21, Walter left his home and Quaker family in Leeds, Yorkshire, England, around 1867, to make his livelihood in the United States. From New York, he took a job driving a wagon team west, and remained sixteen years in the West, in Texas, Arkansas, Oklahoma, and Kansas, doing diverse jobs, including teaching English to reservation Indians. By 1883, he arrived in Florida, traveling by steamboat on the St. Johns River and overland by mule-drawn wagon to Cocoa. Pleased by what he found, he began applying for land through the 1820 Land Act, selecting 40 acres of land in Wabasso obtained February 13, 1884. He also purchased 225.46 more acres of land through the 1820 Land Act, from 1884 to 1919, in Indian River, Brevard, St. Lucie, and Martin Counties.

By 1887, he began setting up in business as a merchant. That year, Kitching and E. E. Hill of Cocoa began operating a floating store for settlers along the Indian River in the Trade Boat *Wave,* advertising in the *Florida Star* newspaper to create customers. "Walter Kitching with E. E. Hill will make regular trips southward as far as Jupiter calling everywhere with Trade Boat *Wave,*" was the ad in 1887 newspapers. They carried all kinds of staples and fancy groceries, dry goods, hats, shoes, hardware, and tools. Kitching dissolved his partnership with Hill in 1888 or 1889 and went into partnership with Col. S. F. Travis of Cocoa. They purchased a larger boat *Sparkle*, but that proved to be too small, so they built a yet larger vessel: the two masted, shallow draft, 56-foot schooner, *Merchant.*

Depending on the weather, winds, and vagaries of such an occupation, a trip from Cocoa to Jupiter and back usually took 30 to 40 days; the trade boat arrived about once a month. Kitching blew on a conch to let prospective customers know he was coming. If they had no docks, customers rowed out to the ship. As well as providing all necessary supplies, Kitching was also a Notary Public, witnessing legal documents such as deeds, and then delivering them to the proper agencies. He also performed marriages. Often he would send postcards ahead to settlers along the coast, notifying them of the dates when he expected to reach them.

As he continued acquiring land, not all land acquisitions in this sparsely settled area were peaceful, as was reported in the *Narrows* column in the *Florida Star* from April 5, 1888. George King contested a claim of Walter Kitching's to a homestead on the west side which was awarded to King. King sold his current land to John H. Stiff, and moved to the new site adjacent to a hammock with oaks, maples, mulberry, and cabbage palmetto. After his house was finished, he set out a grove of orange and lemon trees, moving his apiary of Italian bees to the new home on the west side.

The newspapers could not be trusted for all news. On April 1, 1892, newspapers reported the death of Walter Kitching, quoting an article from previous issue of *Public Spirit*, which stated that a telegram had been received from Eden reporting his death. Sylvanus Kitching in Sebastian was contacted and he informed the press that it was not true, and that Walter Kitching was still alive.

By 1892, Kitching capitalized on the coming railroads, beginning construction of a general store on his Potsdam (Stuart) property at US Hwy 1 and West 4th. In his Mercantile Store, the main floor was divided into dry goods, hardware, and grocery sections. In an attached shed, he had stock feed and fertilizers. Indians came to his store, bringing hides for sale, and purchased goods from him. He offered the St. Augustine, Jacksonville, and Indian River Railway, soon to become the Florida East Coast Railway, cash and right of way land in exchange for a railroad dock and depot on his property when it came through in 1893.

That year, he met Emma Jane Michael from Frost Proof, who was visiting her Michael brothers John and Stephen, who were living near Wabasso. They married in February 1894, traveling by train to honeymoon in St. Augustine. Emma traveled with Walter on the *Merchant* until their home on the St. Lucie River was completed. Realizing that economic changes would be brought about by the forthcoming railroad, and tiring of the long trips, Kitching turned the *Merchant* over to his nephew Alfred Michael in 1894, who continued the relationship with Colonel Travis in Cocoa. At age eighteen, Alf purchased the *Merchant* from his uncle and ran it with a crew of five and merchandise worth $5,000. The birth of Walter and Emma's child Sarah Josephine in 1895 was an added incentive to give up trade boat travel. By 1898, according to a letter written by Sylvanus Kitching, Walter had a pineapple plantation not as susceptible to frost as his own, as Walter's was further south. Walter was also president of the first Stuart bank, and donated land for the Methodist church there.

In 1888, Walter Kitching wrote a letter describing the Indian River area to *The Home and Farm*, published in Louisville, Kentucky. As a result of this letter a number of families came to the area from Kentucky and neighboring states. It described the Sebastian of that day:

> Indian River, Florida.
>
> Perhaps your readers may be interested in hearing from Indian River. This is a salt water sound, 140 miles in length by one to five miles in width, and so straight that a line stretched the entire length would not necessarily touch either shore. The waters are well stocked with fish, green turtle, oysters, crabs, etc. The most numerous fish are mullet, sea trout, channel bass, cavally and pompano. Mullet are very easily caught by throwing a cast net into a school of them. Those who fish for the markets catch large quantities with a seine. Oysters are simply delicious for six or eight months of the year. You can load up a boat either with the aid of oyster tongs or by wading in the shallow water. They are free for the gathering, and many people make a fair living by boating them to the numerous hotels and

boarding houses. One of my neighbors cleared $60.00 per month by gathering and selling oysters last winter.

Of course the aim of every man is to have a good bearing orange, lemon or banana grove. We give preference to the lemon in this vicinity. It bears sooner than the orange (in three to four years from the bud), is more prolific, it thrives with less culture and fertilizing, it bears heavier crops than the orange and it ripens its fruit from July to September, being the time when the imported crop is nearly exhausted and the price at the highest. Bananas bear in nine months after planting the suckers, and are good paying crop, as also are cabbages, tomatoes, etc.

The price of land on Indian River varies according to location, natural advantages, thickness of settlement, etc. Fifty dollars an acre is the average price of lots on the river front, but a quarter of a mile back from the river thousands of acres can be bought near this settlement at from $10.00 to $15.00 per acre, of the richest vegetable and banana, also high orange and lemon, land. Clearing is an expensive item. Timber lands cost $30.00 to $40.00 to make ready for the plow, though some adopt a cheaper plan by felling the timber and brush and piling in windrows, then grubbing a space about 6 feet wide every 20 or 30 feet for the tree rows, and gradually clearing the ground of roots by periodical cultivation of the trees with a hoe.

The healthfulness of this country cannot be excelled. Malaria and kindred diseases are almost entirely unknown. At present the only railroad is at Titusville, the county seat, but other lines are advancing towards us, which, ere long, are expected to traverse the entire length of the river. We have about a dozen steamboats of various sizes and hundreds of sailboats varying in length from 15 to 60 feet.

At this point, Indian River is separated from the Atlantic Ocean by a peninsula from 100 yards to a quarter of a mile wide, and salt-laden breezes lovingly caress, and at the same time moderate, the summer's heat. We had no frost last winter, and our highest temperature last year was 94 degrees. The mean annual temperature is about 70 degrees. This is truly a delightful climate, the invalid's sanitarium, the tourist's delight, and the poor man's home. Sportsmen can kill a deer, bear, wild cat or alligator almost any way.

W. KITCHING, Sebastian, Florida

Vero Beach Press, June 18, 1925, p. 7. Reprint from *The Home and Farm*, published in Louisville, Kentucky, 1888

Promoters and Visitors

With the advent of easier transportation, more people turned their attention on Florida. The abundance of bears, panthers, bobcats, mosquitoes, and alligators was minimized or ignored. Cheap land, fertile soil, virgin natural resources, mild climate, healthful air, and fantastic hunting and fishing were touted across the United States. And everyone came. How could they resist the reports they were reading?

Promoters loved the Indian River area as the exemplar of all of the many virtues of Florida. The year 1881 saw the creation of the Indian River Agricultural and Immigration Society, formed to promote settlement in the Indian River area. This was a successful venture, as by December of that year, every steamboat brought settlers. Early developers and promoters, in an attempt to convince prospective settlers that they were not a problem, maintained that the mosquitoes of the area were small, frail, clumsy, and did not cause malaria. Palmetto hats and switches, smudge pots, and netting were used to combat them. The unfortunate earlier names of Mosquito County and Mosquito Lagoon were not mentioned.

Dr. James Alexander Henshall

Dr. James Alexander Henshall described idyllic southern Florida hunting trips that he took two winters in 1879-80 and 1881-82, describing himself as an angler, sportsman, yachtsman, naturalist, and physician. The accounts of these trips were originally published in two sporting journals, and later as a popular book, *Camping and Cruising in Florida.* The first winter he and his traveling companions, patients of his that he brought along for the curative properties of Florida winter weather, made their way by rail and steamboat to Titusville. There Henshall purchased a skip-jack yacht that was cat-rigged, 18 feet long, with a 15-inch draft, named the *Blue Wing*. Their objective was to sail south to Biscayne Bay and the Florida Keys, and back up by way of the St. Johns River to Jacksonville. From the Indian River, they traveled down the St. Sebastian River. They passed the cabin of Mr. Kane (Cain) one-half mile down on the north bank. Traveling down the north fork, they found a clear spring on the bank. Henshall described an area that teemed with all manner of wildlife, including fish, manatees, tarpon, pelicans, cranes, herons, 'possums, land tortoises, deer, snakes, turkeys, cranes, egrets, herons, ibises, paroquets, buzzards, and immense alligators. Settler Tom Sellers and his family lived at the head of the North Prong. Henshall treated Sellers' sick child, and borrowed his dogs for deer hunting. The group experienced the trembling and rumbling sound from the earthquake that struck on January 12, 1880. When they headed back out, at the mouth of the St. Sebastian River, they passed the fine hammock of Mr. Gibson. A few miles below on the Indian River, they arrived at Barker's Bluff, where the cabin of Arthur Park stood, opposite Pelican Island. Using the pelicans for target practice, they continued south.

Dr. Henshall's second trip was made in the small five-ton schooner *Rambler* in 1881-82, accompanied by his ailing wife. They sailed down the Indian River to the St. Sebastian River and down the North Prong to their old Cabbage Camp just above the mouth of the North Prong past Mr. Kane's cabin on the main part of the river. Mrs. Henshall had an unfortunate encounter with some of Mr. Kane's black hogs. On another part of their winter journey, they poled three or four miles up the South Prong, following its loops and bends. The banks were high and covered with dense trees, bushes, and vines. Back onto the Indian River they approached Pelican Island, which was covered with nesting brown pelicans. Two years prior to this trip there had been no nesting birds, due to hunters. The rookery on an adjacent island held egrets, cormorants, and man-o-war hawks.

In his last chapter he wrote: "The wealth and glory of the vegetable kingdom, the varied and curious forms of animated nature and the balmy atmosphere and sunny skies of the southern seas must be realized by appreciative senses to do them justice." To the ailing he recommended Florida's air, sunshine, exercise, nutritious food, and good water.

C. Vickerstaff Hine

C. Vickerstaff Hine described in his book *On the Indian River* his trip which was a vacation to cure bodily ills, down the Indian River by canoe around 1889. He brought his own canoe with him from Chicago, custom fitted and 14 ft. long, with sails. To reach the Indian River, he traveled by rail and steamboat from Chicago to Titusville. He traveled down the Ocklawaha by steamboat to the St. Johns where he changed steamboats for the leg to Titusville. He considered Titusville to be the metropolis of the Indian River area. He spent two months on the Indian River in his canoe. He called the people of the Indian River area "semi-amphibious." The river was the great highway; every house had its own pier and boat. The water was so clear at 20 (sic) feet deep that it seemed to be only a foot down. The fish could be clearly seen. The St. Sebastian River widened into the broad St. Sebastian Bay where it joined Indian River. Along that river he found an enormous variety of wildlife, fruits, plant life, and flocks of birds.

1884 Promotional Guide

Max Bloomfield produced a tourist guide published in 1884 that primarily featured St. Augustine, but also promoted the Indian River area. Titusville, formerly Sand Point, on the Indian River was the eastern terminus of the Indian River Railroad. The other principal settlements on the Indian River at that time were Georgiana and Eau Gallie. None of the other settlements springing up along the Indian River, such as Sebastian, were mentioned. He considered the Indian River area a sportsman's paradise abounding in game and fish, the most inviting area in Florida. Like many others, he noted that the difficulty of transportation, which formerly deterred many from visiting that portion of the state, was eased by the advent of steamboats and railroads, creating ever-increasing numbers of visitors each season to its many and varied attractions.

Pelican Island

With the arrival of increasing numbers of naturalists and sportsmen to the Indian River area, Pelican Island gained fame, to its detriment. Depredations put the brown pelican population in jeopardy. By 1885, concern echoed in the newspapers. The *Florida Star* reported that for two years previously, the pelicans had ceased breeding on the island because of the continual harassment and shooting by Northern tourists. It stated that the birds did come back that year to nest. There were pelicans, egrets, cormorants, and man-o-war hawks on a small adjacent island. Some of the collectors, ornithologists and naturalists that visited the area were George Field, Arthur Howell, A. C. Bent, and later, George Nelson.

William Henry Jackson

It is difficult to imagine the magnitude of the impact of the new phenomenon of photographic images on middle-class Americans in the mid-1800s. Invented in 1839, glass plate photography was a complicated, expensive procedure accomplished by professional photographers. However, it brought to the average American the reality of other, romantic, unknown places, and the reality portrayed by William Henry Jackson and others like him, was wondrous.

Post-Civil War, the great westward expansion and migration began. Young men streamed west to make their fortunes. Industrialists focused upon exploitation of western resources, financing geological surveys with artists and photographers to document their discoveries. Railroads crossed the continent and financed artists and photographers to illustrate their brochures. Insatiable curiosity and the romance of unexplored, primitive frontiers seized the American imagination. William Henry Jackson rode the crest of this phenomenon to become one of the most successful and popular landscape photographers of his time. He traveled on countless expeditions funded by the government geological surveys or the railroads. His were among the earliest photographs of America's vast wilderness, including the Rocky Mountains, the Yellowstone River, American Indians, and other frontier images. Thousands of copies of his photographs and those of other photographers in the form of stereographs, postcards, books, booklets, and pamphlets were printed and sold.

Florida began to garner attention as another romantic, unspoiled frontier. Jackson's first Florida expedition was in 1887. He made many winter expeditions into Florida on paid commissions, during which he sought more unspoiled wilderness. During 1885-1892, he spent winters in Mexico, California, Louisiana, or Florida. His long and favorable connections with the western railway systems carried over into Florida. He received commissions to promote Florida railroads and hotels to stimulate the interest of tourists and developers in the state through his photography. Memorable photographs of the St. Sebastian and Indian Rivers are part of his heritage from the side trips he took on these commissioned journeys. He traveled by a rental steamboat called the *Cleo*, built in Melbourne. The *Cleo* is a focal point in his photographs of the Indian and St. Sebastian Rivers. Florida landscape images portray a mysterious, haunting beauty unspoiled by the encroachment of civilization. As a counter-balance, his commissioned photographs of hotels invited guests to enjoy civilized, comfortable surroundings. Many of his photographs of Florida still exist, and still excite the imagination. Detroit Publishing Company, the owner of many Jackson photographs, dates the photographs of the Indian River County area from 1880-1897. The Hales biography dates them at either 1887 or 1889.

In 1888-89, George Eastman, founder of Eastman Kodak Company, invented flexible transparent film negatives and the Kodak camera for photography. This easier method of photography ushered in the era of the amateur photographer, and the complicated, glass plate photography by professionals eventually began to phase out. The Kodak camera became a staple of travelers and tourists everywhere, who were no longer dependent on the professionals for a picture.

Naturalists

Easier travel to Florida was also a boon to the naturalists everywhere who wished to observe firsthand the abundant and unique flora and fauna of the state. They also saw the advantage of a winter expedition with no snow. In 1882, there was a very large breeding pelican population, according to Robert Lawrence of New York. Noted naturalist of the American Museum of Natural History, Frank M. Chapman, sojourned at Oak Lodge during his Indian River expeditions, as did many other naturalists. Professor Jenks stayed at a place on the shore, or at Oak Lodge during the many years he wintered in the area, forming a mounted collection of numerous local bird and animal specimens. Mr. Baker, another guest, collected birds for Southwick. He stated that the only roosting place of brown pelicans was at Pelican Island. Naturalist William Beebe was another guest at Oak Lodge. Brown University and the United States National Museum funded a collecting expedition for George W. Field in 1888, headquartering at Oak Lodge.

Chapman went on an expedition in a small cat boat with a guide to the mouth of the St. Sebastian River on March 11, 1889, five miles south on the opposite shore of the Indian River. His guide was a nephew of Latham, searching for Carolina Parakeets. He found 50 in flocks of 10 to 20 at the head of the St. Sebastian River, a few miles west of Wabasso. Parakeets were very easy to shoot. Chapman shot only what he thought he needed, but later another hunter came in and took all of the rest to be sold, sealing the extinction of that species. Chapman also collected specimens of the South Florida cotton rat, field mouse, and beach mouse while he was at Oak Lodge that same winter. He reported that sandhill cranes and herons were scarce, having retreated into the more inaccessible prairies due to hunters.

Post-Civil War, promoters were even advertising Florida in England. In 1886, an exhibition of North Florida pictures were projected on a screen in the Exhibition Hall of the Photographic Society of Great Britain. In 1888, O. Pierre Havens, a leading American landscape photographer, left Savannah, Georgia, and settled in Jacksonville, becoming the leading photographer in Florida. Flagler used his photographs in his brochures.

Even with all of the national interest, Sebastian was still having trouble making it into print. *A Tourist and Hunter's Guide to Indian River Country 1889-1890* contained small descriptive paragraphs of towns along the Indian River, but made no mention of any towns between Melbourne and St. Lucie.

10

The Fruits of Civilization—Steamboats Rule the Waterways: 1880s

Travel and Transportation, Commerce

What a wonderful time to be in Florida! In the 1880s, the Indian River witnessed an explosion unlike anything seen before or since, caused by steam. The steam engines of the boats and trains transformed the area, and the two began an intense rivalry in Florida, to the benefit of its inhabitants. Commercial ventures were growing and prospering. Towns took on character and shape. Imagine the excitement of the vision of the first steamboat or first train to people in an area with little contact with the larger world on a day-to-day basis.

People were pouring into Florida due to increased ease of travel by rail and steamer. Fernandina was a hub for most of the travel to other parts of Florida. Central Florida was a popular destination for tourists in the winter season, and large resort hotels sprang up. In the winter, Jacksonville contained people from all over, sportsmen, tourists, crackers, speculators, and bunco artists. This was not true for Sebastian at the beginning of the decade.

Travel Problems

Travel was still a confusing combination of multiple forms of travel to the Indian River area in the early 1880s, all of which were inadequate. Access to the area remained extremely difficult. Railroads and roads were needed. There were many ideas of how improvements should be made to waterways. An intracoastal waterway was on everyone's mind. Steamboats needed less treacherous waterways. Boating on the waterways was unreliable and dangerous, with tortuous channels, shifting shoals, shallow water, and unpredictable winds.

Gardner S. Hardee chaired a committee for recommendations on an intracoastal waterway. A proposal was made for a continuous waterway between Jacksonville and Miami down the interior of the eastern coastline. This was to be accomplished by dredging canals connecting the various natural waterways along the east coast of

Florida. In 1881, the Coast Canal Company began work on an intracoastal waterway. In 1889, the Florida legislature passed an act to complete the entire Intracoastal Waterway from St. Augustine to Biscayne Bay within five years. The Coast Canal Company hired Rittenhouse, Moore & Company of Mobile, Alabama, to begin the work. However, many years passed before it became a reality. Eventually, the Corps of Engineers took over the work and completed the Intracoastal Waterway in the 1930s.

The Haulover Canal needed improvements. There were many complaints; it was too narrow, not deep enough, and strong currents occurred due to the fact that the Indian River water level was 2 or 3 feet higher than that of the Haulover. In 1881, proposed improvements to Haulover Canal were made by J. F. LeBaron, an engineer. In 1886, the Coast Canal Company used the steam dredge *Chester* to clear the Haulover, but it rapidly silted in again and the Company cleared it again in the 1890s.

The usefulness of an open inlet at Gilbert's Bar was again addressed in 1885, when another attempt to open it failed. It was dredged open again in 1892. In 1886, there was an unsuccessful attempt to open the Sebastian Inlet to improve fishing and travel. The St. Sebastian River had no bridge, only a barge, pulled by mules.

Trade Boats

The rivers were still the best means of transportation and communication, and nearly everyone used them. Practically every settler had a pier on the Indian River to which small vessels could come. Traveling trade boats brought supplies and services. Scheduled steamer traffic was rare until the mid-1880s. Mail had a loose schedule, subject to weather and other delays.

John McLean and others followed soon after the Abbots and Captain Hogg to cash in on the success of trade boat commerce. He ran the sloop *Agnes*, beginning about 1880, operating out of Daytona. W. S. Norwood and Company sold from the trade boat *Osceola*. G. B. Rumph of Titusville ran the trade boat *Irene* for several years, but sold it to the Florida Canning Company which continued to trade on the river after 1890. Another trade boat operator was J. Hector Cornthwaite. Mary Baird ran the *Mary B* with her two sons. Captain McNeil operated the *Norma*.

A trade boat was described by Charles Gifford in Newman's book: The trade boats traveled the river from Fort Pierce to Titusville. They had shelves all around and had sufficient headroom to stand erect, providing nearly all necessary items, which were furnished by a man in Cocoa. The boats took three men to run them who lived onboard. The boats stopped along the river and sold to anyone, and people rode out in skiffs to meet them.

The larger towns had doctors and dentists who also traveled up and down the Indian River tending patients. Dr. F. H. Houghton found a rather unique way to provide his dental services with the trade boat *Dentos*. He advertised ahead of time what his schedule would be. Traveling by boat to provide his dental services from Halifax to

Lake Worth, he stopped at docks along the way, staying as long as necessary at each. If needed, a patient could get on at one stop, and travel to the next to get off, having a tooth pulled or cavities filled while they traveled. In the 1880s, the temperance movement was gaining adherents, and organizations formed in Titusville, but it did not succeed at that time. Trade boats regularly peddled liquor along the Indian River. They were gradually replaced by stores and offices in towns, as towns grew and transportation improved in the mid-1880s.

Steamboats

The steamboats on the Indian River were vital to the development of the area. They carried passengers, freight, produce, and mail. By 1880, the population had grown to the point where steamboat operators could make a profit and more steamers began to ply the Florida East Coast. A vast improvement over other previous marine craft, they replaced the use of barges and smaller craft, due to their large capacity, speed, and the fact that steamboats were able to run up and down river equally well. They also had the extremely shallow draft needed for Florida waterways. In *Steamboating on the Indian River*, Fred Hopwood noted that the golden steamboat era came between the years 1880-1889, when over 25 steamboat companies set up business on the Indian River. More than 200 steamboats plied the Indian River before the end of the era. All settlements on the river extended their docks into the middle of the river to make it easier to catch the attention of the steamboat captains. There were more than 100 landings along the Indian River. Often there was a sign at the end, with the word "Landing" in the name.

Railroads

Railroads were the ideal solution to travel woes, and the Internal Improvement Fund was renewed and land grants were resumed to encourage railroad extension into Florida. Railroads and their developers began to consider the growing lucrative Florida trade. Shaking off the failures that dogged the 1870s, railroads flourished, and the greatest railroad construction was in the 1880s, when 75,000 miles of track were laid in Florida. Many small railroads began crisscrossing the state. In the year 1800, 500 miles of track were laid in Florida; in contrast, in 1810, 2,489 miles were laid. In the winter season of 1881-1882, railroads advertised their Florida routes as the most convenient and comfortable. Consolidation of some lines began in 1885.

Because in part of the complexity of travel in Florida, the steamboat and railroad companies of the 1880s became an intertwined combination of both rail and water travel. Small companies that began as either rail or steamboat merged with others, forming larger and more complex systems during this decade.

Some Failed Attempts

There were quite a few companies that failed soon after beginning. Around 1881, the Sanford and Indian River Railroad was chartered by an Orlando syndicate, and started grading from Fort Reed toward Lake Jesup in 1882, but never actually laid tracks. The Leesburg and Indian River Railroad hired laborers but never laid tracks. The Palatka and Indian River Railroad planned to run from Titusville to the St. Johns River in 1881. It was taken over by the Jacksonville, Tampa and Key West Railroad.

Early Starts

Some companies started small in the decade. W. H. Churchill, who had operated a tram road in the 1870s, became president of the Indian River Railway and Transportation Company in 1881. W. S. Norwood's hack line was running from Titusville to Enterprise where connections could be made with the DeBary Line. Thomas W. Lund's Pioneer Line transported passengers and freight from Titusville to Salt Lake by hacks and wagons. Connections were made with vessels from there. From 1881-1883, the Tropical Florida Railroad was organized, running from Ocala to Wildwood and Panasoffkee. The Jacksonville, St. Augustine, and Halifax River Railroad opened in 1883, which was suited only for materials. Henry Flagler wanted a better railroad to get to St. Augustine where he built the Ponce de Leon Hotel in 1885, one for passengers between Jacksonville and St. Augustine. He gained control of that line and refurbished it. In 1886, Flagler took over control of some other lines and started south, 110 miles of railroad from Jacksonville to Daytona, and made history in Florida.

Early Independent Systems

The *Cinderella*, one of the independent operations run by Captain A. W. L. Ostrander, was a luxurious steamboat that arrived in Titusville on September 17, 1882. She was fast, light, steel-hulled, and 115 feet long, with a speed of ten knots, and built in Bordertown, New Jersey. She had ten staterooms, a pantry, and a saloon. She had difficulty negotiating the shallow parts of the Indian River because she was too heavy, and was too wide for the Haulover Canal. *Cinderella* left after one year to navigate the deeper St. Johns River. In 1883, *City of Palatka* began semi-weekly service on the St. Johns River, and in 1884, *City of Monticello* began service there as well.

The steamboats *Indian River* and the *Haulover* ran in the early 1880s. They had a 12-foot beam and 60-foot length, too large to pass through the Haulover Canal. Both were owned by the Fischer family of Titusville. The *Haulover*, operated by Jacob Lorillard, carried freight and passengers down the Halifax River and through the Mosquito Inlet to the Haulover Canal, where it met the *Indian River*. C. F. Fischer was captain of the *Indian River*. The *Indian River* would then take on its passengers and freight to Titusville and points south. The *Indian River* made a weekly trip from Titusville to Sebastian, then called at New Haven. In 1884, the U.S. government dredged a wider and deeper Haulover Canal, allowing both boats to be used for the entire run. 1885, the *Ino* was a sternwheeler built on the Halifax River to run on the Indian River with the *Frostline,* owned by H. Q. Hawley.

Florida Railway and Navigation Company

The first state system emerged in 1884, the Florida Railway and Navigation Company, created by Sir Edward Reed. It ran lines crossing the whole northern and central part of the state with 509 miles of track. It went into receivership in 1886, and became the Florida Central & Peninsular Railroad Company in 1888.

The Economy Takes Off

Eighteen eighty-six was the tipping point in Sebastian's economy, due almost entirely to the advances made in transportation that opened the area with easy access. Sebastian and the Roseland area went from subsistence farming and local trade to interstate commerce, due to the advent of easy shipping by train and steamer. Rich, virgin soil, and mild climate practically guaranteed good harvests. Sebastian was recognized; it made it into the directories. More and more people moved in.

Problems Addressed

After several failed proposals, in the banner year 1886, the Haulover Canal was cleared with the steam dredge *Chester*. However, complaints continued that the canal could not effectively carry the steamboats. There was a proposal to cut a new canal. The completion of rail service to Titusville and the Titusville railroad dock to accommodate steamers was completed in 1886.

Roads

Road traffic involved horses, mules, or oxen in this decade. Into the late 1800s, wild marsh ponies were common in Florida, and they were particularly well suited to the marshy area of Indian River County. They were small and light, with large hooves which kept them from floundering in the sandy, marshy soil and poor or non-existent roads. It was thought they were descendants of escaped Spanish horses.

More roads were being cut. In the 1880s, new roads were created by petitioning the county commissioner. If the petition was approved, a three-member road committee was appointed to obtain the right-of-way, and to lay out the route. No public outlay of funds was utilized; roads were primitive. After the 1885 state constitution was implemented, a state road law was passed requiring all able-bodied adult males to give a certain number of days each year for work on the public roads. This was unsuccessful. Coupled with the demand for better roads, this lack of success in requesting voluntary labor led to taxes and public road departments for road improvements. Bicycling was a popular fad in the 1880s which required a smooth road surface, as well. A Good Roads Convention was held in 1897 in Orlando. More and better roads were needed; the consensus was that roads should be paved with crushed shell.

Progress

By 1888, tourists were flooding into the county by rail and steamboat. Throughout the United States and particularly in Florida, word spread of the completion of rail service to Titusville and the opening of the Inland Waterway, even though it was not quite finished. The Traveling Passengers Association of the United States and Canada organized parties of 100 for its Florida tour, stopping at Rockledge. Pennsylvania Central Railway stopped in Titusville on its organized excursions to Florida. Steam yacht *Vera* carried Rochester tourists down the Indian River. Privately owned luxury yachts docked on the Indian River when traveling. The visit of President Grover Cleveland to Rockledge in 1888 received national news coverage.

However, the larger steamboats and the increase in the volume of traffic called for the need to improve the waterways for this more dependable transportation. They had to contend with shifting sand bars and poorly marked channels. Slowly, special dredges began to be used to provide these improvements, widening and deepening waterways, removing obstructions and snags. The government was slow to act, and by the time the Army Corps of Engineers was given the responsibility for clearing rivers in 1900, the steamboat era in Florida was nearly over. The end came in 1894, caused by railroad competition and freezes, although a few continued to operate until 1900.

Railroads improved service, and began standardizing as they expanded into Florida. In 1886, most of the railroads converted to standard-gauge tracks, with 4 feet 8.5 inches between rails, making it easy to switch trains from one set of tracks to another, instead of switching contents from one car to another. In 1887, the first Florida Railroad Commission was created to regulate railroad passenger and freight rates and operations. Increases in railroading increased hazards. Passing trains burned some buildings to the ground.

In the mid-1880s, some of the systems began to combine rail and steamboat modes of travel, to ensure smoother transitioning from one part of the distance traveled to another. The state exploded with many little systems and combined systems, some of which directly affected travel to the Indian River area around Sebastian.

When Frank M. Chapman traveled from Gainesville to Micco in 1889, the trip from Gainesville to Titusville was on the East Coast Railway, and from Titusville to Jupiter Inlet he traveled on a stern-wheel steamship on the Indian River.

Enterprise to Titusville Railroad

The Enterprise to Titusville Railroad offered subscriptions to have it built by January 1, 1886, and $30,000 was raised. Construction began immediately, with 300 workers clearing, grading, building bridges, and laying track. It was completed by the deadline.

In 1887, the St. Johns and Halifax Railroad reached Daytona, and the Jacksonville, Tampa and Key West Railroad reached Sanford where it connected with other railroads going south and west. The coming of railroads slowed the traffic on the St. Johns.

Indian River Steamboat Company

The Indian River Steamboat Company was organized early in 1886 as an extension of the Jacksonville, Tampa and Key West Railroad on the water. Captains Richard P. Paddison, Steve Bravo, and A. W. Buie were some of the most recognized commanders. As the area grew, so did the need for freighters. The *Progress* captained by Steve Bravo was profitable for the Indian River Steamboat Company until they went broke in 1896. Their small steamboat *SV White* was ideal for working the Indian River. The Indian River Steamboat Company also owned the Celestial Railroad (The Jupiter and Lake Worth Railroad), which ran from Jupiter to Lake Worth, with stations named Jupiter, Venus, Mars, and Juno. There were also connections further south. The whole system was called the Tropical Trunk Line System and served the Florida east coast until Flagler built his railroad in the 1890s.

Atlantic Coast, St. Johns and Indian River Railroad

The Atlantic Coast, St. Johns and Indian River Railroad was chartered in 1883. On July 23, 1885, the *Florida Star* included in the list of subscribers R. A. Hardee and W. M. Fee, from the Indian River area, who donated to the Atlantic Coast, St. Johns and Indian River Railroad Company. It was leased to the Jacksonville, Tampa and Key West Railroad as a branch line. At Titusville in 1886, the company built a 1500-foot dock into the Indian River and laid track on it so that the trains could run out over the water to meet the steamers which the company would be operating. This made Titusville a supreme hub of transportation in the Indian River country and began a decade of unparalleled Indian River steamboating. It opened up the Indian River area to settlers, commerce, and tourism.

Jacksonville, Tampa and Key West Railroad

When the Jacksonville, Tampa and Key West Railroad came to Titusville, the *Haulover* and *Indian River* served as the railroad's southernmost link. When that railroad acquired the Indian River Steamboat Company in June 1889, it put an end to the operation of the *Indian River* and the *Haulover*. That company had greater resources and more boats and became the dominant operation on the river. The *Loxahatchee* was the largest and most unusual of the steamers built by the Jacksonville, Tampa and Key West Railroad to transport railroad equipment from Titusville to Jupiter, and was also used as a barge to service other boats. She could land freight on shore in as little as 2 feet of water. The *Chattahoochee* was purchased and berthed at Jupiter as a floating hotel for travelers on the rail and steamboat systems.

From 1886, the Jacksonville, Tampa and Key West Railroad and the Indian River Steamboat Company Railway Mail Service had the contract for mail delivery as far south as Titusville and major towns along the river until 1893, when the Colegrove Mail Line took over the contract for mail delivery south of Melbourne.

Tropical Trunk Line System

The Jupiter and Lake Worth Railroad merged with the Jacksonville, Tampa and Key West Railroad, creating the Tropical Trunk Line, which started in Jacksonville where passengers and freight took the Jacksonville, Tampa and Key West Railroad to Enterprise. From there, passengers traveling to Titusville could board the Indian River Express. From that point, the next leg of the journey south was by steamer; the *Rockledge, Georgiana, St. Lucie, St. Augustine*, and *St. Sebastian* plied the 140-mile journey to Jupiter.

Richard P. Paddison was captain and owner of the *Rockledge*, a stockholder of the Tropical Trunk Line, and superintendent of the Indian River Steamboat Company. The *Rockledge* was built on the Cape Fear River in North Carolina. She was 136 feet long, with an iron hull; it was a side-wheel steamer first named the *Governor Worth*, serving Jacksonville to Sanford on the St. Johns River. After being refurbished and renamed *Rockledge*, she arrived on July 28, 1886, and became known as "the Queen of the River," because she was a favorite of local residents. President Grover Cleveland visited the Indian River area in February 1888 and traveled on the *Rockledge* on his tour. After that trip, the *Rockledge* was sold and became a freighter. Later it became a floating hotel at the end of the Indian River named the Lake Worth Hotel. Flagler had the *Rockledge* towed to Fort Pierce and later to Stuart to be used to house railroad workers. Then it was towed to Miami and served as the city's first hotel. In 1913, she was towed out to sea and sunk.

After sale of the *Rockledge*, the *SV White* was purchased by the Indian River Steamboat Company and used for the entire route. She was small, 75 feet long and 18 feet wide, with a draft of only 30 inches, which meant she could run through the

Narrows at full speed. Her captain was Charles Fischer, son of Captain Herman Fischer. It later served as a mail boat and tow boat. She continued to work on the river after the Indian River Steamboat Company was out of business.

The *St. Lucie* was built in Wilmington, Delaware. Arthur Lindsy was the first captain of the *St. Lucie,* according to Charles Pierce. She was later captained by Steve A. Bravo for the Indian River Steamboat Company. The *St. Lucie* was the most popular steamboat on the river, mainly due to Captain Bravo. She was 12 feet long, had a beam of 24 feet, and had 14 staterooms and a large hurricane deck. She drew only 35 inches of water and could travel almost anywhere on the Indian River. *St. Lucie* was the first new steamer to arrive in Titusville, according to Charles Pierce. In Pierce's unpublished manuscript *On Wings of the Wind,* he described the *St. Lucie*:

> With flags flying, bright red hull and snow white upper works,
> her polished brass gleaming and sparkling in the bright sunlight,
> she made a picture never to be forgotten.

Captain Steven A. Bravo

Captain Bravo's Spanish ancestry was clearly apparent. He told wonderful stories, had a tremendous voice, was an entertaining host, had an anecdote for all occasions, and a big smile. On one trip of the *St. Lucie,* a man was heard yelling from the top of a tree. They approached, and found a bear crouched at the foot of the tree. Captain Bravo shot the bear and rescued the man.

Captain Steven A. Bravo was from Dr. Andrew Turnbull's New Smyrna Colony. He was a skipper for the Indian River Steamboat Company. At different times he was captain of the *St. Sebastian,* the *St. Augustine,* and the *St. Lucie.* Bravo's brother Johnny sometimes took over the helm of the *St. Lucie,* according to Evard Geer, and sometimes George Williams, who was famous for his ability, was at the helm. Bravo worked for Henry Flagler during the Spanish-American War out of Biscayne Bay. When Flagler's railroad came through, he sailed the *City of Key West* for Flagler between Key West and Miami. The *St. Lucie* was brought down by Flagler to haul materials between Miami and Key West. Bravo was also captain of the *St. Lucie* when it was caught in the 1906 hurricane and went down. Thirty-seven of the 120 on board drowned at that time.

Other Steamboats

The *St. Lucie* was so successful that she was joined by two sister ships, the *St. Augustine* and the *St. Sebastian.* All of the steamboats of the Indian River Steamboat Company were named after Indian River towns. The *St. Augustine* was faster, and the *St. Sebastian* was longer. The Indian River Steamboat Company was in operation on the Indian River with its three boats until 1895, when it was declared insolvent.

The *St. Augustine* was bought by the Indian River and Biscayne Bay Navigation Company as a passenger ship and ended up rusting away on the Loxahatchee River. Captain George Gleason skippered the *St. Sebastian* in the late 1890s. Three years after the 1895 bankruptcy, the *St. Sebastian* went back into service on the river for a short time and served in the Spanish-American War, eventually ending up as a ferry in Fernandina. The *Santa Lucia* came 3,000 miles down the Ohio and Mississippi Rivers, around Florida and up the ocean to the inlet to serve the local traffic. The *Santa Lucia* was one of the best-known freighters, owned and operated by Captain Paddison. It was purchased by the Florida East Coast Railroad to transport railroad supplies and building materials from Eau Gallie to Lake Worth. Captain Alex Goode skippered the *Santa Lucia* for a while. In 1895, it was transferred with the *Sweeney* to the Indian River to transport building materials to the new town of West Palm Beach.

Captain A. W. Bouie was a skipper of steamer *Santa Lucia* when it was owned by the Indian River Steamboat Co., and was captain of the small mail boat *Cleo*. By 1889, he was the sole operator of the *Cleo*. He and his boats had a reputation for being on time. He later supervised the operation and maintenance of the Celestial Railroad.

East Coast Transportation

The East Coast Transportation was organized in 1889. They purchased the *Sweeney*, a 134-foot vessel that was 34 feet wide and drew 22 inches of draft. The *Sweeney* came to Indian River on October 28, 1890, to carry passengers and freight. She had beautiful staterooms, a large dance floor, and awnings on her decks. The *Sweeney* was famous for its annual excursions from Titusville to Oleander Point for the celebrated May Day picnics. The *Sweeney* had a sister ship named the *Denny* which was less desirable, as it had a draft of 36 inches and was more likely to go aground in the lagoon.

East Coast Transportation was a competitor to the Indian River Steamboat Company for freight and passengers. This competition caused their failure. Moreover, the Jacksonville, Tampa and Key West Railroad also failed by late 1892. By 1895, the Flagler railroad and freezes of 1894 sealed their demise.

Indian River and Biscayne Bay Navigation Company

A new steamship company was formed, named the Indian River and Biscayne Bay Navigation Company. It ran the *Progress* and freighter *Sweeney*, renamed *Della*. She ended up as a quarantine ship and sank in Key West Harbor in 1909.

Steamship *Panama*

Sebastian hit the news with an unexpected windfall for local residents on Friday, October 28, 1887, when the steamer *Panama* went aground on a reef in the ocean opposite Sebastian, about due east of Pelican Island. The *Panama* was a Spanish vessel carrying a large mixed cargo and passengers from New York to Havana and Central America. Trying to float the ship free of the reef, Captain Luciana Alcatena ordered the cargo thrown overboard, which started washing up on the beach. The keeper of the Indian River Inlet House of Refuge, Henry B. Archibald, was one of the first on the scene. He organized salvage parties and arranged to have passengers and crew helped ashore. Goods salvaged were intended to be held for the insurance company agent. Paul and Gottlob Kroegel, David and Mercer Gibson, the Cains, Kitchings and Captain Frank Forster were among those early to arrive. Word spread all up and down the coast, however, bringing scavengers and wreckers from as far away as Titusville to Jupiter. It was impossible to control, and much of the cargo was carried off. Some people obtained clothing and household items. Cain salvaged a sewing machine on board. It became the community sewing machine for the settlement and the Cain daughters became sailmakers for Paul Kroegel's boatyard. The Krogels got some dishes and cutlery. Someone opened a wine cask and people started drinking on the beach. By Monday, the *Panama* was free of the reef and headed south, minus her cargo.

Economy and Commerce

With better transportation, it was possible to begin shipping fragile commodities to northern markets, energizing growth. Everyone, no matter the size of the real estate, engaged in some sort of agriculture, even though clearing the land was difficult. Individuals hunted or fished for market as well as for their own families. By the 1880s, more commercial products were going to market. The dramatic increase in transportation was a great boon to commerce of all sorts. Increased population also provided customers locally. Steamboats and railroads could carry large enough loads northward to be profitable.

Agriculture was booming. Mrs. C. W. Baird was a vegetable and truck farm grower. Mrs. S. F. Brown grew oranges and pineapples. Dempsey Cain was an orange and vegetable grower. D. P. Gibson grew bananas, coconuts, oranges, pineapples, and vegetables. Walter Kitching grew bananas and coconuts. Gottlob Kroegel raised bananas, oranges, pineapples, and vegetables. Mrs. M. C. Hosch was a coconut, orange, and pineapple grower. W. H. McCall grew bananas and oranges. August Park was a banana, pineapple, and vegetable grower. R. B. Spratt had orange groves. E. H. Woodruff raised pineapples.

Citrus

Citrus groves were maturing and producing large crops. In 1881, J. F. LeBaron's *Survey of Agricultural Production* enumerated 204 orange groves along the Indian River, making citrus a dominant commercial crop. The 1886 freeze hurt younger citrus trees, but older ones survived. Marketing and transportation were still difficult, but constantly improving. The Indian River Fruit and Vegetable Growers Protective Association was formed in early 1888 to address the problems of growers.

Vegetables

The settlers learned by trial and error the differences in Florida farming. They discovered that it was necessary to fertilize and control weeds; deer, cattle, and hogs ruined the fields, and crops were more susceptible to cold and freeze than citrus. Beans and tomatoes had the most acreage and production. Farmers also grew and shipped cabbage, cucumbers, eggplants, onions, watermelons, guavas, and bananas. They found that tobacco was not successful in the Indian River area.

Pineapples

Pineapples did not succeed long-term. Growers started producing pineapples around 1878 or earlier, but most pineapple production was in the southern part of the county. Pineapples were difficult to work with, but brought a good price. Cheaper foreign competition and shipping difficulties eventually ended pineapples as a major crop.

Cattle and Livestock

The open-range cattle grazing that began around the 1850s continued. The western part of Brevard County produced more cattle herds, whereas growers prospered more to the east of the St. Johns River. Unexpected hardships hit Florida farms; alligators and panthers ate the pigs, and coons and possums got the poultry.

Commercial Fishing

Ice and railroads made commercial fishing feasible. Before the 1880s, turtles were a major commercial product shipped north, and one fishing group at Indian River Inlet existed. Serious commercial fishing began in the 1880s with George Scobie's oystering at Titusville. He shipped his first 5 gallons of oysters north on the first train out of Titusville in 1886. The catch went out in barrels packed in ice. The Parks shipped out 2,500 turtles in 1886. R. G. Hardee and A. M. Sample created the Sebastian Fish Company. They had 20 boats operating between Sebastian and Fort Pierce.

Timber

The extensive forests of virgin pine were used for local lumber. Saw mills sprang up. Before the existence of saw mills, people imported lumber or used salvage from wrecked ships. Wood was cut for buildings, to fuel trains, and to lay tracks. By the 1890s, elsewhere in the country, the demand grew for yellow pine lumber, turpentine, and rosin. Tracts of land would be bought, turpentine extracted for a number of years, and then the weakened trees would be clear cut for lumber. Convicts were leased by state and local governments for this work. Roseland was one such place. The convicts were housed in a long, low, barracks-style building, the Stockade. It had a high tower and fence and stood on what is now the southeast corner of Berry Avenue and Gibson Street. It was said that they were afraid to escape, due to the alligators, bears, panthers, and other wildlife in the area.

Entertainment and Activities

Ease of travel meant increased access for social activities, and enough individuals to form group activities. As population in Brevard County rose, the 1880s and 1890s saw the rise of many activities and entertainments, although it took longer for them to arrive in Sebastian. Settlers had to travel to other parts of the county to partake in the fraternal orders and social organizations such as the Indian River Lodge, F&M, Masonic Lodge, Eastern Star, Knights of Pythias, Daughters of Jericho, YMCA, Independent Order of Truthtellers, and literary societies. Groups and towns had local bands. Locally, social hops were held. People swam, went visiting, and had picnics. National holidays were celebrated much as today, with speeches, parades, picnics, races, and other activities. Yacht clubs, boat races, and regattas existed in many communities all along the river. Gun clubs formed. Hunting and fishing parties were common. Baseball was popular.

In his book *On the Indian River*, C. Vickerstaff Hine described an article in *Indian River News* concerning a Sunday-school Convention held at East Melbourne on June 6, 1889. People came by boat from all up and down the river and camped out the night before to be ready for the convention the next day. This was the first annual convention of the Indian River Sabbath School of Melbourne. This group was organized as an auxiliary to the State Branch of the American Sabbath-School Union. There was a delegation from Sebastian, and James A. Groves of Sebastian was selected as one of the officers of the association.

11

The Decade of the Railroads: 1890s

The 1890s was a period of growth and consolidation for Brevard County and Sebastian, and it was a beginning for Roseland. Overshadowing all was the revolution in transportation, the arrival of the railway in 1893, the area's link to the larger world. It brought faster, streamlined connection to the rest of the country. It carried in manufactured goods, settlers, land speculators, tourists, sportsmen, and naturalists, and sent north the catches of fish, oysters, and turtles, and agricultural products of citrus and other fruits and vegetables. The towns along the railroad flourished. However, a nation-wide depression and devastating freezes in this decade were extremely damaging to the economy.

Panic of 1893

The growing economy of Florida was severely set back by the panic of 1893 and ensuing depression. A sharp New York stock market plunge in 1893 set off a panic of selling that caused the stock market to crash. This resulted in a credit crisis and the failure of a huge number of businesses, including banks and railroads. Unemployment was widespread. This depression lasted for about four years, ending in 1897. The effects spread throughout America, including Florida.

Great Freeze of 1895

While still in the grip of the depression, the freezes of December 1894 and February 1895 caused front-page headlines. Alachua County, at that time the state's leading producer of citrus, was hardest hit. The trees there were completely destroyed, as well as in Marion and Orange Counties. When trees thawed out, they burst apart with a shocking cracking sound, completely destroying them. Some of the Titusville groves survived. South of the St. Lucie inlet, there was no lasting damage.

The Indian River groves received much less damage, and not all were hurt. Some groves survived, but some were abandoned. Some growers began replanting with bud wood from the groves of Dempsey Cain, the Ercildoune Frost Proof Plantation, and Mrs. Eason, known as the Hirsch Grove, all of which survived in better condition. As a consequence of this disaster, the entire citrus industry shifted southward. These freezes were even more damaging to truck farming than to the groves, which convinced many farmers to switch to citrus groves. The combination of the depression and freeze jolted the economy, causing even greater bank failure and unemployment.

There was one positive result. The freeze improved fishing, as it killed off the worthless catfish and toad fish, leaving mullet and trout alive. Dead fish were hauled from the shore by the wagonload and used for fertilizer. The freeze, coupled with the decline of steamboating, drove some of the growers to commercial fishing.

There were more freezes to contend with in this decade. The 1898 freeze brought the first snow to Brevard County, and there were other freezes in 1899 and 1900. In the 1890s, there was more economy in Florida to be damaged by adverse weather than there was in the earlier severe freezes in Florida of 1747, 1766, 1774, and 1835.

Many people did not give up, and worked to overcome the hardships. An *Indian River Advocate* newspaper ad by one Cocoa entrepreneur in December 6, 1895, in part stated "Bear in Mind … that I am not out of business" in large type.

Brevard County

Due in no small part to the railroad, population and economy along the east coast were booming, much of it centered on the needs of the railroad, and the needs of the individuals brought in by the railroad. Railroad camps of workers needed servicing. Train engines burned wood, increasing timbering and the number of sawmills. Ice houses were needed to keep shipments fresh. Hotels and apartments were built to house newcomers, tourists, sportsmen, and naturalists. Roads received some attention; state funds were used for some of the most trafficked roads to lay a three-inch base of palmetto fiber topped by a layer of shell to meet county standards.

County finance problems involving county commission expenditures and county debt in the hands of County Commission Chairman Robert S. Morrow came to a head, involving stormy meetings in 1892 by the Brevard County Reform Association. Heated political feuding continued by many groups, much of which centered in Titusville. The sale of liquor became legal again in the early 1890s. The Licensed Saloon Keepers Association was organized in the early 1890s to eradicate the illicit speakeasies and trade boat sales that had sprung up during Prohibition, with little success. Titusville's reputation remained shady in the 1890s. Murders were frequent along the building of the railroad, one of which involved a lynching of the killer. In 1895, most of Titusville burned to the ground, perhaps caused by suspected arsonists that were nearly lynched. Financial shortages caused by the county treasurer set off another furor in the mid-1890s. Melbourne, incorporated in 1887, was growing.

The Spanish-American War had a local effect, as many trains ran through the Brevard County towns transporting soldiers to Miami in 1897. The wood-burning passing trains burned some buildings to the ground and damaged others. Home guards sprang up as many became concerned with coastal defense when the War Department refused to send aid. They saw no action in this short-lived war, however.

Around the turn of the century, there were signs of economic recovery in the county, and a change was made to elected county officials as opposed to appointments by the governor. Redistricting reflected the changed population demographics, shifting away from cattle in the west, toward increasing population in the east.

Sebastianites still had to travel for social services in this decade. According to the *Florida Star*, there were seven physicians licensed to practice in Brevard County in 1890. They were B. R. Wilson, J. B. Screven, and W. S. Graham serving Titusville; G. W. Holmes and C. A. Henz in City Point; and J. O. Scofield and W. L. Huglett in Cocoa. Dr. F. H. Houghton offered dental services on board his floating dental apartments. Titusville dentist Dr. F. W. Craven spent two days in Sebastian pulling teeth in May 1896.

Education in Brevard County schools was being upgraded; the Brevard Teacher's Institute held a workshop in December 1892 for an exchange of ideas and mutual improvement amongst educators in the county. It was a move away from utilizing students who had just graduated from high school as teachers. A law passed in 1899 allowed the formation of special school tax districts, which was approved by all precincts. This created consolidated schools and brought some stability to education. Funding to hire teachers was assured. It also meant that some students had to travel longer distances to school; some boarded with families in town during the school sessions.

Sebastian

This decade, Sebastian boasted of four stores, two hotels, a boarding house, a school, and two churches. Central Avenue was added to Louisiana Avenue and Main Street as thoroughfares. Two railroads ran through. The railroads undoubtedly contributed to Sebastian's growth. They supplied the easy transportation access it had lacked before. Support services for the railroad were springing up, although agriculture and fishing dominated commerce. Civic and social activities were providing a civilizing atmosphere; the town of Sebastian was maturing as it grew. The newspapers of the 1890s contained information about the day-to-day lives of its citizens. In the *Indian River Advocate* were details about who was visiting friends, who stayed at the hotels, and the status of local projects such as the railroad installation or road building. Cattle ate gardens, houses burned, boats were built, and crops were sent by rail. All of the minutia of daily life could be found in the local news.

Stores, Boarding Houses, Hotels

Sebastian had a downtown. In it was Sylvanus Kitching's store that was prospering. He had the upstairs of his store divided into rooms for guests in September 1893; however, when the hurricane of October 11-12, 1893, struck southeast Florida, the Kitching store was blown off of its blocks into the river. Water flooded to the top of the counters; stamps, stamped envelopes, and postcards were ruined. When he submitted his claim for damages, he estimated he lost $2,000 in goods and property. By 1895, Kitching had prospered and made improvements to his store and home. Seeing the changes that would come when the railroad arrived, the Kitching building was moved by Sylvanus and his son Stanley with rollers, from the river up to its new location on Main Street, close to the railroad. Business was good, and in 1896 he expanded his store's services; he had a third-story floor laid on his building, which made a grand hall. Their second-floor hotel was now named the Palm House. In August of that year, Miss Edith Kitching was managing it in her mother's stead while her mother was visiting out of town. A popular continuing entry in the *Indian River Advocate* was the list of current guests at the Palm House.

Sylvanus Kitching hosted a grand ball at the Palm House on Christmas Day in 1896. That year he also had a large cistern built. He had a civilizing influence on the town; a sign in Kitching's store read: "Gentlemen will please deposit their superabundance of secretious saliva in the expectorating receptacle." Kitching's wife Martha never really adjusted to life in Sebastian, as Sylvanus confided in a letter to his friend in 1898. However, she had her own interests. Apparently Martha kept up with the latest in medical innovation, as Mrs. S. Kitching advertised providing electrical treatments for rheumatism, paralysis, general debility, acne, or eczema in the *St. Lucie County Tribune* from May 21, 1899.

There were more signs of booming civilization in Sebastian. In the 1890s, William C. Braddock added competition for the sale of merchandise when he opened his store on Main Street.

In May of 1896, Hall & Edwards opened a meat market that was able to get Chicago steak to sell to residents, but it was short lived. By August of 1896, a third general store was added for a short time, that of James Morrow. That month he built an addition on the south side of his store, and enclosed his house and yard with a fence. No doubt the fence was necessitated by the fact that at the time, livestock were still allowed to roam freely. Individual property owners were obliged to erect fences to keep the animals out. This was a continuing complaint. The *Florida Star* reported on March 31, 1899, that R. A. Hardee was getting a petition signed to have hogs excluded from within one and a half miles of the Indian River. The Hardees also had a hotel on Main Street, as well as their fishing business.

Carlile House

Mrs. Carlile's Boarding House was a popular place to stay for newcomers to Sebastian. The Semblers first stayed there when they arrived in 1901, according to Cora Sembler Sadler. There was a long bunk room on the second floor, and the kitchen and dining room were in a separate structure. Many of the other residents were bachelor fishermen. It was later owned and run by A. J. Semblers, and the building has had many owners since then. At one time, it was a gift shop. It still stands, on the corner of Truman Street and North Central Avenue at US Hwy 1, an excellent example of the Cracker House style, updated.

Churches

In 1895, a second church was added to Sebastian. The Rev. S. F. Gove officiated at the new Baptist Church at Sebastian. The church was built west of Kitching's store on land donated in 1896 by Captain Christian F. and wife Elise S. M. Fischer of Titusville.

According to the Church Register of the Sebastian Methodist Church, and the Methodist Archives of Florida Southern College, the first service in the Methodist Church was held by Rev. C. F. Blackburn in 1893, before the church was even completed. Rev. Blackburn had been sent to officiate at the establishment of the church, and had only a Bible, folding chair, and a vase of flowers. Parishioners sat on planks laid over nail barrels, and the flooring was temporary, consisting of planks laid over dirt. The church was soon finished. The Methodist Church had a parsonage added on a corner lot by the railroad in July and August of 1896. It gained many new members in the 1890s. George B. Hall and Meta B. Barnett were married there in 1893, as were Arthur K. Kroegel and Ida Johnston in 1898. Katie Park was baptized there in 1895.

Cemetery

Over the years, neighbors asked to use part of August Park's land for their burials, and in 1895, this land was donated for the Sebastian Cemetery. Park's house was built east of the cemetery, on the Indian River. August Park died January 12, 1895, when a tree fell on him, and he is buried in the Sebastian Cemetery, in the Park Section, as is Polly Ann Park, who died in 1898.

Indians

Indians were present in the area, as reported in the *Indian River Advocate* on November 6, 1896. There were about 25 Indians camped out on the Sebastian River west of Sebastian. They had plenty of ponies, wagons, chickens, etc. with them, and, according to the newspaper, seemed to be enjoying themselves immensely. They traded with local merchants.

Civic Matters

After Sylvanus Kitching, Henry B. Howard was Postmaster in Sebastian from 1893 to 1896. He was followed by William C. Braddock, who was Postmaster from 1896 to 1899.

From 1899 to 1902, James Morrow, formerly from Georgia, was Postmaster. He was also a farmer and shopkeeper. Sebastian was beginning to govern itself, needing more than postmasters. In the 1890s, it began adding more offices. W. Owen Jacobs of Sebastian was appointed Justice of the Peace by the governor for District 7 of Brevard County. Town offices were voted upon; candidates for town offices were Chas. Park and C. V. Sherwood for constable, and G. H. Edward, B. F. Hardsty, and H. B. Howard for justice of the peace. Fifty votes were polled on election day in August of 1896.

School

In mid-October of 1893 school opened, conducted in the Indian River Land and Improvement Company building in Sebastian. Miss Willie May of Rockledge was the teacher. Classes were held there until the new school was erected. As of the first of November of 1893, there were 25 pupils at the Sebastian school in town and eight in the school on the Sebastian River. In October of 1895, Miss Jennie Parham was appointed as teacher for the Sebastian school. School closed April 23, 1896, for the year and Miss Parham returned to her home in Stinson, Georgia. Keeping the school in Sebastian open was often a matter of finding someone to teach and obtaining operating funds. School did not open the first week in October of 1896, as it had no teacher. It opened the first of November with sixteen pupils, when Miss Ladye Skipwith of Nashville, Tennessee, was hired. In December of 1896, there was a severe outbreak of measles among the students and general population, and the school closed for a week, reopening with a small attendance. Miss Jennie Parham taught two more years at Sebastian.

One of the teachers of the school was Professor Benjamin F. Hardesty, a former Sergeant in the 1st Special Louisiana Battalion of the Confederate Army from 1861-1865. He was a member of the Brevard School Board, reporting on Sebastian school at the regular meetings. He and Mrs. Ella Hardesty were also early members of the Sebastian Methodist Church. Carpentering was one of his skills; he helped with the enlarging and remodeling of the church in 1901. Benjamin died in 1917 and was buried in the Sebastian Cemetery, in the Park section. Ella died in 1923 and was buried next to her husband.

The new school building also offered as a venue for social activities. In September of 1896, a social was held by the Ladies' Parsonage Society in the school on a Saturday night, and another one was held later in the month to raise funds for the parsonage.

Ivey and Cassie Lawson

There were several influential families that moved to Sebastian during this decade that helped shape Sebastian's character and form. The Lawsons were the first of these notable families to arrive at the turn of the decade. Ivey Lawson was one of the sons of H. Briggs Lawson, who had been one of the mayors of Hahira, Lowndes County,

Georgia, and one of the founders of the Methodist Church in Hahira, along with Stephen Vickers. Ashley Lawson was the first settler of Hahira, and a settlement sprang up around his house; West Lawson and H. Briggs Lawson were among the first to follow. By 1880, H. B. Lawson and family were in Brooks County, Georgia, which had split off from Lowndes County in 1858. Ivey had moved to Quitman, and he and his wife Cassie (Amanda) Lawson left Quitman, Georgia, on January 1, 1889, stopping in City Point for several months until daughter Ruby was born. They then continued their steamboat journey to Sebastian with their family, except for Parris. They had sent their twelve-year-old son Parris ahead by wagon with their household goods. The Lawsons left behind a beautiful colonial home in Quitman, Georgia, to live in a palmetto shack until their new home was built in Sebastian. In Georgia, Ivey grew peanuts and tobacco, and owned a commissary. In Sebastian, Ivey supplied wood to the steamboats and railroads, and became a citrus grower. Cassie was a charter member of the Sebastian United Methodist Church in 1891. In 1892, Ivey Lawson built a house "entirely covered with paper," as it was phrased in the *Indian River Advocate.* Ivey Lawson obtained a land patent for 80 acres in 1899. The Lawson's glowing description of the Sebastian area was instrumental in convincing other South Georgia families to move there, such as the Ryalls. After Ivey's death, Amanda made her home with her daughter, Mrs. W. C. Braddock. The Lawsons are buried in Sebastian Cemetery.

Parris and Bamma Vickers Lawson

Twelve-year-old Parris was given the responsibility of driving his family's household goods from South Georgia to Sebastian with two friends when the family decided to relocate in 1888. He arrived in Sebastian in December of 1888. Parris always worked a variety of jobs. He was employed at the Ercildoune Lodge as a general handyman and bellhop for about two years, from 1893. He also had citrus groves and grew vegetables. Parris was a carpenter, working on most of the buildings erected at that time in Sebastian, including remodeling the Methodist Church in 1909, and building the Woman's Club and the Sunday School rooms of the Methodist Church in 1926. He put his hands to other types of labor, as farmer and handyman, including plumbing and concrete work. He served as city clerk, election clerk, and city councilman.

Bamma Vickers' brothers George F. and Frank C. Vickers arrived in Sebastian around 1903, and the rest of the Vickers family arrived in 1908. Parris and Bamma had known each other in Hahira, Georgia, and were married soon after she arrived in Sebastian. The ceremony was held July 15, 1908, in the Sebastian Methodist Church. After marriage, Bamma helped with their support. She had a dressmaking and millinery shop in the living room, and worked in the local packing houses. The Lawsons boarded local schoolteachers in their home as well. Bamma was a founding member of the Sebastian Woman's Club, the oldest in Indian River County, organized in 1914. She also taught Sunday School. In the 1920s and 1930s, the Lawsons provided a free public children's library in their home. In 1931, Parris bought a car. They both served at an observation post in 1942 at Archie Smith's, part of the Air Warning System. Parris died at age 85 in 1962, buried in Sebastian Cemetery with his parents, his wife Bamma Vickers Lawson, and his son Basil. Bamma was feted by the whole city on her 100th birthday, and died in 1985, only one-week shy of 103 years of age.

The Ivey and Parris Lawson houses were built near each other in the Vickers Brothers Subdivision on the sand ridge. The two houses were moved south 150 to 175 feet to Old Dixie Highway, and one still remains there, the Parris and Bamma Vickers Lawson House, which achieved the distinction of listing on the National Register of Historic Places. The National Register described the history of the house as a two-story, wood frame house with two porches, a tin roof, and a brick chimney. It was built around 1911, facing the railroad, and moved to US Hwy 1 around 1919. It was one of the first houses in the Vickers Brothers Subdivision, which was platted from 1911 to 1921. They moved their house to be next to Bamma's parents who had just built on Old Dixie Highway, which was becoming the main road and most prestigious location in Sebastian. The kitchen of the Lawson house was originally a separate building, but was joined to the house when it was moved. It received some modernizing upgrades since that time, such as water, sewer, and electricity.

William Christopher Braddock Sr.

Soon to settle in Sebastian after the Lawsons was the Braddock family. The William Christopher Braddock, Sr., family had lived in Seville, a small town near DeLand, Volusia County, Florida, an area rife with fighting, killing, and cattle rustling, during the range wars. They owned land in Volusia County and had a farm, cattle, and general store. William C. Braddock was a private in the 2nd Florida Cavalry of the Confederate forces from 1861-1864. While Braddock was in the war, his wife Victorine stayed in the Florida swamps near Seville and lived off the land with children and servants.

After the war, Braddock returned to Seville, built a hotel, and had a general store. Around 1891, after a devastating freeze, he and his family moved further south to Sebastian. They came down the Indian River by barge, carrying with them their horse, wagon, household goods, and some of their sixteen children. Sometime after their arrival in 1891, William purchased and began operating the Hardee general store on Main Street in Sebastian. The post office was in his store, and their home was on the second floor. The *Indian River Advocate* reported in September of 1896 that W. C. Braddock was disposing of his stock and general store merchandise to W. A. Landes, and would devote his time instead on raising vegetables commercially. In the 1900 census, living with William and Victorine were children Ada, Scott, Irene, and Wallace. In 1911, they moved to Lakeland. William C. Braddock Sr. went blind in his later years. He died in 1925, and was buried in Lakeland, as was Victorine, a few years later.

William Christopher Braddock Jr.

William Christopher Braddock Jr. was born in Florida in 1876. He arrived in Sebastian with his parents in 1891. He married Kate Lawson in 1898 and had sons Leroy and Maurice. She was the daughter of Ivy and Cassie Lawson. They came from Georgia to Sebastian in the early 1900s. Will was a fisherman whose residence was near that of his parents in 1900. With him at that time were his wife Kate and nine-month-old son Leroy. He later owned a store, grew tomatoes, and had a tomato packing house. William Braddock was the brother of the George Braddock who lived on Louisiana Avenue. Their brother Scott Braddock died from a fall in Daytona Beach at the time he was living in Sebastian. Bachelor brother Wallace also lived in Sebastian.

George Byrd Hall

George Byrd Hall arrived in Sebastian early in the decade. He was born in 1866 in Georgia. Meta Barnett was born there as well. He arrived in Sebastian around 1892-1893. He and Meta married April 2, 1893, the first marriage in the Sebastian United Methodist Church. George and Meta Hall joined the church in December 1893. Per the 1900 census, their daughter Julia was born in Florida around 1898.

Meta Hall was a school teacher. She and George held old-fashioned ice cream socials on the church grounds on Saturdays to raise money to buy benches for the church. She was one of the small group of women who organized the Methodist Church.

George was a citrus farmer, owner of the Klondike Grove; his business was known as G. B. Hall & Co., of Sebastian. The Klondike Settlement plantations began approximately eleven miles west of Winter Beach. Other plantation owners in the Klondike Settlement were Judge Minor S. Jones of Titusville; E. W. Hall, a tax collector; and John C. Jones, a postmaster and the son of Judge Jones. Judge Jones was the first, with land purchased in the late 1890s.

By April of 1900, George B. Hall had obtained his Klondike plantation that he developed with orange groves and vegetables. He had a large potato crop and cucumbers. P. P. Lawson was his assistant. By November of 1900, he had moved onto his Klondike property, perhaps staying for the harvesting season. In November of 1900, Mr. Hall shipped his first oranges. He had mules and wagons that hauled his citrus to Sebastian where it was boxed in his packing house for shipment north. His stall for his mules and his packing house were on Main Street. On the north side of Main Street was the Kitching store, then the packing house, stalls, and barber shop owned by Hall, and finally the Hardee store on the east end. The packing house was later moved to Rte. 512.

On August 12, 1910, Meta and George Hall purchased land in Block A of Hudson's Addition. George's parents, Enoch Warren Hall and Julia Ward Hall, were also residents in the Sebastian area. Enoch died at age 75 in 1912. Julia died at age 70 in 1916. George died in 1915, at age 49, and Meta died at age 39 in 1912, all of them within five years of each other. All are buried in the Sebastian Cemetery in the Park section. When the George B. Hall estate settled in 1918, some of his property went to M. M. Miller, J. D. Yongue, and George Mason.

Murray Hall

Murray Hall was born in Onarga, Iroquois County, Illinois, around 1865. He originally worked for the Illinois Central Railway and other railroads in Illinois. In 1879, he relocated to Fairbanks, Marion County, Florida, coming to Florida to work for the Jacksonville, Tampa and Key West Railway. In 1888, in Seville, Florida, he met and married Sarah Braddock, one of the daughters of W. C. Braddock, Sr. They lived there until 1896 when they moved to Sebastian. The Halls first visited Sebastian in February 1896, when Murray purchased 10 acres of land from Gottlob Kroegel as of March 1. Mrs. Hall and two children returned to her home in Seville to prepare for moving to her new home. In May, Mrs. Hall had returned from Seville to Sebastian.

In July 1896, Murray Hall accepted a position with the Florida East Coast Railway in Miami, and later he was posted to Sebastian where he was a telegrapher and the first station agent in Sebastian. They had a large two-story house near the W. C. Braddock home, and raised four children: Elton, Emma, Gwendolyn and Margarita, all born in Florida. That station was important to the lives of the Sebastian inhabitants. Nephew Maurice Braddock would go to Hall's station office to listen to the baseball games. Telegraphers also brought frost warning information, as well as other timely information. The Halls donated land for the Macedonia Baptist Church in 1907, and Hall had a house on Palmetto Avenue that he rented to the George Knight family. The Palmetto Avenue house was built in the late 1890s and still exists. It is one of the significant properties listed in Old Town Sebastian West on the National Register of Historic Places. In 1914, when Fellsmere began to grow, Murray quit working for the railroad and began working for Mr. Fells. He moved his family to Fellsmere, where he had a successful real estate business. He moved to Fort Pierce in 1921, where he again had a successful real estate business, and became a city commissioner. He died there in July of 1941.

The Fosters

The religious community benefited from such supporters as the Fosters. In the late 1890s, they joined the James Groves family on Louisiana Avenue. Ernest and Abraham Foster were brothers of Mrs. James A. Groves. They purchased land from the Groves homestead and built homes on Louisiana Avenue. Ernest and Luella Foster had orange groves, as did Abraham and Alice Foster. Their sister Joy Foster married Jimmie Graves. Alice's sister Ida Johnston went to live with the Fosters. She had moved to Sebastian with the Groves, as did their sister Helen, who was a spinster who became a missionary in Brazil.

Abraham was born in Louisiana, and moved to Sebastian from Opolousa, Louisiana, following the Groves family from there in 1897. Abraham Foster married Louisiana-born Alice May Johnston on August 9, 1906, in the Methodist Church. Oliver Fauss officiated. Abraham was a carpenter as well as a grower, and built houses for many of the local residents, including the Arthur Kroegel home on the ridge. Paul Kroegel helped Abraham build the Foster house. It had a split shake roof, yellow pine frame and exterior, with an octagonal parlor in front. It was raised up off the ground for air flow underneath, to make it cooler in the summer, typical of many houses of the period. Abraham and Alice were members of the Sebastian Methodist Church, as were Ernest and Luella. Abraham was on the church board, and helped remodel the church in 1909. Alice worked for the Woman's Missionary Society for the church. Alice died in 1940, and Abraham died in 1956. Both are buried in the Sebastian Cemetery

Real Estate Investors

Out-of-state investors found the area around Sebastian inviting for development. Not all of them were successful. However, in the following 20 years, more and more land was developed and platted in the area.

James A. Hudson

James Hudson was a developer from Jefferson County, Arkansas, who purchased and platted two parcels of land in Sebastian in 1891. The first was along the Indian River, platted December 6, 1891. His property along the waterfront sold well. When Thomas New's will was probated in January of 1886, to settle a debt with the Pittsburgh Book Directory of the Methodist Protestant Church Company, that company was awarded title to the deeds to settle his debt. James A. Hudson was the purchaser of the Thomas New Estate property on February 11, 1889, for $1,500. This was comprised of three parcels of land of approximately 72 acres. This land became part of Hudson's developments.

Hudson's Addition

On February 13, 1896, Hudson purchased from Serena Fisher of Baltimore, Maryland, land which was originally a land grant to John Baird in 1884. This became Hudson's Addition to Sebastian. The *Indian River Advocate* announced the platting of Hudson's Addition on June 19, 1896. W. C. Braddock and James A. Hudson had the land between S. Kitching's and W. C. Braddock's surveyed and cut up into building lots. This was land north of Main Street, bounded by Louisiana Avenue to the east, west of the railroad tracks. East-west streets were named Edwards, Arkansas, and Hudson Streets. Ring

Street ran north-south through the subdivision. It was platted on March 8, 1897. The land was subsequently sold in 1901 to Frederick M. Hudson and William H. McBride. This was attested to at Jefferson County, Arkansas.

The *Indian River Advocate* on July 3, 1896, related that G. H. Edward's residence in Sebastian burned to the ground in a matter of minutes from a cooking fire, and that he had no insurance. By July 17, the lumber had arrived for Edward's new house to be built in the north part of Hudson's Addition, south of Sylvanus Kitching's home; by July 24 work was still being done on Edward's two-story home. The siding went up at the end of July. Although the painting was not yet done, in August, he moved in. He planted orange trees in 1897.

Cincinnatus Farms

A far more ambitious development project was attempted west of Sebastian, untimely ended by death. In 1895, W. W. Russell of Cincinnati purchased 115,000 acres of land west of Sebastian, with an eye towards developing a community there. The prior owner was the United States Printing Company. He began with a survey of the land in May of 1895. The surveyor's report was encouraging; the land could be drained inexpensively. This proved to be inaccurate. Russell created the company Cincinnatus Farms to direct the reclamation of the land. By November of 1895, the imminent construction of a railroad from Sebastian to the property was reported in the *Indian River Advocate*. The project was more complex and expensive than anticipated. Work on reclamation and the railroad ceased five years later in 1900 upon Russell's death. There were many claims against the Russell estate and it was tangled in litigation. In 1910, E. Nelson Fell acquired the land and began the Fellsmere Farms Company, and later created the town of Fellsmere.

Kitching

Another little settlement sprang up without the help of investors. In the 1890s, Sylvanus Kitching's store was the beginning of the Kitching settlement southwest of Sebastian. Sylvanus Kitching opened a store on the Sebastian River about four miles from Sebastian in May 1896, so that workmen on the Cincinnatus Railroad would not have to walk to Sebastian to get supplies. It had a sawmill camp and a stop on the railroad in addition to the store. It was another early attempt to extend settlement west of Sebastian. Stanley Kitching was placed in charge of the store. It was intended to be only temporary and closed when the workers moved on. It was opened again in October of 1896 for the next group of workmen. A small settlement named Kitching, or Eureka, later flared briefly at this location. It was a regular stop for the Cincinnatus Railroad, and in the 1910s, for the Fellsmere Railroad.

Roseland

At last, Roseland was officially on the scene, not merely as an adjunct of Sebastian. Although there were settlers in this area prior to this time, Roseland came to life as a town in the 1890s, when it acquired the post office. Soon thereafter, it added a dock, railroad station, school and E. M. Stoke's general store on the east side of the railroad tracks. Roseland was also home to the Old Stockade, a convict camp. Investors brought more growth in this area; the New Rochelle group created the Trilby Plantation, and Lawrence Moore added the Ercildoune and Frost Proof Plantation. Bay Street ran from the railroad depot to the Ercildoune.

Dempsey Cain is forever a part of Roseland's history. Roseland acquired its name in 1892, from the rose bush at the side of the Cain residence, when Will Underwood, Charles Mallory, and Dempsey Cain had to decide on a name for their new post office when filling out the application on the Cain porch. Roseland finally had a large enough population area to qualify for a post office. The application was sent in December of 1891. Roseland obtained the status of a named post office on March 1, 1892, and William C. Eason, who owned land in the Roseland area, was appointed postmaster.

Dempsey Cain

On May 4, 1891, pioneer resident Dempsey Cain acquired of 135.28 acres of land on Orchid Island, roughly across from Barker's Bluff, Certificate No. 10577, through the Sale of Public Lands Act of 1820. The Cain property on the north side of the St. Sebastian River continued to be the family's residence. However, that land did not have a clear title until after Dempsey's death, due to the fact that it was Fleming Grant land. In 1913, both his land and John Baird's were part of the Fleming Grant title difficulties encountered by the Florida Land Development Company in clearing the original title.

Robert Bowler, in the Cain household, was born in Florida around 1864, the son of Celia Padgett Bowler Cain, by her first husband, Robert Bowler. He was living with Celia and Dempsey Cain in 1885 at age 21. In 1891, he acquired a land patent for 79.45 acres on the barrier island on the ocean across from Sebastian. In 1896, Robert Bowler established a wood station in Roseland and was cutting wood for the railroad. Dempsey Cain Sr. died on February 2, 1902, and is buried in the Cain Cemetery in Micco. In the 1910 census, the Cain family consisted of Celia, sons Robert Bowler and Dempsey, daughters Lillian and Lora, and the Grant family that Lora married into, with two children. This was a household of eight individuals. Robert was a 48-year-old farmer, apparently unmarried, and Celia was 64. Celia Cain became blind a few years before she died in 1925, and she is buried with Dempsey.

William C. Eason was postmaster of Roseland for just one year. He owned land in the area near the mouth of the St. Sebastian River on the south side around 1890, but may have left the area a year or two later, as the *Indian River Advocate* reported that his property and the Blackshear properties, including the Roseland Dock, were leased to C. A. Mallory, and that Mallory had contracted to have the dock extended for steamboat traffic. The Eason property was eventually purchased by Lawrence Moore and became part of the Ercildoune Plantation.

In September 6, 1893, the office of postmaster was turned over to John L. Hoefler, who held the office until 1895. William P. Underwood was Postmaster from 1895 to 1901, when Alfred W. White was appointed.

Civic Matters

David Gibson donated land for a school on March 5, 1884. In the beginning, grades 1-8 were taught. Roseland students attended high school in Vero Beach or Wabasso. Not all innovations were immediately in use, as noted in the *Indian River Advocate* in 1895: "We have an express office now and are waiting for someone to send us something." Mail was arriving on a daily basis in 1896; the mail boat *W.S.M.* was making daily trips to the Narrows and returning, and making special trips to Woodley on Sundays. John L. Hoefler was made justice of the peace October 6, 1893, for the 8th district. In November 1896, W. Ely was appointed Justice of the Peace, and that same month, individuals voiced their displeasure at the fence law that required property owners to fence their own property to keep out the hogs and cattle of others that were allowed to roam freely. A public dock was started in Roseland, and by January 1897, it was reported nearly finished in the *Indian River Advocate.*

Roseland Roads

Roseland began acquiring its roads in the 1890s, but not soon enough for some. The *Indian River Advocate* reported on January 16, 1896, that Mr. A. E. Bogue of Melbourne thought he saw what might have been several poor attempts of roads around Roseland, or several places that might have been mistaken for roads. The combination of the railroad and new land purchases spurred the need for roads. The *Indian River Advocate* tracked the progress of roads. By the end of January of 1896, D. Cain was in charge of clearing land and creating a route to the depot. By October, work was being done to improve Bay Street, originally named Rocky Road. In November of 1896, a public dock was started in Roseland, and Quinn Gibson cleared a 12-foot road from the depot to the dock. The land around the post office was cleared, and the bank along the railroad graded and planted with grass. In December of 1896, Messrs. Moore and Ruffner had Bay Street cleared from the Drake place to the Mallory Plantation, which resulted in a good road all the way from the depot to the Ercildoune Inn. Traffic increased on the county road, due to the Ercildoune ferry across the Sebastian River.

David Peter Gibson

David Peter Gibson continued on in the Roseland area, but his crops suffered in the big freeze of 1895-96. To cover debts, he sold some of his land and mortgaged his house property. He fell behind on the payments; however, apparently Gibson was not evicted from the property as he was still there in 1901. Some of Gibson's property was later purchased by Donald MacDonald, who as a boy had visited his uncle Judge Northcott on the land. Around 1896, Gibson engineered another improvement to the inlet, but the result remained little more than a shallow cut. The Sebastian Inlet Association organized a dredging of Gibson's Cut in 1899, removing almost 7,000 cubic feet of dirt, which the ocean soon closed again. Sometime after 1901, he disappeared. There was a riot of speculation as to the reason for this. He may have finally been arrested and imprisoned around the time of WWI.

Elmer M. Stokes

Elmer M. Stokes came to Roseland some time before 1896 when he met and married Esther Cain, daughter of Dempsey Cain. He was working on the railroad extension in 1896, first at West Palm Beach, and then at Miami. He made the trip back to Roseland in April a couple of times, first to visit Dempsey Cain, his father-in-law, and then a week later when his wife was ill. He returned to West Palm Beach when she recovered.

By June of 1896, his work on the railroad extension at Miami had finished, and he moved his family into the McCole place on the Indian River. He had a small truck garden, but gave it up, frustrated by the free-ranging cattle that ate his garden. In July of that year, he got a contract cutting saw logs for the mill in Vero. He got a job in Woodley in October of 1896 working at the sawmill, and he moved his family and shipped all of his household goods there. They remained in Woodley, with occasional visits to Roseland until 1902, when they moved to Roseland. He was appointed postmaster in Roseland in 1902. He remained in that position until his death in 1913.

Col. Henry D. Ruffner

Col. Henry D. Ruffner and wife Joanna also settled in the Roseland area in 1896 as seasonal residents. Henry Ruffner attained the rank of Lt. Colonel of the 26th Virginia Cavalry in the Confederate Army, serving from 1862 to 1865. After he mustered out, he was a silver mine operator in Colorado, and then lived in Charleston, West Virginia, with his family. In the 1870 U.S. Census, Henry D. Ruffner, a 34-year-old farmer, was living in Charleston with his 30-year-old wife, Sallie, and their children, Augustus and Virginia. Subsequent to the death of Sallie, he married Joanna Abbott, 34 years his junior, a marriage he arranged with her father in exchange for an owed debt. Two years later, Henry and Joanna decided to move from West Virginia to Florida, and settled at Titusville. After the big freeze of 1894-95, they moved further south and relocated to the Ercildoune area, on the bluff formerly owned by D. P. Gibson, with its citrus groves and pineapple fields.

Colonel Ruffner purchased the Blackshear orange grove in October of 1896. He arrived at Roseland with his wife for the winter, along with a large number of barrels and boxes, and several wagonloads of furniture. They built their home on the Indian River overlooking the bluff. That same month he began preparing the ground for potatoes and beans for the commercial market, and started improving his grove. In December of that year, Walter Gibson built an oyster pen and got a boatload of oysters for the Ruffners. In April of 1897, the Ruffners went back to their West Virginia home, but said they intended to try a summer in Florida. The Ruffners spent most of 1898 in Roseland, except for July and August, when they returned to their Charleston home.

Ruffner bought the Jacobs' place on the Indian River from A. S. Packard of Connecticut in October of 1898. The Ruffners' home on Indian River Drive was purchased from Allen Campbell in 1918. It is still in existence and was restored around 1960. They had a yacht and entertained friends from West Virginia. They had many pets, including an alligator named King Bulger, a deer, and a pelican. Both Henry and Joanna were entertaining storytellers known for their hospitality, and Joanna was noted for her vivacity and West Virginia accent.

The Roselandites

In the 1890s, Roseland merited its own column in the *Indian River Advocate,* wherein the everyday life of Roseland's inhabitants was reported. The Roseland area was maturing and growing, and by and large, it was prospering. People were improving their holdings and social life was blooming.

Owen Jacobs was clearing land on the hammock and putting in orange trees on his Indian River Plantation in 1893. In the Roseland area, the group of men from New Rochelle, New York, were building cottages on the Mallory Plantation. The Mallory and Jacobs families were in the social news. Mallory leased the Blackshear and Eason properties, including the Roseland Dock, and contracted to have the dock extended for steamboat traffic. Mrs. Roy of Chicago purchased the Mallory place. In 1895, several alligators more than 12 feet long were killed in the Sebastian River. Heavy rains washed out crops in September, and a bug infestation caused a total crop loss for Cain. Postmaster W. P. Underwood received a shipment of eight elegantly bred pigs.

On May 29, 1896, "No rain no mosquitoes and no people in Roseland, nothing but heat and horseflies," was a report in the *Indian River Advocate.* In October 1896, Englishman Allen E. Campbell, born circa 1864, leased the Hirsch Grove, and that same year built a lovely two-story frame home on North Indian River Drive. The January 1897 cold snap damaged some vegetable crops. In March of 1898, Mrs. M. C. Epsom, owner of the Hirsch Grove, was in town examining her property, and continued Campbell's lease on the grove. H. B. Howard was looking for land for a sawmill site in Roseland in 1898. Roseland's only bicycle was in for repair. On March 17, 1899, William Ayers, a piano tuner from Brooklyn, was doing business in Roseland.

Alfred White from England went to Canada, New York, and finally, to Florida, where he stopped in Roseland. There he met Katherine Cain; they married in 1898. They moved to the south side of the St. Sebastian River. He died in 1902, and she took over the management of three orange groves for absentee owners on the south bank of the river in the area between the railroad tracks and what would become US Hwy 1, to support her family.

Unfortunately, when the Historic Property Survey of 1989 of Roseland was completed, it was found that no buildings remained in Roseland from the 1880s and 1890s. The survey reported that the earliest remaining buildings in that area were two from 1900, the Ruffner House on North Indian River Drive, and one on Roseland Road that was considered typical of that period.

The New Rochelle, New York, Investors

Investors discovered Roseland and settled in. A large group of investors from New Rochelle, New York, became interested in the area around Roseland and the rivers. Many of them interested themselves in several projects. They were Thomas, Drake, Alexander Hudson, Mrs. A. Hudson, Henri Van Zelm, H. H. Todd, Banker W. W. Bissell, T. Daly, and Mr. Greenbeck. Some of them bought property in the area. W. W. Russell of Cincinnati, Ohio, joined some of these investment projects.

The Sebastian River Land & Improvement Company of New York was incorporated in 1893 by New Rochelle, New York, residents Thomas Drake, Alexander Hudson, and Henri Van Zelm, who invested in the Sebastian area real estate. This company was formed from the Indian River Investment Company, after the death of James W. Todd in 1893. He had been responsible for its organization and acquisition of the Wauregon development. In November of 1896, in the Roseland area, the company cleared land from the depot to the Drake place, in expectation of beginning building that winter, per the *Indian River Advocate.*

Trilby Plantation

The land where the St. Sebastian River and Indian River joined was described as a high bluff, 20 feet above the water line, with natural terraces. At that time, there were already cottages there, with beautiful gardens surrounding them, and orange groves that were frost-proof. The title had been in dispute for many years, but the New Rochelle, New York group, Messrs. Drake, Dailey, and Todd, and Mrs. A. B. Hudson with her daughter, Alice, arrived in Sebastian in mid-February of 1896 and settled title disputes satisfactorily. Their intention was to develop the area as a beautiful, enticing community.

In March of 1896, Banker Bissell, T. S. Drake, and others of the investment group went to Roseland to complete the deal. Mr. Goode, a Melbourne real estate broker, was involved with Drake, Bissell, Todd, and Hudson in closing on their adjoining properties. All of them planted orange trees on their property. By June 15, 1900, the Trilby Plantation facing Sebastian Bay was controlled by the Sebastian River Land Improvement Company, with owners T. S. Drake, W. W. Bissell and H. H. Todd.

Drake was the only one to build a house, Trilby Cottage. Many of the investors visited him there. Some visitors were Elliott Folks, Mr. White, and Mr. Greenbeck. By 1898, Trilby Cottage was growing twelve kinds of roses. There was a fire there in March 1899, and the storehouse burned, but the house and kitchen were saved. Drake and Todd went to Melbourne for new supplies for replacements of everything.

Ercildoune Hotel and Plantation

The Ercildoune was the property of Chicagoan Laurence C. Moore. His property encompassed purchases from Charles A. Mallory and Elizabeth A. Mallory, Thomas C. Knight and Emma M. Knight; James W. Hamilton and Katherine A. Hamilton, and M. C. Eason and W. C. Eason. The Ercildoune Plantation, owned by Moore, consisted of the Ercildoune Hotel and the Frost Proof Grove of 500 bearing citrus trees which were planted some years before the hotel's opening. No doubt because of its favorable location, the grove was not damaged by the freezes of 1894 and 1895, and remained in good condition into the 1920s.

The word Ercildoune is Celtic for prospect bluff. It was named for a Scottish prospect bluff, Erceldoune (or Ercildoune), now called Erlston, located in the Borderlands. In the 13th century, it was the home of Thomas the Rhymer and was located on a bluff at the confluence of two rivers, the same configuration found at the confluence of the Sebastian and Indian Rivers where the Ercildoune Hotel and Plantation was located.

Everything about the new hotel being completed was news. The *Indian River Advocate* in 1893 stated that Mallory had leased the Blackshear and Eason properties, including the Roseland Dock, and had contracted to have the dock extended for steamboat traffic. On October 18, 1895, it reported, "Mrs. L. C. Moore returned to Ercildoune on Saturday last, but her trunk wandered around on the railroad until Tuesday, when it was captured at Sebastian."

The Ercildoune was obviously a well-advertised and desirable hotel. The *Indian River Advocate* followed closely the development of the Ercildoune Hotel and the surrounding grove, and nearly every issue carried the steps in its development. In September of 1895, it reported that L. C. Moore was going to erect a one-story hotel for 35 guests. The contractor was chosen, B. F. Hardesty of Sebastian, working with an anticipated completion date of December 1, 1895. In October, men began working on the property and lumber was expected to arrive in a few days, supplied by G. F. Paddison. Rain in late October and November delayed work, and water was running high in the Sebastian

River. The well-known contractor and builder P. H. Hall was working on construction, and it was almost finished December 27, 1895, running past the expected completion date. Moore was obtaining the needed permits for a roadway on the north shore from property owners to connect with the county road and wanted to hire a barge, to establish the Ercildoune Ferry at that time. Moore treated his carpenters to a trip up the Sebastian River in the launch *Tartar* one day.

On January 10, 1896, plumbing and furniture were being installed. Even before it was finished and the furniture had even arrived, on January 24, 1896, the Ercildoune had its first bridal party, a couple from Chicago. Furniture for the Ercildoune arrived February 14, 1896. On February 21, the Ercildoune was not finished, but was accepting guests. By March 6, guests were arriving.

The Ercildoune was reported completed on September 11, 1896. In October, improvements were being made to the building and grounds, and a lawn was being put in. In November, Moore obtained a shell crusher to pave the walks and drives around the Ercildoune. On January 8, 1897, it was reported open and fully equipped.

The Ercildoune Hotel Season of 1896-1897 printed brochure featured its many attractions. The Frost Proof Orange Grove of 500 trees and Ercildoune Plantation were part of the Ercildoune Inn Property. Ease of travel to the Ercildoune was emphasized, via the Florida East Coast Railway from Jacksonville to Roseland, a seven-hour journey.

Described in the brochure, the Ercildoune Inn of the Ercildoune Plantation stood on a 40-foot bluff above the St. Sebastian and Indian Rivers. It was 200-feet long, and had 16 rooms and a 12-foot veranda. The rooms had two iron beds with the "best hair mattresses." Each room opened onto the veranda and had both a bath and closet. The inn was constructed of cypress and pine and had a central lobby with a coquina fireplace. Plumbing was exterior.

All necessary conveniences were available; Southern Express had an office in Roseland, there was a telegraph office three miles south, and there was a post office in Roseland. Ercildoune Cottage contained the Plantation headquarters.

It was considered a sportsman's paradise for hunting and fishing. There was a wharf for boats. The *Queen* offered cruise trips to the Bahamas and *Tartar* was available for river cruises. In its heyday, it was a favorite vacation spot with such illustrious guests as President Grover Cleveland and the famous actor Joe Jefferson. According to the brochure, Lawrence C. Moore was the Proprietor.

12

Pelican Island and The Feather Wars: 1890s

In the 1880s, Queen Victoria's influence on ladies' fashions began to wane, and a trend towards extravagance and opulence in dress began to take over. This was exemplified in the Edwardian Age that placed an emphasis on high fashion of formal dress as a badge of social status, with the correct clothing worn on all occasions. Exotic plumage from all types of wild birds to top ladies' hats became the height of fashion. A vigorous national economy that allowed extravagance, the growth of international commerce, and the excesses of ladies' fashions led to the Feather Wars and several laws concerning preservation of national wildlife.

The Naturalists and Ornithologists

In the 1890s, many individuals began to take note of the effect of human activities on the wildlife population in the nation. Due to the possible extinction of bison, bird species, and others, a gradual trend was commencing towards recognition of the need for conservation. First outcries were against the amateur sportsmen and commercial plume hunters, and later, against the collecting methods of the ornithologists and naturalists.

Dr. Morris Gibbs

Naturalist Dr. Morris Gibbs was one who began to sound the alarm. He made several journeys to Pelican Island, staying at Oak Lodge on these trips, publishing his findings in a series of articles. Reporting in *The Osprey* on an excursion February 17, 1891, to Pelican Island, Dr. Gibbs deplored the wholesale destruction of birds by tourists who regarded wanton shooting an acceptable pastime, and by plume hunters who were satisfying women's fashion trends, as opposed to the actions of legitimate collectors who were furthering scientific knowledge.

Tourists dotted the peninsula with dead birds and mammals shot for sport and left to rot, he noted in 1894 in the *Kalamazoo Gazette*. Pelican Island was described by him as an immense rookery with 5,000 to 8,000 birds. A score of other species of birds wintered there; the author recorded over 30 species. In 1894, he wrote in *The Oologist* of his stop at Oak Lodge, where there were 10 to 20 people there consistently in the winter months. Gibbs visited Pelican Island, where he witnessed a whole party of sportsmen firing volleys of shot. He stated that "the Rookery had been known to exist for over 20 years and birds have been shot and robbed of their young annually for over a decade, and yet they persist in mating in the same situation each winter and spring." As many as 10,000 birds had been reported. Residents informed him that there were three or four times as many birds in previous seasons. Around 4,000 were in sight on that trip. Dr. Gibbs secured 200 fresh pelican eggs to take back home for his cabinet in Michigan.

L. W. Brownall

In an 1894 trip to Pelican Island, naturalist L. W. Brownall reported seeing 1,000 birds in a flock. He collected 125 sets of eggs.

Frank M. Chapman

In the 1880s and 1890s, Frank M. Chapman, an associate curator of the American Museum of Natural History, was a frequent visitor to the Florida East Coast. On his trips, he stayed at Oak Lodge, the local gathering spot for sportsmen and naturalists. Chapman spent much of his time at the Kroegel homestead, where Paul Kroegel and he became friends. He made frequent trips to Pelican Island to observe and obtain specimens for the museum. He began his studies with a gun and a camera, collecting complete sets of species for the habitat displays at the museum, but by 1900 his thinking had changed, as had the national mood, and he began working with many cameras, but no guns.

In Frank Chapman's first visit to Pelican Island in 1889, he traveled to Titusville by railway, and by stern-wheel steamboat from Titusville to Jupiter Inlet on the Indian River to Micco, where he stayed at Oak Lodge. Professor John W. P. Jenks was also in residence there, creating a mounted collection. Mr. Baker was there as well, collecting birds for Southwick. Mrs. Latham, the proprietress of Oak Lodge, was something of an amateur naturalist, helping those who were her guests. In anticipation of their arrival, she collected several sets of a series of turtle eggs for a period of 60 days, showing their different stages of development from earliest to hatched. She sold these sets to Chapman and Jenks. Prior to Chapman, there had been very little collecting of mammals in Florida, and he found five new species of mice and rats, which he presented to the scientific community. In the 1890s, he began a series of extremely popular lectures on natural history around the continent for the American Museum of Natural History. He continued his collecting trips as well.

On his second trip to Pelican Island in 1898, he honeymooned with his new bride Fannie, who began a lifetime of assisting her husband in his pursuits. On their honeymoon, she began skinning the birds to be mounted. The two of them went in the *Lida* and anchored off of Pelican Island to begin the most complete study of brown pelicans ever made.

Frank Chapman wrote extensively of his findings regarding the habitats and nature of birds in his book *Bird Studies with a Camera*, published in 1900. He devoted a chapter to Pelican Island and bird migration habits. He was vehement in his denunciation of wanton destruction of birds and their eggs by sportsmen and naturalists alike. Chapman's lectures and writings were influential in making many others aware of the plight of the birds at Pelican Island. He inspired others to become involved, including members of the American Ornithologists' Union and Florida Audubon Society. Chapman was also a friend of President Theodore Roosevelt, who supported conservation and later created the first National Wildlife Refuge at Pelican Island.

A long-standing Christmas tradition was spotlighted during 1900 and eventually went out of fashion. It had long been the custom for hunters to gather on Christmas Day in teams, and compete to shoot all of the wild birds and fur-bearing animals they could find. The results of these competitions were then published in sporting magazines. Frank Chapman in his *Bird Lore* (later *Audubon*) magazine proposed in 1900 that this tradition be changed instead to an annual bird count.

The Feather Wars

The Feather Wars were a long, gradual battle begun in the 1880s, an awakening to the consequences of wanton destruction of wildlife. It began slowly attracting more and more influential members who wrote, lectured, formed societies, and lobbied to spread their ideas of conservation.

Audubon Society

The Audubon Society was and is one such group. It had its beginnings in a short-lived Audubon Society formed in 1886 by George Bird Grinnell, a noted editor and sportsman. The inspiration for the name was the famed painter of birds, John James Audubon. A year later, Grinnell began the *Audubon Magazine* with articles of news and editorials opposing the unrestricted slaughter of birds and calling for bird protection. Much of his opposition was directed at the gunners who served the millinery industry, providing feathers for women's attire. However, this society and the magazine were gone by 1887.

The idea of an Audubon Society was picked up again in 1896 by a group of Boston sportsmen and society women concerned with the growing threat to wild bird populations. They formed the Massachusetts Audubon Society to promote their agenda against bird depredations. This idea proved popular in other states, and more and more states formed their own Audubon Societies. These groups began to educate the public and promote changes in the laws regarding wildlife.

Another pro-bird conservation magazine was started in 1899 on a nationwide basis, the bimonthly magazine *Bird-Lore*, begun by Frank Chapman. It had a section providing news from the various state Audubon Societies, creating the first unified nation-wide forum for these groups. This magazine was successful, and eventually changed its name to *Audubon*.

In 1905, the National Association of Audubon Societies was formed, with William Dutcher as its first president.

William Dutcher

William Dutcher was a New Jerseyan who farmed, and later worked in the insurance industry in New York City. He had a life-long interest in ornithology and bird preservation, and was involved in many societies to that end. He was first president of the National Audubon Society, and was called the father and originator of bird protection in America.

One example of his work was in 1897, when William Dutcher, as Chairman of the Committee on the Protection of Native Wild Birds, presented a paper "To Protect the Wild Birds; Report of the Committee of the American Ornithologists' Union at Its Congress," at the American Ornithologists' Fifteenth Congress. In it was a design to combine a Bird Day with Arbor Day, and it detailed the ongoing work of the Audubon Society.

William Temple Hornaday

William Hornaday was the most combative conservationist of his day. He was born in Illinois in 1854, and by 1874, he had undertaken his first expedition to Florida, to the Everglades to collect specimens for Ward's Natural Science Establishment of Rochester. Much of his life was spent in similar expeditions all over the world, collecting materials for natural science exhibits. He published books and articles of his travels. From 1882 to 1890, he was the chief taxidermist of the National Museum (Smithsonian) in Washington. In 1889, he was its director. He studied and published works on bison extinction, and worked to establish protected bison herds.

In his 1894 stay at Oak Lodge, Hornaday wrote for the *Indian River Advocate* that protection and preservation were needed for Pelican Island. He described a slaughter by a steam launch and two sail boats that visited Pelican Island, where about 100 shots were fired, killing birds. At that time, approximately 1,000 birds were present, whereas two years prior Maurice Gibbs estimated 4,000 were there. In another article, he claimed that plume hunters had killed 71% of the wading bird population of Florida in the 1880s and 1890s. From 1896-1926, he was the director of the New York Zoological Park (Bronx Zoo). He was instrumental in obtaining the passing of the fur seal treaty to save them from extinction in 1911. In 1913, he created the Permanent Wildlife Protection Fund.

Theodore Roosevelt

The conservation movements were fortunate that Theodore Roosevelt became president in 1901. As well as a politician, he was a soldier, outdoorsman, naturalist, and explorer, sympathetic with the aims of the various conservation societies. During his presidency, he greatly expanded the system of national parks and forests.

Concerned Public Cries for Action

Many newspaper articles called for protection of Pelican Island birds, such as that in the *Indian River Advocate* of April 27, 1894. Mark V. Barrow wrote *A Passion for Birds* in 1988, regarding the groups that sought to limit the killing of birds by ornithologists and naturalists, not only sportsmen. In an article regarding a 1900 trip to Pelican Island, Frank Chapman reported in *Bird Lore* that in 1898, 845 nests were counted, with 251 of those nests occupied. In 1900, 710 nests were counted, with 179 of those occupied. On October 14, 1900, the *New York Times* printed an article on another Frank Chapman lecture on Pelican Island. On February 20, 1901, the Springfield *Republican* printed an article on a lecture by Charles Dennison Kellogg on the study of birds on Pelican Island and other areas. The St. Albans *Daily Messenger* reported on the brown pelican on September 20, 1901, "Like his white brother the bird is likely to be exterminated in Florida." The article continued, stating that the brown pelican now had only one rookery convenient for slaughter by reckless gunners during the incubation period. Many women's groups joined the plea for change.

The Laws

Public opinion began to swing in the direction of conservation, and many movements to protect wildlife gained momentum as more joined their ranks. Lobbying by the pro-conservation groups began to have a positive effect, creating state and national laws. From 1895 -1905, some states adopted their own bird protection laws. In 1900, Congress passed a powerful protection for wild birds, the Lacey Act, which banned interstate commerce of birds killed in violation of state laws.

Pelican Island: First National Wildlife Refuge

Pelican Island became a locus of the pro-conservation fervor. Located in the Indian River off the southern part of Sebastian, just north of the Narrows, it is a mangrove island in shallow water still frequented by great numbers of many types of waterfowl during the winter-breeding season. Pelican Island is the largest of three breeding grounds for brown pelicans. It was feared that without action to preserve Pelican Island, the brown pelican would become extinct. Pelican Island endures in spite of the hunting over the years, rescued due to the actions of so many. President Theodore Roosevelt declared Pelican Island to be the first national wildlife refuge in the United States on March 14, 1903. In 1909, the refuge was expanded to the other nearby mangrove islands, and in 1966, it was added to the National Register of Historic Places. More area was added to it over the years.

In 1903, newspapers all over the United States reported formation of the national wildlife refuge at Pelican Island. *DeLand Weekly News* reported on May 8, 1903, "Pelican Island has been designated as a government reservation—no shooting allowed at or near island without permission of the warden."

The *Tampa Morning Tribune* reported on May 17, 1903, "March 14, 1903, White House, Theodore Roosevelt: 'It is hereby ordered that Pelican Island in Indian River, in Section 9, Township 31 South, Range 39 East, State of Florida, be, and is hereby reserved and set apart for the use of the Department of Agriculture as a preserve and breeding ground for native birds.' (signed) Theodore Roosevelt." This news and text was reported in numerous newspapers around the country. Paul Krogel was appointed warden of Pelican Island.

Document from the Department of Agriculture:

> Mr. Paul Kroegel of the State of Florida is hereby appointed Warden in Charge of Pelican Island Reservation, Florida, in the Division of Biological Survey in the United States Department of Agriculture at a salary at the rate of One ($1.00) Dollar per month, to be paid from the fund appropriated for General Expenses of Biological Investigations.
>
> He is hereby requested to take the Oath of Office immediately and file the same, together with a statement of legal and city residence and personal record, with the Appointment Clerk in the Department of Agriculture, and report for duty in writing, to the Chief of the Division of Biological Survey, and be subject to the rules and orders of the Secretary of Agriculture. This appointment to take effect on April 1, 1903. (signed) James Wilson, Secretary of Agriculture.
>
> United States Department of Agriculture, Washington, D.C., March 24, 1903.

The Aftermath

The May 25, 1859, Plat Map 13791 of Township 31 South Range 39 East, surveyed by William S. Harris, contains the notation added to the plat, "Pursuant to order Mar. 14, 1903, reserves Pelican Island in Sec. 9 for use of the Dept. of Agriculture as a preserve and breeding ground for native birds."

In the chapter *The City of Pelicans* in his book *Wild Wings: Adventures of a Camera-Hunter Among the Larger Wild Birds of North America on Sea and Land,* Herbert K. Job related his trip to Florida from New York in 1903. His group stayed at Oak Lodge and took a small sailboat down the Indian River to Pelican Island, where they took photographs of the brown pelicans, using cameras that took pictures with plates. He estimated that there was approximately a one-third increase in the number of nests from Chapman's 1898 estimate of 845 nests in the four years since then. He believed this to be true due to better enforcement of strict laws in Florida against the destruction of plume-bearing birds, and a growing understanding of the value of wildlife to attract tourists.

In 1905, Chapman received permission to return to Pelican Island, where he stayed in a blind and photographed and observed the birds. He returned in 1908, continuing his study, taking motion pictures. In 1914, when he returned, he and Kroegel counted 1,600 dead or dying young pelicans that mysteriously starved to death. One thousand healthy adult birds were at the other end of the island. The last time Chapman visited Pelican Island was in the 1930s. In modern times, as many as 25,000 birds nest on Pelican Island.

Chapman continued to write about Pelican Island. In *Camps and Cruises of an Ornithologist*, he wrote that in 1858, Dr. Henry Bryant wrote of his visits to the island and noted the presence of pelicans, three kinds of egrets, herons, roseate spoonbills, Man-O-War birds, and white ibis. When Chapman visited 50 years later, only the pelicans remained. Several sources reported that the pelicans left for two years when the large "NO TRESPASSING" sign was erected, and the birds did not return until it was removed and replaced with a more modest sign. Prior to that, the only other time the brown pelicans failed to nest was once after a season of wholesale slaughter.

Chapman had access to Warden Kroegel's meticulous records on bird populations. He observed that the pelicans all migrated together at one time. Flocks of 500 to 1,000 birds normally arrived around November 1, and after about a week, landed and began nest building. The first eggs were normally laid by December 1. The 1907-08 season was exceptional; around 7,000 birds arrived earlier, but only about 1,500 nests were built for approximately 3,000 birds. There was no explanation for what happened to the other 4,000 birds.

Not all results were positive, and poaching continued. Three game wardens were shot by poachers, Guy Bradley in 1905 in southern Florida, and in 1908, Columbus G. MacLeod in Florida and L. P. Reeves in South Carolina. Their killers were never convicted. In 1909, protection for Pelican Island was strengthened to make it unlawful to harm the birds in the Pelican Island Refuge in any way. In 1911, the Audubon Act (Ducher Law) proposed by William Dutcher was enacted to prohibit the sale of native wild birds in New York State, which effectively ended the use of feathers in ladies' hats there, except for feathers of farm-raised birds such as pheasants and ostriches, which was still legal. However, these measures did not stop the killing. Hornaday campaigned for more extensive laws in New York, and more states joined in. Imports continued, however. After controversy, the Wilson Tariff Act passed in 1913, containing a section that banned import of wild birds for any purpose. The Migratory Bird Act in 1913 placed all migratory birds under federal jurisdiction, which imposed more hunting restrictions. More refuges were created around the country. In 1925, the Brevard Reservation at Mosquito Lagoon became a National Wildlife Refuge. Unfortunately, despite these efforts, shooting continued after it was made a refuge. By the 1920s, due to social pressure, feathered ladies' hats were no longer in fashion and had mostly disappeared.

Paul Kroegel

Paul Kroegel was born in Germany January 9, 1864, and arrived in the Sebastian area at age sixteen, with his father, Gottlob. From first sight, they were drawn to Barker's Bluff with its magnificent view of the Indian River, and that is where the two of them made their home. Pelican Island was directly east of their home, with its vast flocks of migratory birds.

Captain Paul Kroegel had his own cargo line while still in his teens, operating from Titusville to Key Largo. He studied navigation and seamanship, obtaining his captain's license in 1885. He built a 60-foot schooner that he used in this business. The *Irene* was one of his earliest boats, and with it he ran shipments and mail from Titusville to Key Largo. He would deliver mail cargo in the Keys and return with boatloads of pineapple slips in the 1885-1890s period. From Titusville to Stuart, he ran in the Indian River, and at high tide he crossed into the Ocean at Gilbert's Bar and followed the coastline using celestial navigation at night. He traveled as far as Key West, carrying mail, freight, and passengers. The advent of the railroad put an end to this lucrative shipping business, however. He built a boat modeled on the lines of the famous *Mystery* to carry mail. In 1896, he finished building his mail boat *U.S.M.,* and with it made daily return trips to Narrows, and made a special trip to Woodley on Sundays. The *Yellow Kid* was also built by him in 1896.

A man of many interests and abilities, Paul started his own agricultural pursuits. The pineapple industry was booming during the late 1800s, and Paul began his own pineapple plantation in Oslo, where he homesteaded 160 acres of land, acquired on May 16, 1898. He also had citrus groves, kept bees, and sold honey to Ohio during WWI, when there was a sugar shortage.

The Lawson family arrived in Sebastian around 1889 from Tifton, Georgia. Paul began courting their daughter Ila, and by July of 1900, their house was nearly completed.

Paul married Ila Lawson in October of 1900, in her parents' house. They had a party at their new house after the wedding, a "chivaree," with music and dancing.

At his home in Sebastian on Barker's Bluff, Kroegel began a boatbuilding business. He was skilled as a carpenter, and built buildings as well as boats. He built a skipjack launch for L Moore of Roseland in 1900, among others. After the advent of motors for small boats, Paul Kroegel became a mechanic to keep all of the boat motors that he had installed on the fishing boats running. Paul Kroegel put a Sintz motor in the sloop *Mist* in 1893. The Sintz Gas Engine Company in Springfield, Ohio, was a pioneer in marine engine manufacturing, formed in 1885.

At the request of the Audubon Society he built a motor boat, the *Audubon,* and delivered it to Cape Sable for Warden Guy Bradley, who used it for plume hunters patrol. After Bradley was shot and killed by the plume hunters in 1905 in south Florida, Paul acquired the boat and used it in his own patrolling as warden.

Kroegel was a member of the salvage crew of the *Mary E. Morse* that went aground on a reef just offshore from Sebastian in September of 1900. Also in the crew were H. B. Howard, Stanley Kitchen, Ray Ellis, and Fritz Leicht. They used an old Civil War tugboat, *The Three Friends,* to pull it off the reef at high tide. All the lumber floated ashore in the process. With his proceeds from this work, he bought furniture for his new house for his new bride.

In the 1880s, the boat channel in front of Gottlob's house was less than 200 feet from Pelican Island, and sportsmen would use the pelicans for target practice. Gottlob would drive them off with a 10-gauge shotgun. By 1900, Paul was a self-appointed guardian of Pelican Island. He also ran off hunters with shotgun. He was friends with Frances Eleanor Betts Latham, owner and proprietor of Oak Lodge hotel, and met many of the writers, naturalists, and professors who came to study Florida's flora and fauna. Artist Luis Agassiz-Fuertes came with Frank Chapman to the Kroegel house, painting birds that illustrated Chapman's magazine *Bird Lore.* Many other naturalists, publishers, photographers, and ornithologists came to the Kroegel home in 1905, often as many as 20 at a time. Indians also came to visit, camping out in tents. Photographer George Shiras III was one of the visitors, the creator of the *National Geographic* magazine. Through Frank Chapman, he campaigned to obtain funds for the protection of Pelican Island.

Paul Kroegel was warden at Pelican Island until 1926. As with many stories, there are two versions as to why he stopped being warden. In one, he resigned due to physical infirmity, and in the other, funding was cut for his position when the pelicans stopped roosting at Pelican Island in 1925 and relocated to Mosquito Lagoon to its newly created National Wildlife Refuge. The pelicans later returned to Pelican Island, but his position was not reinstated. Perhaps both are true.

The County Commissioner appointed J. O. Fries, Paul Kroegel, and R. G. Hardee to mark and lay out a road between Sebastian and Wabasso in 1901. Paul continued to be a man of many interests and abilities. As well as being warden, in 1905 Paul was appointed county commissioner for the newly created St. Lucie County. Paul and his father Gottlob and brother Arthur worked on a survey crew in 1910 with Surveyor Elmer Robb, Bruce and Robert Ryall, and George Vickers. Paul played the accordion for dances at Titusville, sailing there in his boat. In 1914, Paul Kroegel bought one of the first cars owned in Sebastian. It was a Ford touring car from Jacksonville, and he learned to drive it on the way back, taught by the hired driver. He and his family were avid bicyclists. He also learned photography from George Nelson and was responsible for many of the local photographs taken of the day.

Arthur K. Kroegel

Arthur K. Kroegel was the younger brother of Paul Kroegel. After coming to the United States with his father and brother, Arthur Kroegel, age two, lived with his aunt and uncle at Crestline, Ohio, before he came to Sebastian. After his arrival in Sebastian, Arthur lived with his father Gottlob until he got married, as did his brother Paul. Arthur K. Kroegel and Ida Johnston married May 12, 1898, at the United Methodist Church, a few months after she moved to Sebastian. Ida came from Louisiana with the Groves family when they moved to Sebastian. On May 16, 1898, Arthur acquired 160.96 acres of land south of Oslo. Paul built Arthur's and Ida's home, close to Paul's home.

Arthur and Ida were members of the Sebastian United Methodist Church. He carried the mail from Sebastian to Fort Pierce on a boat built by Paul, and had groves. Arthur and Ida later had a one-story house built on the ridge for them by Abraham Foster, as Ida did not like living on the river. It was later remodeled into two stories. Their daughter, Helen, was born 1908. After Ida died in April of 1925, he married again, and moved north, but a year later, Arthur moved back and lived with his daughter Helen and her husband. Arthur lived in Sebastian 71 years, and died December 26, 1955. The Roy James family eventually purchased that house on the ridge.

13

Evolution into the Railroad Lifestyle: 1890s

By the 1890s, steamboat travel was reaching the peak of luxury travel in Florida. The boats were bigger and more magnificent, the routes and connections were better, and service was more frequent. However, railroads had come to Florida and were marching across the landscape, heading further and further south. For a while, through mergers and agreements, the two forms of transportation worked well together, but eventually the speed and greater capacity of the railways doomed steamboat commerce. Roads had barely started to be a competing factor. With these advances in travel, commerce and individual mobility flourished in Florida.

Steamboats and River Traffic

Indian River steamboat traffic reached its pinnacle in this decade. Their arrivals, departures, and passage down the Indian River constantly merited notice in the *Indian River Advocate.* The Jacksonville, Tampa and Key West Railroad took over control of the Indian River Steamboat Company in 1889. The whole system, called the Tropical Trunk Line System, served the Florida east coast from its commencement in 1886 until it went broke in 1896. Colegrove Mail Line took over mail delivery from Jacksonville, Tampa and Key West Railroad and the Indian River Steamboat Company south of Melbourne after 1893. The *St. Augustine* and the *St. Sebastian* steamships advertised connecting with all trains at Titusville and Rockledge in 1998. Competition between various railroad and steamship lines was fierce. The 1894-95 freezes and the Flagler railroad brought about the end of the Indian River Steamboat Company. Eventually, railroads doomed all steamship travel. The railroad and steamboats did not completely do away with old forms of transportation and commerce; Mrs. Chase ran a trade boat in the 1890s which sold dry goods and millinery on the river.

Other riverine improvements and activities continued in the 1890s and were reported in the *Indian River Advocate.* The dredge *E.C.I.C.* dredged the mouth of the Sebastian River in July of 1893. R. B. Spratt moved to Sebastian in 1893 to help supply wood to the numerous steamers. Stanley Kitching ran the sloop *Mermaid* up to Eau Gallie, taking passengers up and bringing gasoline on his return in 1893. Indianapolis visitors staying at the Palm House were taken on the *Arrow* by Stanley Kitching to view Pelican Island, where they saw about 3,000 birds. The river was still an important factor in everyday life.

The Sebastian River was crossed by a self-service ferry before a bridge was erected across, a barge with a wire pulley system. Later there was a ferry attendant with horses to pull the barge. Bob Bowles was the first ferry operator. Don R. Beaujean operated a ferry many years, and in later years gave scenic tours on the *Atlantic*, a gas-powered motor boat. He arrived with his parents from Melbourne around 1890. They settled on land purchased by his father from Captain David P. Gibson in 1988, a quarter-mile south of the location of present-day Sebastian Inlet, on the barrier island.

The arrival of the railroad in the mid-1890s and the influx of investors made the area around the confluence of the Sebastian and Indian rivers a hotbed of activity. From the very first, when Marr and Canova moved there, it was a desirable site. It this decade, it came into its own. However, not all growth proceeded seamlessly. Accidents happened, weather did not cooperate, some things did not move fast enough, and some were not feasible through lack of funding.

Inlet to the Ocean

Opening the Sebastian Inlet was again promoted in 1896 as an aid to tourism, and another failed attempt was made at creating an inlet to the ocean. On March 5, 1897, the Roseland Inlet Company incorporated in New York with the purpose of creating an inlet from the Indian River to the ocean. During their first meeting, they appointed W. W. Russell of Cincinnatus Farms a director. The other directors were Mssrs. Todd, Drake, and Bissell, and Mrs. A. Hudson of New Rochelle. In April of 1897, it was reported that the Roseland Inlet Company was looking for additional subscribers.

Haulover Canal and the Intracoastal Waterway

In 1892, fear of railroad competition fostered renewed efforts to improve conditions for steamboat traffic. There were complaints that steamboats could not get through the Haulover Canal because of its lack of depth and narrowness. Moreover, the Indian River was silting in, making it shallower. Private citizens contracted to have the Haulover Canal dredged open again so that the *Sweeny* could get through, hauling pineapples from Eden to New Smyrna. The U.S. Army Corps of Engineers started work after negotiations with the Coast Canal Company and brought the dredge *Suwannee* into the Indian River to open a channel 5-feet deep and 75-feet wide, but lacked funding to finish. In 1895, Henry Flagler invested in the Coast Canal Company, providing more funds for its work. By 1905, the Coast Canal Company claimed a uniform 6-foot depth from the Haulover to Grant's Farm, and its dredge *Florida* was clearing a similar channel southward toward Jupiter, finishing in 1912. The Intracoastal Waterway was ultimately taken over and completed by the U.S. Army Corps of Engineers in the 1930s.

Henry Flagler and the Florida East Coast Railroad

Henry Flagler and his railroad brought permanent change to Florida. He was born in 1830 in western New York, the son of a poor Presbyterian minister. At age fourteen, Henry traveled alone to stay with his half-brother in Republic, Ohio. Flagler wanted to make a name for himself. He had his own business by age 21, and was a partner of John D. Rockefeller at age 37, selling crude oil. Together they organized the Standard Oil Company. He was extremely wealthy by the winter of 1883-1884, when he first visited St. Augustine. That same visit, he planned his first Florida hotel in St. Augustine, the Ponce de Leon Hotel. This magnificent enterprise opened on January 10, 1888, and the first all-Pullman train from New York to Florida ran that year. This hotel was one of the first buildings in the country to be made of poured concrete. He began adding other hotels in Florida. Sebastian history would have taken a very different course if Flagler had built a hotel there.

Flagler first took over existing railroads in the 1880s, and in 1892, he began building his own. He bought his first railway in 1886, the Jacksonville, St. Augustine and Palatka. In 1888, he added in a road route from Palatka to Daytona, and changed the name to the Jacksonville, St. Augustine and Halifax River Railway. As he built or acquired hotels, he added rail lines to reach them. By 1890, Flagler added a hotel in Ormond to his holdings and consolidated several existing rail lines into his Jacksonville, St. Augustine and Halifax Railroad that ran from Jacksonville to Daytona.

He was authorized by charter to build from Daytona to Miami. From 1890-1892, his railroad did business with steamers on the Indian River, and he invested in a few small steamers for his own trade. The Halifax and Indian River Railway was incorporated in 1891 to build from Daytona to Titusville. In 1892, Flagler incorporated the Florida Coast and Gulf Railway Company, and acquired the property and franchises of the Halifax and Indian River Company. He changed the name in 1892 of the Florida and Gulf Railway Company to the Jacksonville, St. Augustine and Indian River Railway Company. This name remained while Flagler was building the railway through Brevard County.

He advertised reaching Palm Beach by rail on November 1, 1893, but did not manage to do it. The first train through from Jacksonville to Rockledge arrived February 6, 1893. Eau Gallie was reached June 26, 1893, with train no. 27; Melbourne October 2, with train no. 27; Sebastian December 11 with train no. 23; and Fort Pierce January 29, 1894, with train no. 23. Each temporary terminal of the railway had a connecting steamer for the balance of the trip as his railway advanced down the coast. Palm Beach was reached April 2, 1894, with train no. 23.

By 1894, the railroad company was reorganized as the Florida East Coast Railroad. Palm Beach hotels, The Breakers and Royal Poinciana, were started in 1893, before the rails were laid and materials were shipped by a combination of steamboat and by land to build these hotels.

The Railroad in Roseland

The *Indian River Advocate* followed the progress of the railroad to the St. Sebastian River. By July 21, 1893, the men accomplishing the grading of the track had finished, and the tie cutting gang had arrived. The cross-tie men would be next. By September 29, the pilings were all driven on the Sebastian River railroad bridge and cap sills were being put on. By October 13, track was running to the Sebastian River Bridge. It was a wooden bridge with a large draw so that boats could navigate the river.

The railroad and its activities vitalized the Roseland area. By 1895, a depot for the East Coast Line was erected, and in January the following year, a 250-foot platform and freight station was built at Roseland. That year there were rumors that the Cincinnatus Railroad would connect with the Florida East Coast Railway at Roseland instead of Sebastian, which would have been a boon for Roseland. Quinn Gibson, son of David Gibson, oversaw the railroad water pump and bridge per the newspaper reports, a position he held for 32 years. He also was responsible for keeping the kerosene lights lit, and he cut the wood for the boilers that generated for the steam engines running the pump.

The Railroad in Sebastian

On December 11, 1893, Sebastian history changed forever when the first train of the Jacksonville, St. Augustine and Indian River Railroad arrived. Henry B. and Emma Howard not only donated land for the Methodist church, they also deeded a right of way for the Jacksonville, St. Augustine and Indian River Railway Co., a strip of land 100 feet in width, on either side of the railroad on December 28, 1893. A wooden depot was built there.

At first, outgoing railroad mail was picked up from a hook on a pole, and incoming mail was tossed off the train in a sack. Later, more services were added. The railroad station stood on the south side of Main Street, east of the railroad tracks. It had a wooden sign with the number "338" on it. This number signified that it was the 338th depot erected by the Florida East Coast Railway. It also had a large "Sebastian" sign. After a few years, the depot proved inadequate. The replacement depot and freight warehouse were built after delays in 1896, located roughly in the area south of Main Street, east of the railroad track. The carpentry work was completed by January 24, 1896, and the slaters and painters finished their work soon after that. This new depot was considered a big improvement over the old one that leaked, per the *Indian River Advocate.* By May of 1896, it was decided that the railway platform was not long enough, as passengers had to wade through heavy sand when leaving the platform.

The ease of travel by rail created a new societal division. Alfred Michael stated that those who settled after the railroad came in were considered "newcomers." Other changes occurred. When the railroad arrived in 1893, a number of buildings were moved to be next to the railroad, and new construction now fronted on the railroad instead of on the Indian River Lagoon or on the Sebastian River, completely altering the community focus. The train cut through lives. In 1896, one of D. P. Gibson's young steers was hit and killed by the train, and W. C. Braddock's cow was killed by a freight train. Passing trains occasionally caused fires. Men who had been cutting wood for fuel for the steamboats now cut wood for the trains.

Sebastian River Railroad Bridge Tale of Frustration

The *Indian River Advocate* related in continuing entries a saga, the tale of frustration of drawbridge repair to the Sebastian River railroad bridge. On November 15, 1895, the drawbridge was not working on the Sebastian River railroad bridge, and East Coast Line engineers were expected to work on it. The draw section had blown down during a storm and the railroad cleared the debris off the tracks very quickly after and rail traffic resumed. However, the drawbridge portion was not repaired and boats could not get through. Nearly every edition of the *Indian River Advocate* reported the status of this problem, in a continuing series of entries about the frustration. In July of 1896, it still was not fixed, and boats still could not get through. In that month, R. G. Hardee anchored his sailboat *Dora* near the railroad bridge, waiting for the drawbridge to be repaired. In September of 1896, railroad workers came to clear away the drawbridge wreckage, but did not repair it. By that time, two boats were moored there, waiting for it to be repaired. In October and November, some work was being done. They were working on in again in February of 1897. At long last, in April of 1897, the sloop *Minerva* passed through the drawbridge. The woes continued. In the *Florida Star* from July of 1898, it was reported that the railroad bridge would be partly rebuilt during that summer, and that part of the timber for that had arrived. In September, several carloads of timber for bridge repair were coming, but work on the bridge was postponed for several weeks. Work resumed at the end of September and would be done in a few days. Apparently, it was finally finished, after only three years …

Railroad Shipping

Entrepreneurs in Sebastian and all of Florida were quick to take advantage of the scale of shipping made possible by rail. By the winter of 1893, the Flagler railroad was hauling

Indian River oranges, and by the next summer, it was hauling pineapples. By 1895, 2,500,000 pounds of fish were shipped north: mullet, pompano, sheepshead, sea trout, and oysters. Goods were moving from Sebastian as well. That year, Sebastian sent its first shipment of fish north by rail.

The *Indian River Advocate* in 1896 reported the prosperity of rail traffic that affected all areas of Sebastian life. G. H. Edwards was successfully shipping beans. R. A. Hardee & Co. was shipping fish in large quantities, and had a fine delivery wagon. Conductors said that they had put off more freight in Sebastian than at any place between Titusville and Palm Beach. Sebastian had three carloads of freight coming in. Hall & Edwards was receiving Chicago steak. Merchants were getting in goods almost daily. R. M. Wilson received a carload of furniture from New York.

Sebastian and Cincinnatus Railroad

A railroad spur from the Florida East Coast Railway line in Sebastian was deemed to be the best means of conveying men and materials to the impenetrable swampland that was to become Cincinnatus Farms, the development begun by W. W. Russell in the 1890s, west of Sebastian. This track ran west from a point south of Sebastian, roughly in the area that is now Rte. 512. In March of 1896, A. O. and W. W. Russell obtained a right-of-way title from Tallassee for their railway to Cincinnatus Farms. In May of 1896, H. B. Howard received the contract for the first mile of ties, per the *Indian River Advocate*. That same month, a crew of 100 cross-tie men set out the ties. They camped near the county bridge and the Kitching store four miles west of Sebastian. The right-of-way was finished and the grader was working. Frank Hunter hauled timber for the railroad bridge across the Sebastian River. By June 19, the ties were nearly all cut and were being delivered, and began being laid by June 26. Two carloads of railroad spikes arrived in August. The first five miles of track to the Sebastian River were completely laid by October 2, 1896, and then the pile driver began sinking the pilings for the bridge. Iron was laid on the tracks in November. By the end of November, the track had been laid for ten miles. W. W. Russell died in 1900, and all work stopped on his projects. It was another eleven years until this rail spur project was taken up by Nelson Fell, for his Fellsmere Farms.

Roads

In the 1890s, travel into Florida was still accomplished by a combination of rail travel, steamboat, and small boat, as described by Allen H. Andrews, an Estero publisher, in his book *A Yank Pioneer in Florida*. However, when Andrews described an ox-drawn wagon as an "oxmobile," he made quantum change in language, inspired by the introduction of Henry Ford's first automobile in 1892. Automobiles, trucks, and tractors arrived in Florida hot on the heels of the railroad, and again life was forever altered. Horses, wagons, and popular buggies were eventually edged out.

To begin with, Sebastian roads were a loose network of footpaths and trails for wagons and horses. Early roads were built by felling trees and pulling the stumps, or going around them. Undergrowth was removed and the ground was plowed and leveled, with a drainage ditch to keep it dry. These streets remained unpaved for a considerable time, as sand roads that were rutted and frequently muddy. Crushed shell from the Indian middens was added later. Passing of conveyances coming from the opposite direction had to be carefully planned.

After Louisiana Avenue and Main Street (which ran only from Louisiana Avenue to the Indian River to begin with) was Depot Street, later changed to Palmetto Street. Louisiana Avenue and Main Street were extended. Finally, Central Avenue was added, running north and south. Subdivision platting added more streets. Hudson's Addition, platted in 1896, added Edwards, Arkansas, Hudson, and Ring Streets.

Improvements were made to the Sebastian Bridge in August of 1893. There was a growing demand for a road running the whole length of the county on the west bank of the Indian River. The legislature called for a bond in October of 1895, but this was rejected by the voters. It was to be a shell-paved road. However, shell paving of roads proved to be controversial. Nevertheless, better public roads were needed. A three-mill tax was levied, and individuals had to donate rights-of-way without compensation. The county road running the entire length of the county along the west bank of the Indian River was built and maintained that way in the 1890s. It was completed by the turn of the century. R. A. Hardee was given the responsibility for obtaining the right-of-way. R. B. Burchfield was the surveyor. When Henry T. Gifford and S. T. Hughes built a part of the road from Sebastian to Fort Pierce, they cleared a 10-foot-wide swath through palmetto and brush, measured the road, and set up painted mile markers from saplings. They were paid $22.50 per mile.

The expansion of roads demanded ordinances. In the late 1890s, Titusville enacted an ordinance to keep horses and mules off the streets. In April of 1896, the Sebastian Welfare Committee worked on a new road along the riverbank from Hardee Street to S. Kitching Street, a shelled road 9-feet wide. Also in 1896, R. A. Hardee began building a road with private funds to run westward from Sebastian. It was in competition with the Sebastian and Cincinnatus Railroad, which had been opened that year.

Gone and Forgotten?

Where or what was Launa? The *Indian River Advocate* noted in April 1896 that Captain R. A. Hardee was working on the county road between the Sebastian River and Launa. *(Launa: this is an Icelandic Old Norse word meaning "to reward".)*

Flying

In another confusion in travel, "S. Kitching made a flying trip to Cocoa this week." In *Indian River Advocate*, several Sebastianites were noted making "flying trips" out of town in 1896. As airplanes hadn't come to Florida yet, it seemed a bit odd. With a little research, it was determined that as well as meaning to hurry, "flying trip" was also a current slang term, referring to a book published in 1891, *In Seven Stages: A Flying Trip Around the World*, written by Elizabeth Bisland. A publisher asked Ms. Bisland to leave one evening for a trip around the world, to beat the current speed record. This trip was made with conventional modes of travel, train, ship, etc., not by air. The telling of this journey proved to be a popular book, with several editions published. The Wright brothers began their experiments in powered flight in 1896, but did not achieve their first flight until 1903.

A Growing Civilization

Florida's railroads affected more than just Floridians. Northern diets were changed forever by the arrival of relatively inexpensive fresh produce in winter from Florida. As many as three crops a year of truck farming could be grown and delivered quickly by refrigerated railway. However, ice came from a plant in Titusville. Sebastian had no ice for one week when it broke down in September of 1896. These freshly grown items and fresh seafood became available to the general populace up north, not only at the exclusive northern hotels. Moreover, with the advent of the railroads, goods produced in the north flowed more readily into Sebastian.

As the area matured, farmers adjusted to the unique agricultural differences in Florida. Rich soil and mild climate made growing easy, but there were unexpected problems to overcome. Destructive wildlife of all sorts was plentiful in the area, including insects, wildcats, alligators, and snakes. Bears were everywhere. The *Indian River Advocate* reported that the numerous Sebastian wildcats ate the poultry; Ivy Lawson killed a catamount bothering the neighbors' chickens on August 21, 1896. It also reported a large rattlesnake killed by Dempsey Cain with a hoe on July 24, 1896. Horse flies and mosquitoes dictated that even in the hottest weather, individuals had to be completely covered; mosquito swarms could kill animals. Alligators dotted the waters. Hurricanes could wash everything away.

Citrus and Truck Farming Industry

Indian River citrus was gaining national recognition as a marketing entity. In 1892, the Indian River Orange Growers Association was formed to protect their trademark due to continuing infringement concerns. In 1909, the Florida Citrus Exchange Convention was held in Tampa to organize a system of common advertising and marketing, similar to that of California.

After the advent of the railroad, most commercial products were sent north by railway. Prior to the arrival of the railroad, the Indian River Steamboat Company transported the citrus crops northward. The main issue among growers and farmers was dissatisfaction with freight rates and the damaging handling of produce. They were able to exert enough influence to have a Railroad Commission created by the 1890 legislature, but the railroads were more influential and not much was accomplished.

Success in agriculture was a balancing act between man, nature, and happenstance. In April of 1896, due to dry weather, pineapple crops were lost and citrus trees were suffering, per the *Indian River Advocate.* Also reported in 1896, the Blackshear Grove, purchased by Mr. Ruffner that year, was doing better than when it was managed by W. Gibson.

Fishing

Naturalist Morris Gibbs reported in his *Fair Florida* article in the *Kalamazoo Gazette* on February 11, 1894, that gill nets were set out for a fish haul, which was usually three to six kinds of fish. The edible catches were channel bass, mullet, sea trout, sheepshead, sailor's choice, mangrove snapper, and catfish. Moreover, sawfish as long as 12 feet were caught in the net. Sharks were common. Oysters and crabs were plentiful. Schools of huge porpoises were seen in the ocean, and some were seen in the lagoon. They could be shot easily.

Commercial fishing took hold with the advent of the railway. Mattie Braddock began as assistant postmaster, as H. B. Howard left the post office to devote all his time to his fish business in 1893. He built a large fish packing house over the water for himself and W. H. Hartley, and he used his pile driver to finish Captain Hardee's dock.

In 1895, there were 254 residents and nineteen firms engaged in the fishing industry in Brevard County. That year, 2,659,815 pounds of fish were shipped out of Titusville, Cocoa, Eau Gallie, Melbourne, Grant, Sebastian, Fort Pierce, Eden, Jensen, and Stuart. The first shipment of fish out of Sebastian by rail was on September 11, 1895. From Sebastian alone, 103,890 pounds of fish were shipped that year. August Park, the Hardees, and H. B. Howard were commercial fishermen responsible for part of Sebastian's haul. Charles Peake of Sebastian continued his commercial turtling. In 1896, R. G. Hardee added a large refrigerator to his fish house, and received two tons of ice for it, per the *Indian River Advocate.* That was also a very good year for harvesting and selling oysters by many individuals, as reported in the news.

Fishing was done in the Indian River, with nets hung from outrigger arms on the boats. Mullet and trout were the primary catches, and a good day's catch of mullet was 1,000 or 1,500 fish. The fish were packed in 200-pound barrels with ice brought in from Fort Pierce until ice plants were started locally. The barrels were taken to the railroad depot by mule-drawn wagons.

In 1897, a U.S. government survey concluded that the waters were not being overfished. By the 1890s, permits were issued for planting artificial oyster beds along the Indian River, due to their growing importance and commercial demand. All fisheries experienced the same problems with marketing and transportation as citrus growers. In the 1890s, the Florida Fish Company formed in Jacksonville and marketed most of the fish from the Florida east coast.

By 1901, seining was prohibited by law in the Indian River, delivering a blow to the local economy, and creating an uproar amongst commercial fishermen. This led to fishing as a sport, developing as a commercial venture on the Indian River. After the Sebastian Inlet was cut, local fishermen went out into the ocean about ten miles for grouper and snapper.

Ice Plant

Man-made ice and refrigeration had been around since the 1860s, but ice plants were not in common use in Brevard County until the advent of the railway and increased shipment of commercial goods requiring refrigeration. Formerly, natural ice had been brought from the north by ship. In 1888, Titusville had an ice factory. Fort Pierce acquired one also. With large-scale commercial shipping by rail came an urgent need for ice and shipping containers. Ice plants were started in Sebastian and other towns along the river in response to the need. The development of artificial ice was a boon to the shipping of fish, oysters, and turtles to market, preserving the catch. These plants were run on cord wood, supplied by locals who might also bring ice to the fishermen as they brought in their catch of the day, and take the catch the train depot for the fishermen. A whistle-blast for each 100 pounds of catch by the fishermen signaled the amount of ice needed. The Harry Sample family moved from Hopewell, North Carolina, to Sebastian and built an ice plant and barrel factory in 1896 in response to shipping needs.

Daily Life

Despite freezes and the depression, Sebastian and Roseland inhabitants appeared to be prospering. Wells were being dug and homes were being built; businesses were modernizing and expanding, meeting the monumental changes of the decade. This minutia of daily life recorded by the *Indian River Advocate* provided a rich, full picture of everyday life.

Eighteen ninety-six was a good year for local doings. H. B. Howard's house, one of the largest in town at that time, was finished by April. It was completed with a two-story veranda around it. It was the local opinion that well digging produced better water than that from a driven pump. W. C. Braddock, S. Kitching, and G. H. Edwards all had wells dug. The W. W. Russell home was finished in June. Hy Benson was stricken with meningitis and was dangerously ill at Palm House, but later recovered in August. C. S. Roberts moved into the Indian River Land and Improvement Company's house just north of S. Kitching's store in October. A rather unusual and ominous message was in the newspaper in 1897. "There are some lead dollars from 1800 in circulation—beware!"

Leisure Activities Recreation and Entertainment

As population grew, so did local forms of entertainment. Moreover, in these prospering communities, individuals could indulge in more pleasurable activities. Along with picnicking and boating parties, more organized events were added. Sebastian's literary society was formed in the 1890s. With roads, bicycles came into use in the 1890s, and bicycling clubs formed. The bicycle race in Jacksonville in 1896 was advertised locally. Hundreds of people passed through Sebastian on the F.E.C. excursion train going to the Jacksonville bicycle races. Gun clubs were organized. Hunting and fishing parties were common. Brevard County placed a $5 bounty on bears in early 1890s, as they were so plentiful. They were a ready target when they dug along the beaches for turtle eggs during the turtle nesting season. Fire fishing for mullet in the evenings was in vogue in August 1893. Horseback riding was popular. As ever, national holidays were celebrated.

Y.P.S.C.E. (Young People's Society of Christian Endeavor) had an unusual sociable in February 1896. Each member was decorated in his or her fad. "Some of our girls have very strange fads," stated the author of that column in the *Indian River Advocate*. That month, a dance was given at the new depot to dedicate it. Another dance was held two months later at Hardee Hall with 20 couples.

Boat Racing

Yacht clubs and boat races and regattas existed in many communities all along the river. The *Indian River Advocate* posted the boat race entries. The regatta in April of 1892 filled the newspaper columns for months prior and after. In March was the Sebastian Regatta Club planning meeting that set up the schedule of races. Special boats were built to compete in these races. Henry Park and W. L. Torbert were building a catamaran to run in the regatta. A lengthy article appeared describing the races of the regatta, and the dance following the race. In 1895, the fish boat race was postponed. Some of the longest articles in the newspaper were boating articles about races, and the relative merits of the various racing boats.

14

The Maturing Society: 1900s

At the turn of the century in Florida, the growth of the 1890s continued, cities developed, and population continued to increase. This new century was a period of optimism founded in a belief that hard work and self-reliance were the keys to a fruitful life. Individuals took their civic responsibilities seriously, and promoted the welfare of their emerging communities. Governments at federal, state, county, and local levels were expected to provide support and improve public services, safeguarding natural resources. At the federal level this led to more national preserves and parks.

The great promise of the railroads in Florida during the prior decade was somewhat dimmed. Railroad interests still fueled many political decisions in Florida, as it held a large amount of Florida real estate. However, many of the large tracts of land given to the Florida East Coast Railway contributed nothing to Florida's growth, and the railroad did not have the expected impact, due to high shipping costs and inadequate services.

There was a greater impetus for progress and industrialization in the state, with more state services desired, but with low taxes. Taxes were lowered, coupled with revenue brought in with the addition of special taxes on licenses, company charters, and such other items.

In this period of 1900-1910, there were many advances in science and technology around the entire country that were slowly filtering down into Florida. These were eagerly greeted as they became available and affordable, such as the automobile, telephone, and electricity. The state population had grown to 752,619 in 1900. That year, due to the shifting center of the Florida population, a vote was made whether to move the state capitol, but it remained in Tallahassee.

In his tenure as governor from 1901-1905, William Sherman Jennings brought several important changes to the state. He instituted primary elections, and created a board of control over education. It was possible to obtain a teaching certificate by finishing a nine-week normal course at Stetson University. However, it was not necessary to graduate high school first to qualify. He implemented drainage of parts of the Everglades, which was considered a step forward for land reclamation. This program was continued by the next governor, Broward.

Leading Florida from 1905 to 1909, Napoleon Broward proved to be a popular governor due to his progressive ideas for state government which struck a responsive chord in Floridians. He had no railroad connections, and he too favored a popular drainage program for land reclamation. The Everglades Drainage District was formed to create a series of canals for this purpose. Education was promoted and child labor was prohibited. In 1906, a pure food and drug law was enacted. An automobile speed law required motorists to stop if requested by a horse's owner when his horse was restive from the auto's presence, and required a speed of no more than four miles an hour at a bridge or curve. More care of the poor in the county was fostered. Sebastian Inlet received attention; the Chief Engineer of U.S. Army, Maj. Shunk, investigated and prepared a negative report on the feasibility of an inlet to the ocean across from the St. Sebastian River on March 2, 1905. The jetties would need extensive work.

There was an important advancement in medicine in this decade. In 1909, the *St. Lucie Tribune* reported that the successful Pasteur treatment for rabies went into effect in Florida, and could be administered from Jacksonville, instead of in Atlanta in person. As of July 9, 1909, after being bitten, the individual's wound was to be treated by his local doctor, the dog's head was to be packed in ice and sent to the laboratory of the State Board of Health, and if found rabid, the Pasteur treatment was sent to the doctor. Once a day for 21 days, the individual went to the doctor to be treated. This new treatment routine was deemed unique in the world.

Brevard County

In 1900, there was a redistricting of Brevard County, changing Sebastian's district. The revised District 3 was comprised of Eau Gallie, Melbourne, Malabar, Micco, Banyan, and Sebastian.

During this period of local history, Brevard County followed the custom of leasing their convicts as laborers; prisoners were let to the highest bidders. Organizations paid the county for their labor and provided room and board in secure locations until their sentences were served. This reduced county costs of maintaining jails. The turpentine industry used them around the state, including in Roseland. Convicted killers, as well as those convicted of lesser crimes in other counties, were being sent to convict camps. St. Lucie County also followed this practice. On July 15, 1910, the *St. Lucie Tribune* reported that some convicted gamblers were sent to Roseland convict camp for 90 days. State legislation in 1909 required state supervision of the camps. The many abuses of the system in the turpentine industry brought harsh criticism, and Florida ended the practice in 1918. As a result, Brevard County began using the convicts on county road projects, and finally stopped the leasing of convicts altogether in 1923.

Road Travel

The first automobiles arrived in Brevard County around 1905. Before automobiles, roads were traveled by wagons and carriages, and by horses, mules, or oxen. The most useful vehicles had a high wheel carriage. In the 1890s, there were some road improvements made; however, the first law in Florida regarding roads only mandated that stumps in the road bed could be no more than 12 inches high. Only the most traveled roads were graded. Most roads were unpaved and generally followed the easiest course, around trees and large bushes, and consequently might follow a sharply winding, meandering path. These roads might also contain hidden stumps in the high grass center ridges. Bridges were created only over those places where the water was too deep to drive through.

Consequently, these roads were a nightmare for the first automobiles. Many of these roads navigated by wagons were impassable by automobiles that were less maneuverable and had a lower carriage. Crossing water could flood the autos, killing the engine and miring the wheels in mud. A horse team might be needed to pull them out. Ford Model T's were popular because they had a higher carriage and could more easily navigate the winding roads. They were also very reliable. Clearly, however, road changes would be demanded following the advent of the automobile.

1905 St. Lucie County

Increasing population brought the desire to create a new county. From the late 1890s to the early 1900s, the population in the south end of Brevard County continued to grow, and people wanted more specific representation. This desire to split off was opposed by northern Brevard, but the bill passed to form St. Lucie County from the southern part of Brevard County in 1905. This new county included land from the Sebastian River south as far as Okeechobee. Its county seat was Fort Pierce, which had become incorporated as a city in 1901. The population of St. Lucie County in 1905 was less than 1,000. Its main development at that time was along the Indian River and the Florida East Coast Railway. Pineapples were the chief crop and the most important industry countywide. Commercial fishing was also prominent. Citrus growing was gaining importance. Brevard County assumed its present-day size. There was a mumps scare in 1908.

The first St. Lucie County Commissioner for Sebastian was Paul Kroegel. R. G. Hardee was the first tax assessor. The county was officially created effective July 1, 1905, but its formation was celebrated on July 4 with daylong festivities. Downtown Fort Pierce was the center of the commemoration, with a parade with floats, a grand marshal, and speeches by C. T. McCarty and Claude Olmstead. Boats, horses, and wagons were decorated. Cannon fire and games took place. Picnics were held and everyone celebrated. Sebastian, Narrows, and Quay were some of the new voting precincts formed in the new county. In 1909, there were 40 registered voters in Precinct No. 1, the Sebastian and Roseland area, per the *St. Lucie Tribune* report. Reporting the lists of registered voters and appointing voting inspectors helped insure honest and accurate voting results, addressing past problems of voting misconduct.

During this decade of the century, prohibition was a contentious subject, and reactions were volatile on both sides of the subject. Governor Broward campaigned for state-wide prohibition. At the time, each county in Florida could vote whether to be wet or dry. Nationwide prohibition was not enacted until 1919, and was the law until 1933. The result of prohibition was continuing rebellion in the form of rum-running and speakeasies. When it came to a vote in the new St. Lucie County, Sebastian reported by telegram that it voted 41 dry and 3 wet April 17, 1906, in the *St. Lucie Tribune* voting returns. "St. Lucie goes into prohibition by a landslide" was the headline. No precinct in the county voted a wet majority; the results were 313 against selling and 182 for selling.

New technology was beginning to be recognized. In 1909, a network of hard surfaced roads was considered a necessity to keep up with the times. Electric power distribution had been around since the 1880s, but the technology was a little slow in reaching the area. It was not until the around 1916 that use of electricity and electrical appliances became widespread in St. Lucie County, and Sebastian did not have its power plant until 1925. "Electricity" was more of an exotic catchword in this decade. "Electric Bitters" was advertised in *Ft. Pierce News* for health, a spring tonic drink that cured many bodily ills. "Tanglefoot Electric Fly Paper" was advertised, as well. Electric lamps were beginning to be used for automobiles and were in the auto ads.

Civilization was intruding into the wilds in 1905. A Florida East Coast Railway train narrowly missed hitting a bear on the railroad tracks. Deer were considered common on the tracks, but bears were not, according to the *St. Lucie Tribune*.

Sebastian

Sebastian was growing and expanding its services. In this decade, Sebastian had a population of 100. The town consisted of two grocery stores, a meat market, several hotels, the Sebastian school, the train depot, G. B. Hall's packing house and barber shop, the Methodist and Baptist churches, and Mrs. Carlile's boarding house. Perhaps the greatest addition to Sebastian was a medical doctor for the first time, Dr. David Rose. Dentistry was available in Melbourne, as advertised in the *St. Lucie Tribune*: "Dentistry at a reduced price. Floating dental office, *Dentos*, now located at Melbourne." Telegraph and Western Union Express were available at the depot. The Postmaster was R. G. Hardee from 1904-1906. Main Street, Louisiana Avenue, Palmetto Avenue (originally called Depot Street), Central Avenue, Edwards, Arkansas, Hudson, and Ring Streets were the existing streets. An ice house was built in Sebastian; S. N. Gladwin supervised the construction of the ice factory. It was situated opposite the railway station and completed in June 1902. Fish camps lined the Indian River, and citrus groves and truck farming were everywhere. There was a cattle ranch west of town. The Florida East Coast Railway ran north to south through town, and the abandoned Sebastian-Cincinnatus Railroad tracks ran from Sebastian to the west to Eureka and the defunct Cincinnatus

Farms development beyond. Rental houses were in demand. In 1906, Sebastian was a part of a U.S. Geodetic survey. Precinct voting inspectors in July of 1906 were Ed. L. Haynes, G. H. Hall, and T. B Hicks; P. P. Lawson was clerk, according to the *St. Lucie Tribune*. W. C. Braddock was appointed District Registration officer for Sebastian, per the *Ft. Pierce News* in 1908. By 1909, the first non-railroad bridge over the Sebastian River was created.

In November of 1906, the Florida East Coast Automobile Association proposed an endurance run for automobiles from Jacksonville to Miami that would go through Sebastian. Rightly concerned about the condition of the roads, a letter of inquiry was sent regarding what would be found in St. Lucie County. The reply given by C. T. McCarty, reported in the *St. Lucie Tribune*, had this to say about Sebastian and Roseland at that time:

> On entering the county on the north you are ferried across the Sebastian River, there being no bridge convenient. Roseland is the first settlement in the north end of the county, and at that point can be found Ercildoune Inn, conducted by Lawrence C. Moore and one of our enthusiastic good roads men. Col. H. D. Ruffner and other progressive citizens reside there. For the first miles to Sebastian you encounter very soft sand for the greater part of the distance. Fairly good hotel accommodations can be found at Sebastian and facilities for supplies, repairs, etc. South of Sebastian 6 or 8 miles mostly good road brings the driver to Wabasso.

Land was being subdivided and sold for residential lots. *Hall's Addition* was platted August 16, 1907, and the *Estate of August Park Subdivision* was platted November 1907, which consisted of land from Fleming grant line on the west, to the Indian River on the east.

Pelican Island was the first National Wildlife Refuge in 1903. Paul Kroegel was its first warden. The massive task of dismantling Barker's Bluff to sell the shell for road surfacing began in 1908 and was not completed until 1913.

Town Buildings

Sebastian's downtown had renovations and expansion. Mrs. Jones had a hotel in Sebastian that was sold to Mr. Baughman in 1905. She moved to Miami. Mrs. James A. Hudson, a former Sebastian resident, stayed at the Baughman Hotel that year, among other guests. Kitching's Palm House hotel had many guests, and the Sembler House was a new hotel in 1906. The Kitching and Braddock general stores were in operation, and Sebastian again had a meat market in 1906. The *St. Lucie Tribune* stated "We hope it will last longer than the previous one." Oscar Gaffney had a barrel factory on Palmetto Avenue near the railroad tracks. E. B. Sembler occasionally ran it for him when he was away.

Sylvanus Kitching

In the 1900 census, Sylvanus Kitching and his family still resided in Sebastian. Sylvanus Kitching filed his will on October 17, 1901, in which he bequeathed to his wife Martha all of his property, real, personal, and mixed, so long as she remained unmarried and virtuous. However, if she should marry again, she would be confined to her dower or child's part as she might elect. When she died, the whole of his estate was to be left to his daughters, divided equally, provided that they remained unmarried and continued to lead a virtuous moral and religious life. If any of them married, they forfeited their portion to their unmarried sisters. To his sons, he left only the sums of 25 cents each because he knew they would take care of themselves, and help their sisters. The will stated that the balance remaining was left to his sons.

Kitching's son, Stanley, moved to Stuart in 1902, where he became a leading merchant and mayor of the city. He married Naomi Neal when he was 49. In the Spring 1904 session of Brevard County Circuit Court, Sylvanus Kitching formally severed his ties with Edward VII, King of Great Britain and Ireland, and became a U.S. citizen. Martha Kitching remained unhappy with Sebastian and Florida, and desired to return to England. She moved to Stuart in 1904 with some of their children, and then returned to England for a visit, from August 1904 to February 1905. She died in Stuart November 29, 1906 at age 52 of cerebral apoplexy superinduced by Bright's Disease. She was buried at Fernhill Cemetery in Stuart.

Sylvanus remarried after the death of his wife. According to the 1910 census, 61-year-old Sylvanus was living in Sebastian with his 41-year-old wife, former Virginian Martha V., and Martha's 20-year-old daughter from a prior marriage, Beatrice Aikin, who had been born in Florida.

Walter Baughman

The Baughman and Owen families moved to Sebastian in 1904 from Georgia. Walter Fred Baughman and Eva Isabelle (Belle) Owen married in Georgia some time before 1897. Sons Leon and Alton were born in Georgia. Baughman settled first on property he acquired west of Sebastian on the St. Sebastian River, where he grew sugar cane to make maple syrup and sugar. The Baughman's lived there briefly, moving later to Palmetto Avenue at Louisiana Avenue in Sebastian, and then to a house further down on Louisiana Avenue. Baughman had a dairy in Sebastian and delivered milk to customers. He also had the Baughman Hotel, a store in Eureka, and some teachers boarded with the Baughmans. Walter died in Augusta, Georgia, in 1958 and was brought back to Sebastian for burial. He was a member of the Methodist Church and Woodmen of the World. Belle died in 1947, and they are buried together.

The Palmetto Avenue house was subsequently owned by councilman Harry Sallee, and later by Fern DeVane. It was an excellent example of a side-gabled rectangular plan building with double-hung windows and a metal roof, and was one of the significant properties listed in Old Town Sebastian Historic District West, placed on the National Register of Historic Places January 6, 2004. However, it was later demolished. The house on Louisiana Avenue was later owned by John and Jackie DeVane.

Dr. David Rose

The arrival of Dr. David Rose in 1908 was extremely welcome to the inhabitants of the Sebastian area, as there was no doctor from Melbourne to Fort Pierce until his arrival. Dr. Rose delivered his first baby in 1908, Mildred Park. He bought land, intending to become a citrus grower in the Louisiana Avenue area, but soon began practicing medicine when patients flocked in, and his citrus grove was not sufficiently profitable. He became certified to practice medicine in Florida. Much of his practice took place under primitive conditions in the field, and was every type of doctoring imaginable, from delivering babies, to typhoid fever, to snake bites, to work accidents. He saved many lives. The worst of the patients were sent elsewhere to a hospital. He made house calls in Charlie Sembler's boat, on horseback, by buggy, and later by one of the first automobiles in town, a Model T Ford, to see patients. Florida East Coast Railway was one of his clients for its employees for many years.

The Rose family was Scots in origin, from Ontario, Canada, as were the A. G. Roses, seasonal visitors to Sebastian with a house on Palmetto Avenue, not far from Dr. Rose's home. After receiving his degree to practice medicine, Dr. David Rose practiced in Chicago and Oklahoma City. In 1905, he married Sarah Wentworth. After a visit to Sebastian, the Roses determined to live there, and bought the five acres of land on Louisiana Avenue. In addition to their house and barn, the Roses built a house for their daughter. The Rose's home, built in 1910, also served as his office. Much later, the barn built around 1909 that housed the Rose's horse and buggy, was converted to a house, now known as the Edith Suddard House.

Both Roses were very involved in civic matters. Dr. Rose was a president of the Sebastian Board of Trade, member of the Board of Public Instruction and State Welfare Board. He was also one of the group of citizens that left Vero on a special train for Tallahassee to argue in favor of creating a new county on May 4, 1925. Sarah Wentworth Rose had been a teacher in Chicago. In Sebastian, she was the first president of the Sebastian Woman's Club, organized early in 1914, in the Rose home. She also wrote news for the *Ft. Pierce Tribune*. In 1927, she was elected president of the county Federation of Women's Clubs; however, Sarah Rose died in an automobile accident shortly after her election to the county office. Dr. David Rose died in 1942, and is buried in Sebastian Cemetery.

Andrew Jackson Sembler

Andrew Jackson Sembler, born in New York in 1829, was the first of the Sembler family to move to Florida in 1880, after his first wife, Emily Knapp, died. He settled on land near Lake Eldorado, where he became a successful citrus grower. In 1889, he married Sarah Eloise Stansborough. The freeze of 1894-1895 destroyed his grove, and he then started a grocery store in Tavares. He and Sara Eloise later moved to Sebastian sometime after 1900, where his son Edwin Benjamin Sembler, and grandchild Charles William Sembler, lived. At the time of the 1910 U.S. Census, Andrew and Sara Eloise were living with son Edwin and family next to Dr. David Rose. Andrew and Sara Eloise acquired the Carlisle House, which they operated until his death from heart disease in 1911.

The Churches

The Sebastian Methodist Church on Louisiana Avenue was refurbished. Rev. W. T. Lane was responsible for the remodeling of the Methodist Church, enlarging it in 1901. A group of local citizens aided him in this venture, Parris Lawson, James Stinson, carpenter B. F. Hardesty, Frank Vickers, and George Vickers. Although Methodist ministers normally had only a one or two-year tenure at any one place, W. T. Lane was also on the list of registered voters for both 1902 and 1909. The Methodist Church was an important part of the lives of the Sebastianites. The Ladies of the Methodist Church met in November 1905 and organized a W. H. M. Society for the purpose of improving the church property. That same month, a Pound Party was held at the parsonage to add items to the parsonage larder. The second meeting of the Woman's Home Missionary Society met at Mrs. Grove's home on November 19, 1905. The fencing material for the church was received and installed in 1906. More remodeling was undertaken in 1909 by local citizenry under the supervision of George Vickers.

Two more churches were added to Sebastian this decade. In the beginning, services of the Congregational Church were held in the Sebastian school building. In 1901, land was donated by James A. and Mary R. Hudson, on north Central Avenue. A wood frame church with a bell tower, painted white, was completed in 1903, and the first services were held in March of that year. Its first minister was Rev. Weatherwax, in 1902. This church lapsed in 1906. In 1907, Murray and Sarah Hall donated land for the Macedonia Baptist Church, which was built in 1908. The Sebastian Methodist church donated the first benches and a bell for the bell tower, the one originally donated to the Methodist church by the Groves. Later, another larger church was built over it and subsequently moved to another location.

School

With an increase in population, there were more students. Local school boards had to provide funding for longer school terms and a more varied curriculum, and the tax districts had to raise money for larger and more expensive school buildings. A second teacher was added, assistant to the principal at Sebastian. A report from November 19, 1904, by the Brevard County Superintendent of Schools to the State Superintendent, stated that seven new schools had been added, one of which was Sebastian's. Sebastian's school system was improved; a two-room, two-story wooden building with a belfry was built near the railroad tracks on Louisiana Avenue. Supervisor G. B. Hall was getting the school ready for opening in September of 1905. County Superintendent of Public Instruction Platts paid a visit to the new school at the end of September. There were two teachers that year, Ella Singleton and Mrs. G. M. Stewart. B. F. Hardesty of Sebastian was a member of the county school board and reported on Sebastian's school from 1905-1908. The teachers appointed for the 1906-1907 school term remained Miss Ella Singleton, principal, and Mrs. G. M. Stewart, assistant. Fundraising helped pay for school improvements. In October of 1905, the School Improvement Society was organized, and that month teachers and children of the school hosted an event with ice cream and literary entertainment to raise funds for a fence around the school property, which was erected in February of 1906. In April of 1909, Sebastian petitioned the Board of Public Instruction to become a Special Tax School District.

The school became an integral part of Sebastian life. The third generation to be named Billy Bowlegs, of the Seminoles, often went to the school and sat in the classes along with the students. This school was a venue for entertainment before the Town Hall was built in 1914. The School Debating Class was entertained by teacher Miss Ella Singleton at the home of Mrs. G. B. Hall in October 1905. The play given by the Ladies' Aid Society at the school in February of 1906 was considered a success. In 1906, there was a school picnic to celebrate Thanksgiving with songs, recitations, and a talk by Rev. W. A. Myers, followed by dinner and sports with prizes awarded, as reported in the *St. Lucie Tribune*.

Photographers

Much of what we know of our past is thanks to photographers. In the 1880s, William Henry Jackson portrayed the area's pristine wilderness. In the early 1900s, there are a few local photographers that chronicled the area's early history, such as George Nelson, Paul and Rodney Kroegel, and George Knight.

George Nelson

One of the major impacts to the Sebastian area came from a naturalist who researched there. His photographs and those of the Kroegels have left a lasting image of the era.

George Nelson was born in Vinalhaven, Maine, in 1875, and made his home in Lexington, Massachusetts. His interest in wildlife and wilderness travel developed at an early age. Prior to 1900, George Nelson was a naturalist on an expedition to the Galapagos Islands to study the Galapagos tortoise, which was nearly extinct at that time. In 1900, at age 24, he held the title of ornithologist with the Maynard-Pratt Scientific Expedition to Florida.

In 1901, he was hired by the Harvard University Museum of Comparative Zoology as a preparator. In that position, he mounted specimens that other naturalists brought to the museum, including one dinosaur skeleton; he also collected and prepared his own specimens. He made many winter trips to Florida to study the birds on Pelican Island, no doubt inspired by the years of controversy surrounding it and its final creation as the world's first national wildlife refuge in 1903. His collection trips also took him to Bermuda, the Dominican Republic, and Swan Island. His many photographs and specimens swelled the Harvard museum with many previously unknown specimens. His fine work in mounting the specimens was praised in the museum reports, and he was noted for his hand-painted glass photographic slides of specimens. Many of these slides were used in lectures and his photographs appeared in journals. He wrote scholarly articles and was a popular lecturer.

Nelson became close friends with the Kroegels during his trips to Sebastian. He stayed with them during many Florida winters, profiting from their closeness to Pelican Island and availability of their fine boats for transportation. He made many such trips, photographing and collecting specimens. He and Rodney Kroegel often collected specimens in the marshes west of Fellsmere and around the whole area for the Harvard Museum. He made extensive study of the Pelican Island birds for his work as Harvard preparator.

He created his own home base in Sebastian for his winter visits that became a meeting place for other naturalists. By 1910, Paul built a house for him near the Kroegels on property he purchased from them. George built a second, larger, two-story home by 1925. A darkroom was also constructed, used by George and the Kroegels. He infected Paul and Rodney with his love of photography, and taught them how to photograph and develop the pictures. He is responsible for many local photographs taken in this period. He was also an ardent fisherman and outdoorsman. His boat was named *Let's Go.*

During his later years, he shifted his work from preparing and mounting current specimens to work with fossils, due to chronic arsenic poisoning from the preservation process. In 1937, Nelson was made Preparator in Chief of the Harvard University Museum of Comparative Zoology, a position he held until 1946 at age 70. At retirement, he became a permanent resident in Sebastian until 1952, when he sold his home and moved to Vero Beach. He remained a popular local lecturer and fisherman. He died in Vero in 1962.

Rodney A. Kroegel

Rodney Kroegel was an intelligent man with wide-ranging interests and abilities. He had an abiding love for Sebastian and the local heritage. He kept up with all the latest innovations in technology. The son of Paul Kroegel, he was born on March 9, 1903, and lived most of his life on the Kroegel homestead in south Sebastian on the Indian River. At an early age, he was influenced by the many scientists and naturalists that came to the area to study the flora and fauna. He helped George Nelson collect specimens and learned photography and film developing from him. He was in charge of Nelson's studio when Nelson went north. Rodney began photography using the glass plate negatives common at that time, but soon moved to flat film. He found, however that this early film had its problems; it was volatile. It warped and created many photos out of focus. The clearest and most enduring photographs of that era seen today are the ones made with glass plate negatives. He became a professional photographer, and on Sundays, individuals would line up at his studio to have their photographs taken. Many of these were portraits done on postcard photographic stock in common usage at the time. Copies could be made for mere pennies, and were very popular for advertising as well as personal use.

Rodney embraced the developing technologies. He repaired small electrical appliances and he built a radio. He ran the hand-cranked projector at local movies shown while Meta Chesser played the piano, the only sound for the silent movies. A self-taught electrician, he wired local houses for electricity, and did plumbing. Sebastian Electric and Plumbing Company was owned and run by him until the late 1970s. The War Department accepted him for Citizen's Military Training Camp in 1923, and he spent the month of August in Anniston, Alabama, at Camp McClellan. In 1927, he and Nora Etters married, and they moved into their new house built that year on the Kroegel homestead. Their children were Wayne, Douglas, and Janice. Douglas moved to Tampa, and Wayne lived in Wabasso. Janice married John Timinsky, and stayed in Sebastian. Involved in civic matters, Rodney served on the Pelican Island Preservation Committee, was a member of Lion's Club, and was a charter member of the Sebastian Volunteer Fire Department. Moreover, he belonged to Early Settlers of the Lower Indian River. Nora was a member of the Sebastian Sewing Circle.

In 1997, while Rodney was hospitalized in Tampa during a visit to family, his house was burglarized and burned, and all was lost. He died on December 30, 1999, in Tampa. In 2011, the remainder of Rodney's house was demolished. Rodney's sister, Frieda, married Treley Thompson, who was drafted in WWI, and served in the Navy as a Seaman 2nd Class in 1918. Treley was the manager of a packing house.

George Washington Knight

Another photographer, George Washington Knight, seems to have been an insouciant, intelligent man, one of the Floridians who was always on the move, never stopping for very long in one place. His father was murdered when he was a baby. At a young age, George was apprenticed to a wheelwright, and learned blacksmithing and how to make whiskey. His first wife was Emma Johnson, and with her their son John was born. She died in the childbirth of twins. He and second his wife Sarah Jane Sexton were both second-generation Floridians who came from Calhoun County Florida. In the early 1900s, George designed and built a mill with a hydraulic turbine for milling lumber, sawing ties for the Panama Canal Railroad. The wood was taken by oxen down to the river and floated down to where sailing ships took it to Panama. George traded the mill in for a waterfront plot of land in the Park Estate in Sebastian, land which had been owned by A. Ford. Ford's camera and photographic developing equipment were included in the trade.

Around 1907, the Knights came by rail down the coast to Sebastian, where George built their small waterfront house with a darkroom on the Ford land. He became an avid photographer. Three years later, their daughter Mae met and married Charles W. Sembler, who came with his family in 1901. George and Sarah had five surviving children after Mae. Apparently, George was a lighthearted man. He was known to have a good singing voice, was fond of traveling and visiting friends, and went to all-day Baptist revival meetings when in the Panhandle. He also gardened, fished, and built boats. George was a founding member of the local chapter of Woodmen of the World in 1909, and served as a school board trustee.

Sarah, who was often sickly and pregnant, contracted typhoid in 1910, and Mrs. Henry Park took care of baby Gwendolyn Knight. Around this time, the Knights left the waterfront home and rented a house on Palmetto Avenue from Murray Hall. Around 1916, George and family moved to Southport, Florida. Daughter May stayed in Sebastian with her husband, Charlie Sembler, and Gwendolyn went back to live with Mae. Sarah died in Southport shortly after arriving. George's third marriage was to Luella Sexton Willis, Sarah's sister. He made tombstones for unmarked graves in Southport, and built his own coffin, which he kept in the dining room until his third marriage, when it was moved to the garage. He died at age 93.

Harry Hill

Harry Hill was a professional photographer in Fort Pierce from 1905-1937, owner of "Florida Photographic Concern." He was made the official photographer of the Florida East Coast Railway Key West Extension. In 1914, he created four albums of F.E.C. photographs.

Roseland

By the turn of the century, Roseland was growing. Roseland in this decade boasted of E. M. Stokes' general store and post office, the railroad depot for the Florida East Coast Railway, a public dock, and the Old Stockade. There was also the Ercildoune Inn, Trilby Plantation and other groves, and a ferry crossing the Sebastian River. Berry Street ran from the depot to the Ercildoune. A tramway was built from the dock to the depot for handling fish. The bridge was being worked on by Mr. Boone's crew of fifteen. The Blackshear land was sold at public auction in June of 1909. Students were schooled in Sebastian. Wauregon was in this area but was failing.

The Stockade in Roseland was still in operation as a prison camp for convicted criminals that were leased out to work. They were taken across the Sebastian River by barge each day to work tapping trees for turpentine, and returned to the camp each night.

The first attempt to plat and subdivide Roseland in 1903 failed. That year, surveyor J. O. Fries created a plan of Roseland for J. M. Swain, nine blocks along the south bank of the Sebastian River, which included the northern part of Wauregan. Two companies acquired Swain's land, the Florida Development Company and the Berry Land Company, both owned by developer A. A. Berry of Clarinda, Iowa. However, at this time, the plan failed. Berry renewed his efforts in 1910.

Roseland Residents

Upon the Stokes' return to Roseland in 1902, Elmer M. Stokes was made Roseland postmaster. The Stokes family lived upstairs and had a small store and post office in the first floor of their home, which was behind the freight depot in Roseland, just east of the railroad, on the south side of the St. Sebastian River.

David P. Gibson and his wife Ellen were on their property at the time of the 1900 U.S. census, but David was gone by 1902. E. A. Gibson died August 31, 1907. She was a devout Baptist. Quinn Gibson, son of David P. Gibson, continued his position as bridge tender and water pump manager in Roseland for the Florida East Coast Railway. There were two boilers and two pumps at the Roseland station. Quinn was single at the time of the 1900 census, but married Christine a little later, around 1900, and had a daughter, Josie. In October 1906, Quinn completed an addition to the Register cottage, and moved in with his family. They were members of the Sebastian Methodist Church.

Jack Hardee's house burned and everything was lost in June of 1906. He had land on the west side of the Sebastian River in the Roseland area. He was distantly related to the Sebastian Hardees. The Bowlers and Cains also were living on the west side of the Sebastian River. Lawrence C. Moore and his wife Francis were doing a thriving business at the Ercildoune. Alfred White died in 1902, but widowed Katherine continued with their groves.

In the Indian River Drive Area of Roseland were some elegant houses. Judge Elliott Northcott built his one-story wood frame winter residence in 1904 there, a square building with a chimney in the center of the house. It was later purchased by Donald McDonald. Also on Indian River Drive was the Allen Campbell house, Bellevue, which was built in 1896 and later purchased by the Ruffners.

The Jesse Yongue family added the lovely house Riverside to Indian River Drive, built in 1909 by Jesse. Florida-born Jesse built it to be hurricane-resistant, and added a widow's walk to the second story with an excellent view of the ocean. He was employed by the Florida East Coast Railway to build railroad bridges and owned rental properties. He had groves and a packing house behind the house, a pineapple field near Fort Pierce, and a theater in Ybor City. He took his civic responsibilities seriously; he was one of the first county commissioners, and a champion of the Red Cross. After Jesse died in 1934 at age 63, wife Janie first rented the house out, then sold it to their friends, the Hanshaws.

Eureka, Kitching Settlement

In the 1900s, there was a railroad track running west from Sebastian with no trains. Cincinnatus Farms was defunct; Fellsmere Farms Company had not started yet. There was still, however, a community called Eureka, or Kitching. This spot was named Eureka by the settlers it attracted. Walter F. Baughman, as well as Stanley Kitching, had operated stores there. It also had a post office. There was a spring north of the bridge called Kitching Spring. The Drawdys, Trolls, McFees, and Davises were all there a short time. The Hairs, Millers, and Beugnots all arrived around 1909, settling in Eureka. Mary Vickers was a teacher at the Eureka school for one year, and Mr. Mathis also taught there. The school, which began in 1905, was only open for four or five years until it was burned down by some disgruntled teens in 1909. There was no church, but Sunday School classes were held in the homes of the Trolls or McFees. The Gant and Creary families ran sawmills for the lumbering industry in the pine woods along the South Prong of the Sebastian River. Charlie and Bessie Taylor lived a little further north on the Sebastian River, arriving around 1910. The Van Antwerps, as well as two Matthews' families, lived to the north of this settlement.

Miller Family

Benjamin Miller, his wife Tootie Gore, and their family were farmers who arrived around 1909 in Eureka. They had two sons and a daughter living with them, Gordie, Doodle, and Josie. The Millers and Beugnots worked at the Creary sawmill across the river from Roseland during the year it was in operation. They rafted the logs up to the sawmill. The Millers were still in Sebastian at the time of the 1920 U.S. Census. Benjamin W., age 66, was born in South Carolina. He was a truck farmer who owned his own home and land with a mortgage. His wife, Susan A. Miller, age 42, was born in Florida, as were all their children. Living with them was their son James R. (Doodle), a 27-year-old laborer; Josephine (Josie), age nineteen; Benjamin G. (Gordie), a seventeen-year-old laborer; and Milo, age fourteen. It is not known if Tootie was Susan's nickname, or if Susan was a second wife. Benjamin W., who died in 1924, Susan A., who died in 1960, and B. Gordon Miller, who died in 1970, are all buried together in the Park Section of the Sebastian Cemetery.

Beugnot Family

The Beugnots were in Florida by 1908, when their daughter Martha was born, and settled near Eureka in 1909. The Beugnots farmed the land, and on April 13, 1916, a homestead patent was issued to Henry E. Beugnot for 160.24 acres. Henry was born around 1867 in Indiana, of German descent. He and his wife Wiley Frances Beugnot were in Georgia by 1889, when their first child Charles was born, and the next six children. They left Georgia, where he had worked in a sawmill for many years, to go to Florida around 1908. He later gave up farming and the Beugnots operated a logging business, rafting the logs down to the Creary sawmill. He was a ship's carpenter and working for wages in 1920. Their children were Charles L., Mary P., John T., Wiley E., Alva C., Henry A., Farris L., Martha L., and Alice C. Wiley F. Beugnot died in 1938 and was buried in the Sebastian Cemetery. Henry was not buried there, but son John and his wife Perla are buried next to him.

Hair Family

The Hairs were one of the families that chose to settle in the sparsely populated Sebastian River area around Eureka. Thomas Guilford Hair was born October 12, 1876, in Manatee County, Florida. His father, Streety Ashford Hair, brought his family to Brevard County around 1881 from Manatee County. The Hair ancestors and related families were cattle ranchers in Hillsborough, Manatee, and Desoto Counties, and successive generations raised cattle for more than a century. On December 23, 1897, Guilford Hair married Montie Adeline Willis, born April 22, 1897, in Osceola County. Her parents were early homesteaders from Early County, Georgia.

Guilford and Montie Hair were settled on the Sebastian River by 1909, the year they bought property from Mr. and Mrs. W. F. Baughman. The following year, they purchased more land from Mr. and Mrs. C. C. Warren. The Hairs farmed, raised cattle, and contracted to butcher beef for the railroad company. They had nine children, five of whom went to the Eureka School.

Mosquitoes!

The topic of mosquitoes in Sebastian deserves a chapter all to itself. The Seminole Wars and mosquitoes are credited with delaying the settlement of Florida, putting it almost in last place amongst the other states. Indian River County was part of Mosquito County from 1824 to 1845. Thereafter, county names were chosen that were more attractive and less suggestive of harsh realities. Today, it is impossible to imagine what a threat mosquitoes were to early Florida settlers. Swarms of mosquitoes killed chickens, dogs, and cattle. Cows would stand in the river at night to avoid being bitten. People protected themselves in many ways.

A topic of many of Marion Ball's interviews with long-time Indian County residents in the 1980s and 1990s was how they formerly coped with the scourge of mosquitoes. Richard Milton Jones said that they bought B brand insect powder, put it in a can lid, and lit it. The sand flies didn't like the smoke, and people could hardly tolerate it either. However, it was not very effective against mosquitoes. Thomas R. Cadenhead Jr. related that they were so bad that you had to wear a helmet with screens over your face, and everyone had a smudge pot by the door. According to James Baldwin, the salt marsh down by the river was where the mosquitoes came from. They used palmetto brushes at the door to brush the mosquitoes off before they went inside. You couldn't talk or work without having a veil over your face, according to Ernest Barnwell.

Humor was one way of coping with the scourge. *St. Lucie Tribune* columnists bantered back and forth about mosquitoes in 1905:

> Rain and mosquitoes are plentiful, the former much needed.
>
> *Narrows* column, July 28, 1905

> Some Sebastianites are 'fever bound' in Louisiana. Too bad. We hope that they will not bring any infected stygomia, anophelis, or any other kind of mosquitoes in their grips. Ours are bad enough and numerous enough, thank you.
>
> *Sebastian* column August 18, 1905

> We don't believe there is any place in the state that can beat us in truck farming, and we know that they can't beat us with mosquitoes. 'The worst I ever saw them,' is what everyone says.
>
> *Narrows* column, August 25, 1905

> Last week Narrows was inquiring for their 'lost, strayed or stolen' mosquitoes. Guess some of them came here as we have had an oversupply of a most vicious kind here lately. Wish the owners would come and get them. 'No charges' to pay.
>
> *Sebastian* column, September 9 1905

> Rain! rain! oh, my! and mosquitoes. Sebastian need not claim any of ours. We have them every one.
>
> *Narrows* column, September 15, 1905

> The Narrows correspondent said the mosquitoes had all gone. Well, we suppose they have, for we had a light shower of them here a few days ago. We would be glad if they would go back home, for they have steel pointed bills and we do not like them a bit.
>
> *Ft. Drum* column, September 15, 1905

Anna Pearl Newman relates some of Charles Gifford's tall tales about mosquitoes in her book *Stories of Early Life Along Beautiful Indian River:*

> Once I took a picture of our grapefruit stand. The mosquitoes were as thick as could be. I sent the picture to friends and asked them if they could see the grapefruit on the trees, as the fruit was still green. The reply was: 'Couldn't see the fruit, but there was sure a nice flock of turkeys under the trees.'
>
> I had the first fruit stand. It had a palmetto roof. Pelicans would fly north and would light on the fruit stand and call to the young mosquitoes, thinking they were her babies, to fly north with her.
>
> We used to sit around and watch the mosquitoes play games under the trees. The one that got the most oranges on its bill won the game.

Early developers, in an attempt to convince prospective settlers that they were not a problem, maintained that the mosquitoes of the area were small, frail, clumsy, and did not cause malaria.

15

Commerce and Social Life: 1900s

The most common and most successful commercial ventures in the area of Sebastian and Roseland were fishing, citrus groves, and truck farming. Mild weather, fertile land, and pristine waters practically ensured success. Many of the local civic leaders were also hard-working commercial successes who devoted their time to several varied enterprises. Social life flourished in this expanding economy.

Fishing

Around 1901, two of the most prominent and long-lasting fish companies were begun, those of E. B. Sembler, and T. B. Hicks, adding to the many other established fish companies, such as that of R. G. Hardee and the Parks. Many individuals hired on in this lucrative industry. Rapid transportation by rail and ice plants were a boon for the fragile cargo, and the whole area teemed with fish in the rivers. Fish camps were situated up and down the Indian River. "Run boats" would collect fish from the camps each day and bring them to the packing houses where they were processed and packed in ice in wooden barrels for the trip north. On August 4, 1905, 50 barrels of fish were shipped from Sebastian.

The industry had its ups and downs. In October of 1905, the Sebastian Inlet was dug and dredged open, and remained open for a short while. An inlet to the ocean would make ocean fishing possible in the Sebastian area. On May 17, 1909, a state law went into effect prohibiting catching fish with the use of haul seines or drag nets in all of the fresh or salt water within Brevard, St. Lucie, Palm Beach, and Dade Counties, within 20 miles of the coastline.

Robert George Hardee

Robert George Hardee, known as "Bob" or "Cap," was a son of Robert A. Hardee, and was born in 1872 in City Point. His family moved from there and founded Hardeeville, which was later renamed Rockledge. While there, he was employed as a mail carrier, traveling by boat to communities up and down the Indian River. He relocated to Sebastian with his family. At age 28, in 1900, he married Clarissa Maskery (May) Kitching, who was born in 1882 in England, the daughter of Sylvanus Kitching. Bob and Clarissa had two daughters: Meta, born around 1902, and Teresa, born nineteen years later, around 1921.

R. G. Hardee was heavily vested in the civic affairs of the city and county. In 1893, concerned with the impact of the Florida East Coast Railway on boat traffic, he advocated for a drawbridge for the train track across the St. Sebastian River, to ensure free access. He was the first Tax Assessor of St. Lucie County, when that county was formed July of 1905. Hardee was Sebastian postmaster from June 9, 1904, to September 17, 1906. He served twice on Sebastian city council and was one of the representatives who went to Tallahassee to form Indian River County in 1925. In 1916, R. G. Hardee was the vice president of the Sebastian Board of Trade. He was on the original Board of Directors of the Indian River County Mosquito Control District when it was created by the Florida Legislature in June of 1925.

An astute businessman, he succeeded in many ventures. He planted citrus groves and was a commercial grower. Hardee Packing House was his. He dealt in fish wholesale and had a packing house at Jupiter, and floating fish houses. *Eagle* was his ship that carried passengers and cargo. His dock at the end of Main Street, the Eagle Company Fish Dock, was used by local and other boats. His Hardee Service Station was a popular gathering spot next to the Hardee Oak, which he had planted, and he became an agent for Standard Oil Company in 1909. He added an oil house to his dock. Real estate was another of his ventures, subdividing some of his land to be sold as lots in Edgewater Park and Hardee's Addition. A large half-page advertisement in the *St. Lucie Tribune* read "Grand Auction Lot Sale Bob Hardee's Addition to Sebastian, Florida," slated for March 22, 1913.

A symbol of his business success, he built a two-story, fourteen-room, colonial-style mansion on Main Street between US Hwy 1 and Indian River Drive. It had four fireplaces, white columns on the front, and a white picket fence. This was built when the Hardee's daughter, Teresa, was four, circa 1925. Unfortunately, it was destroyed by a fire in 1936. He also had an elegant yacht known as the *St. Sebastian.*

Robert G. Hardee died in July of 1947 and was buried in Sebastian Cemetery; Clarissa died in 1977 and is buried next to him. The Hardee name can be found in downtown Sebastian on commemorative plaques. The large live oak tree near the Chamber of Commerce Building is the Hardee Oak, and over the years, it has survived efforts to remove it. In 2016, it was 125 years old.

Simeon Alfonso Park

Florida-born Simeon Park, son of August Park, was a wholesale fish dealer and fisherman with several fish houses. This family business was one of the oldest in the area, beginning with August Park, in the early days of Sebastian. Simeon's fish were shipped in barrels to New York City or Georgia by the train carload. He met Martha Raulerson at a Masquerade Ball, and they married in 1903 in the Sebastian Methodist Church. She was also a native

Floridian. For many years, she was a social columnist for the *Press Journal*, and entertained the Busy Bee Sewing Circle at her home. She was also one of the election inspectors. In 1925, she was on the Christmas Tree Committee of the Woman's Club, which met in the Sebastian Town Hall at that time. Their Woman's Club building was not erected until 1928. In 1926, she attended the Federation of Women's Clubs meeting in Fellsmere. Also involved in civic affairs, Simeon was a member of the Sebastian city council. They had two daughters, Lenora and Mildred. The couple had their second house built on property facing the Sebastian Woman's Club, on South Central Avenue (US Hwy 1), not far from the railroad tracks. Simeon died at age 86, in 1963, and Martha died in 1969. They are buried together in the Park section of the Sebastian Cemetery.

Edwin Benjamin Sembler

In 1901, Edwin B. (Ned) Sembler and his son Charles moved from Millbrook, New York, after his wife Cora died, leaving behind Ned's young daughter Mary with relatives. He stopped at Palatka and Titusville. In Titusville, he partnered in commercial fishing with T. B. Hicks, but left to go to Sebastian. Hicks followed shortly thereafter and they continued the commercial fishing venture, Hicks & Sembler, or Sembler & Hicks. E. B. Sembler was given a permit to carry a Smith & Wesson revolver in February of 1909, per the *St. Lucie Tribune*, and he was a registered voter. By 1910, he was married to Evie Martin. That year, their household next to Dr. David Rose's consisted of three generations of the family; living with them were son Charles, still single, his father, Andrew J. Sembler, and his wife, Sarah Eloise. The Hicks & Sembler sawmill was operated at the Sebastian Bridge west of Sebastian. Edwin's father, Andrew Jackson Sembler, later moved into the Carlile House.

The Semblers had an eventful year in 1911. When Charles and Mae moved to Wabasso after their marriage, the lumber business and sawmill was moved to Wabasso in August 1911, and was in operation in early September. Lumber was provided by the sawmill for the Flagler railroad, Fellsmere railroad, and the town of Fellsmere. In 1911, Hicks and Sembler were also involved in real estate, and in November of that year, sold a lot to Albert Cain, fronting the shell road in the north part of town where he built a residence. Andrew Sembler died in 1911. In 1912, both the Edwin and Charles Sembler families followed T. B. Hicks to Roseland, and purchased the Gibson house from Hicks. They began supplying shell for road building, supervising the removal of shells from Indian middens. With the onset of WWI, Edwin moved to Jacksonville to work in the shipyards. He returned to Sebastian after the war and resumed working with his son. They rented docks, then acquired a dock in the north part of town for the fishing concern of Sembler & Sembler, wholesale dealers in salt water fish. In 1928, the business suffered a setback when the hurricane destroyed the fish house and dock. The business, however, continued. E. B. Sembler died at age 75 on November 18, 1941, and is buried in Sebastian Cemetery.

Charles William Sembler

Charles William Sembler was born in 1889 in Millbrook, New York, and traveled with his father and stepmother to Sebastian in 1901. In the 1910 census, Charles was single, living with parents and grandparents next to Dr. David Rose. He suffered a serious injury to his knee and was taken to the Florida East Coast Hospital (railroad hospital) in St. Augustine in April of 1910, where he was operated upon. He kept his leg, but could no longer bend it and suffered a long recuperation.

Charles married Margaret (Mae) Knight, daughter of George Washington Knight, on Valentine's Day in 1911 in Sebastian. They were quietly married at the parsonage by Rev. Woodrough. Only close relatives of the bride were present, perhaps because of grandfather Andrew Sembler's illness. After, the couple moved to Wabasso and lived in the Vreeland cottage west of the railroad. A week later, the "tin pan brigade" serenaded them one night at their home until the Semblers could stand it no longer and invited them in for wine, reported the *St. Lucie Tribune*.

At the onset of WWI, when Edwin left for Jacksonville, Charlie was recuperating from typhoid. Charlie and Mae moved to Grant, where they lived next door to Roy O. Couch. Charlie was employed by Couch, doing a variety of jobs, one of which was Couch's project to open the Sebastian Inlet. Charlie operated the dredge invented by Couch for a year, but this labor was ineffective, as sand filled in again as quickly as it was removed. Many local individuals labored at this attempt with them, but it ultimately failed. After the war, when his father returned to Sebastian, Charlie and Mae left Grant and returned to Sebastian as well, where the Semblers resumed the fishing business. He became assistant manager of Indian River Fisheries in 1930. Charlie was a school trustee and one of the original city councilmen when the city of Sebastian was formed, and remained one for 20 years. Charlie and Mae had six children, and are buried next to Edwin in the Sebastian Cemetery.

Thomas Branch Hicks

Thomas Branch Hicks was a civic leader and an important figure in the Sebastian fishing industry. His parents, Mary Jane Turner of Georgia, and John E. Hicks of Kentucky, were living in Gainesville, Florida, when Thomas was born in July of 1872. By the time he was 28 years old, he had established himself in the commercial fish business in Titusville. In 1900, he had employed, and then partnered, with Edwin (Ned) Sembler in Titusville. When Ned moved on to Sebastian with his son in 1901, Hicks expanded his fishing business to Sebastian, where Sembler lived. When he met Edwin's sister Frances Mabel there, he changed the central location of his business to Sebastian, and they married on September 25, 1902, in Sebastian. Their first child, Mattie, was born in 1903, and Edwin followed in 1905. In 1910, Hicks bought the house and part of the estate of the late D. P. Gibson. He renovated it and made it their home. That year, William H. Lancaster, age 76, boarded with them. Emily was born in 1914. Somewhere around that time, Pauline Ganoe, daughter of a friend of Mabel's, came from Higley to attend school and help keep house. Her sister Annette did the same a few years earlier, as there was no high school in their home town. Hicks purchased more land, including one acre in Hudson's Addition in 1918. He owned cottages that were rented out.

Hicks began diversifying and expanding his businesses in 1906. Indian River Cooperage and Co. incorporated for the purpose of making fish barrels in November of 1906. Its original headquarters were at Eau Gallie. Hicks became vice president, and a director, and held stock in the company. The following other fish dealers also took stock in the company: Indian River & Lake Worth Fish Co., E. A. Holt, Lars Jorgensen, J. T. Tucker, Eagle Fish Co., Sebastian Fish Co., W. F. Anderson, O. Roch, I. D. Jandreau, H. E. Crooks, E. J. Ricou, R. White, and W. B. Cross. This barrel factory went into operation in Eau Gallie and another one was built to open in Sebastian the following February, a 30 x 60 foot building. From time to time Hicks did road work, paid from the Road & Bridge Fund.

The Hicks fish business continued to grow. T. B. Hicks & Co. moved its business to Oslo and began shipping fish from there in 1909. Ned Sembler became his partner. The wholesale fish business extended to Fort Pierce. In 1925, he bought a Chevrolet truck for the fish business.

Hicks became part owner of a sawmill west of Wabasso with Ned and Charlie Sembler. Lumber was being made at Hicks & Sembler's mill by December of 1910. Their lumber used to build houses in the newly developing Fellsmere, and the hotel building that still exists there was made with Hicks & Sembler lumber. It also cut cross-ties for the Florida East Coast Railway. In August of 1911 the sawmill was moved to Wabasso and was in operation by September.

As well as being involved in Hick's fish business, Ned Sembler also sold caskets, and Mabel helped him prepare bodies for burial in Ned's caskets. Mabel also acted as nurse for Dr. David Rose, assisting with births and common injuries. She joined the newly formed Woman's Club at its second meeting. Thomas Hicks was a charter member of Woodmen of the World when it formed in 1909, and became its Secretary. Civic matters were an important part of Thomas Hick's life. He became the first mayor of the newly formed municipality of Sebastian, serving from December 16, 1924, to December 13, 1925, when George T. Badger was voted in. Hicks was active in other civic matters. He served on the school board and was an inspector of elections. He was seated on Grand Juries numerous times.

Groves and Truck Farming

The rich soil and temperate climate insured that in most years, fruits and vegetables would thrive, even in the winter. These winter crops provided fresh vegetables to the rest of the country locked in snow. Pineapples were a major local crop, as were tomatoes and beans. However, the cold wave of January 1900 damaged the groves and truck farming, bringing about a change in production. Truck farming moved south of the St. Sebastian River after the devastation of the freeze. The groves suffered as well, but there was an excellent orange and grapefruit crop in 1905, and by about 1907, the citrus industry production had recovered. In 1908, Florida's production of citrus was six million boxes. Florida Citrus Exchange was formed in 1909, and met in Tampa to tackle the problems inherent in the growth of the industry, including the need to improve marketing and sales techniques. Facing the same needs, many local sub-exchanges were formed as well. The Indian River Citrus Growers Association also filed for corporate status that year.

On December 21, 1906, the *St. Lucie Tribune* listed growers on the north end of St. Lucie County:

> R. A. Hardee of Sebastian has one of the largest groves of orange and grapefruit.
>
> W.C. Braddock Jr. has groves of oranges and grapefruit, and grows vegetables, including eggplant. He is the largest shipper of fresh eggs, shipped daily, on the east coast and is a leading merchant.
>
> G. Kroegel has a 10-acre grove on the riverbank sheltered by a large shell mound.
>
> Foster & Groves has an orange and grapefruit grove on the ridge high above the town, surrounded by shade trees and tropical fruit trees, and has flowing wells of pure water.
>
> G. B. Hall & Co. has a fine grove west of town, has a large packing house, and is a shipper of fruit and vegetables. Hall has a specialty of shipping direct to hotels.
>
> Others include W. T. Laine who grows oranges and vegetables. Ivey Lawson and G. A. Braddock ship oranges and grapefruits.
>
> In Roseland Col. H. D. Ruffner has a hospitable house and is one of the best orange growers in the state. He has all kinds of fruit, as well.
>
> A.E. Campbell has a fine grove adjoining the Ruffner grove.
>
> Robert Bowler is a grower with orange groves, and vegetables, especially eggplant.

Vickers Family

The Vickers family had wide-ranging commercial interests in Sebastian. They were from Hahira, Lowndes County, Georgia, close to the Florida state line. Drew Vickers was an early settler in that county, circa 1821. Descendant Stephen Vickers and H. B. Lawson were two of the trustees and on the board of stewards of the Methodist Church in Hahira in 1891, and Mr. and Mrs. Stephen Vickers, Mr. and Mrs. H. Briggs Lawson, and Mrs. W. F. Lawson were some of the charter members. When Stephen Vickers married Sarah Folsom, C. W. Ryall was her legal guardian. Stephen and Sara Vickers had three sons, George, Frank, and Everett. George Vickers had been a millwright in Georgia, and Frank had been a farmer. George and Frank left Georgia and farmed in Dade County for a few seasons, but decided not to settle there. They worked along the way as they headed north again and stopped several places, including Sebastian, where they were acquainted with the Lawsons from their home town. The two brothers determined to live there around 1903, and went back to Georgia and convinced their parents, Stephen and Sara, to move to Sebastian around 1908, when they arrived by rail. Everett and unmarried daughter Bamma Vickers moved with them, too. Bamma married Parris Lawson, whom she had known previously, in July 1908 in Sebastian. Daughters Alma and Mary Jane were already married and stayed behind.

According to the 1920 U.S. Census, the Vickers household in Sebastian consisted of Stephen, wife Sara, and sons George and Frank, living in a rental property. The census must have caught them just prior to moving into the house on Central Avenue. Stephen was retired, and George and Frank were single and fruit growers. Their residence was near the W. C. Braddocks. By that time, Bamma and Everett were both married, with their own households.

Stephen and Sara Vickers

The Vickers retained close ties with their prior home in Lowndes County, Georgia, as they made frequent and lengthy visits back. It is likely that Stephen Vickers maintained business holdings in Georgia for some time after their move, as well as returning to visit their daughters and other relatives. In 1919, Stephen Vickers built a large two-story frame home on Central Avenue (US Hwy 1), where they resided with sons George and Frank. This lovely residence is one of the significant properties listed in Old Town Sebastian Historic District East, placed on the National Register of Historic Places on August 4, 2003, and is considered an excellent example, as is the Bamma Vickers Lawson House. George and Sara continued to live there after the death of Stephen in 1924. Sara died in 1931.

George Vickers

George Vickers entered into many business ventures with his brother Frank, including the stores, real estate, and citrus groves. Some of his business ventures were done on his own. He made many trips back to Lowndes County, Georgia, often with his parents. In 1907, he purchased the Norwood property south of Sebastian. He hauled shell for the roads. The remodeling of the Methodist Church in 1909 was under his supervision. After the incorporation of Sebastian, he was elected the town marshal. George never married, and continued to live with his parents. He died January 31, 1960, in Sebastian. By the 1920s, Frank and George were concentrating on their groves and the store. In 1925, they purchased 55 acres of citrus grove property south of Sebastian from G. A. Braddock, and became citrus growers with extensive grove property.

Frank Vickers

With his family, Frank Cox Vickers was born in Lowndes County, Georgia, February 16, 1878. He and brother George formed Vickers Brothers and were involved in many business ventures around the area. He became one of the prominent growers in the county. He remained single until November 28, 1927, when he married Estelle Lassiter in Jacksonville, Florida. By the time of the 1930 census, they were living in a rental home on Main Street. Frank died May 1, 1973, in Vero Beach. Frank and Estelle are buried next to each other in the Sebastian Cemetery.

Everett Western Vickers

Everett Vickers, born September 30, 1891, in Lowndes County, Georgia, was twelve years of age at the time his brothers left for Florida. He stayed in Georgia, and arrived in Sebastian with his parents. On April 21, 1914, he married Mary Elizabeth Edwards in Sebastian. In May of that year, he built a large bungalow a few lots north of the Town Hall on Central Avenue. Everett worked at a variety of jobs, including road work and managing the stores. In 1916, the *St. Lucie Tribune* carried an advertisement for Everett W. Vickers, fire insurance agency and notary public, in Sebastian. He invested in real estate, purchasing and reselling the Gibson house. He also made periodic trips back to Georgia. As of the 1920 census, he owned his own farm and was a fruit grower. By 1930, he remained a grove owner, and remained in the Central Avenue house.

George Aldridge Braddock

George Aldridge Braddock was one of the sons of William Christopher Braddock, Sr. He married Rebecca Poppell of Seville. He and his family lived in Titusville until 1904, when they moved to John's Island, and from there they moved to Sebastian in 1907. The George Braddocks first lived in a small house on Louisiana Avenue, until their larger house was built in 1909, which is still standing on north Louisiana Avenue, a large, two-story, Georgian Revival-style house. It has front porches on both stories and a widow's walk at the top. The Braddocks had four children, George, Geraldine, Janelda and Dixie. G. A. Braddock acquired a large fleet of fishing boats on the Indian River and had a dock there. Additionally, he had a large citrus grove, a dairy, and raised chickens. He also grew and shipped mangoes.

He was the Sebastian commissioner appointed to the board of the Indian River Farms Drainage District to assess the proposal to add canals to the area. The proposal was accepted March 30, 1920, and bonds were issued to cover the expense. After Indian River County was formed in 1925, George A. Braddock was appointed as a county commissioner in the new County by Governor Martin. He became hard of hearing as he got older, and was struck by a train near his home in 1949, at age 81. He is buried in the Park Section of the Sebastian Cemetery, as is Rebecca, who died in 1945.

George & Elizabeth Martin

Perhaps George and Elizabeth Martin were city dwellers advised by their doctor to seek a milder and more healthful environment than could be found in New York City. They left Manhattan in 1905, when George was 64 and Elizabeth was 58, purchased land, and began by growing potatoes for market in 1906. He graduated to a grove and was a successful fruit grower for many years. George had a long illness in 1920; however, they had made a successful transition from urban life. Elizabeth died in 1923, and George died in 1925. They are buried together in Sebastian Cemetery.

James Leonard Stinson

The longtime Sebastian resident James Leonard Stinson started out with an important piece of Sebastian real estate, but he had troubles in his life and was not successful. Up until sometime in the 1900s, James Leonard Stinson lived in Georgia. He was born there on April 6, 1861. Around 1883, he married Susan A. Stinson, who was born in Alabama on July 13, 1863. At the time of the 1900 U.S. Census, James, Susie, and their children James Monroe Stinson, age thirteen, Augustus (Gustavus A.), age eleven, Josephine O., age eight, Albert L. (Albert Leonard/Lennard), age seven, Ilai, age four, and Margaret, age one, were living in Talbotton, Georgia. They were all born in Georgia. Farming cotton there became unprofitable for them, and a short time after that census, the Stinsons moved by train to Sebastian. For a time, they lived in a rented house. On December 13, 1909, Stinson was granted a Homestead Act land patent of 160 acres of land in Sebastian in the area around what is now the eastern part of Rte. 512.

At the time of the 1910 census, the Stinsons were living in Sebastian with the Simeon Park family, the Hartmans, and the Kroegels for neighbors. By 1916-1918, James farmed his land, and worked in the Hardee groves. He was an inspector of elections in 1916-1920. Son Albert was a fruit packer and daughter Josephine was teaching; she had received her teaching certificate and begun teaching school by age sixteen. Margaret was a student. Son James was a fisherman. Josephine met Joseph Gibbs of Vero and they married on Christmas Day, 1917. It was not a good year for son James and daughter Margaret, however. In 1917, James Stinson went on trial for having sex with an underage female, and his sister Margaret had a son, John A., out of wedlock. James Monroe Stinson joined the U.S. Navy and served as a seaman second class from April 17, 1918, to November 11, 1918, at Naval Headquarters District 7, Key West, Florida. Ilai F. Stinson served as a private in the U.S. Army Infantry from October 6, 1918, to April 16, 1919. The Stinson brothers Gus and Albert were raising peppers and other vegetables on the Lennard A. Stinson place north of Wabasso in 1919. Lennard also had property and peach orchards back in Georgia.

By January of 1920, James L., Susie, and Margaret were still in Sebastian, living in a rental house. James was a house carpenter and doing road work for wages. He installed a light plant for the Micco Garage. Margaret Stinson was working as a clerk, unmarried, living with her parents, and she had a three-year-old son, John A. Stinson. Margaret married Sidney D. Gaines of Vero on June 2, 1920. It was a quiet home affair with family attending. Gus, Albert, Albert's wife Effie, Katie, and Ilai all lived in Wabasso, farming. Josephine and Joe Gibbs moved to Daytona.

James Leonard Stinson died in 1935, and wife Susie died in 1932. They are buried next to each other in the Sebastian Cemetery, along with Albert and Effie Stinson, James Monroe Stinson, and Ilai Stinson. With them are Thomas Lennard Stinson, who was in the U.S. Navy in WWII, and Katie Stinson. Buried not far away are James and Susie's son Gustavus A. Stinson, his wife Ophelia, and Mildred, born in 1907. Sidney D. Gaines, husband of Margaret, is also buried in Sebastian Cemetery.

Cattle Industry: Daniel Sloan

The Sebastian Ranch Company was a prosperous cattle ranch in early Sebastian, located two miles west of Sebastian on Fellsmere Road in the area of what is now Fleming Street. In 1918, it had 639 head of cattle. Cattle were allowed to roam free; fencing of cattle did not become a law until much later. The ranch was started by Daniel Sloan, who was born in Dade City, Florida, on October 5 of 1857 or 1858. Arriving around the turn of the century, he spent the rest of his life there with his wife Margaret who was born circa 1864, in Florida. He was considered to be a prosperous businessman. He died on Jan 23, 1919, and was buried in Sebastian Cemetery. William and Margaret had three daughters, Celie, Edna, and Viola.

Arthur Orville Sloan

Their son Arthur Orville Sloan was born February 19, 1900, and was a rancher on his father's ranch. He married Frances F., who was born in Florida circa 1903. Around 1918, when he was eighteen and she was fifteen, they married. In 1920, after his father's death, Arthur did not continue as a rancher. He worked as an operator at Western Eyrins and he and his family lived in a rental in Fellsmere, according to census records. They had a baby, Morpha (Martha). At the time of the 1930 census, Arthur and family were living in a rental in Sebastian, and he was a river fisherman for wages.

William M. Sloan

Sebastian had another prosperous Sloan family who arrived around the turn of the century, probably related to the Daniel Sloans. William was born October 12, 1857, in Sanford, Florida. He too had property on Fellsmere Road where he was a grower. He was also a prominent merchant. On February 20, 1878, he married Elizabeth Sullivan, who was born August 7, 1856, in Orlando, the daughter of J. L. Sullivan, Sheriff of

Orange County. They had seven children. Mrs. R. G. McCain of Sebastian; Mrs. J. F. Tucker of Ft. Drum; Mrs. J. M. McCain of Melbourne; Miss Lillie Sloan of Sebastian; L. A. Sloan of Fellsmere; W. P. Sloan of Sebastian; and H. R. Sloan of Sebastian. The Sloan family had extensive property interests, groves, business buildings and investments in Sebastian and other towns. Elizabeth Sloan died September 29, 1920, and William died August 21, 1924. His funeral was one of the most attended services in Sebastian. Husband and wife are buried together in the Sebastian Cemetery.

Cattleman James Raulerson

James Raulerson was one of the Civil War Veterans of the Confederate Florida Infantry who eventually made his home in Sebastian as a cattleman. In the 1900 U.S. Census, he and his wife Welthean were living in Acron Lake, Florida, with their daughter Martha M. James was born in Georgia in October 1844. Welthean was born in Georgia in January 1855. They were married in 1874. They had two other children not living with them in 1900, Emmet and Lenora, who lived in Sanford. Sometime after 1900, they moved to Sebastian and were neighbors of Murray Hall and William N. Sloan. Martha married Simeon Park in 1903 in the Sebastian Methodist Church.

Social Life

In this decade, prosperity gave impetus to a flourishing social life, duly reported in the *St. Lucie Tribune* and other newspapers in the area. There were many social and civic groups in operation and many types of entertainment. Moonlight beach parties were popular. Friends and family were visited locally and outside the state. Party trips to the oyster beds and oyster roasts were popular. There was a fish fry down the Sebastian River in July 1906, but the boat motor failed and oars had to be used. Dances and picnics were held.

Church socials and dinners continued. Fundraisers were held and civic improvement was in vogue. It was possible to travel to Fort Pierce to see silent moving pictures by 1906. Silent films were shown in the schoolhouse in the evenings. Hall and Younge gave their motion picture show to a crowded house in 1906. "The Motorist" came out in 1906, as did the blockbuster "Life of a Cowboy." In 1908, "The Tempest," "The Adventures of Dollie," and "Her First Adventure" were movies shown. A Fort Pierce bookstore advertised a list of 48 books and 13 magazines for sale in 1906. A sampling of the titles included *Awakening of Helena Richie, The Girl from Tim's Place, Black Spaniel, Starve Crow Farm, The Gambler,* and *Breakers Ahead.* The 1905 State Fair in Tampa was attended by Mr. and Mrs. Ivey Lawson. Individuals met to form a Temperance Club in July 1906. M. E. Hall purchased a stereopticon outfit.

J. W. Sherrill, deputy organizer of Woodmen of the World, arrived in Sebastian and organized a lodge of about 20 members. On April 9, 1909, application was made for a charter for the temporary organization of Woodmen of the World in Sebastian, with sixteen members. Temporary officers were Con. Com., C. Shemuce; Adv. Lt., G. W. Knight; Banker, W. F. Baughman; Clerk, W. C. Smith; Escort, H. J. Park; Watch, Jesse C. Fulford; Sentry, A. C. Kroegel; Physician, Dr. Rose; and Managers, Jas. L. Stinson, S. A. Park, and T. B. Hicks.

The School Improvement Society had a meeting in May 1906 hosted by Mrs. G. B. Hall and Shields Clarke. "Your hobby" was the feature of the evening. Prizes were given for the most striking costume representing the hobby and for the most answers to questions about a penny. Miss Johnson won for her costume, which represented ferns and geraniums. Another May meeting of S.I.S. had gramophone music for entertainment and refreshments of pulled candy and cake. S.I.S. had a book social in June 1906, hosted by Mrs. M. E. Hall and Miss Braddock. The special feature of the evening was a book guessing contest.

Chautauquas

By and large, around the turn of the century, most entertainment Floridians enjoyed had to be made by themselves. However, a national phenomenon made its way into Florida, revolutionizing and stimulating thought, the Chautauqua. A Chautauqua was an exciting breath of culture and entertainment from the more civilized parts of the country, and many individuals made the trip from Sebastian and Roseland to other towns to partake in these annual events.

The concept of a Chautauqua began on the northern shore of Lake Chautauqua in New York State in 1874, as a Methodist Sunday school retreat by Reverend John Heyl Vincent. (Chautauqua is a Seneca Indian word that translates as "bag tied in the middle," which describes the lake's shape.) These summer retreats of religious, inspirational, and educational experience gradually added cultural and entertaining elements to the curriculum by the late 1870s. These summer programs attracted thousands of people by the early 1900s. This popularity prompted other communities to form their own Chautauquas and to request Chautauqua lecturers to come to their towns to speak. Theodore Roosevelt called Chautauquas, "The People's University."

Thus, the circuit Chautauqua concept was born. Circuit Chautauquas were a group of individuals who traveled throughout the summer months, predominantly to small mid-western rural towns. At each town on their circuit, they presented a "Chautauqua Week" of lectures, music, humor, drama, and children's programs. The programs and performers changed from season to season; politicians joined the circuit in an election year; World War I topics were timely in the war years. Vaudeville performers and opera stars might do a season of Chautauquas.

Costs were kept down by standardization and a full booking schedule that was organized by the Chautauqua bureaus. Bookings were guaranteed a year in advance. Mass mailings were sent out, made possible by the railroads. Extensive advertising campaigns were undertaken in each town. Towns had to guarantee a minimum fee in order to be included. They traveled primarily by rail. Crews set up 80 x 120 foot tents. Lighting was gasoline lanterns, and later, portable electric lights. Seating was planks or chairs. An elevated platform held the performers. Personal conduct had to be exemplary. These Chautauquas brought adult education and entertainment to small rural areas. They broadened thought, and updated the habits, dress, makeup, and speech of people across the country. They provoked change and discussion and molded public opinion. They entertained. Gradually, southern states were added to circuits, enabling them to continue their programs in the winter.

Melbourne was one of the towns that created its own Chautauqua. It formed the East Coast Chautauqua Assembly in 1897 to organize local Chautauquas. It held its first one that year. An undated publicity brochure stated that the "Chautauqua of the Tropics" had formed three years prior, and that its President was E. P. Branch of Melbourne. It said that due to the immense popularity, the Chautauquas would be continued and a Chautauqua Park would be created by 1902, managed by Dr. W. L. Davidson of Cuyahoga Falls, Ohio, and would contain a large and modern auditorium. The Chautauqua of the Tropics continued each winter for two weeks. In 1906, it featured children's classes, lectures on bible study, and physical culture. Music was provided, and a moving picture. In the 1920s, the organization branched out and was meeting in Titusville as well.

Vero brought in circuit Chautauquas. By 1919, the Radcliffe Chautauqua out of Washington, D.C., brought its three-day programs to Vero and Fort Pierce in February. Performances were in a tent, the school building, or hotel. There were daily concerts and lectures on varied topics, such as "The Challenge of Destiny," "The Greatest Thing that Men May Know," "Home Making," "The House Around the Corner," "The Problem of the Unprepared," "The Red Cross—a Record and a Prophecy," "Scientific Mysteries," "Home Care of the Sick," "Pushing Back Horizons," and "Electrical Wonders." The programs changed each year. They included: poetry readings, choirs, lecturers, yodelers, a pianist, a writer, jesters, Swiss hand-bell ringers, actors, impersonators, a magician, and an Arctic explorer. These Chautauquas stimulated and educated. The Vero Woman's Club helped organize reception of the event and found fee guarantors who made up the difference for costs above the ticket take. Radcliffe came back to Vero nearly each year thereafter in February for three days, until 1927, when Vero Beach began booking the Redpath Chautauqua instead. They performed yearly in Vero Beach through 1929, but cancelled thereafter due to the inability to guarantee the required fees.

Chautauquas reached their zenith in 1924, and gradually diminished thereafter, due to the depression and the advent of radio and movies which provided cheap, year-round entertainment and education for all.

16

The War Years and More: 1910s

Much of what happened in Florida from 1910 to 1920 was directed by nationwide events. WWI affected every part of American lives, not just the warfare, but also the methods of materials production, new inventions, and the economy. Prohibition became the law of the land shortly thereafter. Telephones, electricity, automobiles, and biplanes came to Florida. Freezes, floods, and influenza left their mark. However, it was also the beginning of the great land boom.

In 1909, Albert Waller Gilchrist took office as Florida's governor. Under Governor Gilchrist, telephone and telegraph rates became controlled by the Railroad Commission. Road construction was supervised by a state road commission enacted in 1913, and served in an advisory capacity to counties. WWI interrupted before much was accomplished on this. Election laws were overhauled in 1913, making the counties responsible for appointment of election officials and reporting results, rather than the state. Campaign fund limits were set. He also sponsored legislation to safeguard public health.

Women's issues were in the news. Women's suffrage was as much a hot topic as prohibition, but equality was not. Banking got a boost, too. A 1910 bank advertisement in the *St. Lucie Tribune* encouraged ladies to have their husbands open a checking account for them, as it was easier to pay bills by check than by cash. Family issues were going to court. For example, J. Byrd was arraigned before Justice Laine and went to trial on the offense of deserting and failing to support his children, as reported in the *St. Lucie Tribune* in 1915.

In 1916, Floridians elected a Prohibition Party Governor, Sidney J. Catts, who led Florida through the war years. He also endorsed women's suffrage. Prohibition was entered into law in Florida, effective in 1919, echoing the national law. The Volstead Act pronounced the ban on alcoholic beverages in the United States on January 16, 1919, and a year later the country went dry. Prior to prohibition going into effect, there was much public pressure to ban liquor, and temperance groups were springing up everywhere. Many of the Florida counties had already elected to be "dry."

An important product in ship building was collecting turpentine for pitch, used in caulking ships, among other uses. In order to contain costs, Consolidated Naval Stores

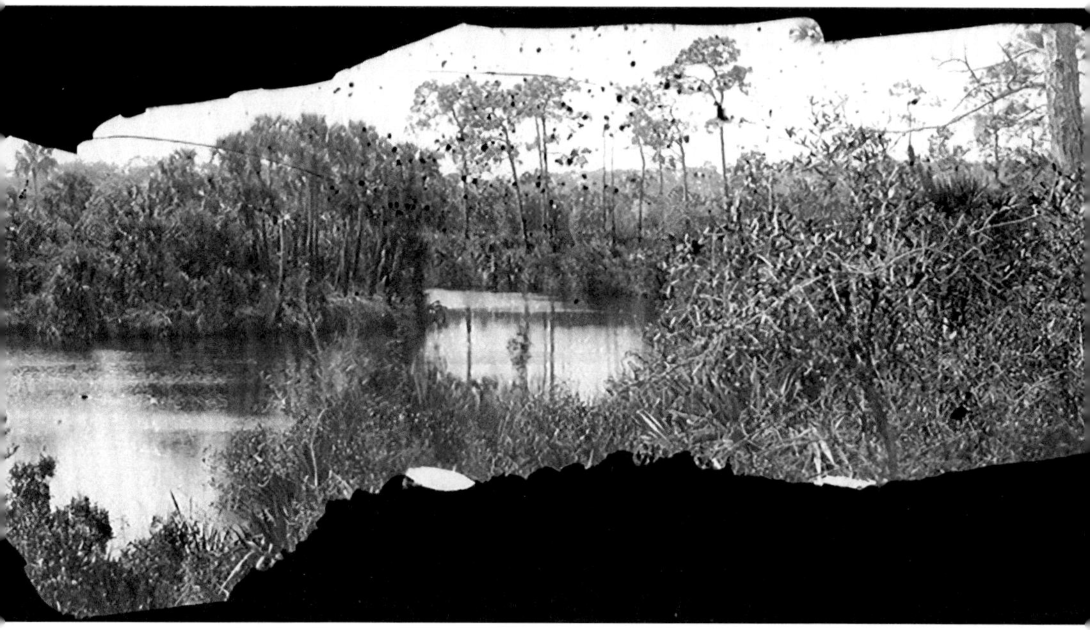

1 St. Sebastian River (RK)

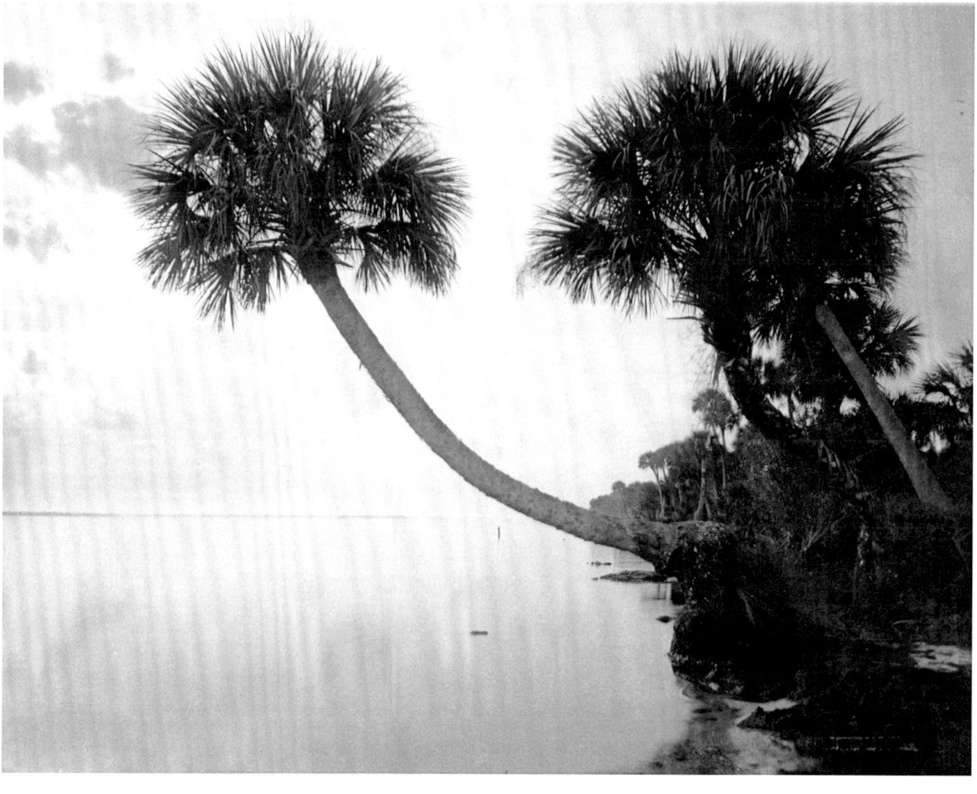

2 Palmettos, 1880s (WHJ)

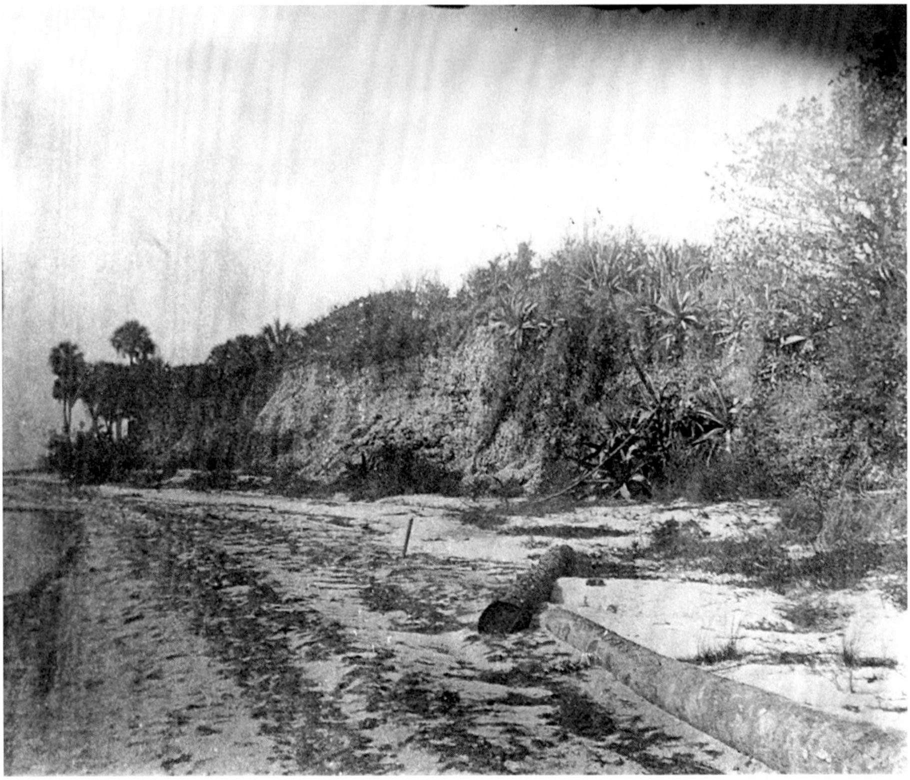

Above: 3 Barkers Bluff, 1900s (RK)

Below: 4 1715 survivors' camp marker (EES)

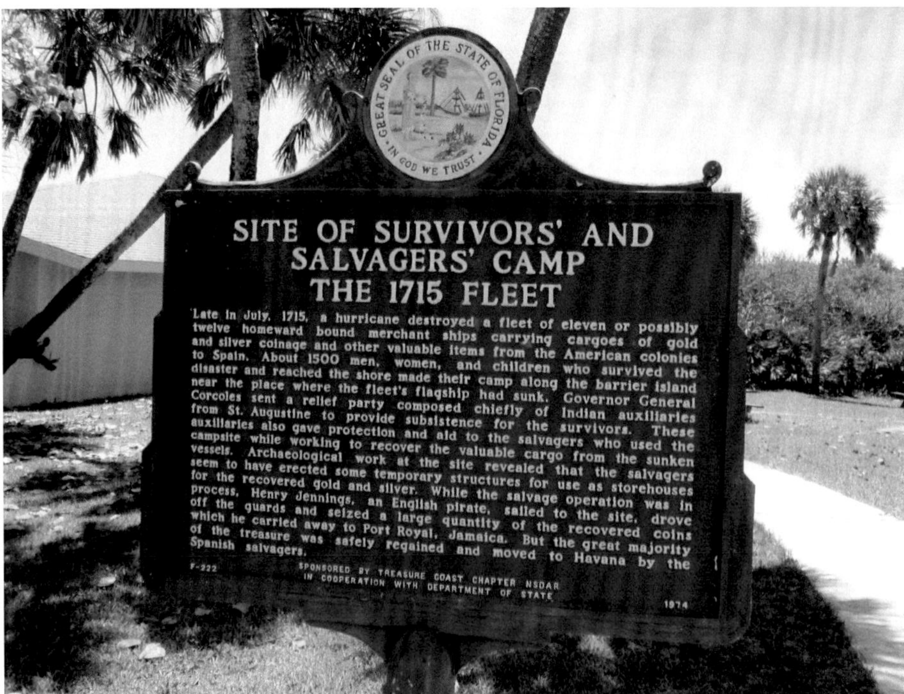

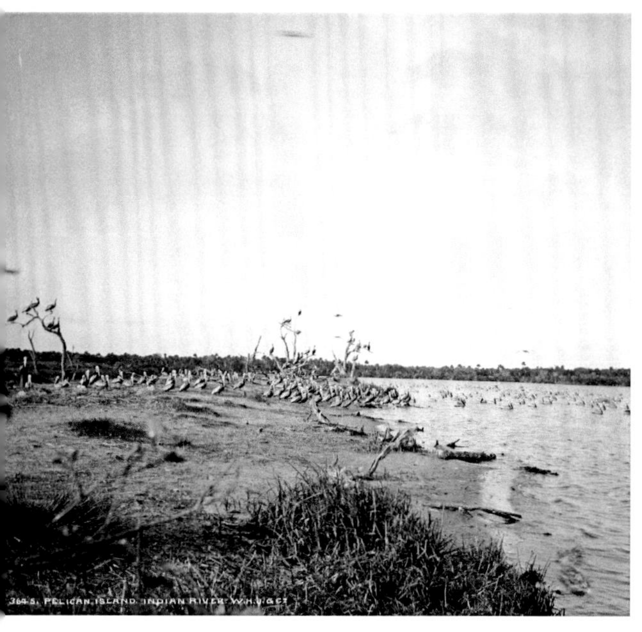

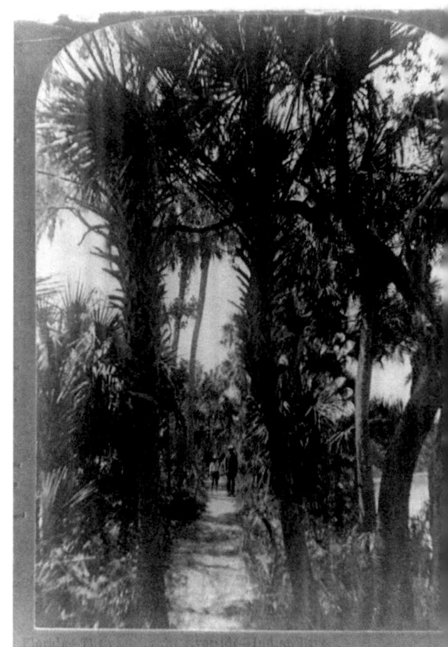

Above left: 5 Pelican Island, 1880s (WHJ)

Above right: 6 Path by the Indian River (GB)

Below: 7 Palm trees on the river (AC)

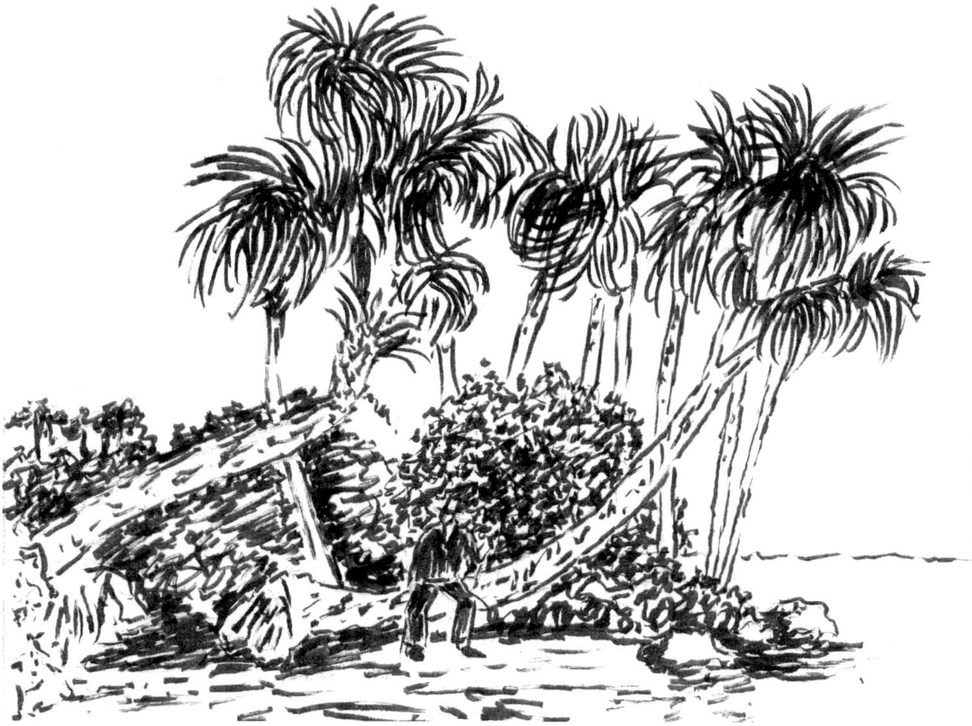

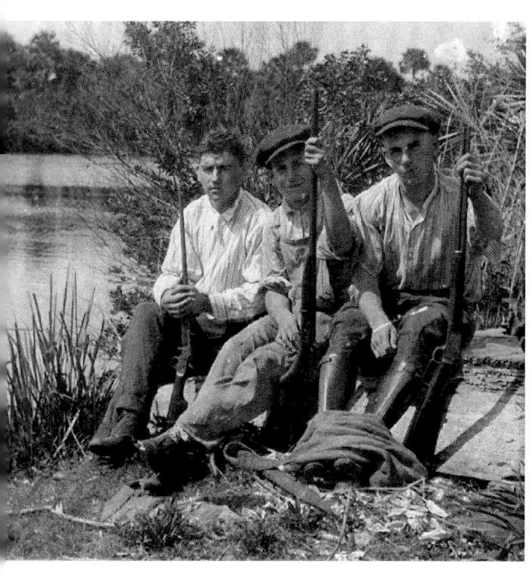

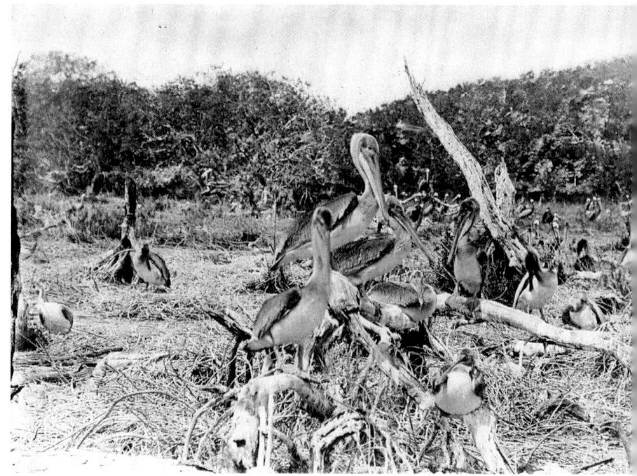

Above left: 8 Pioneer spirit (RK)

Above right: 9 Pelicans, Pelican Island (RK)

Below left: 10 Prohibition—not for everyone! (RK)

Below right: 11 Charles F. Gottlob Kroegel land patent, 1889 (GLO)

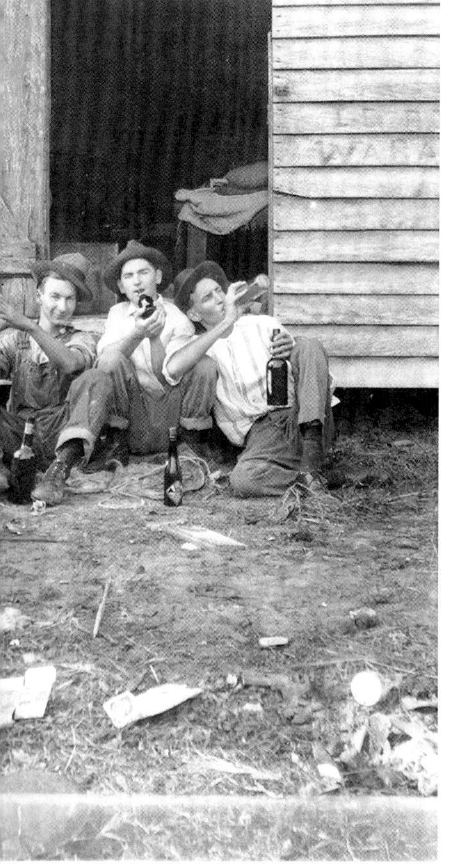

301

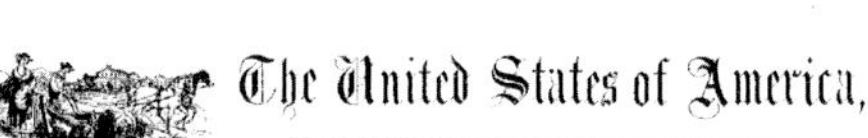

The United States of America,

TO ALL TO WHOM THESE PRESENTS SHALL COME, GREETING:

Homestead Certificate No. 6387
Application 10633

Whereas there has been deposited in the GENERAL LAND OFFICE of the United States a CERTIFICATE of the Register of the Land Office at Gainesville, Florida whereby it appears that, pursuant to the Act of Congress approved 20th May, 1862, "To secure Homesteads to actual settlers on the public domain," and the acts supplemental thereto, the claim of Charles F. G. Kroegel has been established and duly consummated in conformity to law for the Lots numbered one, two, three and four of section eight in township thirty-one south of range thirty-nine east of Tallahassee Meridian in Florida containing one hundred and forty three acres and eighteen hundredths of an acre

according to the Official Plat of the Survey of the said Land returned to the GENERAL LAND OFFICE by the SURVEYOR GENERAL.

Now know ye, That there is therefore granted by the UNITED STATES unto the said Charles F. G. Kroegel the tract of Land above described; TO HAVE AND TO HOLD the said tract of Land, with the appurtenances thereof, unto the said Charles F. G. Kroegel and to his heirs and assigns forever.

In testimony whereof I, Benjamin Harrison President of the United States of America, have caused these letters to be made Patent, and the Seal of the General Land Office to be hereunto affixed.

Given under my hand, at the City of Washington, the twenty-first day of June, in the year of Our Lord one thousand eight hundred and eighty nine, and of the Independence of the United States the one hundred and thirteenth.

L. S.

By the President: Benjamin Harrison

By M. McKean Sec'y.

J. M. Townsend, Recorder of the General Land Office.

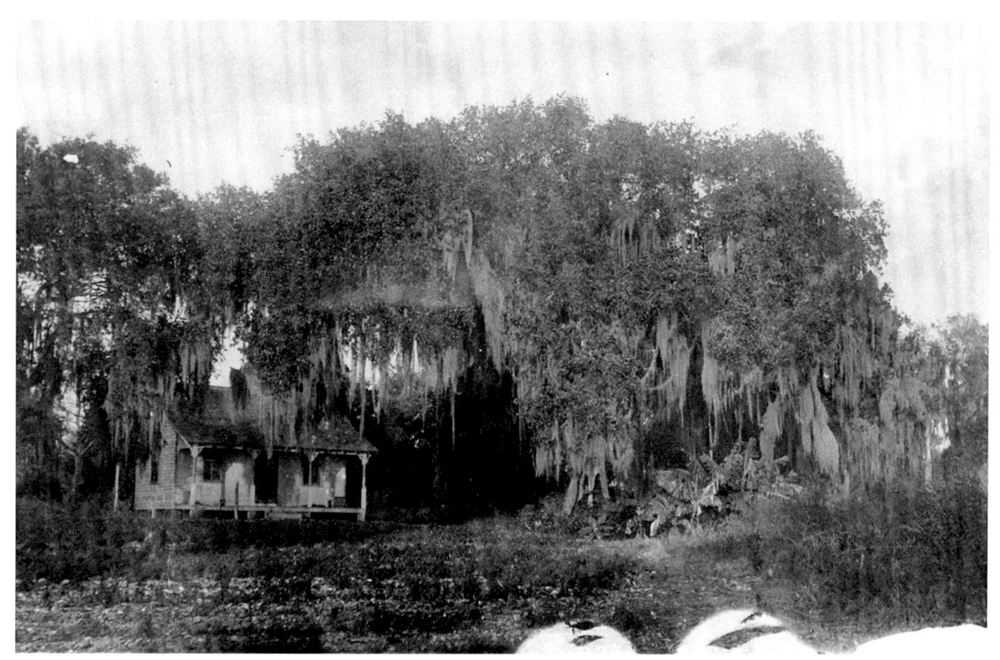

12 Charles F. Gottlob Kroegel home on Barkers Bluff (RK)

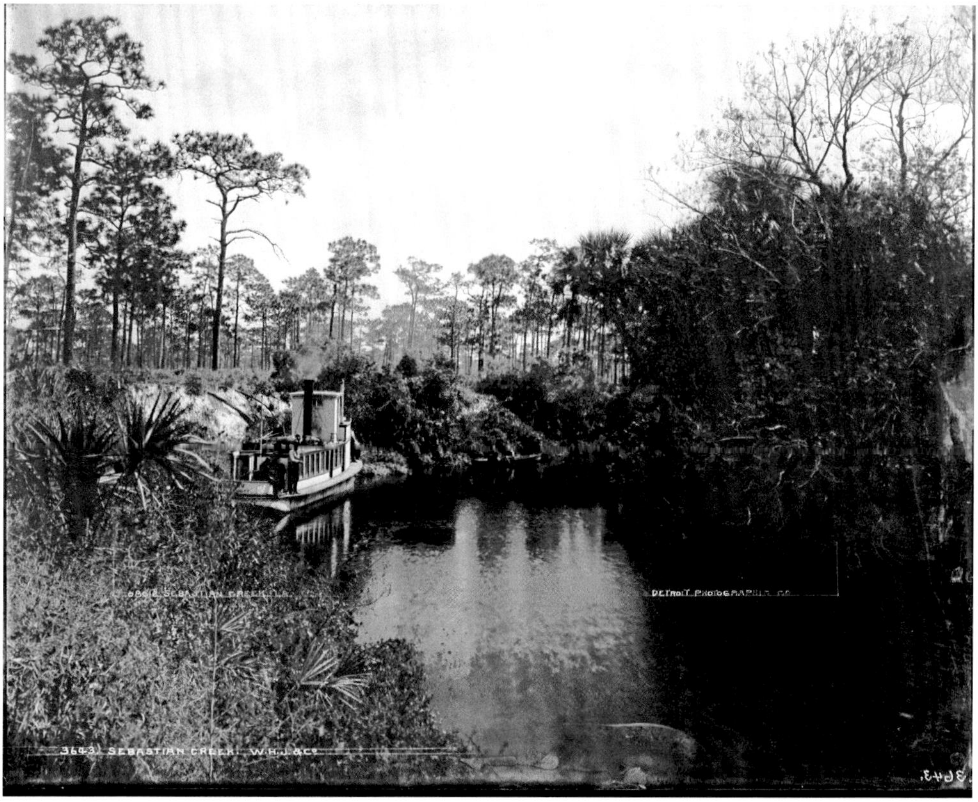

13 Sebastian Creek, Sebastian and steamboat *Cleo*, 1880s (WHJ)

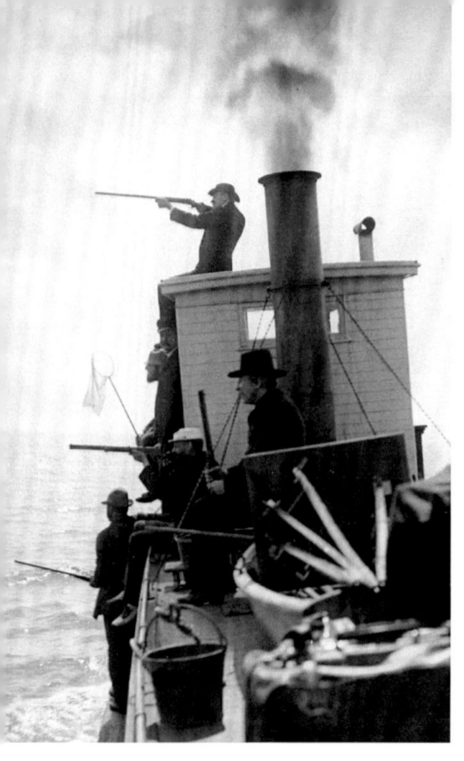

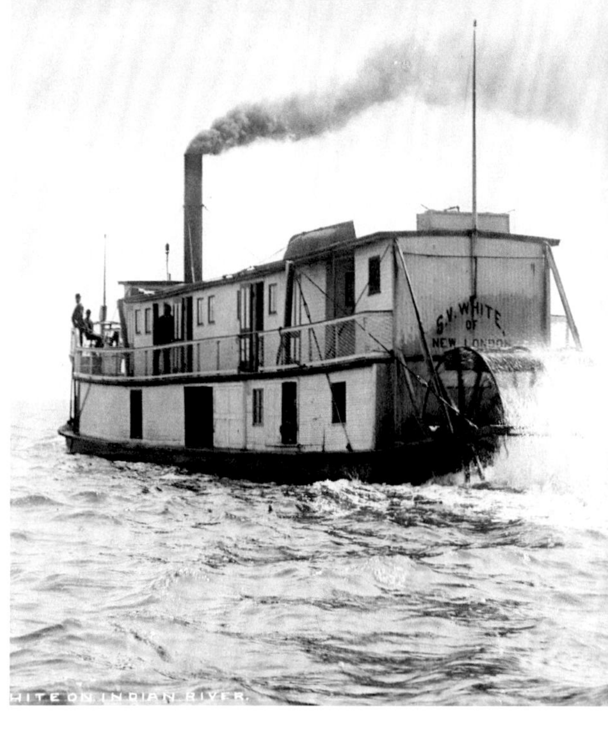

Above left: 14 Duck shooting on Indian River, steamboat *Cleo*, 1880s (WHJ)

Above right: 15 Steamboat *SV White* on Indian River, 1880s (WHJ)

Below: 16 Kroegels and Lawsons gathering holly (RK)

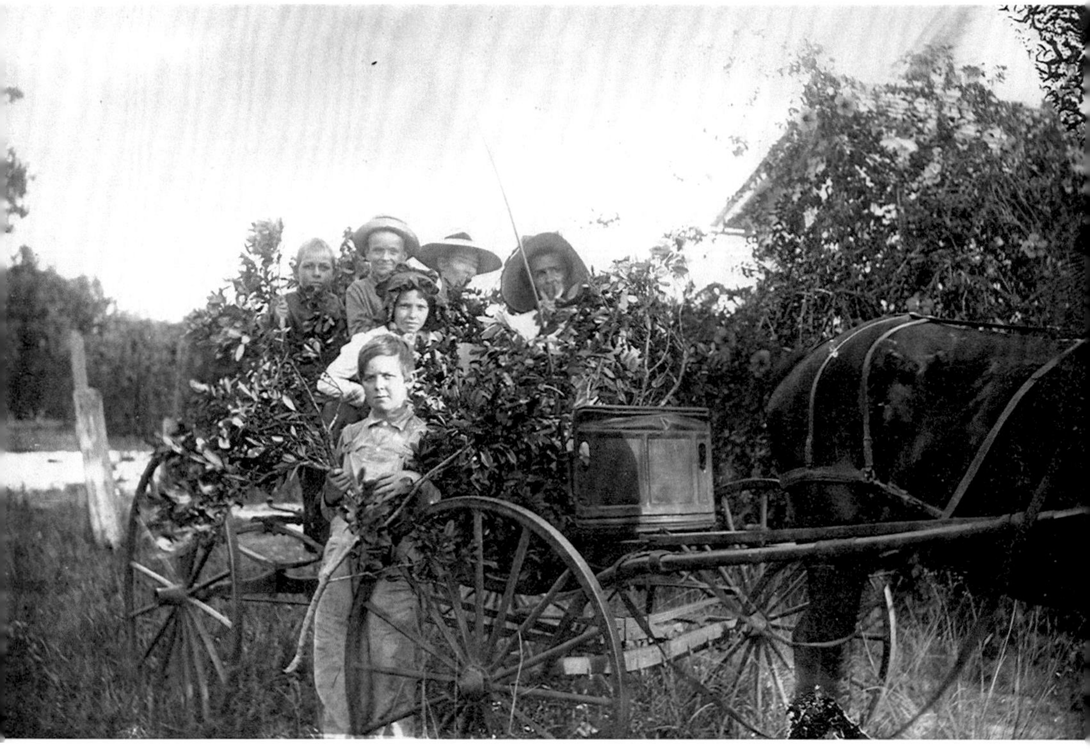

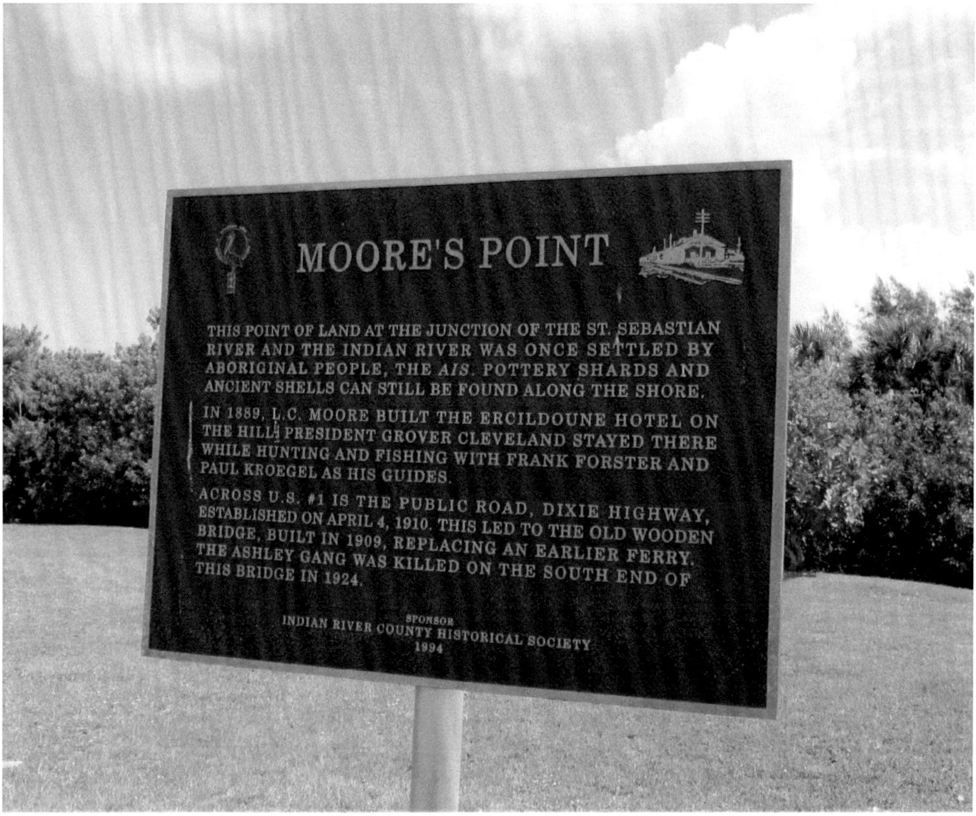

17 Moore's point marker (EES)

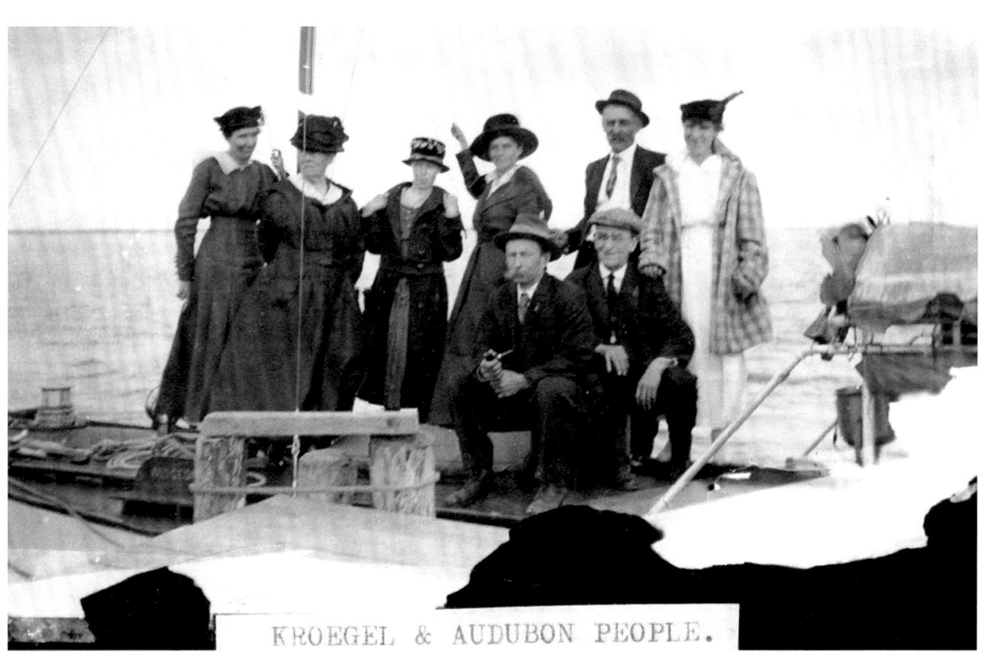

18 Paul Kroegel and Audubon people, 1900s (RK)

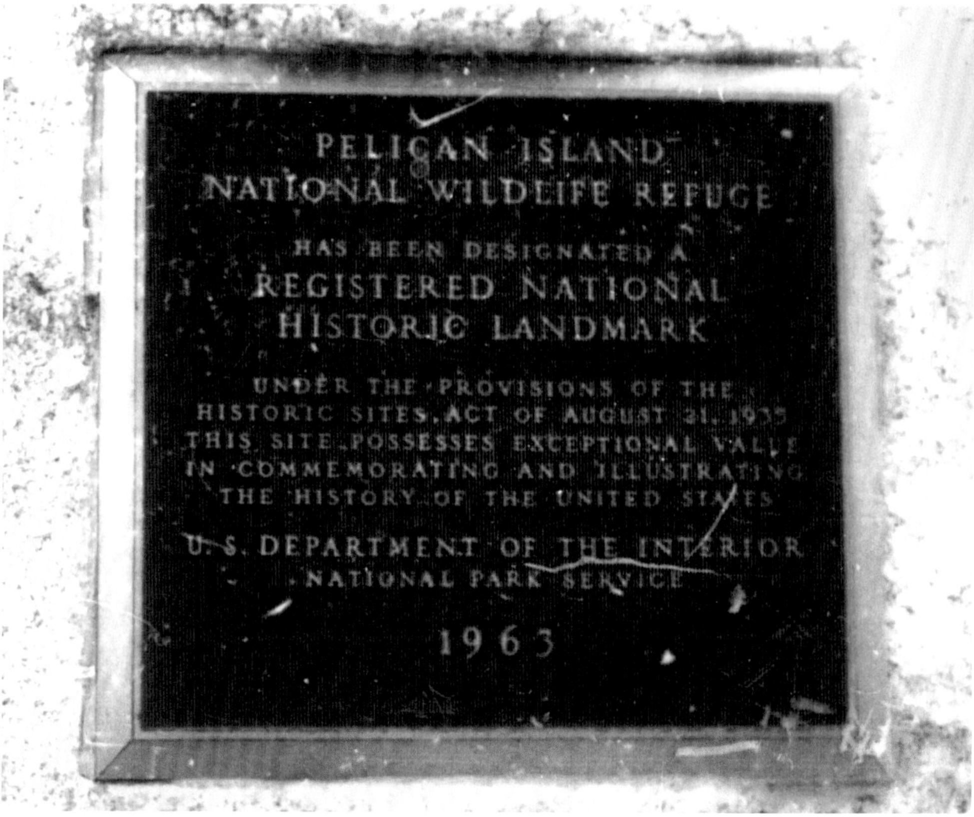

PELICAN ISLAND
NATIONAL WILDLIFE REFUGE
HAS BEEN DESIGNATED A
REGISTERED NATIONAL
HISTORIC LANDMARK
UNDER THE PROVISIONS OF THE
HISTORIC SITES ACT OF AUGUST 21, 1935
THIS SITE POSSESSES EXCEPTIONAL VALUE
IN COMMEMORATING AND ILLUSTRATING
THE HISTORY OF THE UNITED STATES
U.S. DEPARTMENT OF THE INTERIOR
NATIONAL PARK SERVICE
1963

19 Pelican Island marker (RK)

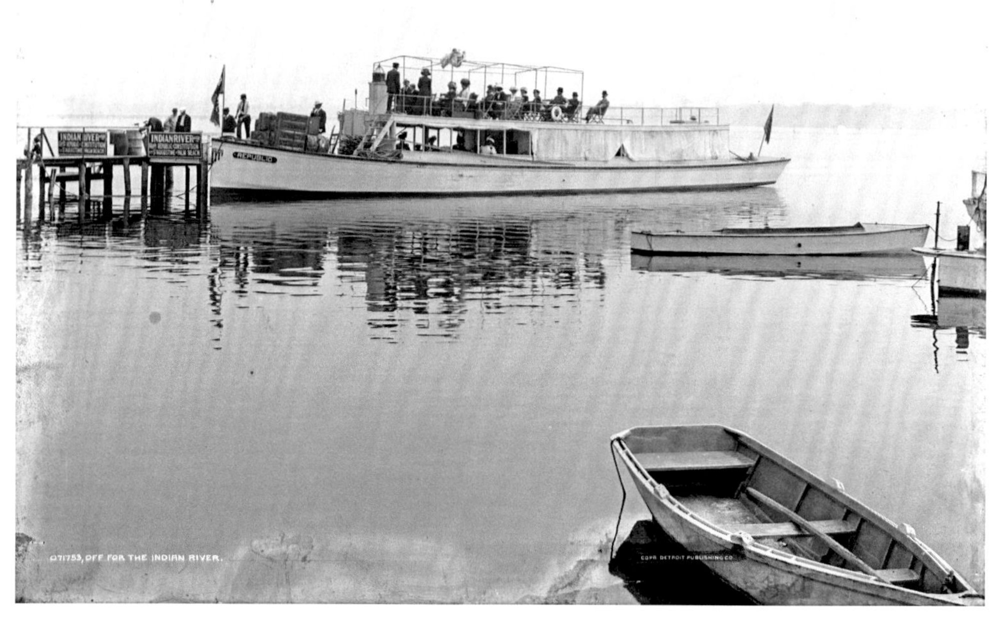

20 Off for the Indian River, 1880s (LOC)

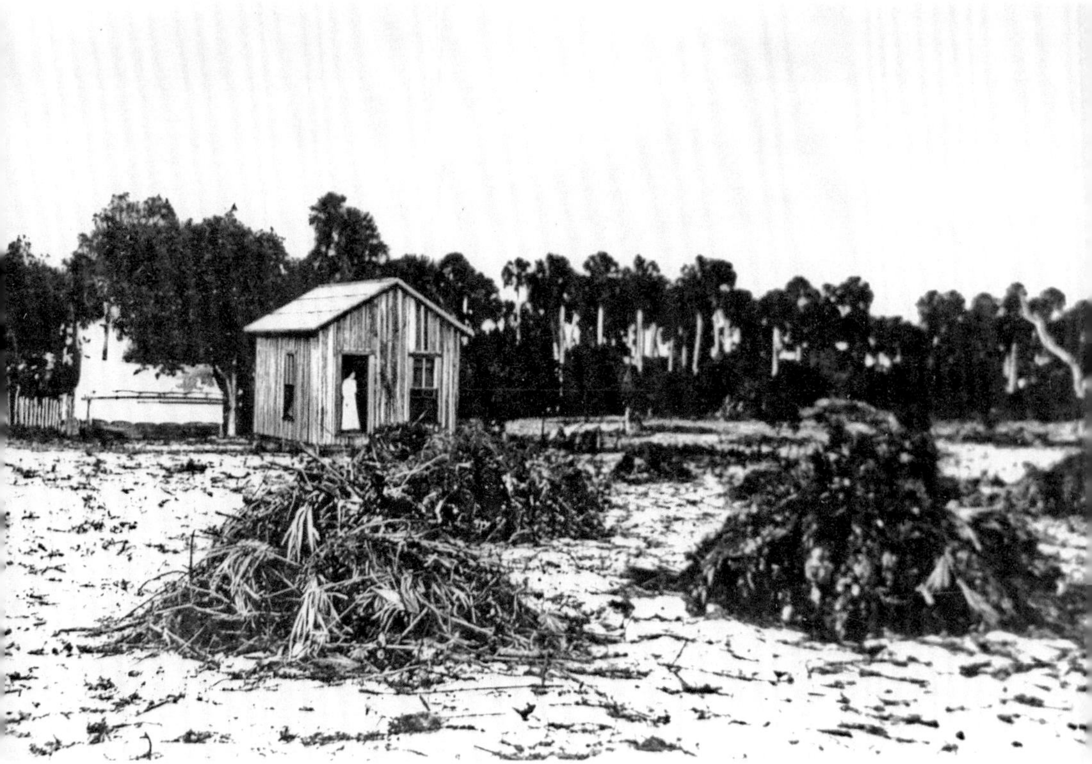

21 Gaffney home, 1900s (RK)

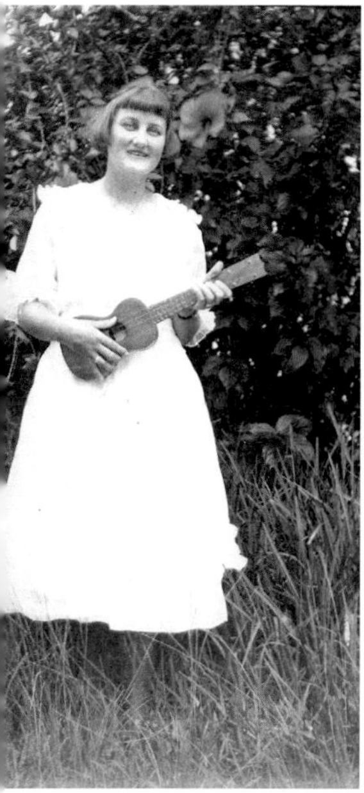

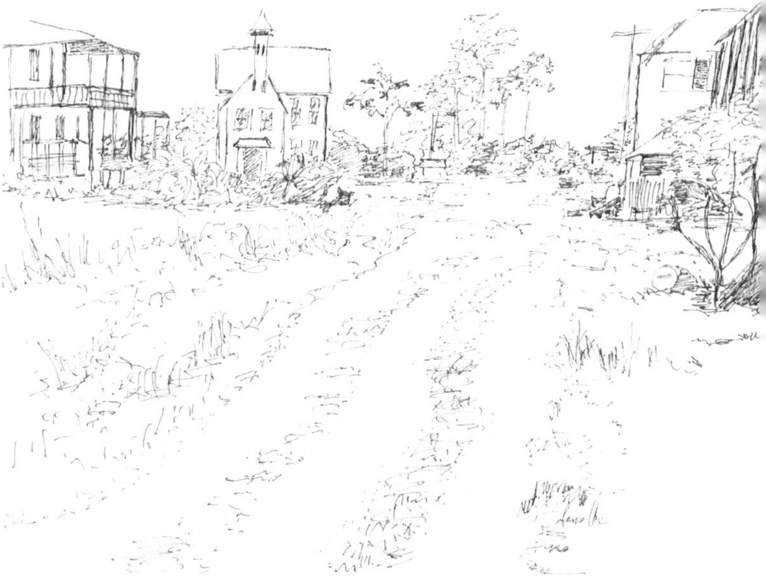

Above left: 22 Lucy Yongue with ukulele (RK)

Above right: 23 Main Street Sebastian looking west c. 1912 (AC)

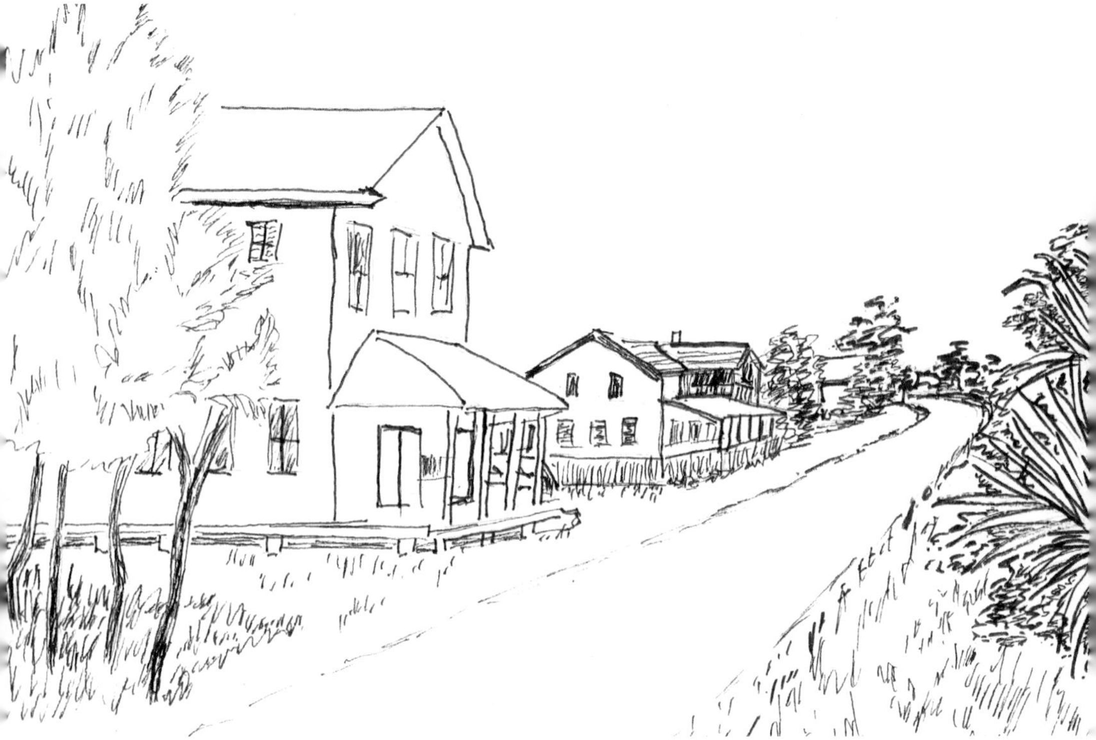

24 Central Avenue Sebastian looking north c. 1920 (AC)

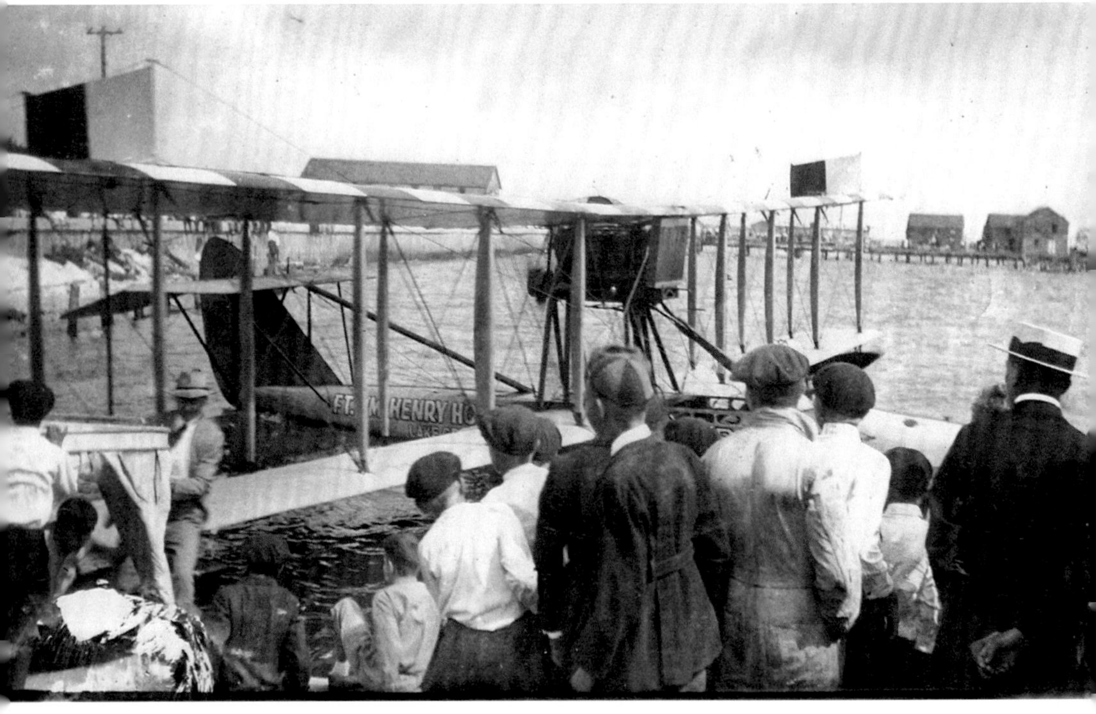

25 Aeromarine Flying Boat, 1923 (RK)

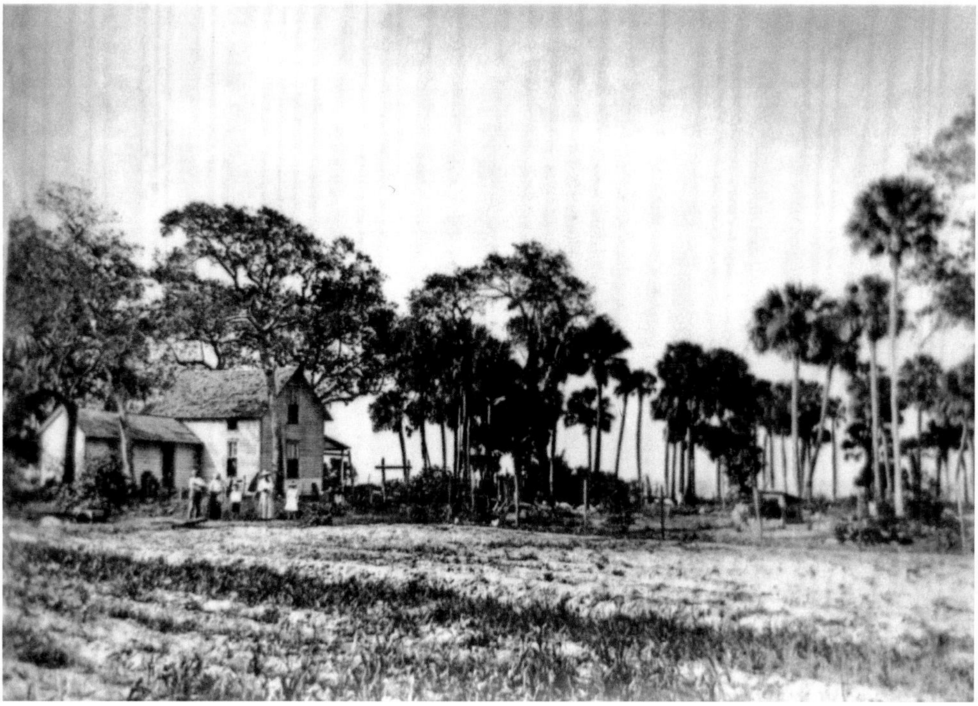

26 O. A. Hartman home, 1910s (RK)

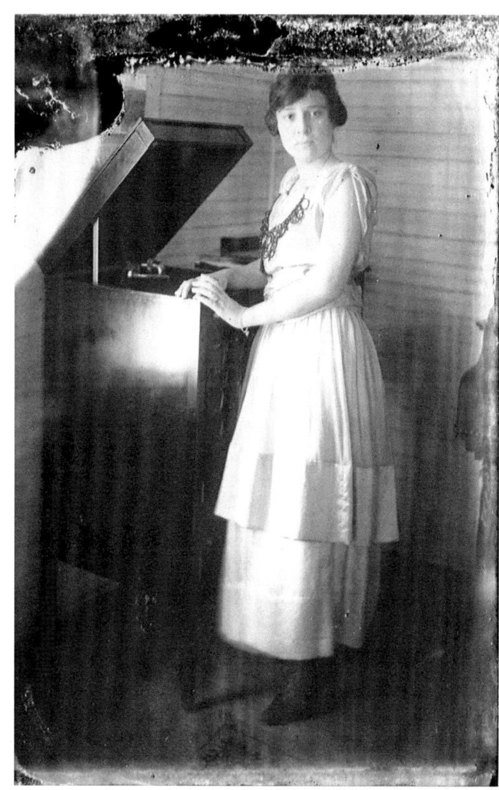

27 Mattie Hicks with record player (RK)

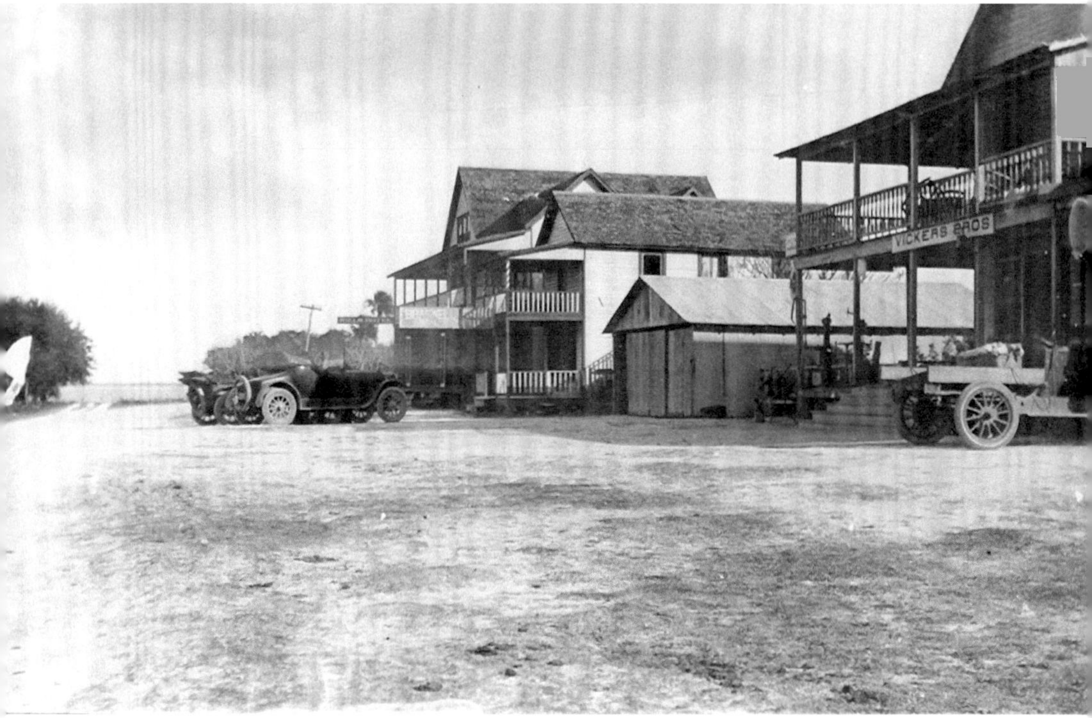

28 Vickers Store, Main Street Sebastian, 1920s (RK)

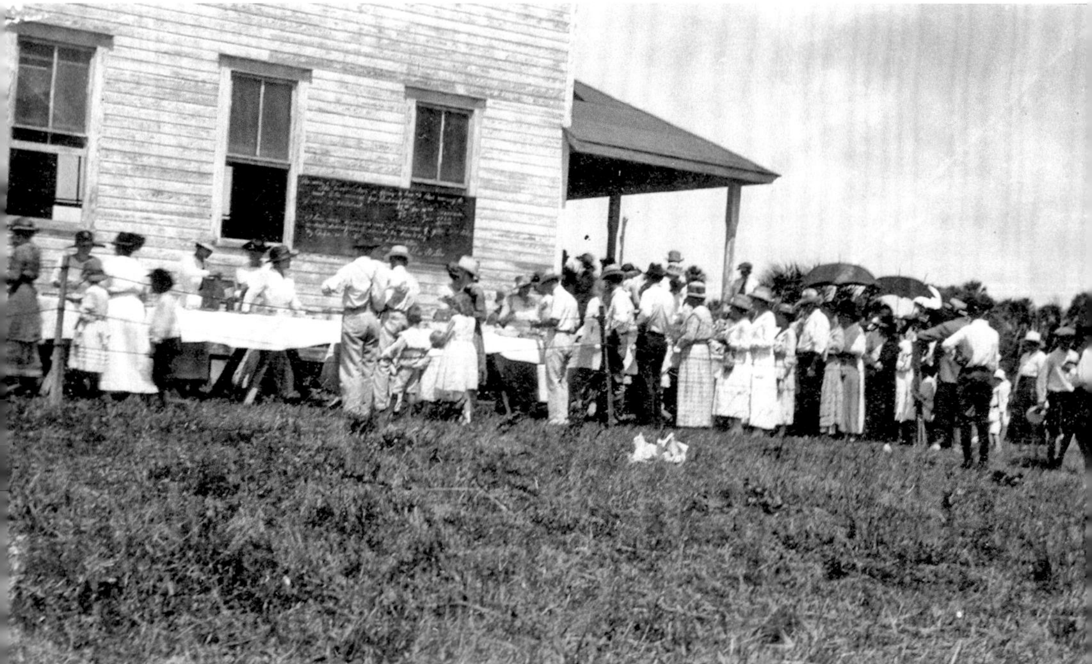

29 Political rally at City Hall, Sebastian, 1920s (RK)

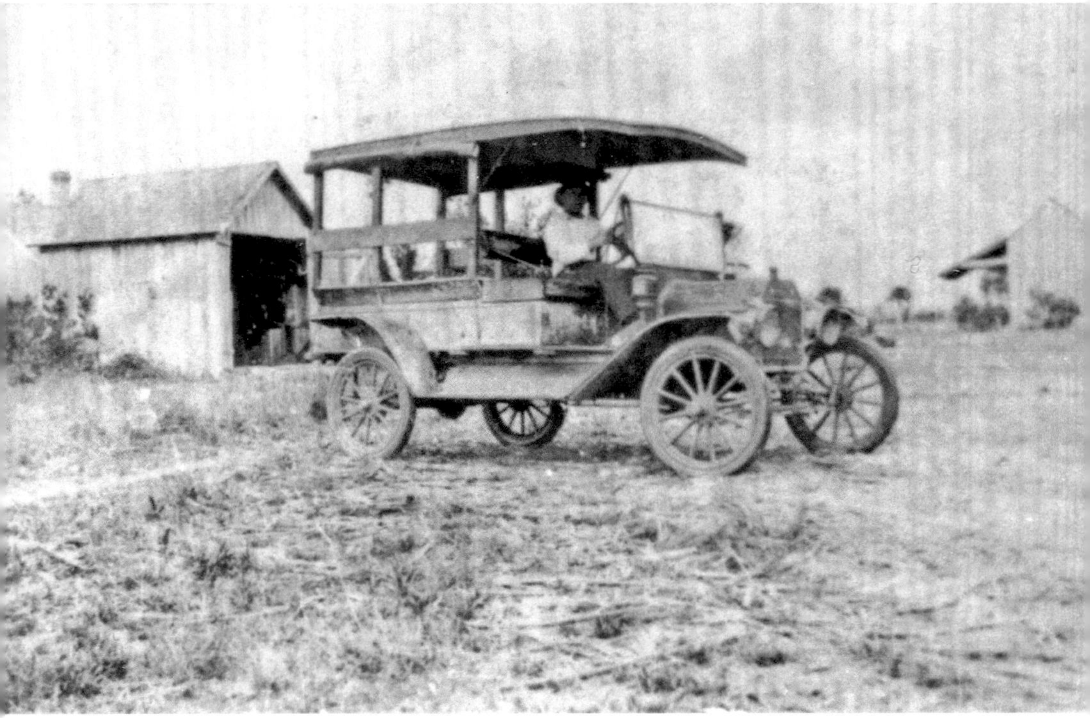

30 Rodney Kroegel with Model T delivery truck, 1920s (RK)

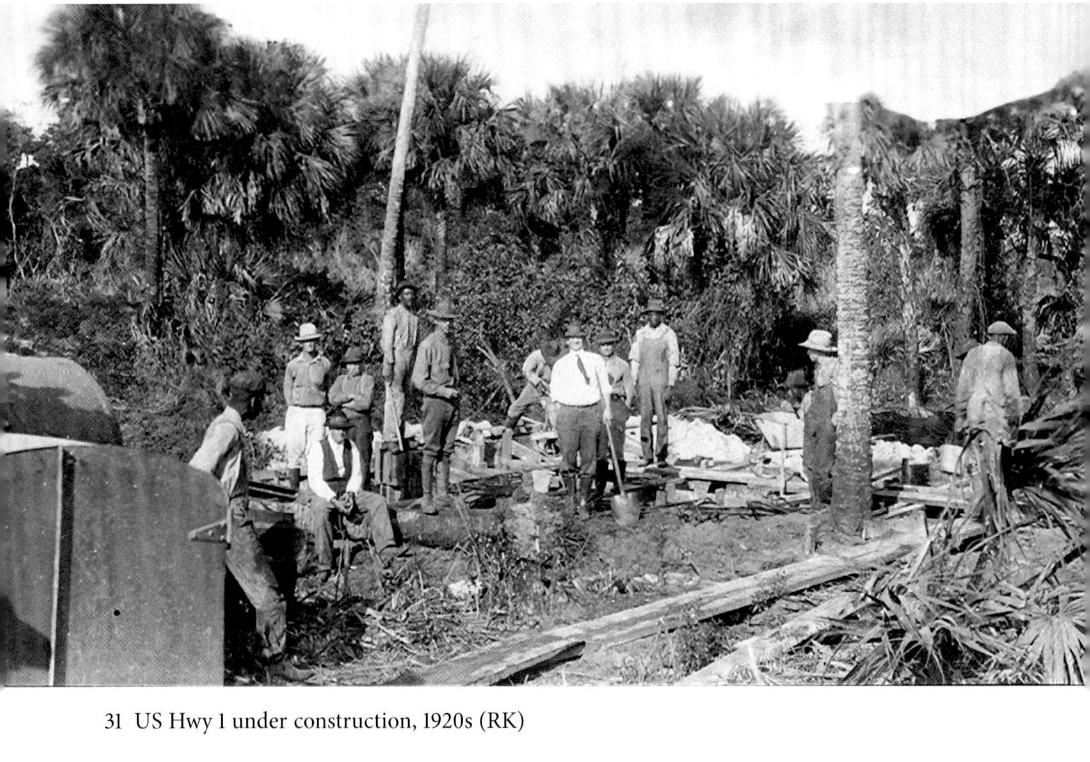

31 US Hwy 1 under construction, 1920s (RK)

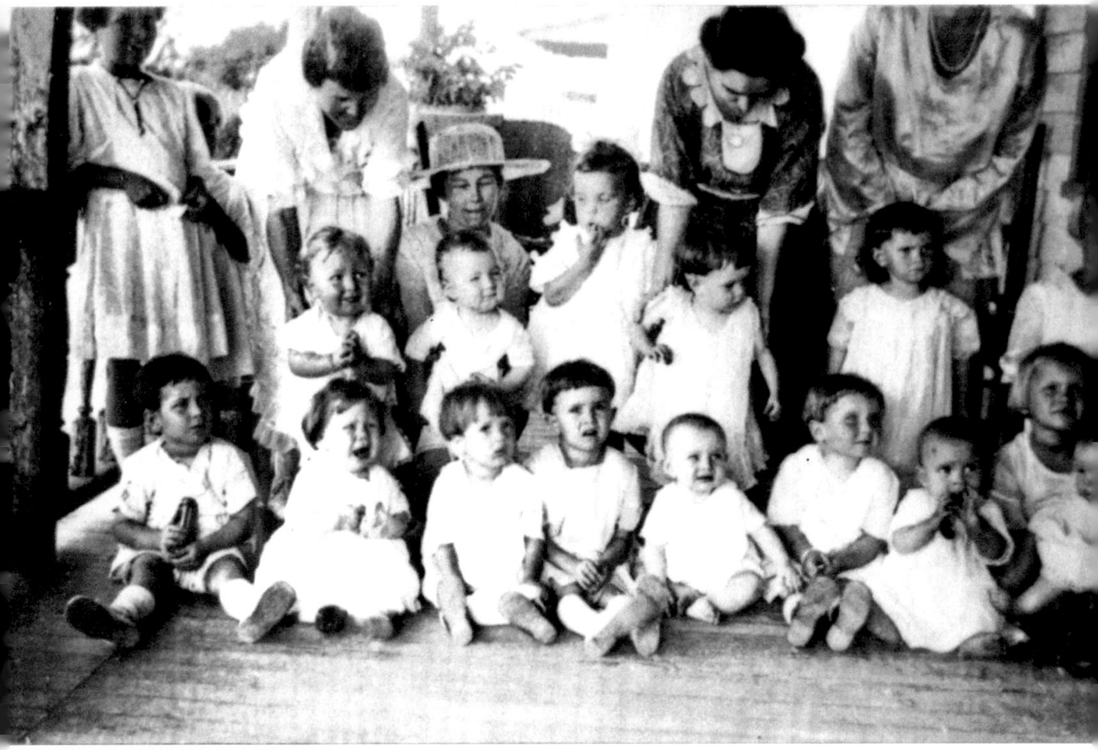

32 No wonder the population was growing! (RK)

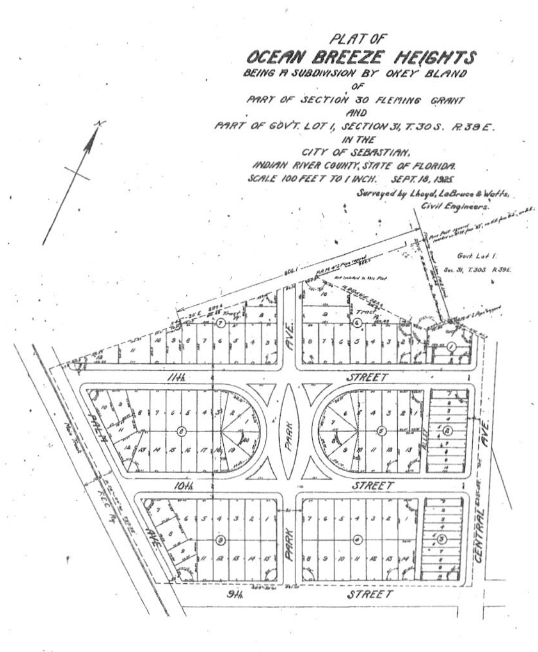

33 Plat map of Ocean Breeze Heights subdivision, Sebastian, 1925 (OBH)

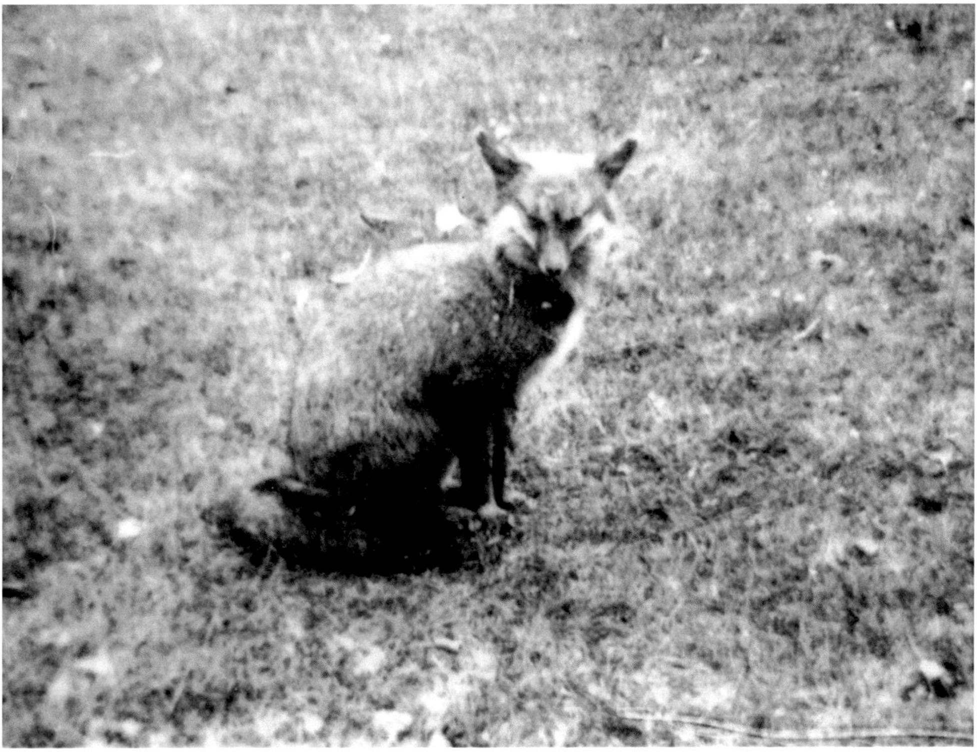

34 A pet fox (RK)

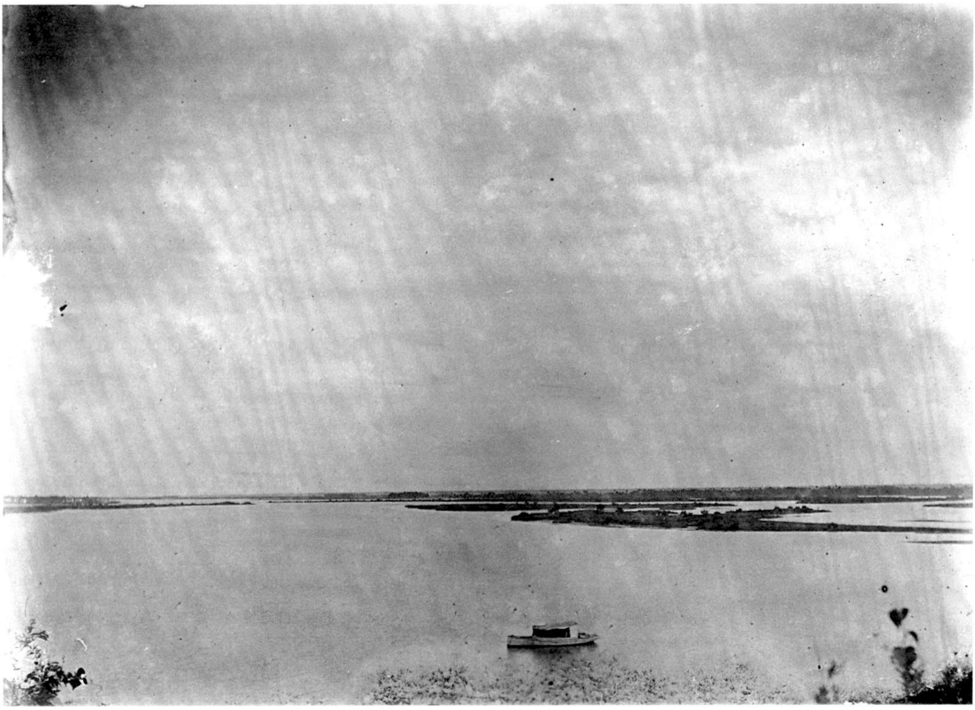

35 Indian River (RK)

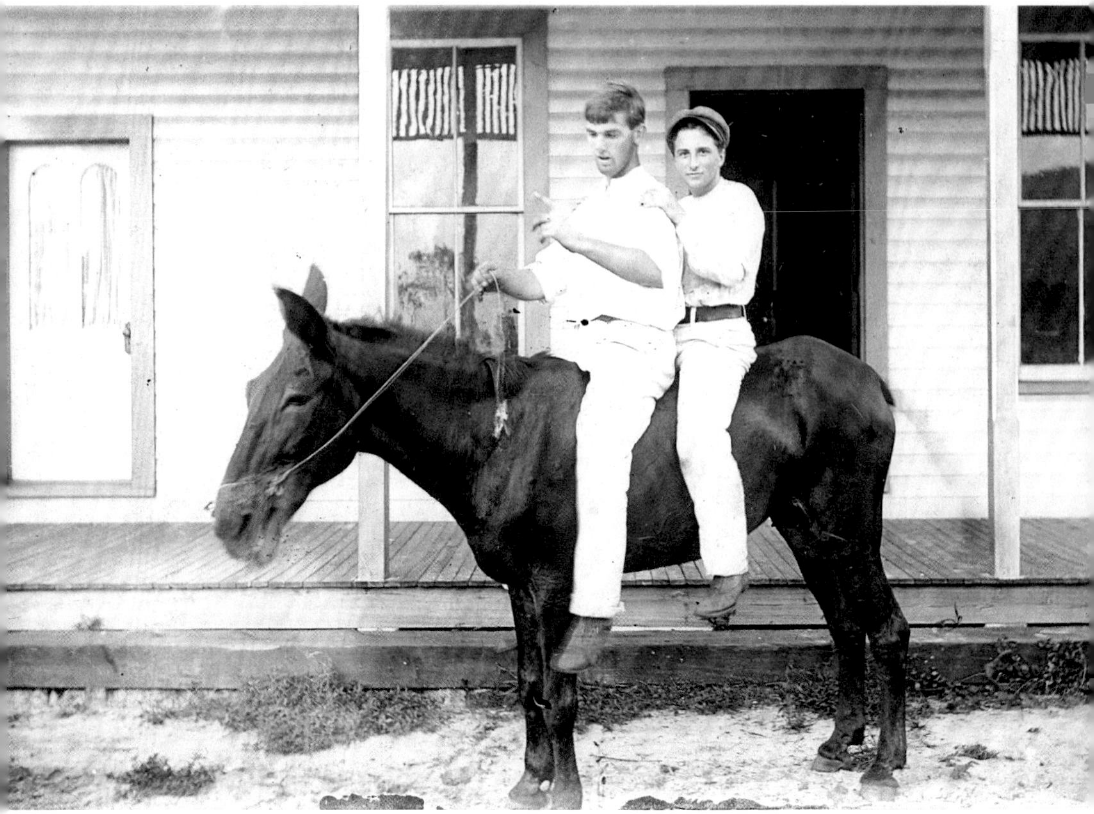

Above: 36 Wells and Middleton on a mule (RK)

Below left: 37 Dixie Highway along the Indian River (AC)

Below right: 38 Sebastian Creek (AC)

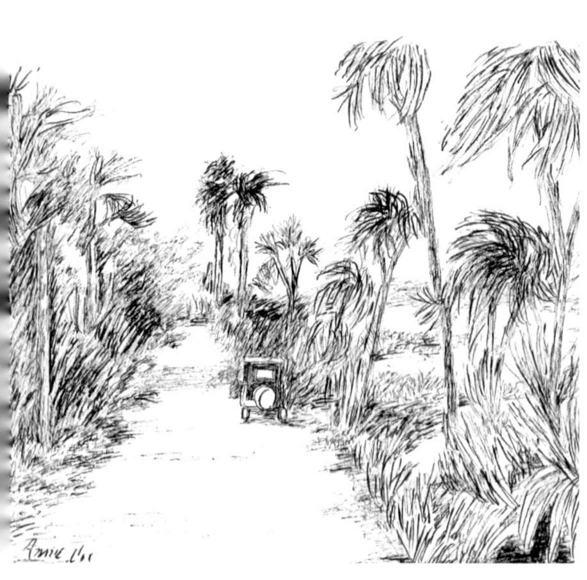

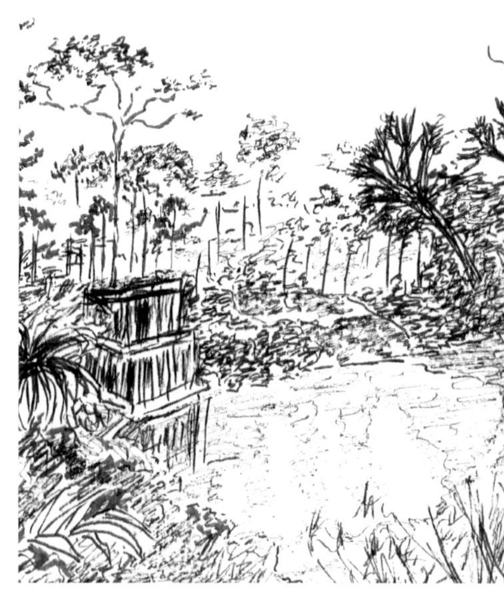

Company began purchasing Florida timberland and turpentining. They created a subsidiary company, Florida Pine Company, instead of leasing the work to independent contractors. Florida Pine Company was incorporated on July 17, 1907. This proved to be a very profitable venture for Consolidated, as convicts were subleased to do the work, considerably cutting costs. Florida Pine Company continued to operate until it was dissolved June 4, 1936. A state bill providing that all counties would work their convicts on the roads, and prohibiting their lease, did not pass in 1911; however, the leasing system was abolished in Florida in 1918. Florida was one of the last states to abolish this practice due to its financial success. The convict lease system was repealed in Florida, although not all counties stopped the practice until 1923.

Other changes were made during the term of Governor Sidney J. Catts. He made attending school compulsory. A licensing system for teachers was put into place. In September 1915, examinations were given in Fort Pierce for the licensing of teachers. Also under Catt's term, counties received financial aid for road and bridge construction. On November 18, 1918, a temporary war-time prohibition to save grain went into effect. After WWI, state growth and the economy were dominant issues. In December 1919, Florida held a very successful State Fair Expo in Jacksonville.

Nationwide entertainment was alive and growing. Daily attendance at moving picture shows reached 25 million in the United States according to estimates reported in the *Ft. Pierce News* in December 1917. Another state-wide issue in 1918, an influenza epidemic erupted in the state, mainly centered in Jacksonville. Within four weeks, 30,000 contracted the disease, and 464 died. It returned in 1919 with 621 cases and 64 deaths.

St. Lucie County

Fort Pierce, the county seat, was the largest town in St. Lucie County and the first to incorporate, in 1901. On May 17, 1909, a new county courthouse was voted upon by the county commissioners under chairman Paul Kroegel; the contract was let, and purchasing of materials was begun by July 2, 1909, according to the *St. Lucie Tribune*. It would have every modern convenience. The county expended over $50,000 in Fort Pierce on the impressive courthouse and jail near the center of the city overlooking the Indian River. Fort Pierce spent $100,000 in municipal waterworks, an electric light plant, sewerage, and several miles of street paving and cement walks, which were laid by 1912. The Florida East Coast Railway determined to make Fort Pierce the center for repair work for its southern division from Fort Pierce to Key West. It built a new large depot at Fort Pierce, extending the yards and enlarging the round house and repair shops over 30 acres of land. Employees moved to Fort Pierce for the convenience. Fort Pierce population jumped fivefold by the middle of the decade.

By 1913, ushering in the real estate boom in the county, four significant residential and farm communities had been planned by out-of-state developers. Fort Pierce

Farms started in 1910 northwest of Fort Pierce. St. Lucie Gardens at Walton was next developed by the Franklin Land Company and the Coldron Land Company. Fellsmere followed with its town, farms, and gardens. Indian River Farms Company in Vero was flourishing. Extensive promotion and advertising was undertaken to stimulate growth. White City, four miles southwest of Fort Pierce, began as a center for truck farming, followed by more truck farms directly west of the city, after the railroad company had started the work of drainage. Citrus and the fishing industry were prominent ventures throughout the county.

The work of the Indian River Farms Company in 1915 provided a surprise; the digging of the Indian River Farms Company drainage canals in Vero uncovered human skeletons of the early Pleistocene era, as well as many extinct species of a variety of animals that stimulated scientific interest.

St. Lucie voted "dry" on the prohibition issue, even before it became national and Florida law. Some alternatives to hard liquor were offered, such as in an ad in the *Fellsmere Tribune* that ran in 1916 for "Paloma," touted as being a new, non-alcoholic, non-intoxicating sparkling bottled beverage. The advertisement stated that it was made from wheat, corn and rye, not malt, with no narcotics, chemicals, or flavoring extracts, and it was not medicated or compounded. It sold for 15 cents a bottle. The beverage does not seem to have become popular.

The convict leasing camps continued in St. Lucie County in this decade, although public opinion was changing. Convicts were beginning to be leased for road work, rather than work in turpentining. In St. Lucie County, bids were opened for the hire of county convicts for road work, and F. E. Bridges' bid was accepted for the term of one year by the county commissioners in February of 1910. On July 15, 1910, the *St. Lucie Tribune* reported that some convicted gamblers were sent to Roseland convict camp for 90 days. A man convicted of the illegal sale of liquor was put to work on the roads. Florida Pine Company's bid for the leasing of convicts was accepted in 1911 by St. Lucie County commissioners.

Sebastian

Sebastian was maturing as a town in the 1910s. Its population was 323. Its attractive downtown area included several stores: Kitching's, Vickers', Tompkins', and Harvey Deal's stores. It also included a post office with Maude Park as postmistress, Sembler's Boarding House, Sebastian Hotel, Palm House, the Grove Hotel, and a Board of Trade. It built a town hall, which held dances, plays, committee meetings, and silent films. Sloan's added a grocery and hotel in 1919. There was a school and two churches, Methodist and Baptist. Other civilizing services were Vickers' Sebastian Garage, Gaffney's barrel factory, Southern Bottling Works and Sebastian Bottling Works. There was Taylor's barbershop and Baughman's dairy. A medical doctor, Dr. Rose, was in residence, but there was still no dentist. For dental work, it was necessary to travel to Fort Pierce, or to Dr. Wilcox in Roseland, in 1911. Mrs. R. G. Hardee had to go to the hospital in Jacksonville in February of 1916 for appendicitis, a problem too complicated for local medical treatment. The Sebastian National Loan Association formed. The major streets were Main Street, Palmetto Street, Louisiana Avenue, and Central Avenue. More streets and homes were being added as land was platted and subdivided. The railroad ran trains west to Eureka and the developing communities of Fellsmere and Broadmoor, and the Florida East Coast Railway ran through north-south. The train depot held a telegraph office. Along the Indian River were many fish houses, Hardee's Packing House, and an ice house. In the surrounding area were many groves, farms, and cattle ranches. Storch Brothers of Chicago owned a Sebastian packing house in 1919. M. M. Miller ran the Square Deal Nursery.

Hotels

Sebastian offered many choices for lodging. The Grove Hotel and Palm House remained popular with travelers, as did the former Carlisle House, now operated by Sembler. More hotels were added.

Sebastian Hotel 1910s

The Sebastian Hotel was a two-story wooden building built in June 1912 that stood on the northwest corner of Central Avenue (US Hwy 1) facing Main Street, north of the post office. A dance was given in the new hotel that month, according to the *Fellsmere Farmer*. That newspaper reported in February 1913 that Mr. and Mrs. Arnold of Sebastian were the owners of the Sebastian Hotel, but that they had moved to Fellsmere and would devote all their time to the Fellsmere Inn, which was sold to them by the Fellsmere Farms Company. The Sebastian Hotel may have become the Mills Hotel, which was owned by Robert G. Mills around 1915 and closed after four or five years in business. The Mills Hotel was then purchased by George Wise in 1919. Subsequent directories in 1920-1922, however, list George Wise as the proprietor of the Sebastian Hotel. In 1928, the Sebastian Hotel burned to the ground.

Idlewild Inn, Mills Hotel, and the Hammons

Robert G. Mills made a brief splash on the hotel scene in the local area when he arrived around 1912, then vanished again six or eight years later. His life was perhaps typical of the rapidly changing fortunes of the times. The Fellsmere Inn, built around 1910-1911, was first managed by Mrs. Harris, who resigned in February of 1912. Robert G. Mills of Roseland took over as manager on February 21, 1912, and began renovating and advertising the Inn's lodging and meals for visitors. He quit as manager in September of that year. He purchased land in Roseland from A. A. Berry in 1913. Mills made plans to open a restaurant in the building previously occupied by Tompkins Store in May of 1913. In October of 1913, the Idlewild Inn in Sebastian was under the management of R. G. Mills, who hosted parties and receptions there through 1914. In 1916-1918, he was manager of the Mills Hotel and its restaurant in Sebastian, running advertisements for it in the *Fellsmere Tribune*. It is not clear whether the Idlewild Inn and Mills Hotel were new buildings, or revamping of another existing hotel. Newspapers, usually quick to herald a new establishment, were silent on this. Robert G. Mills was next heard of in the 1920 census, where he was a single 48-year-old Virginian and manager of the Mills House in Eau Gallie, Florida.

Mr. and Mrs. Eugene Hammon improved their home on Sebastian Avenue in 1916, adding a cottage hotel with ten to twelve guest rooms and porches around the whole house.

Stores

Choice of shopping venues was also expanded. The Kitching store, begun in the 1880s, was still in operation, and remained open until 1925. Braddock's also continued. Several others were added.

Sebastian Mercantile Company

The W. C. Braddock one-room store, the Sebastian Mercantile Company, burned down, but was rebuilt. In June of 1910, his branch store in Fellsmere was one of the first buildings there. In 1910, he put an addition on the Sebastian Mercantile Co. with lumber from Miller & King. The store ran advertisements in the *St. Lucie Tribune* in the 1910s. In September of 1910, it read, "Sebastian Mercantile Co., W. C. Braddock, Prop. Having recently added an addition to our building, we are now getting a large assortment in every line: New Dry Goods, New Groceries, New Hardware. The needs of the people of Sebastian and vicinity have been anticipated and our stock will meet the wants of the people. All goods are guaranteed. Your patronage is solicited. Sebastian, Florida." In 1911, he had new lighting installed by A. B. Lowry of Fort Pierce, and later that year, added a soda fountain.

W. C. Braddock

William C. Braddock Jr.'s two-story brick house was built in 1919 by the Wise Brothers, who were Wabasso contractors, with materials from the Cocoa area. It still remains in downtown Sebastian on US Hwy 1. It is unique as it was the only brick house in Sebastian, the only one with a cellar, and the first with a refrigeration unit. It is one of the noted properties listed in Old Town Sebastian Historic District East on the National Register of Historic Places. William Braddock died in 1940, and wife Kate died in 1948.

Vickers Brothers Stores

George and Frank Vickers worked together on many enterprises while living in Sebastian. They took over the Braddock stores in Sebastian and Fellsmere. At one time Vickers Bros. hauled shell for roads. They purchased groves and also sold real estate, notably in the Vickers Subdivision in downtown Sebastian, platted in 1913.

The Braddock Sebastian Mercantile Co. stores were acquired by the Vickers, and became the Vickers Brothers stores, owned by Frank and George Vickers. All three brothers, George, Frank and Everett, were managers at one time or another in Sebastian. Originally the Sebastian store was a two-story wooden building fronting on Main Street. The family lived on the second floor at the beginning.

The pending sale of the W. C. Braddock stores to the Vickers Brothers received attention from the *St. Lucie Tribune*. The paper reported in January 1911 that Marsh Hall and his family had moved to Fellsmere, and that Mr. Hall was placed in charge of the Braddock store, the Sebastian Mercantile Co. in Fellsmere. At the same time, it reported that Mr. Dunham and his family had arrived in Sebastian, occupying one of the Rose's cottages. He was employed as head clerk of the Sebastian Mercantile Co. in Sebastian.

By December of 1911, Braddock had sold his stores to Vickers Brothers, and George Vickers was busy buying goods for the Sebastian Mercantile Co. The stores had changed names by 1912 to Vickers Brothers, and R. J. Dunham was the manager of Vickers Brothers in Fellsmere, handling the advertising. Vickers Brothers were dealers in general merchandise, with stock that was fresh and up to date, with all sorts of groceries, staples, and dry goods that were constantly on hand, according to the advertising. It also housed the post office. William Ryall was one of the employees. However, by October of 1913, Ralph E. Brown took over the Vickers Brothers Fellsmere store, as George Vickers, who had overseen the store, was taking over management of the Sebastian Vickers Brothers Store from brother Frank. Frank Vickers retired from its management due to failing eyesight, and they let the Fellsmere store go. In 1914, a six-car galvanized iron garage was built near Vickers Brothers in Sebastian so that patrons could have covered parking. In 1916, the *Fellsmere Tribune* printed an advertisement for Vickers Brothers General Store in Sebastian, carrying marine and auto supplies and builder's hardware.

The store was moved, and around 1925, the wood building was torn down and a new stucco building erected. The contractors were Bertling & Ball of Melbourne. The store went through many changes, varying from general store, to selling dry goods, hardware, or groceries; it also served as a space for the post office. The Vickers Building on US

Hwy 1 today is somewhat removed from the original, and has had several facelifts over the years. It was owned and operated by the Vickers family into the 1960s. It was not included on the National Register of Historic Places, due to its extensive renovations.

Tompkins Store

Ernest E. Tompkins' Store in Sebastian, E. E. Tompkins & Company, was on the corner of Main Street and North Central Avenue. It was a two-story wood frame building established some time before March 1912, when Tompkins rented a building from H. J. Parks and opened a general merchandise store in Fellsmere on Broadway. Tompkins was a member of the Fellsmere baseball team in 1912 and one of the subscribers to the State Bank of Fellsmere in 1913. Sometime after 1915, the Sebastian store closed and the building was moved. Doc Sloan, who was a grove owner and bootlegger, lived in the building. Tompkins was living in Fellsmere in 1916.

Deal and Holtzclaw/F. P. Holtzclaw

Deal and Holtzclaw/F. P. Holtzclaw was another short-lived store in Sebastian, but for sad reasons. When his parents contemplated moving to Florida, Paul Holtzclaw and his friend Harvey Deal moved in advance of the family from North Carolina to Roseland in 1911. In August 1915, the two friends went into business together in Sebastian in a grocery store, putting in a stock of goods at R. G. Hardee's building on the corner of Main Street. This was a short-lived partnership, and on February 21, 1916, Deal filed a Notice of Dissolution of the firm of Deal and Holtzclaw. Deal sold his interest in the business and his house to Holtzclaw, and moved back to North Carolina. Less than a month later, on March 19, 1916, Paul married Violet Irene Hardee, and they moved into Harvey Deal's house. Soon advertisements began appearing in the *St. Lucie Tribune* for F. P. Holtzclaw, "dealer in groceries, hay, grain, feed, tobaccos, cigars, gasoline, and oils. Agent for the Royal Tailors."

The Holtzclaws had a baby. For relaxation, they socialized with family and friends, and Paul was an amateur actor, appearing in "The Winning of Latane," a play put on at City Hall. Their new life ended rather abruptly. In 1917, Paul contracted typhoid, and was hospitalized in Jacksonville. That same year, he died, on June 28, 1917, at age 23.

Other Businesses

Other types of businesses were setting up in Sebastian. Sebastian Bottling Works had an intriguing advertisement in the *Fellsmere Tribune* in January 1916: "Why not have satisfaction as well as quality? We are putting out a real prosperity drink. Our line of non-alcoholic beverages is put up in beer bottles. A real satisfying jitney's worth. And then there's Gay-Ola, in a smaller bottle, but a smile in every drop. When you have that all-in feeling, it sets you up and makes you feel just right. Let us quote you prices. Note. This bottle is a business-builder." James J. Gibbs was the proprietor. He was also vice president of the Board of Trade in 1916. Sebastian Repair Shop, with manager Jesse E. Powell, ran advertisements in the *Fellsmere Tribune* in 1916, as blacksmith, wheelwrights, gunsmiths, general repairing, boat building, and representatives for Ferro Marine in Sebastian. The Sebastian National Loan Association formed on December 7, 1916. Its officers were president G. A. Braddock, vice president P. P. Lawson, and secretary/treasurer M. M. Miller. The directors were G. A. Braddock, W. L. R. Barnwell, T. H. Sibley, and J. E. Powell.

Sebastian Town Hall

Sebastian added a civic center to its growing town, the Sebastian Town Hall. This building has variously been called the Sebastian Public Hall Stock Company Building, Sebastian Public Hall, Sebastian Town Hall, and Sebastian City Hall. The *St. Lucie Tribune* carried a notice that sealed bids would be received until November 20, 1913, for the purpose of building a Public Hall in Sebastian. The Sebastian Town Hall was built by the Woodmen of the World on what is now US Hwy 1 in central Sebastian. It was completed in 1914, and was ready for business on March 20, 1914. According to the *St. Lucie Tribune*, it was a large, airy, two-story wooden building, 32 x 64 feet in size, fronting on the East Coast Boulevard. The main floor had an anteroom and property rooms off the main room, which was for town business. The upper floor was designed for entertaining and lodge meetings. It had an 18-foot stage. A dance was held in the hall on March 27, 1914, to celebrate the opening. Many different societies held meetings there, including the Sebastian Public Hall Company. The hall was used for parties, plays, minstrel shows, dances, moving pictures, and other entertainment. Rodney Kroegel hand-cranked the projector for the moving pictures at the Town Hall, shown with piano accompaniment. The top grossing silent film was "Birth of a Nation," starring Lillian Gish, first shown in 1915. The ceremony for first graduating class of the Sebastian School was held in the Sebastian Town Hall in 1918. Six Students were in the class: Meta Chesser, Rodney Kroegel, Cecil Beugnot, George and Maurice Braddock, and Alta Miller. The Town Hall is one of the significant properties listed in Old Town Sebastian Historic District East, placed on the National Register of Historic Places August 4, 2003. It still stands on US Hwy 1.

Municipal offices were moved from there; the *Vero Beach Press Journal* announced September 12, 1947, that Sebastian City Hall had been moved to a business building located on Main Street, which was paid for in full in cash. In January 1957, that paper announced construction of the new Sebastian City Hall and Fire Station by Albrecht Construction Company of Vero Beach, a one-story concrete building at the northwest corner of City Park, facing Main Street and the new US Hwy 1.

Methodist Church

The churches provided a strong central focus for local activities. The Methodist Church hosted many functions in addition to Sunday sermons; some of them were joint functions with the Baptist Church. In May, Children's Day exercises were held at the Methodist Episcopal Church in Sebastian, with a program of songs, prayers, a greeting, recitations, a presentation of flowers, dialogs, and tableaus. Roseland families also attended the Children's Day exercises in Sebastian. The Methodist and Baptist Sunday schools had a joint picnic at Kitching grove on the Old River Road in May of 1916. The choirs of the Methodist and Baptist churches met jointly to practice at the home of Mrs. S.A. Parks in 1916. The young people of the Methodist Church organized a society for church work under the supervision of Mr. and Mrs. W. R. Terrell in February 1916. Rev. Henry B. Boyd was pastor in 1918.

As far back as the 1700s, licenses were granted allowing an individual to preach. The exhorter had to demonstrate improvement before he could become a preacher, and had to undertake a course of study followed by an examination before issuance of a license. An Exhorter's License was granted to Charles E. Taylor in 1918. The license stated that he had been examined by the Quarterly Conference of Sebastian Circuit of the Miami District of Florida, General Conference of the Methodist Episcopal Church South, and he was thereby authorized to exhort, according to the rules and regulations of the Church. Sebastian Teachers Training Classes were held at the Methodist parsonage, and were open to all to provide this training. Taylor became a mainstay of the Methodist churches in the area, acting as a lay preacher in Roseland, Sebastian, and Fellsmere. Charles and Bessie Taylor were one of the families along the Sebastian River between Eureka and Roseland.

Baptist Church

Rev. J. C. DuBose of Fort Pierce was appointed to come to Sebastian on a regular basis in 1916 to give Sunday sermons at the Baptist Church, and river bank baptisms were conducted by him. There was a lecture at the Baptist Church in February 1916 for the support of orphans and planning for their care, by Mr. and Mrs. George W. Henderson of Jacksonville. That month, the ladies of the Sebastian Baptist Church gave an oyster supper at the town hall to pay for new carpeting for the aisles, and for seats. Rev. E. J. Blanchard officiated in the Sebastian Baptist Church in 1918. Some Sebastian residents motored to Quay for Baptist meetings.

School Building

A north wing was added to the two-story wooden school in 1912, doubling the number of classrooms to four, with each classroom teaching four grades. Some of the teachers were recent high school graduates. There were seventeen students in 1914. The teachers appointed to Sebastian's school for the 1915-1916 school term were Professor W. H. Terrill and assistants Miss Marion Leonard of the Intermediate Department and Mrs. Schofeld of the Primary Department. The class roll included Margaret Anne Stinson, Zelpha Alice Bon, Edna Lila Tucker, Nesbit Ryall, and Ernest Edward Haas. Vera Hilde Ashburner of Roseland was class valedictorian. A meeting was held of the patrons of School District 1 in May of 1916 to select teachers for the following year's Fall and Spring terms. Trustees in charge of the meeting were M. M. Miles and T. B. Hicks. Chosen were Mrs. Norma Kester as Primary Department teacher and Miss Marian Leonard for the Intermediate Department. The school principal was not chosen at that time. Student enrollment was 108.

William C. Edwards, Principal

William C. Edwards was one of the more eccentric individuals hired by the school board to teach and act as principal of the Sebastian school. He was an intelligent, educated, vocal man of strong opinions who had difficulty holding down a job. Originally he was an Ohio accountant. When he lost his job due to his radical political leanings, he decided to relocate in Florida. He moved first to Sochoppy in the Florida Panhandle, where he obtained a position as a teacher. His wife Elizabeth was not happy there and returned to Ohio.

He moved next to Sebastian where he again obtained a teaching position. His wife and daughters Mary and Lydia joined him there, in a house on Louisiana Avenue, one of Dr. Rose's rental units. He served as a voting inspector for Sebastian in 1914. In 1914, he was the school principal. As difficult as it was to find and keep educators at that time, William was fired from his position in the school. On July 18, 1914, a vote was held by a special session of school board members on whether to retain Edwards as principal, and the vote was overwhelmingly negative. His appointment to the Fort Drum school was also canceled. In February of 1915, Unity School petitioned to have him appointed as a teacher there. The St. Lucie County school board turned down the petition unanimously. He obtained a teaching position at Barberville in October 1914. By 1918, he had become a farmer. He was appointed postmaster in Sebastian in January 1919, leaving that position in October of the same year. Then he took a position as a bookkeeper for Deerfield Packing Co. in 1922. According to the 1930 census, he was a farmer again, living on Flarido 4 Road in Sebastian. He died suddenly in 1933.

The Edwards children did not have their father's volatile temperament and lifestyle. As expected by their parents, Mary and Lydia taught school prior to their marriages, Mary to E. W. Vickers, and Lydia to Charles Gulledge. Norma moved to Sebastian, and her second marriage was to J. O. Jamieson, a builder who built the churches of Roseland, Fellsmere, and Wabasso, as well as several houses, including the Williams' house in 1918. Three sons, Paul, George. and Ralph Edwards, served in WWI. Paul

Bevan Edwards was employed by the Florida East Coast Railway in New Smyrna as a freight clerk in 1916. He was employed as a fisherman by T. B. Hicks when he joined the Army on December 12, 1917. He served overseas from to January 3, 1919, until his discharge on January 17, 1919, as a Private 1st Class. Ralph W. E. Edwards was employed by A. L. Stinson as a fruit packer when he joined the Army on September 17, 1918. He was ten percent disabled on discharge July 15, 1919. George William Edwards entered the military April 10, 1917, serving on the USS *Reid*. He was discharged in California on January 13, 1918, as a Navy Seaman. William, Elizabeth, and Ralph are all buried together in the Sebastian Cemetery.

Beginning the Real Estate Boom

The 1910s were a period of rapid growth in Sebastian, and many Sebastianites participated in the land boom, selling real estate. Sections 6 and 7 of Township 31 South, Range 39 East in the heart of Sebastian, saw the growth of many subdivisions. *G. A. Braddock Plat*, surveyed October 1912; *T. B. Hicks Subdivision,* December 26, 1912; The *Hardee Addition*, platted January 1913; *Vickers Subdivision*, June 19, 1913; and *Martin Property plat*, August 1913, are part of this activity. Vickers Brothers platted cemetery plots, as well. The Braswell Brothers land opposite the Town Hall was being cleared and subdivided into lots for sale in 1916.

The main residential street in Sebastian, Louisiana Avenue, had several homes added in the decade. In the year 1910, the homes of Charles Hancock, James Gray, Dr. David Rose, and Ned Sembler were added. Walter's Baughman's home was built there in 1912, Lillian Field's was added in 1916, and Charles Taylor's was built on Louisiana Avenue in 1918.

Several residences were added to the north-south thoroughfares. Clarissa Hardee's home on North Central Avenue was built in 1911. A few lots north of the town hall were building homes in 1914. E. W. Vickers built a very large bungalow, and north of him F. P. Park erected a two-story, ten-room house with a room set off on the north side for a post office. He was a fisherman, and his wife Maude was postmistress of Sebastian for several years. Ruth Roundtree Miller's house was erected on Old Dixie in 1917, and the Ardelia Cain and George Cain houses were added to US Hwy 1 in 1918. E. L. Squire purchased a lot on Sebastian Avenue in 1916 and expected to become a permanent citizen, per the *Fellsmere Tribune*.

Sawmills

In booming areas of growth such as in Sebastian and Roseland, a sawmill was a necessity. They consisted of purchased, portable equipment; many individuals started sawmills, moving them around as necessary to obtain business. Some land owners cut their own timber and sent it to a sawmill, to be returned to them as lumber. St. Sebastian River was a convenient mode of moving logs to a sawmill, and several of the mills were located on the St. Sebastian River. Locals hired on as temporary labor. Sawmill machinery was advertised in the newspapers, and could be purchased by catalog or mailed request from cities such as Atlanta or Jacksonville, and delivered by train. This useful business was covered in the *St. Lucie Tribune*. Miller & King moved their sawmill from Gifford to Sebastian in June of 1910, to saw lumber for the Sebastian Fellsmere Railroad Bridge. Hicks and Sembler Sawmill moved from Sebastian in August 1911, where they had provided lumber for the bridge in west Sebastian, to Wabasso. Gant and Creary were other sawmill operators in the area. The Florida Sawmill Association concerned itself with matters of conservation and reforestation in the 1910s.

Vanished

Physical features of a locale can change. Towns and people have come and gone. The prominent hill along the Indian River in Sebastian, Barker's Bluff, was bulldozed to ground level to use the shell to pave roads. River bluffs and old dune lines were smoothed down for the railroads. Broadmoor vanished in the floods of 1915 and was abandoned. Grassland, another small community west of Fellsmere, also failed. Homewood, south of Fellsmere, attracted settlers briefly when Fellsmere and Broadmoor were flooded, but is now gone.

Barker's Bluff

The most notable loss was Barker's Bluff. Long before any Europeans set foot in the Sebastian and Roseland area, the defining topography of the area was made. Toward the southern part stood the most clearly visible landmark for miles around, the Ais shell mound that later became known as Barker's Bluff, on the western shore of the Indian River. From the Ais onward, many individuals utilized this piece of high ground. The Spanish, Seminoles, and early pioneers briefly stayed there. August Park and the Kroegels were the latest, and last.

This significant part of the Sebastian landscape was eliminated in 1908. Barker's Bluff was sold to St. Lucie County for paving material for the first surfaced road that ran from Micco to Stuart. It took more than seven years to completely remove this massive landmark. It was an enormous undertaking to remove this shell midden, which was about 400 x 1,000 feet in size, and taller than the cabbage palms. It required the use of a steam shovel, and a railroad track was laid up to the bluff for as many as eight to ten train cars to carry away the shell, and 50 or so men to do the labor. The shell was crushed to create a hard-paved surface for roads. The section containing Gottlob Kroegel's home was the last to be removed. Gottlob Kroegel's house remained on a small part of the Barker's Bluff for several years after demolition began. Local lore relates that in 1908, a new house was built for him, but he refused to move. On January 1, 1910, he was taken for a boat ride, during which his belongings were moved to the new house, forcing him to comply with the relocation, and the rest of the mound was removed. When Barker's Bluff was in the process of being torn down and sold for road paving, at least two human skulls and bones were uncovered in the shells and photographed.

Roseland

Roseland received new vitality, change, and growth during this decade, due to the vision of A. A. Berry. Unlike Sebastian, Roseland had no difficulty in selecting and keeping the name Roseland, given to it by settlers in the 1880s, even with the advent of developers.

A. A. Berry

A. A. Berry of Clarinda, Page County, Iowa, was the primary motivator behind the development of Roseland. Berry was best known in his hometown as the founder of Berry's Seed Company in 1895, a nation-wide, mail-order farm seed distribution business. In later years, it became a chain of retail stores, Berry's Garden Center. He also started Berry Poultry Farm and Hatchery in Clarinda in 1913.

Berry was born in Ohio of Scottish ancestry. He married his wife Clarie in 1893, and in 1900, he was living in Nodaway, Page County, Iowa, with his wife and three children. This successful businessman set his sights on Roseland.

A. A. Berry's two companies, Florida Development Company and the Berry Land Company, continued their attempts to develop the Roseland area in 1910, when they bought part of Wauregon west of the railroad tracks and coupled it with part of the Fleming Grant to form a tract of 23,000 acres that Berry called Roseland Park. Mr. Leslie was the manager of Roseland Park. This plan never gained traction, and the Roseland Park name died with it.

There had been complications to the title to the Fleming Grant land since the 1830s. An abstract of title was prepared, and a December 23, 1910, warranty deed passed the Roseland land to Florida Land Developing Company and A. A. Berry. However, in 1913, the Florida Land Development Company, A. A. Berry, and wife, Clara J. Berry, had to petition the courts to clear title of Fleming Grant land they had sold. This allowed them to continue with the land development and sales, but title did not completely clear to these lands until President Hoover signed the patent in the 1930s. Another plan for the town of Roseland was formed. A January 1911 plat map was surveyed for Florida Developing Company of Clarinda, Iowa, laying out named roads Roseland, Gibson, Baird, Josie, Dale, and Lewis Streets, and Sebastian, Berry, Nichol, Orr, Crozier, and Elder Avenues. Land was set aside for a college, park, church, and school.

A 1913 revision of a Carter survey for A. A. Berry produced a much briefer plat of Roseland.

There were several variations of the corporate names used in Berry's land development project, but the name that appeared on his sales office building was The Flaland Developing Co. The land began selling, without much done in the way of added infrastructure, clearing, or road building. Some individuals could not even locate the land they had purchased. The lots with frontage on the Sebastian River with groves sold well. The first land sales were in 1911, including a lot to future Judge Milo M. Miller. The following appeared in the *St. Lucie Tribune* on February 10, 1911: "Land sales at Roseland Florida Land Developing Company reported a great many sales in the last few weeks. 2,200 farms of 10 acres each have been sold in and around Roseland. Streets, lots and public grounds have been mapped out. In two weeks land excursions from both the north and west will bring hundreds of people to Roseland, and a booming is expected." This seems like an exaggeration for one month of sales; according to the *Vero Beach Press*, A. A. Berry sold out and moved away from Roseland around 1913.

Flaland Developing Co. Office

The real estate headquarters in Roseland was the Flaland Developing Company Office on the corner of Gibson Street and Berry Avenue, a block west of the railroad tracks. The Company's office was a small one-story wood frame building, with a crow-stepped gabled sign over the front door. H. G. Leslie moved to Roseland around 1911, and became manager of the Flaland Developing Company office. He was a native of Fulton County, Illinois, who went west for four or five years, then moved to Gillette, Arkansas, where he was instrumental in the founding of that town. He was as successful in promoting Roseland as he had been in boosting the growth of Gillette, and land sales boomed. Some individuals promptly sold again; John Anderson traded his house and lot in Roseland for a farm in Kentucky in 1913. Vinton Nichols became the Roseland manager of the Florida Land Development Company in 1913. Roseland began to take on more the look of a town in 1916 and 1917, when P. M. Combs of Chicago, representative of Florida Land Developing Company, arrived and began several improvements, such as lot and street cleaning and painting. A 1916 Florida Land Developing Company brochure quoted in the *Sebastian Sun* on March 31, 1994, gave land prices and had glowing testimonials by local residents. A house with six rooms, a hall, and a porch cost $190.

The Town

Thus, before Roseland had more than a handful of residents, it had a fully laid-out town. Berry's sales and advertising acumen gave Roseland a push towards growth. "Roseland is on the Boom!" was a headline in the 1913 *St. Lucie Tribune.* At the beginning of the decade, Roseland continued to have E. M. Stokes' general store and post office, the railroad station, and dock, all on the east side of the railroad tracks. Bay Street ran from the depot to the Ercildoune. Roseland also had the Old Stockade, originally a prison, near the tracks. On the bayfront was a fish house run by Mr. Youngblood and an abandoned fruit packing house. It had a full set of street names, with some of the streets laid out, thanks to Berry. More was quickly added to the town during this decade. Some of the new establishments and people remained; others were gone within a year or two. Some divided their time between more than one of the towns in the north part of the county, or had homes and properties elsewhere.

The Old Stockade

Before Roseland had a church, prayer services were held in the Old Stockade, the former prison camp located south of Berry Street near the railroad tracks, with the fence and high tower removed once the prisoners were gone. This long, low, wooden structure was renovated to be used as a hotel, and a room on the east end of the building was used for parties and worship services. Sunday School may have been held there as well, until the school was built. Unfortunately, it burned to the ground. Early church services were also held in individual homes.

Ercildoune Hotel

The nearby Ercildoune Hotel had been an ongoing concern since the 1880s. Mr. and Mrs. Len Jones were in charge of the Ercildoune Inn for the winter season in 1913. Popular for decades, it closed around World War I and never reopened as a hotel, perhaps in part due to the advent of the Bay Crest Hotel. J. W. Glass of Decatur, Georgia, owner of the Ercildoune property, arrived in town in April of 1916. J. W. Glass became the owner of the Ercildoune property on April 4, 1916. Later that same year, Professor W. H. Turner purchased the inn and converted the property into a preparatory school for boys. The sixteen rooms were remodeled and the premises were improved. Turner's purchase included 100 acres, 12 of which were grove. The school opened shortly after the purchase.

Roseland Grammar School

One of the first new buildings added to the growing town of Roseland was a one-room wooden schoolhouse, built around 1912 on Dale Street. Sealed bids were requested by the St. Lucie County school board on October 2, 1911, for building school houses at

Eureka and at Roseland. The Roseland Grammar School was in operation until just prior to WWII, and after that time, the children were bused to Sebastian. Roseland Grammar School had one teacher; in 1916, it was Miss Newsome. Student enrollment was fourteen. A growing problem for Roseland was seasonal families whose children attended the Roseland school, but were not included in the taxing district.

After being built, the school was used for many of the town's other functions. In 1913-1914, Sunday School was moved to the school building. J. E. Creary, who owned and operated a sawmill northwest of the railroad bridge, was the first superintendent of the Sunday School. In 1911-1913, Reverend T. E. Weaver of Sebastian Methodist Church held services in the Roseland Schoolhouse every third Sunday evening before the Roseland Church was built. Roselandites also attended the Sebastian Methodist Church. Christmas Tree festivities were held at the school, with exercises by the children, songs, and plays.

Roseland United Methodist Church

One of the Methodist Church's circuit riders visited Roseland, Reverend Patterson of Kentucky, who was one of those evangelist Methodist preachers sent out by the parent church to visit small communities and help parishioners establish a new church. There were 35 charter members who joined March 29, 1914. Reverend Roland accepted seven more into the Methodist Church later on. Rev. M. Crosley conducted services at the school building in Roseland Sunday evening in March of 1916.

On the Berry plat of Roseland, a block was set aside for the church. The land was donated by A. A. Berry in 1915, deeded to the church in the name of its first trustees, W. W. Holtzclaw, N. D. Trull, and A. E. Rankin. This platted land was later exchanged for another, more convenient location. The church was paid for by subscription and built with volunteer labor. Messrs. Fear, Holtzclaw, and Boyd applied the first coat of paint on the new church. The church was built during the pastorate of Rev. H. B. Boyd, who served the Sebastian church 1914-1918, after Rev. Roland. The church was part of the Sebastian charge, and Rev. Boyd divided his time. A large crowd gathered at the river bank to witness individuals being baptized on an April Sunday in 1916.

The first service in the new church was held April 30, 1916. The quarterly conference of the Methodist Episcopal Church was held on Saturday and Sunday at the new, unfinished Roseland church. The conference was officiated by Dr. Siebert, the presiding elder, assisted by Rev. H. B. Boyd, pastor. This was the first church built in this community. Rev. H. B. Boyd conducted a Sunday afternoon service and moved to morning and evening services on the 4th Sunday of the month in Roseland in 1916. Ladies' Aid Society raised funds to fence the church with a chicken supper in 1917, and an organ was obtained for the church through donations that year. It was used for the first wedding in the new church February 27, 1918, between Alma Holtzclaw and William S. Frantz. Mr. Frantz donated the church bell. In 1923, a communion set of silver plate was donated by former Campfire Girls in memory of their guardian Alma D. Holtzclaw Frantz, who died in 1921.

Hotels and Stores

Due to increased population, several small stores were added to Roseland. Moreover, with so many land buyers and visitors to Roseland, hotel space was at a premium. Many little hotels and boarding houses sprang up, and disappeared again as entrepreneurs came and went. One such hotel was the Roseland House. The *St. Lucie Tribune* reported April 4, 1913, that a fire occurred in the Roseland House, with all contents lost. Everyone got out safely, but the building was entirely destroyed.

Roseland Hotel

T .C. Royer was a hotel manager in Roseland from around 1912 to 1915. His name is first linked to management of the Buckner Hotel. In the same issue of the *St. Lucie Tribune* that reported the fire that destroyed the Roseland House in 1913, this advertisement appeared: "The Roseland Hotel is open to the public. Rates $1.50 and up per day. Special rates by the month. T. C. Royer, mgr." This advertisement ran for two years. Royer also took part in Roseland civic matters during his time in Roseland. T. C. Royer was one of the individuals, along with D. Sloan, C. U. Nichol, E. S. Fear, and A. E. Rankin who attended a county commissioners' meeting to ask for a county road with shell surfacing between Roseland and the Indian River in June 1913. This was granted and D. Sloan was given the contract for the construction, which he began immediately. Royer was one of the witnesses in the Hardee case in the shooting of Elmer Stokes in 1913. Also in 1913, Royer was one of the proponents of a special voting district for Roseland, as residents at that time had to go to Sebastian to vote. In August 1913, Royer was hauling the material for his new business building to be erected on the lot just west of his hotel in Roseland which, when completed, was occupied by a barber shop and soft drink establishment. Royer was manager of the Roseland Hotel until February 1915, when he left Roseland to become a farmer in Georgia. The name of the hotel apparently changed to the Roseland House before 1915, as it was the Roseland House that was turned over to Mr. Vaughan of Jacksonville by Royer. Miss Evelyn Vaughan of Jacksonville became the new manager.

Bay Crest Hotel

George and Mazeppa Tuckers' strong drive for business success led them to create the magnificent Bay Crest Hotel in 1914. The Tuckers were one of the southern families that suffered losses from the Civil War in Mississippi. A visit to New Orleans in February 1912 led them to information about the boom conditions in Florida, including land sales and the promising new town of Roseland. Looking for a profitable business venture, they traveled by train to Roseland to scout the possibilities. Upon arriving, it was obvious that there was a niche for a new, luxurious resort for winter guests. The Ercildoune was becoming outmoded. After exploring the area, they settled on a piece of property owned by James Williamson, the section near the present-day Sebastian River Bridge on the west side of the Sebastian River, and purchased it. They planned for a hotel and subdivision of lots for sale on that land. They returned to Pace, Mississippi, by train, and had moved to Micco by June 1913, bringing two workers with them. Jumping right in, they built a camp for the family, started clearing a road down to the river, surveyed land for a subdivision, cleared a lot for the hotel site, and hired an architect and contractors for construction of the hotel.

They returned to Pace, then came back to Micco when the hotel was nearly complete in February 1914. The Bay Crest Hotel was an imposing building constructed of concrete block with 23 rooms on two floors, and a basement and attic. It was finished with hard maple floors and it had a dock with a gazebo down to the Sebastian River. On the south side were several cottages and on the north were garages with a screened pavilion above for parties and dances. The fortnightly dances at the Bay Crest were well attended, and the hotel proved to be a popular spot for dining by local area residents. It was also popular with its hotel guests who were primarily winter visitors who came south by train or in their yachts for the season.

H. Bruntsch Boarding House

At the other end of the tourist spectrum, H. Bruntsch advertised his boarding house, with rooms and meals, in the *Fellsmere Tribune* in 1916; then the Bruntschs moved to their property northwest of town in April of that year.

Hammon Cottage Hotel

Other hoteliers were the Hammons, who were winter residents of Roseland that lived in Astabula, Ohio, in 1910, a family consisting of Eugene Hammon, age 45, wife Lizzie Hammon, age 38, and children, 21-year-old Norman and 14-year-old Theo. They began coming to Roseland in 1912. In 1916, the Hammons made improvements to their home on Sebastian Avenue, and created a cottage hotel with porches and ten to twelve guest rooms. Mrs. Bailey occupied their Roseland home on Sebastian Avenue when they were back home in Ashtabula. N. D. Hammon moved from the Taylor cottage on Sebastian Avenue to the Curtis cottage on Berry Avenue. Mr. Arnold and his grandson moved into the Taylor cottage in 1916. The Hammons opened a hotel in Roseland in the 1920s.

Elmer M. Stokes

Elmer Stokes continued to operate his store and was postmaster of Roseland. He also worked as a ferryman in 1910, paid from the Road and Bridge fund, and he received an extra sum for isolated children. Stokes' son accidentally shot his little sister when he was playing with an old revolver in 1910, a senseless accident. Another tragic shooting occurred in the Stokes family. The *St. Lucie Tribune* related that May 10, 1913, G. J. Hardee shot and killed his brother-in-law, E. M. Stokes, the Roseland postmaster, at the post office with three shots, all of which were fatal. "Baseball Bet Causes Killing at Roseland" was the *St. Lucie Tribune* headline. The shooting arose over a bet on a baseball game between Sebastian and Roseland. Prior to the shooting, Hardee hit Stokes in the face with a stick, they wrestled, and Hardee pulled out his gun and shot Stokes. G. J. Hardee was arrested and taken to St. Lucie County jail in Fort Pierce. A preliminary hearing charged Hardee first-degree murder May 22, 1913, and he was held over for an October trial. At trial, Gardner Jack Hardee was convicted of second-degree murder and sentenced to life imprisonment in the state penitentiary.

Stokes was buried in the Cain cemetery. He left a wife and seven children. Their son, Dempsey C. Stokes, also a Roseland resident, married Ada Sloan of Fellsmere July 14, 1916. A further family misfortune occurred when he drowned in 1928 at the Sebastian Inlet in the ocean opposite the north side of the jetty. His boat capsized in the strong current when his engine stalled. With him was Earl Rosin, who made it to shore.

A. E. Campbell became acting postmaster after Elmer Stokes' death, until Alma D. Holtzclaw took over in August 1913. Englishman Allen E. Campbell, as well as becoming postmaster, was a long-time Roseland orange grower. He was also part of the land-selling staff of the Security Underwriters Corporation of Fellsmere in 1912. In 1918, Campbell sold his orange grove and home to Col. Ruffner, who made the Campbell homestead, Bellevue, his home.

Holtzclaw Store Roseland Bargain House 1916

More than hotels were needed in Roseland, and William W. Holtzclaw filled the niche with his store. He had been a merchant in Boone, North Carolina, and began a store in Roseland after he and his family moved there. W. W. Holtzclaw & Company opened in 1912, a two-story, wooden structure. The family lived on the second floor, and the Holtzclaw store was on the first floor, on Berry Avenue. The advertisements ran in the *Fellsmere Tribune*: "Roseland Bargain House, Will W. Holtzclaw, mgr. groceries, dry goods, notions, feed at bargain prices." Business was so good, at one point he ran two stores in Roseland. His store sold ox feed and feed for mules that were used to haul wood for the railroad.

The store was a gathering spot for young people. Campfire Girl's had an ice cream and fudge sale in the store in May 1916. The Roseland post office was located in his store, and his daughter Alma was the postmistress. His stock arrived by train, mainly from Jacksonville. He operated this store for many years.

William Wesley Holtzclaw

William Wesley Holtzclaw and Mollie Dietz Holtzclaw arrived in Roseland in late 1911, after their son Paul's arrival. On doctor's advice, they sought a milder climate for Mollie's ill health, leaving their store and imposing two-story home in North Carolina. After living over the store in Roseland for few years, they built a more spacious house across the street similar to their North Carolina house. Their daughter-in-law, Mrs. F. Paul Holtzclaw, went to live with William and Mollie after the death of her husband.

Daughter Alma Holtzclaw, postmistress from 1913-1920 in Roseland, became the *Tribune* representative in Roseland and started her own Roseland news column in January 1916. Around 1918, she married W. S. Frantz, engaged in farming and real estate. Another early death, Alma died in 1921 at age 31, and is buried in Sebastian Cemetery, next to her brother Paul.

Roseland boasted of what was probably the first amateur wireless telegraph station in the county. Son Ralph C. Holtzclaw, at age fifteen, became a licensed wireless operator. He constructed his own shop and set up his wireless equipment unassisted. As a service, he provided the correct time of day twice daily, obtained in the morning from Key West and at night from Arlington, Virginia.

The year 1916 saw several arrivals and departures in town; Romer's store was one of the Roseland establishments that came and was quickly gone again in this decade. George H. and Ella Romer purchased land in 1913, and in 1916 and 1917, advertised: "Geo. H. Romer general merchandise, gasolines and oils." His store was on Berry Avenue. They were gone by 1918; Romer's name was removed from the list of voters in October of 1918. Mrs. R. Merchant, the daughter of H. G. Leslie, ran a store in Roseland in 1916, near the railroad tracks. That year she supported community activities, hosting chicken suppers at her store as a fund-raiser for a fence for the church yard, and an oyster supper run by the Ladies' Aid Society, and was not mentioned thereafter. W. P. Walkup was a merchant in 1916 in Roseland. Apparently, Roseland had a dentist for a year, H. R. Wilcox, who advertised and appeared in the 1916 directory.

Roads

Roseland saw some sustainable improvements to its roads in this decade, as noted in the *Fellsmere Tribune* and *St. Lucie Tribune*. In Roseland, street names were placed on posts at street crossings by W. H. Ostrander. Refurbishments were made on Nichol Avenue. In addition, the county commissioners also approved road upgrades. Early in the decade Roselandites had been promoting a road from the town to the Dixie Highway.

Messrs. Ashburner, Romer, and Jones worked at widening and straightening the road between the train depot and the Dixie Highway. In 1913, a proposal was presented to the county commissioners for a shell, marl, or rock road from the Dixie Highway into Roseland. Sloan Brothers completed that hard-surfaced road in 1916. In August 1913, the bridge across the Kimball ditch south of town was completed, making it much more convenient for people to get to town.

Commerce

Although real estate dominated the economy in this decade in Roseland, the profitable ventures that continued before and after the boom were its groves, truck farms, and fisheries. Earlier groves and farms were producing well, such as the Ercildoune's Frostproof Grove, Col. Ruffner's groves, and Drake's and Campbell's groves. More continued to develop in this decade.

Emery S. Fear

The Fears were some of the people from a faraway place that heard the call of Florida. Ohioan Emery S. Fear, age 48, and wife Florence M., 47, were living in Fanning, Scotts Bluff, Nebraska, in 1910. Then they tried Colorado. From Colorado, sometime between 1910-1914, they purchased land from A. A. Berry, and became citrus growers in Roseland. As well as managing their grove, they took part in Roseland life. Emery was a carpenter who helped to build the Roseland Methodist Church with W. H. Clark, and helped Hanshaw build his house. He also helped obtain road improvements from the county commissioners. The Anti-Saloon League of Florida formed local groups in 1918; E. S. Fear was named chairman of the Roseland chapter, and J. A. Groves chairman of the Sebastian chapter. Emery died at age 62, and is buried in the Sebastian cemetery.

William H. Clark

The Clarks were one of the families fleeing northern winter weather, lured by the extravagant promises of A. A. Berry, who stayed in Roseland. William H. Clark, wife Anna Laura, and daughter Garnett, moved to Florida due to the severe winters of northeastern Oregon State, near British Columbia, where he raised horses. In his *Tampa Times* newspaper subscription, he found an advertisement for the A. A. Berry Land Company. Torn between that ad and a Florida west coast subdivision property, the Clarks decided on Berry's land, sight unseen. Clark originally purchased land on the north fork of the Sebastian River from A. A. Berry in 1913; however, that land was too remote and wild. The Clark's settled on a piece of land not far from the location of the present-day Methodist church instead. Clark did some farming and set out one grove, but mainly worked as a carpenter in the area. He was one of the carpenters on the Carlton House and worked on the building of the Roseland Methodist church in 1914 with Emory Fear. He also worked in Miami during the building boom. Per the census, he and Laura divorced by 1930 and he was a carpenter, living in Roseland. Laura was boarding with widow Minnie Hanshaw in a house near his, and was a teacher. In 1940, his home was on the Roseland-Fellsmere Road, not far from his daughter Garnett and son-in-law Lester Hanshaw, and ex-wife widow Annie Laura French, who had married and been widowed in the last ten years. He died in 1952, and is buried in the Sebastian Cemetery, near Annie Laura, Garnett, and Lester.

Lester Adel Hanshaw

Iowa-born Lester Hanshaw became one of the grove owners in the Roseland area. He came to Roseland in 1916 at the urging of his friend Roy Bell, who also moved at that time. Lester purchased land from Milton Hardee, the son of Jack Hardee, that was on the west side of the Sebastian River. Single at the time, he built a house and started a grove there. He enlisted in the Army for WWI, was inducted March 30, 1918, and was discharged April 14, 1919. Both before and after the war, Lester volunteered to work on the Methodist Church. He helped refurbish the church after the hurricane of 1928. Sometime after 1920, he and Garnet Clark married. They moved from the Micco grove property after Garnet and Lester's daughter, Holly, was born. He continued as a grower, and worked as a guide, living in Fellsmere and Wabasso. Around 1940, they bought the Riverside house on the Indian River from the Yongue family, changing the name to Riverview. This lovely, two-story home is still on Indian River Drive. Both are buried in Sebastian Cemetery.

Sebastian River, South Prong Area, Sebastian Creek

Some families preferred an exceptionally secluded existence, away from towns. In the 1910s, there were a few families spread out in the remote area along the South Prong of the Sebastian River, often referred to as Sebastian Creek, between the Eureka settlement and Roseland. It remained a rather lonely wilderness area, and some of the individuals did not remain for very long. During that period, Tom Matthews and his family settled south of the Wimbrow Park area in 1910, and brother John followed with his family a year later, settling next to his brother. Charles Dukeshier and his grandson, Charlie Taylor, bought land in the Wimbrow Park area in 1912. The Matthews families encouraged their Arkansas neighbors, the Van Antwerps, to settle next to them in 1914. The Ashburner family settled on the river closer to Roseland around 1915. Other names associated with that area of the south Prong of the Sebastian River are Crom Elbou, the

Davises, Clark, Bailey, and one of the McCain families. In the 1920s, the Carlton House, or Carlton Hotel, was built on the west side of the river, south of the Wimbrow Park area.

Matthews Families on Sebastian Creek

The Matthews brothers, Tom and John, demonstrated that it was possible to live quite well at a bare subsistence level, with practically no work on their part; such was the bounty of the Sebastian River area of the time. They came from the village of Gillett in Stanley Township, Arkansas County, Arkansas. It was considered an unhealthy area, due to periodic flooding of the Mississippi River.

At the time of the 1910 U.S. Census, both John and Tom and their families were in Gillett. John J. Matthews, age 52, was born around 1858 in Kentucky. His second marriage was to Mary M., age 47. With them were children Daisie and Jennie from his first marriage, and John and Mary's children, Jennie, Cynthia, John, and James. Living next to John and family was 40-year-old Thomas R. Matthews, born circa 1870 in Arkansas and married to May C. Matthews, age 22. She was the daughter of Mary, John's wife. Tom and May's children were Charles, Wesley, and Thomas. In 1910, Tom Matthews and his family left Arkansas and settled on the west bank of South Prong of the Sebastian River, south of the current Wimbrow Park area. John and his family followed in 1911, settling on the east bank. They bought their land from A. A. Berry prior to moving. John was a carpenter and built a large, two-story wood frame house and a boat. The men worked occasionally at small carpentry jobs. The wives maintained the households, kept a small garden, took in laundry, and did housekeeping to provide for the families. They ate wild game and lived off the land.

Charles Dukeshier and Charles Eli Taylor

Charles Dukeshier had been a Private in the 110th Ohio Infantry of Union Army from 1862-1865 during the Civil War. He was one of those veterans drawn to the wilderness of Florida. He set out to fulfill a dream of his after his wife died, that of moving from Iowa to Florida. His grandson, Charlie Taylor, was the only family member who was willing to go with him. Charlie Taylor is representative of the best of the individuals who moved to this area in the 1910s. He embodied its virtues, civic-mindedness, determination, and faith. Charlie had been seeing Bessie Williams, and she agreed to marry him and move with them to Florida. Charlie was nineteen and Bessie was eighteen. Charles and Bessie Williams married in Clarinda, Iowa, on February 5, 1912, and the three of them left shortly thereafter.

Undoubtedly, Dukeshier and Taylor knew A. A. Berry in Clarinda. Charles Dukeshier, in his seventies at the time, traded his Iowa farm to the Berry Land Co. for

10 acres of land along the Sebastian River in the area of what is now Wimbrow Park and the airport. While the land was being cleared and a house built, they stayed in a hotel in Roseland. The wood cleared from the land was sent to a sawmill and brought back down the river to build the four-room house with a porch, two bedrooms, living room, kitchen, and dining area. They had a grove and a wide variety of vegetables, pineapples, bananas, rice, and sugar cane. Dukeshier stayed there for five years, then went back to Iowa for an operation, but he never recovered or returned to Florida. Taylor inherited the Dukeshier land.

Charlie and Bessie lived on that land afterward for a while, then moved to Sebastian in 1918. He built a wood frame house for them on Louisiana Avenue. They had three sons and a daughter. Charlie worked at a variety of jobs, became a barber, and operated barber shops in Roseland, Fellsmere, Wabasso, and Sebastian for more than 60 years. Charlie felt called to become a lay preacher in the Methodist church and received his exhorter's license in 1918. He preached in Sebastian, Roseland, and Fellsmere, and was a superintendent of the Methodist Church for more than 20 years. He served as mayor of Sebastian from 1955 to 1957. Bessie died in 1973. After he retired, he made and sold cast nets at age 86. Charlie remarried at age 86 to Mary, who he met at the United Methodist Church. He died in 1985, at age 93.

Leroy Van Antwerp

Leroy VanAntwerp also wanted to leave the unhealthy lands in Gillett, Arkansas, and was convinced by his friend John Matthews to move to Sebastian. Thus, in February 1914, Leroy, his wife Hattie, and four children traveled to Sebastian. At the time, Leroy was 44 and Hattie was 29. In Arkansas, the VanAntwerps and Matthews were neighbors. Leroy operated irrigation machinery there for the rice fields that had become an important industry in Gillett in 1905. He also cut railroad cross-ties, and trapped animals for pelts.

Staying at first with the Matthews, Leroy cleared the 20 acres of land he had purchased on the Sebastian River and built a two-and-a-half story wood frame house. A tip-top, which was a small screened room at the top where smoked mullet was kept, was entered by a trapdoor. In Sebastian, he and Hattie added four more children to the brood. He continued trapping in Florida, and was gone for as much as three weeks at a time, catching raccoons and opossums. He had a small garden, and small groves of oranges and guavas, some of which he sold in town. There was also sugar cane, which he made into sugar and syrup. Hattie rented a house in Sebastian while school was in session, and worked as a janitor in the school that her younger children attended. She also took in laundry. They bought some groceries in Roseland, and supplemented their diet with hunting and fishing. Their son, Thomas Lehmann Van Antwerp, was drafted in 1917 for WWI in the Navy, and was an Electrician 3rd Class, Radio. He went to the Naval Training Station in San Francisco, and was sent to Harvard radio school in 1918.

That year he shipped out on the U.S.S. *Kroonland*. He was discharged in 1919. Leroy's son, Frank, became a grove owner in Wabasso.

Lionel Ashburner

The respected Ashburner family on the Sebastian River had a colorful history. Lionel Ashburner was born in India around 1872 of English parents. He immigrated to the United States in 1886. His wife, M. Hilda Ashburner, was born in Canada around 1875, of English and Welsh parents. She immigrated to the United States about the same time as Lionel. They married and had their first child, Vera, around 1899 in New York. Son Herbert Elliot was also born in New York the following year. Two years later, the Ashburners were in Virginia where Charlotte was born, remaining there until around 1908, when Edith was born. By 1910, they had moved to Colorado, where Lionel Jr. was born. Moving again, by 1915, Howard was born in Texas, according to the 1920 U.S. Census.

Around 1915, they moved to the Sebastian River a little south of Roseland, where they cleared land and built a large, elegant two-story home on a rise overlooking the Sebastian River. It had a broad porch across the front, and a cellar. It was painted white with green trim. A lawn was started. For a while Ashburner farmed, was a contractor, and worked on the bridge. In 1916, he worked at widening and straightening the road between the train depot and the Dixie Highway. He held other positions, including inspector, inspector of elections, and clerk of elections. In 1922, he was appointed to fill the unexpired term of E. S. Fear when he died, as trustee for the Board of Public Education, and was selected again in 1923. Both they and their children entertained at home, and friends joined them for Thanksgiving dinner.

Hilda's parents were from Richmond, Virginia, Mr. and Mrs. W. Vaughan Lloyd. In 1918, they spent six months with the Ashburners. Their son, E. Vaughan-Lloyd, spent a week there in 1918, then returned to his ship. He was in the U.S. Navy. In 1928, Lionel was selling property. The children married and left home. In 1940, Lionel, age 68, and wife, M. Hilda, age 65, were living on the Roseland Fellsmere Road, on their farm property, with grandson Carlton Hurst, age ten, Edith's son.

Herbert Elliot Ashburner

Herbert Elliot Ashburner, son of Lionel and Hilda, was in military service during WWI. He was drafted into the Navy on February 15, 1918, and made Apprentice Seaman on February 27, 1918. He trained at the Norfolk Virginia Training Station from March 16-31 of that year. From there, he was sent to the Naval Hospital at Hampton Road, Virginia, where he remained until he was discharged on May 22, 1919. He went to his parents' home after his discharge, not completely recovered from a long illness. In 1919 and 1920, he traveled a little. At that time, he was unemployed, and living at home with his parents.

17

The Great War Has its Effect on Transportation and Commerce: 1910s

WWI

One month after Florida's Governor Sidney Johnson Catts took office, diplomatic relations with Germany were broken off. WWI, called the Great War, or the War to End All Wars, began when war against Germany was declared on April 6, 1917. Men were registered for the draft; draftees were called up to duty on July 25 of that year. Florida's first quota was 6,325 men. The men trained at Camp Jackson at Columbia, South Carolina, and Camp Wheeler near Macon, Georgia. A total of 42,030 Floridians were in the armed services for this war; 35,829 in the Army, 5,963 in the Navy and Coast Guard, and 238 in the Marine Corps. One-thousand-forty-six Floridians were killed in action. Five of the 35 flying schools in the U.S. were in Florida at Pensacola, Miami, and Arcadia. By 1919, 921 seaplane pilots had trained at Pensacola. Key West had a submarine and naval training base. Florida's coastal defense became a major concern, and patrols of all sorts were set up. Home Guards were established. No formal rationing was put into effect, but informally, some items were rationed such a gas, energy, and some foods. Sugar was scarce, and its price was high. Prices rose; wages did not.

All men between the ages of 21 and 30 were registered for the draft; however, some of the Sebastian and Roseland registrants appear to be as young as seventeen and as old as 40. Worthy of note was that one, Wiley Beugnot, had only one eye, and Henry Boyd was a Methodist minister. The draft registration process required some personal information from the men, including name, date, place of birth, occupation, employer, and next of kin. This process required the full names of the individuals, not initials or nicknames. Most frequent occupations given locally were fisher, farmer, and railroad employee. Parents or wives were listed as next of kin.

Many draftees were exempted from service. Newspapers of the day provided continuing information as to who was drawn from the draft, or exempted. St. Lucie County had 853 registered men in the county. The first 110 names were drawn to find qualified men, and then the subsequent draft of names was pulled to fill the rest of the quota of 54, as many were exempted.

Service

Not all who were drafted actually served, and others served who were not drafted. Some were both enlisted and drafted. Florida Special Archives Publication No. 28 listed which men were enlisted Florida Veterans of the First World War. The service cards contained information as to where and when they served, and at what rank. The following individuals had WWI Service Cards, fifteen residents of Sebastian and four residents of Roseland who served in WWI, as found in the State of Florida records:

Sebastian:
John Tribble Beugnot, Navy, Apprentice Seaman, discharged at the Naval Hospital at Newport, Rhode Island after 174 days of service in 1917 (drafted)
Charles Lee Beugnot, Army, Private (enlisted)
George William Edwards, Navy, Seaman (drafted)
Paul B. Edwards, Army, Private 1st Class (drafted) (enlisted)
Ralph W. E. Edwards, Army, Supply Sergeant, 10% disabled on discharge (drafted) (enlisted)
Lisbon Futch, Navy, Quartermaster 1st Class (drafted)
James J. Gibbs, Army, Sergeant (enlisted)
Joe E. Goins, Army, Private, 50% disabled on discharge (enlisted)
Arthur C. Hatch, Army, Private (enlisted)
Ezekiel Moore, Army, Private 1st Class (drafted) (enlisted)
Steadman A. Parker, Army, Sergeant (enlisted)
Jesse E. Powell, Army, Sergeant 1st Class (enlisted)
William Rayford Ryall, Navy Coxwain (drafted)
James Monroe Stinson, Navy, Seaman 2nd Class (drafted)
Treley Thompson, Navy, Seaman 2nd Class (drafted)

Roseland:
Herbert Elliot Ashburner, Navy, Apprentice Seaman, discharged at the Naval Hospital at Hampton Roads, Virginia, May 22, 1919 (drafted)
Lester Hanshaw, Army, Private (enlisted)
Milton Jackson Hardee, Army, Private (enlisted)
Thomas Lehmann Van Antwerp, Navy, Electrician 3rd Class Radio (drafted)

The war ended November 11, 1918. In its aftermath, Armistice Day celebrations were held everywhere, along with Liberty Parades. There were speeches, poems, songs, athletic events, races, dances, and refreshment booths. There were Liberty Loan Drives and Victory Drives in 1919. A direct result of the war was the commencement of the sugar industry in Florida and a drop in farm produce prices from their wartime high.

Travel and Transportation—The Age of the Auto

A great concern during this decade was improving the infrastructure needed for transportation. Increases in Florida's interstate and in-state commerce, tourism, and growing population demanded improvements of many sorts. The Inland Waterway, Sebastian Inlet, a bridge over the St. Sebastian River, more roads, better surfacing, and widening of roads were all topics for improvements. The train track west of Sebastian was opened again. Not much attention was paid to the needs of aircraft yet.

The great American love affair with automobiles had begun. A car was a prized possession; garages were built before the house was built. Photographs were taken with the automobile, owners leaning on it, driving it, and standing in front of it. There were more photographs of automobiles than of houses. Both before and after the war, people were more mobile than ever, taking vacations, visiting friends, or going to dinner, church, or to a moving picture out of town. They were free of the travel restrictions that were part of travel by boat or rail.

Roads

One newspaper headline read, "Good roads cut freight bills." This was a decade of the automobile and truck. Demands for more roads were increasing. As early as 1907, road improvements were planned in the county, and by 1912-1913, 62 miles of hard surfaced roads were completed. Concrete was beginning to be widely used in construction, and some streets in Fort Pierce were redone in concrete. Some were surfaced in asphalt and others in marl. The surfacing used depended on the usage of the roads.

There were many notices in the *Ft. Pierce News* of the county commissioners adding new roads in the county, accepting bids for the road construction, many of which were executed by HR Sloan Construction of Sebastian. Many local laborers and subcontractors were hired to carry out the work, paid directly by the county commission. Nineteen sixteen was a busy year for HR Sloan Construction and Sloan Brothers. They were responsible for laying marl on the Sebastian Fellsmere road west of the river, and the bid for asphalting Vero streets. At a county commissioners' meeting, HR Sloan Construction was directed to continue using marl surface on the road between Sebastian Creek and Collier's Slough; it also did hard surfacing in Oslo and more. Work was being done on the Sebastian-Fellsmere road in 1912, and it was completed June 1916.

The most prominent completion was a north-south road through county paralleling the Indian River, connected to the great National Highway from Montreal to Miami. Yet these improvements did not extend everywhere. Hard beach surfaces were often preferred for automotive travel, rather than dusty, rutted sand roads; however, then it was necessary to pay attention to the tides. Not everyone was in favor of the proposed extensions. One fear voiced in the October 11, 1919, *Vero Press* was that such a road system would allow tourists to more quickly leave the county to go elsewhere.

Dixie Highway

The idea of a national highway running north and south through the United States was conceived by Carl G. Fisher, the individual responsible for the creation of the first national highway, the Lincoln Highway, which ran from New York to San Francisco and was dedicated October 31, 1913. The route was marked with red, white, and blue signs reading "Lincoln Highway" and a large "L."

He next proposed the national route to Florida. By 1914, he had obtained enough support to present the idea at the annual meeting of the American Road Congress in Atlanta. In 1915, the Dixie Highway was approved. A new national highway was to be created from Chicago to Miami along the Florida east coast. It would be a section of the "Montreal to Miami National Highway," reported the *Fellsmere Tribune* on May 29, 1915. The fact that 95% of the necessary roads were already in existence along the Florida east coast dictated that it would run there, instead of central or west Florida. The existing roads were considered improved and modern highways, and the complete route through Florida was expected to be completed within one year, according to the Directors of the Dixie Highway Association that was created in Chattanooga, Tennessee. A signage design was copyrighted in 1915 by this association. The signs placed along the route would have a brown bale of cotton on a red background with "Dixie Highway" in the foreground.

The *Fellsmere Tribune, St. Lucie Tribune*, and *Vero Press* followed the progress of this new highway's creation with numerous updates. Auto travelers began asking by 1916 when the Dixie Highway would be completed. Prior to its completion, there was no direct route south, and many roundabout roads had to be traveled. Automobiles were taking over, and roads were needed. In March of 1916, automobile tours of the Dixie Highway were being planned, first from Cincinnati to Miami, and the second, from Miami north, with more tours planned. In Sebastian as well as other towns along the route, committees planned for beautification of the road. The county decided on Australian silk oaks to plant along the route. Local Women's Clubs planned beautification projects.

"Dixie Highway Made Ready for Large Tourist Travel" was the headline of an article from a newspaper from Chattanooga, Tennessee, on April 12, 1916, that was included in the *Fellsmere Tribune* on May 5, 1916. It stated that a record number of tourists were flocking to Florida, and auto travelers were eagerly anticipating the opening of the complete eastern division of the Dixie Highway route to facilitate travel.

The Fellsmere Road Arch Committee started planning an arch to go over the Dixie Highway at what is now Rte. 512, as a gateway to Fellsmere, paid for by subscription. Construction began in July 1916, before it was fully subscribed. The Fellsmere Arch was finally completed March 9, 1919, placed at the beginning of Rte. 512, west of the Florida East Coast railroad tracks.

Railroads estimated 1,000,000 tourists in Florida in the 1916 season arriving by rail. Travel by automobile had not overtaken rail service. Auto travel was estimated at 50,000 visitors to Florida. However, the increases in auto and truck travel were taking their toll on road stability. The surface of current roads was too light for the heavier auto and truck traffic, giving way and washing out. It was suggested that the sand and oil treatment implemented by the Dixie Highway be used on local roads, and that the 9-foot roadways be widened to 15 feet. In December 1916, the Y was completed at the Sebastian railroad terminal to facilitate the handling of traffic.

On July 15, 1916, N. Gillan of Lafayette Indiana, made a record-breaking trip by automobile from Mackinaw, Michigan, to Miami in 69 actual running hours on the Dixie Highway, and was the first car to cover the whole trip on the Dixie Highway. Brevard's section of the Dixie Highway had traffic of 50 to 60 automobiles a day. Many other roads were created by 1919 to connect with the popular Dixie Highway. In Sebastian, the original Dixie Highway followed the route of what is now the named the Old Dixie Highway south of Sebastian, and north on what is now Indian River Drive.

Federal Roads

A Federal Highway Commission was created in 1919 to oversee the creation of a nation-wide road system with the National Highway Bill. It was intended to be an interlocking system of highways joining the main trunk lines of each state with the main trunk lines of other states to form a complete web of highways connecting the whole country together. It was also intended to conform the roads to a uniform good condition.

State Roads

In 1917, the Florida State Road Department was authorized to construct roads. In 1919, it was authorized to increase aid to counties to construct roads, and it assigned numbers to a thousand miles of designated state roads. Florida had 4,767 miles of improved roads, and at that point estimated that it needed another 3,600 miles of roads for a completely integrated system.

In late 1919, the county was a hotbed of controversy over the issue of whether to vote bonds for road construction, which roads, and how much. A resolution was made by the St. Lucie County commissioners for a bond on October 7, 1919, for the Dixie Highway to be built according to federal specifications from the Sebastian River to Vero, and according to State Highway Commission specifications, from Vero to the St. Lucie River, as reported in the *Vero Press*. There was much dispute over the route of the Dixie Highway north of Vero, whether bonds should support it, and whether it was needed. New, good roads were not needed for driving cattle, they argued. One letter to the editor voiced the opinion that "the Dixie Highway will never be of sufficient importance to justify a bond issue in the future." Another bond voted in January of 1920 passed.

Travel Services

A new sort of growth began along the roadways. Instead of centering in a town or hamlet, travel-related services were starting up along the roads, including garages that provided repair services and gasoline, restaurants, and little shops. Increased road travel also brought about increased accidents.

Tin Can Tourists

One of the more amazing developments after World War I was the rise of the "Tin Can Tourists," so-called because of the easy availability and cheap price of World War I surplus tents and vehicles. Coupled with the spread of the highway system across America, a new type of tourist was created. These adventuresome souls camped out, ate at roadside stands, and explored unknown byways.

There were other cars manufactured before Henry Ford's, but his automobile was cheap and reliable. This was due in large part to the means of manufacturing. His automobile factory was the second to utilize assembly-line technology; the first was Eli Whitney. With the advent of WWI, America quickly ramped up its production of war materials, converting and creating factories using this assembly-line technique to quickly turn out tanks, airplanes, artillery, and all of the other materials of warfare. U.S. production of war goods was so successful, in part due to the short duration of the war, that there were thousands of surplus vehicles, tents, biplanes, and other materials at war's end. These items were sold to the general public at greatly reduced prices. Tanks became tractors, and ambulances converted to cargo carriers.

All of the factories that had been created or converted for the war effort quickly adapted to the manufacture of consumer goods, such as travel-related automobiles, tractors, fire engines, road graders, and trucks. The post-war boom to the economy meant that individuals could now afford these "essential" goods. Ford automobiles were most popular and sprang up everywhere. Automobiles became the symbol of the new generation. They created a freedom in that they were faster and did not run on rails. They did not depend on wind, weather, or tides, and had no set schedules. That post-war generation felt the lure of the open road, of escape and adventure. Leisure travel was no longer restricted to the wealthy. Americans took to the roads. They carried surplus war tents and canned foods, traveling light and spending the nights at the side of a road or in a convenient field. Florida was a popular destination, and the Dixie Highway became their route.

In 1919, the Tin Can Tourists of the World formed in Tampa. It is thought that the name derived either from the "Tin Lizzie" auto, or from the tinned foods carried. The society held annual meetings in Florida and Michigan. The members began forming caravans to travel. Florida was supportive of these travelers, seeking the rewards of increased tourism. Along the Tin Can Tourist routes, commerce flourished.

Drawbacks of Technology

Some advances in technology were mixed blessings, as reported in the *St. Lucie Tribune*. New roads were not enough; they now had to be "double tracked," or two-lane roads, to keep autos from hitting each other, and sidewalks were needed for walkers so that cars would not honk at them or make pedestrians leap off the road. The advent of automobiles brought another new phenomenon to roads, the automobile accident. Headlines began appearing such as this one in 1917: "Thos. Dillmon's Car Tries to Climb Palmetto on Riverside Drive—Wrecked."

Indigents

Florida has always attracted those looking for a new life and a way to make a living. Automobiles facilitated this influx. Not only Tin Can Tourists, but also destitute people in automobiles looking to make it rich were arriving and living in their autos or in tents. They created their own burden on the infrastructure of Florida towns, living in makeshift camps with often unsanitary conditions.

Sebastian River Bridge

Following the demand for more roads, bridges were next to receive attention. County commissioners of Brevard and St. Lucie counties began receiving bids on September 5, 1910, for the erection of a bridge over the Sebastian River at Roseland to replace the ferry. The contract was let September 5, 1910, to Radalege & Sons of Eau Gallie. The bridge over the St. Sebastian River was completed by April 28, 1911, reported the *Ft. Pierce News*. It was a wooden structure with convenient approaches at both sides and had a draw of sufficient size to allow the passage of boats. It was replaced by a concrete bridge in the 1920s.

Sebastian-Fellsmere Railroad

When Nelson Fell took over the Russell land tract west of Sebastian to create the Fellsmere Farms Subdivision, he needed access to the land for the massive amounts of men, supplies, and equipment needed to create his vision. Prospective buyers needed easy access, too. The Sebastian and Fellsmere Farms Railroad Co. took over the land and track bed once used by the abandoned Sebastian and Cincinnatus Railroad project, defunct since 1900, when Russell died. Work began on the reconstruction of the railway bed and the railroad bridge in 1910. Miller and King moved their sawmill to Sebastian to saw lumber for the bridge on June 10, 1910. The old narrow-gauge track was replaced. The railroad was completed and in operation September 1910 with two stops, Sebastian and Fellsmere, with a River Bridge stop added in 1912. The track went beyond Fellsmere in 1913 as the town of Broadmoor was built. There was a depot in Fellsmere, and in Sebastian it connected to the Florida East Coast Railway. The railroad had a shed for trains at Kitching, and the Kitching switch located there was a train siding for loading supplies such as lumber. In places, the railroad line was fairly close to the current Rte. 512, but diverged further west.

The railway was designed for both freight and passenger trains. One train was run by a wood-burning steam locomotive. The Fellsmere Railroad Company advertised in 1916-1919 that it had stops at Fellsmere, River Bridge, Kitching, and Sebastian, daily except Sunday, with connections to the Florida East Coast Railway at Sebastian. Deepland, Homewood, and Grassland became other stops.

Florida East Coast Railway

The Florida East Coast Railway provided work for some individuals; Leon Bankman accepted a clerk's position at depot; Snell continued his work at the depot when he came back from his honeymoon in 1916; G. A. Cain inspected ties; R. N. Coleman was a section foreman; R. S. Snell was an agent. That year, Paul B. Edwards left Sebastian to take a job with the Florida East Coast Railway in New Smyrna as a freight clerk. Repair work was kept up in 1916; the Florida East Coast Railway carpenter gang number 1 built an addition to the Sebastian Depot, an Express Shed on the north end. The Florida East Coast Railway bridge gang did repair work in Sebastian. Increased rail service brought its own problems and complaints. Freight trains making flying switches across public roads were vigorously protested. Trains were running over deer and bears.

Sebastian Inlet

Early in the area's history, it was decided that an inlet across the barrier island dividing the Indian River and the Atlantic Ocean near the Sebastian River was an economic necessity both for improved fishing, cleansing the river, and other commercial uses. All early attempts at digging the cut filled in and failed, commencing with New's Cut in 1881, Gibson's Cut in 1886, and others. Attempts were made with pick, shovel, and dredges, but all filled in again.

However, not everyone was in favor of the inlet project. The County Commissioners prepared and approved a resolution in April of 1915 to block the War Department from granting a permit for the creation of an inlet, citing that it was a menace to property owners; the salt water would adversely affect citrus groves. Frank Forster and A. B. Michael made the presentation. This was not agreed to.

The Florida legislature created the Sebastian Inlet District Commission during the 1917-1918 session to address the problem. Opening the inlet had become an economic necessity. The pollution in the Indian River needed to be cleansed out into the ocean and there was a wartime food shortage, which could be solved with the better fishing that an influx of ocean fish would bring. Moreover, fishing boats in Sebastian and Roseland would have ocean access. In May 1918, the Federal Conservation Board approved the inlet, and an inlet district was formed. Carl Schlichtinger of Roseland, one of the officers of the Sebastian Inlet Association, considered that they had a satisfactory program. The first Inlet commissioners were M. M. Miller of Sebastian, Eliot Good of Tillman, and Dr. Preel of Eau Gallie. A few years later, a new commission was created with R. O. Couch a president, Albert Vorkellar as secretary, and Charley Sembler as treasurer.

Work began again on the digging at the Gibson's Cut site opposite the mouth of the Sebastian River in 1917, and newspapers, including the *Miami Herald*, gave periodic reports of the progress. Roy O. Couch spearheaded this next attempt to open an inlet. He operated a machine shop, and was a successful mechanic. The Couch Pump Company was owned by him later on. Couch was also an inventor. He designed a successful pump to drain swamps, a water-powered generator, and, due to his belief in the necessity of opening an ocean inlet, he designed and built a diesel-powered dredge mounted on a barge that was very effective for removal of sand to form the inlet. Charlie Sembler, who was living in Grant at the time with his wife Mae, worked on the Couch Dredge for a year; however, sand filled in as fast as it was removed. A steam shovel was also used in the operation. Many other individuals labored to make the cut.

Eventually, an opening was made sufficient for small boats in late 1918, but it quickly filled in again. In 1919, work began again to open the inlet. To continue the work, Couch and a delegation successfully lobbied in Tallahassee for funding, and a Sebastian Inlet Tax Distract was created in 1919. The cut was opened in 1919, but a few days later the banks caved in and it closed again. Finally, in 1923, a successful inlet was cut. Wave action built up sandbars, but the cut was useful for many years.

Intracoastal Waterway

Long contemplated, actual work first began on an intracoastal waterway in 1881 by a private company, the Canal Company. In payment, Canal Company was given 1,030,128 acres of land by 1912 for 338 miles of canal constructed. This arrangement proved unprofitable, and the Canal Company went into receivership in 1923 and was sold.

Improvement of the Inland Waterway saw an increase in boat traffic. It continued to be used for freight hauling and passenger steamer service in 1911 by the Gulf Coast Navigation Company between St. Augustine and Palm Beach. The Florida Coastal Inland Navigation Company ran ships between Cocoa and Jacksonville in 1913. Many power boats and yachts ran this route as well.

Aircraft

As a sign of things to come, from 1910 to 1912, there were several demonstration landings of the new Wright Brothers biplane; one landed at DeSoto Beach on the sand (now part of NASA). Previously, aircraft were making landings and takeoffs on water as there were no suitable landing places on land.

The Barnstormers

While some were taking to the open roads, the ex-pilots of WWI were taking to the air. They acquired war-surplus biplanes and traveled the U.S.A., landing in convenient fields and selling rides to pay for gas. Many books have been written about their exuberant exploits.

In Sebastian, it was possible to get a ride in a WWI vintage Curtis "Jenny" seaplane from Otis Ashley, whose parents lived in Micco. The model JN biplane was built by Curtis Aeroplane Company of Hammondsport, New York. Thousands were sold post-war at reduced prices and were the airplane of choice of barnstormers. Ashley's was a seaplane, a biplane with pontoons instead of wheels for takeoffs and landings on the water.

The Pathfinder Hydroplane created by Aeromarine Ltd. of New Jersey, and based at Fort McHenry, in Baltimore, Maryland, stopped in Sebastian in 1923 and gave rides, including a ride to the Kroegel family. This design was called a flying boat. The flying boats were aircraft that could take off and land on water, but did not have pontoons; instead it relied on a buoyant main body. The early models were biplanes. They were a popular design for a time, as they did not require expensive land-based runways to operate.

Commerce

WWI had a decided impact on the local economy. Many of the young men went to war and were not producing, and at the same time, the war demanded greater commercial output. Shortages were inevitable. Both before and after the war, however, the area prospered. County-wide, raising pineapples was the chief industry in this decade, followed by commercial fishing. Boats became motorized. Several hundred launches powered by gasoline motors caught and hauled fish to the packing houses at Fort

Pierce, Jensen, Sebastian, Walton, and elsewhere in the county. Indian River Citrus was gaining a name for itself in St. Lucie County. Some groves were beginning to ship 40,000-50,000 boxes of fruit annually. However, the freeze of February 2-3, 1917, wiped out citrus crops, but as it was not as severe as the freeze of 1894-1895, trees were spared. Potatoes, tomatoes, beans, and all kinds of truck vegetables were growing well, and more small farms developed throughout the county.

Sebastian Board of Trade

The Sebastian Board of Trade was created by a vocal and enthusiastic group of businessmen who were supporters of commerce in the area. The Sebastian Board of Trade officers were Dr. David Rose, president; R. G. Hardee, vice president; and J. J. Gibbs, secretary and treasurer. This group advertised itself as "A body of live, wide awake boosters, all pulling together for the good of the community." The group offered information and advice to visitors and prospective buyers.

Fishing

When the inlet briefly opened in 1918 and 1919, ocean fish swam into the Indian River, such as trout, mullet, and sharks. For a short time, fishing boats could go out through the inlet for ocean fishing. Blue fish and pompano were popular catches. When the inlet closed up again, migratory fish like flounder that wanted to spawn in the ocean would congregate on the eastern side of the inlet's location, trying to reach the ocean. They were easily caught. Crabs also walked overland to reach the ocean to spawn. One thousand, five hundred pounds of fish was considered a boat's good night's catch, and many local individuals were engaged in fishing. Packing houses, such as Hardee Packing house, Sebastian Fish Company, and Walter Hawkins Packing House managed the catches, preparing the fish to be shipped out by train with the help of local ice houses and barrel factories.

One of the Roseland fishing concerns was Youngblood Fish House on the bayfront, run by A. L. Youngblood of Gillett, Arkansas, and later Carl Schlesinger. Fern Carpenter of Sebastian took a position as manager of this company in 1916. Allen Cain, Chas Hendricks, and C. E. Henry were some of the local fishermen.

Fernie S. Carpenter

Fernie S. Carpenter made his living in the fishing industry. He owned one of the houses on Palmetto Avenue in Sebastian listed in Old Town Sebastian Historic District West and placed on the National Register of Historic Places January 6, 2004. It is a modest, one-story wood frame house. He and his wife Beedie and son Orva arrived from Arkansas sometime after 1910, and remained in Sebastian. He was a manager of the Youngblood Fish Company around 1916-1918; later, he was a fisherman, and then a laborer doing odd jobs around the time of his death. After he died around 1930, Beedie lived with Orva and his wife, Nettie Ree Carpenter, in the house on Palmetto, next to Fernie's home. Orva was also a fisherman. Fernie, Beedie, and Orva are all buried in Sebastian Cemetery together.

Steadman Parker

Stedman Parker came from a fishing family, but widened his reach much further. The Parker family lived in many places over the years. They were in Sebastian in the 1900s-1910s. John Henry Parker engaged in fishing while in Sebastian with his wife, Hettie. During that time, his son Cecil was also a fisherman in Sebastian, as was William E. Parker, who was a telegrapher for the F.E.C. Railway.

John and Hettie's son, Steadman Parker, was in the U.S. Army during that time. Steadman Parker's enlistment card stated that he enlisted in the U.S. Army at Columbus, Ohio, on June 20, 1916. He served in the Infantry for one year where he reached rank of Sergeant. In 1918, he transferred to the Aero Squadron where he achieved the rank of Corporal. He was honorably discharged August 24, 1920.

Perhaps around 1920 when he was discharged, Steadman married Denise, who was born in England. Their children, Gloria, Steadman Jr., Evelyn, and Dolinda, were born in Florida. In the 1940 U.S. Census, he was a seaman on a steamer, and his wife taught in a dancing school. He was 41 years old in that record. After WWII, he was a Captain of a steamship line. In 1949, he came back to this area and became involved in searching for sunken treasure off the Indian River County coast with Kip Wagner, Jimmy Russell, Carl Wild, and George Bunnell. He continued this interest, and that year Stedman obtained an exclusive exploratory lease from the State of Florida for part of the Indian River County coastline from the Sebastian Inlet south to Ambersands Beach Park to explore for salvage and treasure. Over the years, he had some extraordinary exploits searching for treasure. He began his lifelong interest in treasure hunting when his father showed him the wreckage from a Spanish galleon in 1907. He died in 1966 in Fort Lauderdale, Florida, at age 68.

Citrus

New problems were facing citrus growers and their organizations, the Florida Citrus Exchange, Indian River Citrus Growers' Association, and other groups during this decade. The practice had been to sell the fruit on the trees; buyers would come to the groves to determine purchase and marketing details before fruit was picked. However, the citrus purchasers too often were shipping the fruit when it was still green and immature. Many growers stopped this method of selling, as it was ruining the reputation of Indian River citrus. Moreover, growers petitioned the Florida legislature to create a green fruit bill which was enacted in 1911, limiting the shipment of immature oranges.

Indian River citrus was developing a nationwide reputation for the excellence of its fruit that needed to be protected. To take advantage of this reputation, there began to be instances of actual fraud; other companies and growers not in the Indian River area began selling their fruit labeled "Indian River." Protection was achieved by utilizing and filing unique trademarks for Indian River produce. The Tampa-based Florida Citrus Exchange filed many trademarks with the U.S. Patent and Trademark Office, beginning in 1910, as did other groups and individual growers.

The maturing industry brought regulation as it created jobs. State Inspectors were inspecting groves. More little groves were springing up, and many locals worked in the groves or in packing.

Guy French Davis

Guy French Davis was one of the many individuals in Sebastian that made a comfortable living for himself and his family growing citrus in the rich soil near the Indian River. A native Virginian, he sold his farm and left his hogs in Arkansas where he had been living for more than ten years to settle in Sebastian, and become a farmer and citrus grower. He and his wife, Hattie Odell, married in 1897 in Arkansas, and their four sons, Thomas, Odell, Theodore, and Everett, were born there. The six of them arrived by train in 1910, and rented, then purchased a house and land from Fred Parks in 1911, in the area of present US Hwy 1 and Davis Street. The Davis family remained there, selling their citrus. Thomas died in 1912 at age twelve. Hattie died in 1937. The three brothers were unmarried in 1940, still living at home with their widowed father. Odell was a machinist for Fellsmere Sugar Producers Association, and Theo and Everett were fishermen. The three sons were in the military in WWII; Odell and Everett were in the Navy, and Theo was in the Army. The whole family is buried together in Sebastian Cemetery.

William E. Futch

William E. Futch was one of the many successful citrus growers in Sebastian, but his death received more attention than his livelihood. He was a native Floridian who married Rachel Ida Futch around 1896. They lived in Titusville in 1900, and by 1910, they had moved to Volusia County. They had arrived in Sebastian by 1914, where Futch purchased land near the August Park family and became a citrus grower, raising citrus and a family. This nice, ordinary life had a more noted end, part of a growing problem. On January 14, 1926, a *Vero Beach Press Journal* article was titled: "Sebastian Man Victim of Auto." It stated, "Another sacrifice to the demon speed was added to the list of countless thousands Tuesday morning when William E. Futch, 72, of North Sebastian was struck and killed instantly by a passing automobile." It went on to relate that he was walking on the road when he was struck and thrown by the car. The driver was apprehended and placed on trial.

The sons apparently did not continue with the citrus grove. Son Edmond Futch became a fisherman. Son Lisbon Futch was in the U.S. Navy during WWI. He served on the U.S.S. *Vermont* from April-May 1917, was in the Naval Hospital in Philadelphia for a month, then went back to the U.S.S. *Vermont*. He was discharged August 17, 1918, from the U.S.S. *Vermont* as a Quartermaster 1st Class. As a reservist, he served as an Ensign from January 20, 1919, on *Solace*.

Bayview Grove

The Fields family of White City had a citrus grove and home in Roseland named Bayview in the 1916s. They eventually moved to Miami.

Farming

The soil and climate were perfect for farming, and winter crops continued to feed the north. Many individuals planted truck farms to have a commercial crop while they waited for their citrus trees to mature enough to bear fruit. Many locals kept their hand in with many ventures, including farming, fishing, and taking odd jobs. One of them was a nurseryman with a striking sense of civic and religious duty.

Judge Milo Milton Miller

Milo M. Miller was one of the many strong, successful individuals who helped form both the civic and religious core of Sebastian. He was born in Hadley, Michigan, June 16, 1856. He moved to Missouri where he married Barbara Kuda October 6, 1896. They also lived in Arkansas, and brought their children, Ted, Alta, and Ruby, to Florida in 1910. Miller acquired a 20-acre tract on north Louisiana Avenue in Sebastian where they lived. The two-story wood frame house that was their home no longer exists. For a while Miller did carpentry work, and they took in boarders. He became interested in horticulture and began the Square Deal Nursery, which was very successful. Miller worked with many types of plants, including citrus and other fruits, grafting stock and experimenting. He was elected Justice of the Peace for the north district of St. Lucie County, and he served for fifteen years. He continued to be known as Judge Miller after he left the bench. He was a member of the Episcopal Church and council commander of the local camp of Modern Woodmen. Civic affairs commanded much of his attention. He served for eight years on the board of commissioners for the Sebastian Inlet District and was deeply interested in this project.

He was instrumental in the erection of the community hall in Sebastian and was secretary and treasurer of the Sebastian Public Hall Company board of directors. On the Board of Trade, he served as secretary. He was a member of the Sebastian town council as well. When Sebastian incorporated, he was elected as a member of the city council.

Soon after the incorporation, Judge Miller and family decided to make a move. He sold the North Louisiana Avenue property in 1926 to S. A. Braswell and purchased land on South Riverside Drive at Shumann Drive. At that time, it was not considered part of Sebastian, and he resigned from the city council. The house he built there is thought to be one of the Sears, Roebuck catalog homes. Judge Miller died of a heart attack in May 1929. His funeral conducted by Rev. DuBose was well attended. He was buried in Sebastian Cemetery with Woodman rites, and his wife Barbara was buried next to him; children Ted and Alta, and her husband Curtis Bobo, are there as well.

O. A. Hartman

Hartman was one of those individuals that farmed, and did a little something else on the side. The Hartmans, O. A. and wife Elizabeth, arrived in Sebastian around 1908 and bought the Arthur Krogel home on the river. O. A. was a farmer and sold turkeys. Mrs. Hartman had a store and sold ice cream. Unfortunately, O. A. fell afoul of the laws of the time. In 1910, he was prosecuted for illegal sale of liquor. A jury found him guilty, and he received a sentence of six months in County Jail and a fine. He served the time and paid the $150.00 fine, but was unable to pay the court costs. The Judge discharged him and payment of court costs was waived.

Cattle

For many years, cattlemen in Florida had a very strong lobby, and rights of cattlemen had been paramount. However, with the growth of population and infrastructure, there was a shift in values. Cattle had always been able to roam free, but farmers complained about the destruction of crops. Fences around homes were being trampled and yards were destroyed by the cattle. They were a hazard on roads and railroad tracks. The free-range ordinance was challenged again, but it was upheld in 1910, allowing cattle to continue to roam free. However, in 1913, a law was passed to make it unlawful to let hogs run loose. The question of fencing cattle land was an issue again in the 1920s.

The Sebastian Ranch Company

The Sebastian Ranch Company that had been owned by Daniel Sloan diversified after his death in January of 1919. In October 1919, Sebastian Ranch Co. was engaged in growing potatoes and turpentining two miles west of Wabasso. It was building numerous cottages for its workers.

Lucius Andrew Sloan

L. A. Sloan, eldest son of William and Elizabeth, was born December 15, 1886. He lived in Fellsmere with wife Rosabelle, who was born in 1888, and he was a road contractor and fruit grower in 1917. Moreover, he was part of Sloan Brothers, and was involved in many business and real estate transactions, as well as road contracting. He added 200 head of cattle to his land three miles west of Sebastian on the Fellsmere Road in 1919. L. A. Sloan and his family moved from Fellsmere to a home on South Louisiana Avenue in 1928, which they remodeled. When this house burned to the ground, they donated their piano to the Woman's Club. Lucius died in 1935, and Rosa B. Sloan died in 1981. Both are buried in the Sebastian Cemetery.

William Preston Sloan

William Preston Sloan was the second son of William and Elizabeth Sloan, born December 15, 1886. He lived in Fellsmere with his wife Mattie. In 1914, in Sebastian, he built a two-story, eight-room residence on the north edge of town. In 1917, he was wealthy enough to purchase a racehorse, a mare named Ruby Hill, from the West Coast that he rode, not always traveling by auto. He was a part of the family road contracting business, and part of the Sloan Brothers business ventures. Separately, he also had extensive business ventures. In 1919, he owned the Sloan rental cottages, and added 500 head of cattle to his land three miles west of Sebastian. His Sloan Hotel in Sebastian was planned to open in July but did not open until October 1919. It had waterworks and baths. Mr. Wyse was the manager. It provided nice meals and comfortable rooms overlooking the Atlantic Ocean and Indian River, according to newspaper reports. In 1923, he set out another new grove in Sebastian, purchasing a new tractor to clear ten acres of land. W. P. Sloan was one of the men who chartered the train to go to Tallahassee to lobby for the new county in 1925, and that same year he was involved with Okey Bland's real estate venture.

Harney Rubin Sloan

The youngest Sloan son made a tragic mistake. Harney Rubin Sloan was the youngest son of William and Elizabeth Sloan. Individually and with Sloan Brothers, he was a contractor to build and surface roads all over the county. At times, he was living in Sebastian and at times, in Vero. According to his draft registration form, he was born January 22, 1896, at Fort Drum, Florida. He was single, living in Vero, and his occupation was contractor and builder. Included was the notation "Support of parents."

Harney made a disastrous choice. His claim to be the sole support of his aged parents was disallowed by the draft board, and he vanished. On September 28, 1917, the *Ft. Pierce News* trumpeted a bold headline wondering if he was courting death by his insane act of desertion. He did not show up for his draft induction in 1917. The newspapers continued to follow this case. He hid out in Big Cypress Swamp for three weeks, and then was captured and arrested when he returned to the area to visit relatives. He was sent to Key West and then transferred to Fort Dade, Florida, to face a military court martial on the charge of desertion while drafted. In 1918, he was removed from the voter registration rolls with the notation "gone."

Business Ventures of Sloan Brothers of Sebastian

Sloan Brothers was a company doing road work throughout the county from 1916 through the 1920s. The Sloans had a grocery store in the Hardee building in Sebastian. They were also owners of several buildings around the county. There was a Sloan Building on Broadway in Fellsmere. Ellsworth Weigle's garage moved there in November 1928. The Sloan brothers also purchased two lots in Edgewood, and two rental bungalows were being constructed for them. Miles McNece purchased the Sloan property between 20th and 21st Street on the Dixie Highway in Vero in 1920, using the small building there for his vulcanizing and tire business.

The Sloan Building in Vero may have seen the most activity in a very short period of time, reported in the *Ft. Pierce News*. W. P. and H. R. Sloan were building on their lot adjoining the Edgewood garage on Dixie Highway in 1917, a two-story frame structure that was intended to have a grocery store. A sidewalk was added to the front. Fred Sanders' grocery store and meat market was the first tenant on the entire first floor, and his family lived on the second floor. Peter Sommers leased a room in the new Sloan building to open a restaurant and lunch room later that year. By December 2017, Canfield, Williams Co. leased space in the Sloan Building on Dixie Highway for their Five, Ten and Twenty-Five Cent Store. Mrs. C. F. Linn painted, remodeled, and took over the entire Sloan Building to run a rooming house with an up-to-date restaurant by 1918. Four years later, J. C. DuBose had a business there, as did the furniture store of Yeargin.

18

The National Influence: 1910s

This decade, many outside influences and technology reached Florida. The 1910s were a mix of diverse elements that converged in Florida from elsewhere, from the war to the automobile. One of the strangest new elements to enter Florida was electricity. Entertainment from the rest of the country invaded Florida as well, including moving pictures and Vaudeville acts. Advertising and promotion continued to feature Florida as a desirable destination. More nationwide social clubs sprang up in the growing population.

Electricity

When electricity arrived in St. Lucie County, it was electrifying! Courtesy of local newspapers of the time, the *Ft. Pierce News* and *St. Lucie Tribune*, it was possible to get a first-hand look at the impact electricity had on individuals and towns. The change it brought was overwhelming. The promise of electric power had been around since the 1880s, but the technology was a little slow in reaching this area.

Before the advent of electrical power in St. Lucie County, "electric" found its way into advertising as a catchword with the healthful tonic "Electric Bitters," "Electric" flypaper, and "Stearn's Electric paste rat poison."

Municipal Power

In June of 1912, construction was underway for the municipal plant for water, sewer, and electricity in Fort Pierce, and by Thanksgiving of that year, electricity was turned on. Vero Utilities Company began supplying electricity in 1917. Fellsmere Electric Light & Ice Company also went into operation in 1917. Sebastian was late obtaining municipal electricity. It did not begin until Sebastian incorporation in 1925, when the Municipal Power and Ice Plant was built to supply electricity and ice to the Sebastian area.

Things electrical were slow to appear in news and advertisements in St. Lucie County. In 1914, advertisements by Alcazar Electric Company in Fort Pierce appeared as contractors to install household electrical wiring, and it sold electric lights, fans, ranges and irons, and flashlights. "For Sale" notices for houses advertised electric lighting in the house.

By 1915, more homes and businesses were being wired for electricity, and Mazda Nitrogen lamps were stocked in stores. Electric lamps for autos and Maxwell autos with electric starters and lights were for sale. Electric signs were being erected. For many years, Dr. Boothe, and later Doctors Rollins and Boothe, ran advertisements for electric massages and electrical treatments.

All things electric began increasingly appearing in the newspapers in 1916. Delco-Light advertisements sold a compact electric light and power plant for farms or country homes, manufactured in Dayton, Ohio, and available through salesmen in Vero. It was touted as an improvement over early types of power plants (portable home generators). West Coast Electric Railway Company had an electric railway from Tampa to the East Coast in the planning. An electric corn-popping machine was now at Pioneer Drug Store. Edison Mazda lamps advertised that it produced three times as much light as old-style carbon lamps, and would fit any electrical light socket. The "Spot" barber shop had electrical hair dryers and electrical hair dressers for the ladies. Western Electric Farm Lighting Plants could be purchased in Fort Pierce at the Lektrik Shop, as well as electrical appliances, irons, percolators, water heaters, and lights. Overland Model 25 Touring Car could be purchased with electric starter, electric lights, and 4-inch tires for $695. Electrical effects were promised in an upcoming stage play in Palm Beach. Stetson University and the University of Florida were quick to advertise courses offering electrical engineering study in the College of Engineering in 1916 and 1917. About this time, some realities of the new technology set in. Articles discussing problems with the incompatibility of direct or alternating current found in appliances and sources of electricity began appearing, as did cases of accidental electrocution.

In 1917, advertising and news about electricity took off like a rocket. More home generators were for sale. Individuals in Vero were installing Delco power plants in their homes. The Edgewood Garage installed a Delco-Light Diesel Power Plant October 1917, the first in Vero, and some neighbors used power from the garage. The Live Oak in Vero installed a Delco and was wired for electricity, as were other hotels. Vero Woman's Club was wired for electric lights in club rooms and the library. The lists of things electric that were available grew and grew: electric trains; an electrical railway from Jacksonville to Miami; portable electric sawmills; automobile electric storage batteries that could be recharged and repaired; watches with dry batteries so that they could be read at night; electric pianos; electric multigraphs; electric fans, phonographs, and bells; electric vulcanizing equipment for repair of auto tires; and Hobart Electric Coffee Mill for grinding beans. Many shops advertising repair of electrical appliances were cropping up. Electricity filled every newspaper.

There were drawbacks to this technology, however, as more cases of accidental death by electrocution began to be reported in the newspapers.

What must have been the most disheartening news about electricity was that during WWI, lightless nights were in force and would be strictly enforced by the State Fuel Administrator from the U.S. Fuel Administration Thursdays and Sundays, with no illuminated signs and no white ways or cluster lights. Homes and stores not open could not illuminate. Only lights needed for public safety were allowed, and heavy penalties for violators pertained to all types of illumination. This was announced December 23, 1917, in the *Ft. Pierce News*. Just when all things electrical were coming on the market, the war intervened, turning everything off. Some electrically operated items were late in coming. Air conditioning did not arrive until 1940 in a store in Vero, and in 1949, Bendix washing machines appeared.

Social Life and Entertainment

Social life was active and vibrant in this north end of the county in the 1910s. There were many ways to bring a spark of enjoyment into life. Society was punctuated by many special interest groups and nationwide clubs. Some of these were coupled with civic improvements or raising funds for projects. Newspapers were a popular source for the social news of Sebastian and Roseland.

The newspapers reported these activities, such as the following entries in 1916 and 1917 from the *Fellsmere Tribune*. That newspaper printed a directory of the churches and clubs in the surrounding area:

Ladies' Aide Society met the 2nd and 4th afternoons each month.
Woman's Christian Temperance Union met the 1st Thursday each month.
Methodist Church South met the 4th Sunday each month in Auber Hall, with Pastor H. B. Boyd.
Christian Science met every Sunday morning in the Dixie Playhouse.
Catholic Church met the 4th Sunday each month in the new church.
Masons met the 2nd and 4th Mondays at Vickers Hall.
Modern Woodmen of America met the 2nd and 4th Fridays in Vickers Hall.
Odd Fellows met every Wednesday in Vickers Hall.
Royal Neighbors met the 1st and 3rd Monday each month in Vickers Hall.
Woodmen of the World met the 1st and 3rd Friday each month in Vickers Hall.
Order of Eastern Star met the 1st and 3rd Wednesday each month.
Philathen Class was held the 3rd Friday each month (Methodist Sunday School class.)
Woodman's Circle met the 1st and 3rd Tuesday each month.

Sebastian Woman's Club

The Sebastian Woman's Club was formed in 1914 in the Rose's home. Elected officers were Mrs. Sarah Rose as president, Mrs. Paul Kroegel as recording secretary, and

Mrs. George Braddock as first vice president. Mrs. William Braddock, Mrs. Jesse Yongue, Mrs. Lucy Rogers, Mrs. Paul Holtzclaw, Mrs. Leonard Stinson, Mrs. James A. Grove, and Annette Ganoe were founding members. Many more joined later. They were involved in many civic and beautification projects in Sebastian. Originally meetings were held in the Town Hall. The group raised money for their various projects and to build their own building. They joined with the Board of Trade to beautify the grounds of the school in 1916. The Woman's Club gave a parcel post sale and ice cream social at the hall on August 19, 1916. Proceeds went to improvements to the school grounds. They provided window shades and a flag for the school with funds raised by them in 1917. A clean-up day at the cemetery was organized by the club in 1917.

Some meetings were educational. The State Board of Health provided a lecture on nursing in May 1916. A June 1916 meeting had another talk by the district nurse of the State Board of Health. During one meeting, they had a study of national parks; at another, there were readings and lectures on the study of birds and bird habitats.

Ladies' Aid Society

The Sebastian Ladies' Aid Society was concerned with funding projects to benefit the Methodist Church. They met in the home of one of the members. A sock social was held by Ladies' Aid, with a $10 profit. They also held a chicken dinner in Sebastian Hall. The *Fellsmere Tribune* reported that you would get a supper and pleasant social evening for 25 cents. In 1916, their efforts produced improvements to the Methodist parsonage with paint, a new rug in the parlor, and furniture in the spare bedroom. Moreover, they furnished new kerosene-pressure lights in the Methodist Church. During some meetings, they worked jointly to create a quilt.

The first Ladies' Aid and Sewing Circle in Roseland was organized in October 1915 for the purpose of supporting the Roseland Methodist Church. It met at the home of Mrs. Walter Walkup. Mrs. W. W. Holtzclaw was president, Mrs. Ralph Romer was secretary, and Mrs. Irene Hardee was treasurer. Each member was directed to bring to the meetings sewing or crocheting and a dime, with proceeds going to the church. The group continued to support the church through 1919.

Boy Scouts

Boy Scouts of America incorporated on February 8, 1910. Its aim was to foster self-reliance, citizenship, and good character through a wide range of outdoor and physical activities. A local Boy Scout Troop was organized, led by Scout Master J. J. Gibbs. In 1916, he led a hiking trip to Gibson Springs. William W. Holtzclaw helped found the chapter.

Camp Fire Girls

Several Camp Fire Girls groups sprang up in the area in the 1910s. The organization formed nationally in 1910, designed to be a sister group to Boy Scouts of America. It emphasized camping, other outdoor activities, and environmental education. Clubs were encouraged to adopt a Native American name for their individual groups.

The Wautagua Camp Fire of Roseland was organized in May 1916 at the home of W. W. Holtzclaw. The charter members were Katie and Alfrida White, Joie Gibson, Zelpha Bon, Charlotte Ashburn, Annie Hardee, Lucy Yongue, and Alma, Nell, and Hazel Holtzclaw. One popular definition of Wautagua is that it was an Indian word meaning "beautiful water," and this may be what inspired the Roseland girls to use this name. Promptly after forming, they held a sale of ice cream and fudge to raise funds. They went on a hike to Sebastian in June 1916. In July, they also earned patriotic honors doing street cleaning on Berry Avenue in Roseland. In August 1916, the group hiked over and camped out on the north Fork of the Sebastian River for five days. At the end of their first season of activities, Wautagua Camp Fire Girls held a regular ceremonial in October at the home of Mr. and Mrs. J. D. Yongue. Lucy Yongue received the rank of Wood Gatherer. A new member was initiated and a talk by Mrs. David Rose on Camp Fire works was given with Mrs. Rogers and Mrs. Yongue. The girls partnered with the Ladies' Aid Society and spent a day watering, planting grass, and caring for the Australian oaks in January 2017.

The Hatchinehaw Chapter of Camp Fire Girls of Wabasso held their first meeting at the home of their guardian, Miss Mildred Smith, in June 1916. WoHeLo is an anagram for Work-Health-Love, the watchword of Camp Fire Girls, and was the name adopted by the Fellsmere group. WoHeLo Camp Fire Girls of Fellsmere put on a play called "Any Girl" about Camp Fire Girls in Sebastian Hall in 1918. Several productions of the play were put on.

Other Groups

Many other groups were popular in this decade as centers for social activity. Woman's Missionary Society of the Methodist Church met with a program and installation of officers in 1917. The Epworth League in Sebastian met at Myrtle Braswell's home in June 1916, and Helen Krogel was appointed leader of the Epworth League. Their meetings consisted of songs, readings of papers, scripture readings, and general lectures about mothers and prayers, and other religious topics. Rev. and Mrs. Boyd entertained the Epworth League at the parsonage with an ice cream social. On March 28, 1917, the Epworth League was organized in Roseland by church members for the purpose of training the youth of the community. The Epworth Board was composed of President J. H. McCoy and General Secretary Fitzgerald S. Parker. The Sebastian Camp of the Woodmen of the World held a meeting with election of officers and refreshments in

December 1916. The Sebastian meeting of the Young Ladies Club was held at Margaret Stinson's home.

Sebastian Town Hall Activities

As well as housing offices for civic matters, the Sebastian Town Hall was a very busy hub of social activities, as indicated by these 1916 events. The play "The Winning of Latane" was put on for several showings. E. Mills gave a masked ball. Robert Mills gave a masquerade dance in honor of Meta Hardee's birthday. Numerous other dances were given. Vaudville acts were put on. Li Ho Chang performed acts of comedy and magic. Silent movies used to be shown in the schoolhouse in the evenings, but were later viewed in the town hall. Every December, a Christmas Tree program was held, which included children's performances at the public hall or the school and were always filled to capacity.

Tennis Court

Young people of the area wanted a tennis court in 1916 and set about raising money to create one. They produced a temperance play, "Out on the Streets," with local talent. The showings of the play were a big success. The 25-cent cost of admission went to the new tennis court fund. Vickers Brothers donated the use of their lot near the Town Hall for the tennis court.

The Rest of the Time

Social evenings and dinners with friends were popular. Many individuals visited each other for an evening. Out-of-town friends came to stay for a few days. Weather permitting, beach parties drew everyone, as did boating trips and oyster bakes. A picnic and political rally was held in Sebastian, attended by many locals. Birthday parties and birthday dances were held at local hotels. Many special functions were reported at Thanksgiving, such as dinners at friends' homes, the Yongue dinner party at Riverside with music, or Woman's Club Thanksgiving Dinner with a speaker.

There was a horse racing track east of Fellsmere. Racing enthusiasts from surrounding towns attended the Saturday races. Mr. and Mrs. Sloan, R. G. Hardee, George B. Hall, Cleveland Kitching, W. C. Braddock, and George B. Braddock drove over one Saturday in June to attend the races in 1913. Boats were raced, too. George Vickers bought a new motor boat which hit speeds on the Indian River of up to 12 mph in 1916. Also in 1916, Captain R. G. Hardee purchased a new speed boat and found out that it was not the fastest boat on the river.

Baseball teams were organized. In April 1915, the Sebastian and Grant baseball teams held a game on Saturday; Sebastian won. That year, the Sebastian Athletic Association organized June 28 with ten charter members. H. M. Sallee was president, F. P. Park was secretary-treasurer, and J. J. Gibbs was manager.

Civic

The *Fellsmere Tribune* reported the day-to-day activities of the town. Various groups and individuals volunteered time and materials to improve Sebastian. Projects were set up, and people helped. Every Thursday was declared cleanup day in Sebastian and a group of ladies worked in the city cemetery for two days making improvements in 1916. Mrs. K. M. White donated 20 Australian oaks that were planted on each side of the street from the church to the post office.

Promotion

The mystique of the beautiful, bountiful, tropical wilderness that was Florida continued to be found in many articles and books, all of which fed the boom in tourism and real estate in the 1910s and 1920s.

St. Lucie Tribune

On July 1, 1910, the *St. Lucie Tribune* wrote an eloquent description of Sebastian of the time:

> Sebastian is admirably situated on the bank of the Indian River, but two miles of the juncture of the Indian with the Sebastian River, with a heavy tropical growth along the river front. The larger part of the town is built on the slope between the high red hickory ridge and the Indian River, although there are many fine residences along the ridge.
>
> The chief industry since the beginning of the town has been the catching and shipping of fish, there being at present four wholesale houses, The Eagle Fish Co., the Sebastian Fish Co., T. B. Hicks & Co., and Parks Bros. Of late years it has been found that the soil and climate of this section was most admirably adapted to the cultivation of citrus fruit, and now that industry far eclipses any and everything else. There are many fine groves both of orange and grapefruit to be found in every direction, and the acreage is the second largest in St. Lucie County, being only eclipsed by that devoted to the industry west of Fort Pierce.

Winthrop Packard

Winthrop Packard was one of a small group of Boston nature writers. He was best known for his writings of sylvan Boston in the nature genre, including *Old Plymouth Trails, Wild Pastures, Woodland Paths, Literary Pilgrimages of a Naturalist*, and *Wildwood Ways*. His *Florida Trails* book was considered a literary departure for him. It presented an idyllic vacation trip lavishly illustrated with woodcut pictures and appealing description of flora and fauna along the east coast of Florida. Travel details of hotel accommodations, boat reservations, maps, and plans did not intrude. Intimate details of birds, butterflies, and wildlife abounded. A whole chapter was given over to pelicans and the Pelican Island Wildlife Refuge. The reader could feel his cares melt away in the paradise of east Florida. The picture facing the title page was inscribed: "The road down Indian River winds southward toward the sun." Surely this book inspired northerners to flee the snow and relax along the Indian River in 1910.

Clifton Johnson

Human interest information for travelers in Florida was the way Clifton Johnson described his book, *Highways and Byways of Florida*, published in 1918. Extolling the virtues of the east coast of Florida's mild climate, sunny days, and sea bathing, he stated that the area received tens of thousands of winter tourists every year. He traveled down the Indian River, the great river highway for the local inhabitants, describing the narrow strips of land on the ocean and the safe, placid, beautiful saltwater lagoons sheltering the land fringed with points, harbors, coves, islands, and fresh-water streams. Every house along the river had its own pier and boat. Boats were of all variety, from sail to power boats. The mainland was well suited for residences and the soil unsurpassed for citrus and pineapple cultivation. He described in detail the vast variety of flora and fauna.

In his chapter on Birds and Beasts, he included a description of pelicans and the Pelican Island rookery, which by that time was a government bird sanctuary with a warden. The island was densely populated with brown pelicans. He stated that the warden was able to take a vacation after March, by which time the island was deserted for seven months.

Nevin O. Winter

Nevin O. Winter wrote glowingly of the Indian River area in his book, *Florida the Land of Enchantment*, published in 1918: "Florida has ever been a land of romance." In his chapter on the Indian River, he included considerable description. There were three entrances to the Indian River, at Haulover Canal, Indian River Inlet, also called Lucie

Inlet, and at Jupiter Inlet. The Indian River had almost no tide. Its fishes were described as all saltwater fishes and a considerable part of the bottom was covered with oysters. In the spring, the shores were an entrancing mass of flowers and blossoms of many kinds. The protection of the water made this river one of the splendid fishing grounds of the Florida coast. It was a favorite locality for sportsmen, and a resort for countless numbers of ducks of many kinds. In some places, the river would seem almost covered with them. Also, great numbers of other water birds were found. He described the manatee as "neither wholly animal nor wholly fish, it partakes the character of both."

He stated that the Indian River country was famous for its fruits—oranges, guava, pineapples, cocoanuts, custard apple (wild), and paw-paw. There were plentiful butterflies, and food in abundance for both land and water birds. In February and March, the palmettos were alive with bird life. In the former months, robins would sometimes be encountered by the thousands.

Pelican Island birds returned year after year. On only two occasions had the pelicans been known to be absent from Pelican Island, he related. One season so many pelicans were slain by hunters who desired the wig-quills that the others were frightened away by the dead bodies. The U.S. Government then took charge and made it a reserve. The big sign erected frightened away the birds and the following year the birds did not come. They immediately returned after the sign was removed, he related.

19

Sebastian and Roseland in the Roaring 1920s

The 1920s in Florida was one of the most dramatic periods in its history, with its boom and subsequent bust. The Florida governor during the prosperous boom period was Cary Augustus Hardee from 1921-1925. During Governor Hardee's tenure, Florida was considered a healthful destination in spite of the 1920 Florida influenza epidemic, with 2,541 cases and 79 deaths. Florida grew in population during the decade. The prosperous growth, with grossly inflated real estate prices, continued right up until the bust. More counties were created, and cities incorporated. Governor Hardee prohibited levying state income and inheritance taxes, and outlawed leasing of convicts to private businesses. Railroad services consolidated and expanded. A public road system of 3,254 miles of highway spread through the state helped by a gasoline tax and federal funding allocated for expanded road construction, thus opening the state further to booming commerce and tourism. Women won the right to vote.

Hardee was born on a farm near Perry in Taylor County, Florida, on November 13, 1876. He was the fourth of ten children of James B. and Amanda Katherine (Johnson) Hardee, both natives of Quitman, Georgia, who later moved to Taylor County, Florida. James Hardee was a Civil War veteran. This family was related to the Sebastian Hardees, also from Quitman, Georgia.

Governor John Martin led Florida during its worst upheaval, the boom and bust period. He was a Jacksonville attorney who was born in Plainfield, Marion County, Florida, and became Mayor of Jacksonville two years before his rise to the governorship. Martin became governor of Florida in 1925, at the height of the land boom, and true to his promise, he promoted road building. Wildlife conservation, with deer and quail restocking and fish hatcheries, were financed. Schools received appropriations and textbooks became free for grades 1-6. Southern Bell Telephone Company began an extensive program of laying wires and installing telephones throughout the state in 1925 and 1926. According to the *Vero Beach Press*, 27,141 new telephones were expected to be installed that year, increasing service to every Florida city.

This prosperity was dealt a devastating blow when the Great Depression hit Florida, as well as some natural disasters. The tumultuous, heady rise of the boom period was followed by an equally dramatic crash. The tipping point in Florida was 1926. Real estate sales began to slow, money began to tighten, bank deposits fell off, and there were stock sell-offs. It was fueled by the 1926 hurricane that caused so much damage and a collapse in the financial systems. In 1928, Florida received another hurricane, and the combined results were devastating. The Mediterranean fruit fly scourge in 1929 damaged tourism and ruined the citrus industry. The Great Depression spread across Florida well in advance of the rest of the country. People lost their homes and jobs, and either left the area or were forced into a more primitive mode of existence. Others took to smuggling and black marketeering. Governments went deeply into debt as individuals were unable to pay taxes. Businesses declared bankruptcy. With the crash, fruit flies, and two hurricanes, Florida's government was unequal to the chaotic situation. Hurricane preparedness was unknown at the time. Money was gone and taxes were not being paid. During the first few Depression years, little help was given to Floridians, except for Red Cross. Eventually the federal government stepped in with some financial aid relief. All of Florida struggled until the economy began to recover around WWII. After leaving office of governor in 1929, Martin ran unsuccessfully for the U.S. Senate in 1928, and unsuccessfully for governor in 1932.

St. Lucie County

As county populations grew in the beginning of the decade, regional interests began to dominate. One point of disagreement was mosquito control. The southern part of St. Lucie County argued that it was not possible to successfully deal with mosquitoes, whereas Vero and the northern part of the county believed it was possible to control the threat. Those living in the north end of the county began to resent this division of focus and county control from Fort Pierce. It was felt that Vero and towns to the north were paying for public improvements in Fort Pierce that did not extend to their towns. Stiff fines were imposed on Vero residents for violations, while Fort Pierce residents were not charged for the same violations. Sunday movies were also a conflict. When the new Vero theatre opened on a Sunday, Fort Pierce sent the county sheriff to enforce Sunday closing. This proved to be a final blow.

Indian River County

A group of north county civic and business leaders proposed to form a new county, Indian River County. Some individuals from the northern part of the county were opposed, and many, particularly in Vero, were in favor. Veroites spearheaded a trip to Tallahassee to lobby in favor of creating Indian River County, and a large group of individuals chartered a train to Tallahassee May 4, 1925. Charles W. Sembler and Dr. David Rose of Sebastian were among those that made the trip. Representative Anthony W. Young introduced the bill creating the county that ultimately passed in spite of heavy opposition. Indian River County officially came into existence June 29, 1925. The new county was celebrated with day-long festivities in Vero June 30, with a parade, speakers, food, and more.

Governor Martin immediately appointed five commissioners from around the county to serve until the next general election: G. A. Braddock, J. W. LaBruce, Donald Forbes, John H. Atkins, and O. O. Helseth. Included in the first Indian River County officials appointed by Governor Martin were some Sebastianites: County Commissioner George A. Braddock, and Board of Public Instruction David Rose. Precinct numbers changed in July of 1925; Roseland became precinct 1 and Sebastian precinct 2.

Schools came under scrutiny in the new county in 1927, standardizing more of education. All schools in the county would be open for uniform class lengths, hours, and nine-month terms. With the licensing of teachers, their salaries were rising. A resolution passed that if a school teacher married, the individual's contract was automatically voided. A new contract would have to be executed in the new name. In September 1927, the Institute for Teachers of three counties held a three-day workshop in Fort Pierce for teachers, with speakers and programs on a variety of educational topics such as "Educational Aims for Primary Children."

Mosquito Control District

On June 15, 1922, the *Vero Press* reported steps that were being taken to educate the public about the control of mosquitoes, in the form of lectures, films, and pamphlets from the state. A mosquito control committee formed in March 1923. By May, there was discussion of setting up mosquito control zones in the state. A proposal was drawn up in May 1925 for a Mosquito Control District that would encompass the boundaries of the proposed Indian River County. On June 25, 1925, the *Press Journal* announced that the Indian River Mosquito Control District would be started. The Mosquito Control Board formed in June 1925, including members Dr. L. L. Hutchinson, Alex MacWilliam, and Captain R. G. Hardee. George T. Badger became a member when R. G. Hardee resigned. On April 15, 1926, it was declared that having a mosquito control district was constitutional and that bonds for it were valid. By 1927, a six-week experimentation program was begun to determine how to eradicate the pests, but the problem seemed impossible, as stated in the *Press Journal* at the time. The board tackled the primary question, the source of the mosquitoes. A study found that 90% of the mosquitoes originated in the salt marshes. Those mosquitoes could travel a distance of 40 miles. Fresh water mosquitoes stayed closer to their original source. A cleanup campaign and spraying was instituted, as well as landfill of marshes. A mosquito control ordinance passed in February 1926. Ditches were dynamited to drain standing water in 1930. Spraying was tried, but this killed fish. It was not until World War II and the development of DDT that mosquito control was effective.

Sebastian Before Incorporation

At the beginning of the 1920s, Sebastian was a thriving little town just beginning to feel the effects of the Florida real estate boom, but it had yet to receive the jolt of energy that the change to the new Indian River County and the incorporation of Sebastian would give it. It had all of the amenities. It still had the long-lasting Kitching store and Palm House Hotel that would remain until 1925; it also had the Grove, Sembler and Sebastian Hotels, Vickers Bros. Store, Gaffney's barrel factory, Taylor's barbershop, the Woman's Club, a Town Hall, and others. It had a school, two churches, and a doctor. The two railroads and the Dixie Highway were running through. There were numerous prosperous groves, farms, and fisheries. Sebastian had 72 registered voters in 1920. Sebastian voting inspectors were James A. Groves, J. L. Stinson, G. A. Braddock, and clerk, Everett Vickers. In 1922, Sebastian had a total of 112 registered voters, with 46 new and 20 women, as women could vote then. Some had gone.

Kitching Building

The long-time Kitching store and hotel changed hands. On March 2, 1925, a letter from Stanley Kitching stated that L. A. Sloan bought the Kitching property on the Indian River. Sylvanus died in Stuart in 1926 and was buried at Fernhill Cemetery, as were eight of his children.

Methodist Church

As the population of Sebastian grew, the Methodist Church building needed to expand as well, to meet the needs of its parishioners. In 1926, three rooms, including a Sunday School room, were added to the north side of the church by George and Frank Vickers and Parris Lawson, who had helped with the remodeling in 1901. They were joined by Abraham Foster. The church was completely rebuilt in 1964.

Baptist Church

The Braswells became part of the Baptist Church community. The ladies of the Baptist church served a chicken dinner at noon in the Braswell Building on the corner of Main Street and Central Avenue in February 1926. Mrs. L. P. Doss and Mrs S. A. Braswell were in charge of serving. Other chicken dinners were welcome fundraisers.

The Carlile House

Sam and Esther Braswell acquired the Carlile House sometime in the mid-1910s, living there until they rented it to the Charles Park family around 1919. After the Parks moved out, Sam and Esther Braswell returned there. They occupied it until they sold it to Guy Glasgow circa 1928. The Glasgows remained there until 1955, when they sold it to Mr. Engleson. It has changed hands many times since, and the pretty little building, renovated again in December 1990, still remains.

Sebastian Hotel

Newspapers followed the rapid succession of ownership of the Sebastian Hotel in the 1920s. In 1920-1922, according to local directories, the Sebastian Hotel was owned by George Wise. Abraham Stovitz took charge of the Sebastian Hotel that he had purchased some time ago, and made extensive improvements, according to the *Vero Press* in May 1924. Then, for a period of time, it was owned by Jaska (Jack) Salmela, who sold it to S. A. Braswell in 1926. Braswell turned around and sold it to his friend Mrs. Minnie Bridges, a successful Melbourne realtor, in November that same year. It had been called The Old Sebastian Hotel, but became Hotel Bridges under her ownership. She began making improvements to the property. In January 1927, it burned to the ground, as reported by the *Vero Press*.

George Wise

One of the owners, George Wise, had been an experienced hotelier. Prior to 1919, George and Katherine M. Wise moved from Akron, Ohio, to Wabasso, where they were living when he purchased the Mills Hotel. They then relocated to Sebastian to run the hotel. However, Wise only kept it for a couple of years. Sometime after selling the hotel, they moved to Groveland, Lake County, Florida, where he took up farming.

Jaska Salmela

Jaska (Jack) Salmela and his wife Saime were both from Finland, having immigrated 1903-1908. He was a coal miner and lumberjack in Finland. They met and married in Michigan. They came to Valkaria and later to Grant, where he acquired a homestead land patent for 40 acres in 1918. He tried farming there, but was not successful. While there, he learned net fishing from Charlie Sembler, and he and his family followed the Semblers to Sebastian, moving there around 1920. He continued as a fisherman. He owned the Sebastian Hotel for a few years, and sold it to realtor S. A. Braswell in 1926. After he sold the hotel, he bought the M. M. Miller house in 1926, when Miller moved south. He and his family continued to live there, and he continued making a living from commercial fishing. He and Saime are both buried in Sebastian Cemetery.

Bank of Sebastian

On July 7, 1923, Bank of Sebastian incorporated with the State of Florida. In May 1924, it was announced in the *Vero Press* that contractor Bartow of Melbourne would be erecting the Sebastian Bank building. The structure was to be of hollow tile and stucco, located on the lot just east of the post office. The attractive building was completed and the bank opened in August 1924. It was welcomed with a rush of business the first day it was open, according to Cashier C. M. Warren. The new bank was capitalized at $15,000. It was part of the Witham system, which controlled 200 banks in the states of Florida and Georgia. A stockholder's meeting held prior to the opening completed the organization, electing as directors F. O. Spain, J. P. Anthony, C. M. Warren, C. L. Beaugnot, A. G. Robert, E. W. Vickers, and W. W. Holtzclaw. Unfortunately, this bank went into receivership around 1926.

Chamber of Commerce

The Sebastian Chamber of Commerce was created August 28, 1924, to further the development of their area. It attracted over 30 members by the middle of September that year.

Sebastian Star Newspaper

The wave of enthusiasm also caused the creation of a weekly newspaper in 1924, the *Sebastian Star*. Mrs. Chesser was the editor and it was printed in Eau Gallie. It prospered for two years, but in the face of the oncoming "bust" it was discontinued.

Town of Sebastian Incorporation

Sebastian was incorporated as a municipality on December 6, 1924, as recorded in Vol. 3, Page 1 of the St. Lucie County Record of Corporations. Officials were elected at a mass meeting held in Sebastian Hall. The *Vero Press* reported the proceedings of the public meeting December 11, 1924, that led to the creation of the Town of Sebastian.

Headlines read:

Sebastian Voters Meet to Organize New Municipality

T. B. Hicks elected first Mayor—Other Officers Chosen

Large Number of Property Owners Present at Mass Meeting Monday Night to Vote Forming Town

By a two to one vote of the property owners present the Town of Sebastian was brought into being at a mass meeting held last Monday night at the Sebastian Hall. With the organization of a municipal government overwhelmingly voted, the meeting proceeded to adopt the town boundaries as publicized in the *Vero Press* and to nominate and elect a set of officials. The election resulted in the following citizens being chosen: Mayor—T. B. Hicks; Clerk—L. O. Baughman; Marshal—George Vickers; Aldermen—H. M. Sallee, A. G. Roberts, M. M. Miller, Charles Sembler and C. L. Beugnot.

A roll call showed more than two-thirds of the qualified voters living within the proposed corporate limits to be present. When the question of incorporating was put 42 cast their votes in favor of the proposition and 20 against. R. G. McCain, one of the leaders of the opposition to incorporation, announced that he desired to challenge the qualification of some of those who voted and was instructed to file his objections with the clerk. The meeting then proceeded to transact other preliminary business including the adoption of a name for the new municipality. "The Town of Sebastian" was chosen as its official designation and a seal for the town was adopted.

2nd Sebastian Election

The second election after the city of Sebastian was incorporated was held in the Town Hall December 14, 1925. In the race for mayor, George T. Badger won with 39 votes; incumbent mayor T. B. Hicks received only 34 votes. W. C. Braddock and E. W. Vickers were elected to city council seats. Mrs. P. P. Lawson, Mrs. W. C. Braddock, and her son, Roy, were in charge at the polls. City Marshall John Beugnot also acted in his official capacity.

George T. Badger

The new mayor George T. Badger had purchased property in Sebastian in 1909 and planted orange groves. He was an absentee landowner from Quitman, Brooks County, Georgia, the home county of the Hardees, Lawsons, Vickers, and Ryalls. In 1920, he moved to Sebastian, at first lodging with Albert McCormick, and he engaged in office work. In April 1923, he moved to his cottage south of Sebastian. Later his widowed mother came to live with him, Ida R. Badger. His father had been a Confederate veteran. After succeeding T.B. Hicks as mayor in 1925, such was his popularity that Badger remained mayor until his death in 1940 at age 59. During his active civic life in Sebastian he took part in the formation of Indian River County, was president of the Chamber of Commerce when it formed, and was a member of Sebastian Booster's Club. He consistently promoted Sebastian's growth. He worked for the improvement of the Sebastian Inlet. He was also a member of National Realtors Association, Methodist Church, the Mosquito Control District board, Vero Beach Sketch Club, and Fellsmere Lodge, and was a Master Mason.

Charles L. Beugnot

Another civic leader, Charles L. Beugnot, was born around 1889 in Georgia and came to the Sebastian area with his parents in 1909. He lived for some time with his parents, and worked at many different jobs. Undoubtedly he farmed the family's homestead. He was a logger, served on a dredge boat, and delivered ice for the Melbourne Ice Plant, City Ice & Fuel Company, before Sebastian got its own ice plant in 1926. During WWI, Charles enlisted in the Army and served as a Private. In the 1920s, he became more involved in Sebastian's civic affairs. He became a Sebastian postmaster, serving from 1922 to 1924, and moved the post office back to the Hardee building. In 1925, he was a city councilman, a director of the Bank of Sebastian, and an Alderman. Charles' brother Wiley was registered for the draft of WWI, but did not serve, as he had lost an eye.

John T. Beugnot

Another Beugnot held public office, that of Deputy Sheriff: Charles' brother, John. John T. Beugnot was born in Georgia about 1894, and came with his parents to Sebastian in 1909. He too lived with his parents for some time, and probably farmed the homestead and logged while there. He was drafted for WWI, and served in the Navy as an Apprentice Seaman. He was discharged at the Naval Hospital at Newport, Rode Island, after 174 days of service in 1917. His house at Cross Street and Main Street is one of the significant properties of Old Town Sebastian Historic District West, placed on the National Register of Historic Places January 6, 2004. It is a wood frame front-gabled house with original clapboard siding and double hung windows. In 1925, John was appointed Deputy Sheriff. The *Press Journal* carried a story in 1926 that John, acting in his capacity as Deputy Sheriff, shot two men for reckless driving and speeding. In the article, John was anxious to point out that they were locals, not tourists. For many years, he managed the Vickers store, buying out the business sometime in the late 1930s or early 1940s. Around 1953, when John died, Everett Vickers bought back the merchandising of the store and ran it until the mid-1960s. John was a member of Woodmen of the World. He is buried in Sebastian Cemetery with his wife Perla and his mother Wiley.

Sears Catalog Homes

Two Sebastian homes had an unusual claim to fame; they are thought to have had the special distinction of being Sears catalog homes. The homes of Bill Ryall and M. M. Miller were ordered from a catalog. According to the Sears literature of the day, the building materials arrived by train, with everything necessary to construct the home, including pre-cut lumber, nails, varnish, paint, shingles, etc., and detailed instructions. All materials were pre-cut. Sears estimated that this allowed the homes to be constructed in 352 carpenter hours as opposed to 583 hours for a conventional house—a 40% reduction in time. These homes did not require the use of an experienced contractor, due to the inclusion of all necessary plans, supplies, and pre-cut and fitted materials. All of the latest materials in home building were employed, including asphalt shingles and drywall. Central heating, indoor plumbing, and electricity were all new developments in home design that Modern Homes incorporated. Current popular home styles were offered. Financing included a liberal loan policy. From 1908-1940, Sears, Roebuck and Co. sold about 70,000 - 75,000 homes through their mail-order Modern Homes program. Over that time, Sears designed 447 different housing styles.

William Rayford Ryall

The Ryalls were another of the group of individuals from Lowndes County (later Booth County), Georgia, that settled in Sebastian. The Ryall family moved from Hahira, Georgia, in 1908 on the urging of their friends, the Lawsons, and built a house on Dixie Highway. They brought with them their eight children, Robert, Bruce, Bascom, Katie, William, Nesbitt, Talmage, and Gussie, and purchased grove property with a packing shed in north Sebastian. Son William Rayford Ryall enlisted in the U.S. Navy during WWI in March 1917, serving until September 1919 as coxwain on USS *New Hampshire* and USS *Louisiana.* He lived with his widowed mother Mary and siblings in the family home after discharge. His father, Charles Wesley Ryall, died of a rattlesnake bite while hunting in February 1913, per the *Miami Herald* report. Will and his wife, Lummie, married in 1922. His employment was as an electrician at the power plant in Sebastian. The *Vero Beach Press Journal* reported a tragic happenstance in the Ryall Grove August 10, 1925; in the grove, Will Ryall discovered the body of J. R. Voomar of Detroit, who had been murdered. The Ryalls were not involved in the case. In 1926, Will and Lummie ordered their Sears catalog home and when it was delivered by railroad boxcar, began its construction on Palmetto Avenue. In June, the *Vero Beach Press* reported it was nearly complete. It was a wood-frame, one-story house with an attic with dormer windows. As well as having the distinction of being one of the few Sears catalog homes in the area, it is also one of the significant properties listed in Old Town Sebastian Historic District West, placed on the National Register of Historic Places January 6, 2004.

Judge Milo M. Miller

Another home thought to be a Sears catalog home erected in Sebastian was owned by Judge Milo M. Miller, on Schumann Drive, south of Sebastian proper. By March 1926, the garage was completed and the complete collection of materials needed to construct the magnificent home had arrived by rail. By June of that year, it was nearly ready for occupancy, reported the *Vero Beach Press*. Both of the houses, Miller's and Ryall's, must have been ordered around the same time, perhaps together. They were completed at about the same time, but are different styles. Modifications over the years make it difficult to identify the exact models chosen by the original owners.

Sebastian Improvements After Incorporation

Incorporation created a surge of civic enthusiasm and provided the necessary framework to usher in many changes for Sebastian, and it blossomed. The *Vero Beach Press* detailed the progress.

Municipal Power and Ice Plant

The new town immediately made plans to bring power to the city and created the Municipal Power and Ice Plant to supply electricity and ice to the Sebastian area. On October 15, 1925, Mayor Hicks requested sealed bids for machinery and building and other equipment for a new municipal ice plant. On December 18, 1925, The City Council of Sebastian and the Chamber of Commerce were working jointly to prevent delays in transportation of machines and equipment for the new Municipal Power and Ice Plant, obtaining the necessary permits from the Florida East Coast Railway Co. for shipments from De La Verqne Machine Co., New York City; The Walch and Weidner Boiler Co., Chattanooga, Tenn.; and G. J. Barnett Co., Palatka, Florida. The plant had a 200-horse power DeLa Vergne diesel engine and a 15,000-gallon oil storage tank, with electrical machinery yet to come at that point.

Pole and electrical line installation was also a concern. By March 9, 1926, the Municipal Power and Ice department had received hardware for line construction. It was waiting for receipt of cross arms for the erection of poles to continue to the north end of the city limits. The line running to the south end of the city limits was at that time being surveyed for pole locations. Superintendent Burkhardt planned on following the erection crew with a number of linemen in order that line wires would be up by the time the plant was completed. Burkhardt urged all property owners intending to have their home wired to do so in the near future to avoid rush on service connections. By July, however, C. E. Burkhardt was lured away to a position as engineer with Florida Power & Light Company.

On May 3, 1926, Sebastian Ice Plant made its first carload of ice and it was sold and shipped by train to Fort Pierce. The plant was designed to serve more cities than just Sebastian. The city was able to manufacture and sell more than $1,000 worth of ice per month. Readily available ice reached even the society pages. There started appearing in social columns mention of an iced course served with cake, or a grape ice served with a meal.

Sebastian Electric and Plumbing Company

Rodney Kroegel quickly took advantage of the arrival of electricity in Sebastian, and opened his Sebastian Electric and Plumbing Company. He was a self-taught electrician and he began wiring homes and businesses. Always adept with new technologies, he was also a plumber. Earlier, he learned photography and photograph developing, and running the motion picture projector.

Florida Power & Light Company

Florida Power & Light Company was originally filed with the State of Florida under the name Miami Gas Company July 27, 1906, changing the name to Florida Power & Light Company July 25, 1924; it was reincorporated December 28, 1925. It began buying up local municipal power companies around the state, taking over their existing power plants and equipment, including Sebastian's. Mr. Ellis of the Palm Beach office of Florida Power & Light discussed with the city commissioners the possibility of a franchise with the city in June 1926. By October 1926, it had purchased nine municipal power plants around the state, and it continued adding more. Power lines were being strung throughout the state.

Sebastian Grammar and Junior High School

The 1920-1921 school year in Sebastian commenced with three teachers, Miss Simonek as principal, Miss Alligood, and Miss Ormond. High school for both Sebastian and Roseland continued to be attended in Vero Beach, which became accredited in 1924.

In 1926, work was done to beautify the current Sebastian school grounds and install a playground. Water was supplied by an artesian well dug in 1926 by M. H. Hammon of Roseland. These upgrades continued even in the face of an impending change.

The school system received attention along with the other changes occurring at the town and county levels. In 1926, determination was made by the school board to replace the wooden school building. An article in the *Vero Beach Press Journal* on May 12, 1926, reported that the old school building and grounds were being sold May 18, 1926, and that the new school would be on the R. A. Braddock property west of the railroad track on Main Street, fronting south. On July 20, 1926, bids opened for construction of the new Sebastian school. On August 27 of that year it reported that construction on the new school would begin within the next ten days. However, there were complications regarding the school bonds that were cleared by November 9, 1926. There were also staff turnovers during this turbulent time. In September 1926, Professor McCoy resigned. In October 1926, a new principal was chosen to fill the unexpired term of Principal Koehler; B. K. Platt, a graduate of Peabody Teacher's College, was chosen.

For the 1927-1928 school term, Sebastian now had four teachers. Mrs. Manda Peck was principal, and the three others were Miss Edith R. Martin, Miss Norma Whitener, and Miss Ruth Young. As of June 1927, there were 75 students in the Sebastian school. School trustees Mrs. David Rose and Charles Sembler petitioned for the first school bus for students attending high school in Vero Beach in 1927.

However, there were other problems, and the building of a new school in Sebastian was steeped in controversy, as reported by the *Vero Beach Press Journal* in 1928. The school board had purchased the site for the school west of the Florida East Coast railroad tracks some time prior to 1926 from Braddock, and work was started there. A two-story, hollow tile and stucco building was designed in 1926 by Fort Pierce Architects William W. Hatcher and Lawrence S. Funke. Around March 1928, W. P. Sloan donated land east of the tracks for the school. There were many opinions voiced regarding both choices. A special meeting was convened in March of the school board to hear citizens' petitions regarding both sites, and the board members viewed both sites. The controversy was acute, and the matter was not settled. However, the advice of the school's attorneys was that although there might be litigation and an injunction filed, the board had not been authorized to accept a new site for the building once the first one had been obtained. Contractor W. H. Wallen was under contract, and should continue work at the site already paid for by the board. Work had been suspended for a year on account of litigation. There should be no further delay so that the school would be finished in time for the next school year.

Construction of the new school was finished in 1928 by contractor W. H. Wallen. It was designed in the Mediterranean Revival Style, with patterned stucco exterior walls, terra cotta tower roof, and parapet, with rectangular and arched multi-paned sash windows. The arched entranceway located on the main façade was framed by a pattern of quoins made of plaster intended to resemble stone. A Mission-style shed roof covered with terra cotta barrel tile and supported by large, carved, wooden brackets adorned the entrance way. It had wood floors. This was a dominant style during the 1920s boom period. The building is still in existence, retaining most of its original features. It currently houses the Sebastian Area Historical Museum, Indian River State College classes, and other offices and groups. It is one of the significant properties placed on the National Register of Historic Places August 17, 2001.

For the 1928-1929 school year, Frederick Burrell became principal of the Sebastian school. He had been a principal at several other schools prior to this and a coach at Fort Lauderdale. Lila Drew had charge of the domestic science class, newly added to the curriculum, and Mrs. Frederick Burrell was added as well. Edith Martin and Ruth Young returned from the previous year, bringing the total to five teachers for that school year. There were 93 students in 1928. Hazel Holtzclaw taught in the Sebastian school in 1929 and was promoted to principal a year later.

Indian River County Bank

Soon after Bank of Sebastian folded, Indian River County Bank took over. It filed for corporate status with the State of Florida September 9, 1926, and applied for a charter in Sebastian, with directors E. W. Vickers, C. L. Beugnot, E. B. Sembler, A. G. Roberts, and C. M. Warren of Lake Worth. It was in operation around October 1 in the building of the defunct Bank of Sebastian. Mr. Warren was a former Sebastian resident who was the first cashier at the Bank of Sebastian when it opened.

Sebastian Progress During the Boom Years

The newspapers were quick to report the progress and prosperity of the area's towns in this part of the decade. Sebastianites could be proud of their achievements in creating a modern city. Gone was the leisurely pace of earlier decades; Sebastian was booming! On August 25, 1926, the *St. Lucie Tribune* reported Sebastian's advancement. Sebastian would improve three miles of city streets and the city council accepted the new city jail that was erected on the property occupied by the Municipal Light and Ice Plant. It stated that Sebastian was second in area and third in population in incorporated areas of the county and that it was having a new wave of development. It was replacing the school building, laying out subdivisions; real estate was booming. Fruit growing, winter vegetables, and commercial fishing were the successful leading industries, with 25 train carloads of citrus and 32 train carloads of tomatoes shipped the previous season. In August 1926, Sebastian began improving city streets with paving, sidewalks, and storm sewers. The contract was awarded to Heisley-Fickel Construction Company of Stuart, to begin around October 1, 1926. Main Street was paved with asphalt.

The *Vero Beach Press Journal* of June 14, 1927, gave a snapshot view of Sebastian at its peak, before the crash. "More than One Million Dollars for Improvements around

Sebastian" was the headline. Sebastian had a bank, good churches, progressive mercantile houses, three large packing houses, and a municipal light and ice plant that was a profit-earner for the city. The sixteen-mile Fellsmere Railroad afforded quick transportation to the productive city of Fellsmere. George T. Badger was mayor, and the city council was comprised of president J. L. Montgomery, vice president R. G. Hardee, members S. A. Park and W. C. Braddock, and city clerk A. G. Roberts.

There were new concrete bridges over the Sebastian River for the railroad and Dixie Highway. Indian River Drive was an attractive addition. Numerous fishing docks along the river attested to a thriving fishing business. Agriculture was prospering. A landscaped park was created around the Municipal Light and Ice Plant, and a baseball diamond was planned there, and tennis courts. Sebastian Land Company built an addition to its packing house. According to the *Vero Beach Press,* in April 1927, Standard Oil Company was in the process of building an extensive storage station in Sebastian. Huge tanks were to be installed. East Coast Lumber & Supply built an extensive lumber yard next to the railroad. A railroad siding was at the rear of the building. The building no longer exists.

There were numerous projects planned for which funds would have to be raised. Sebastian at Dixie Highway was the eastern terminus of the proposed Sebastian and Fellsmere cross-state highway to join state highway no. 29 at Kennansville. Sebastian Inlet improvements were planned, as was the development of the Sebastian Drainage District in September 1926. More streets were to be paved, and sidewalks installed. Work was pending on a $40,000 new high school, according to the article.

S. A. Braswell Real Estate Office

Real estate, at this juncture, was extremely profitable. Sam Braswell's Real Estate Office, where he conducted his business, was on the midway section of Main Street, fronting on South Central Avenue. He closed his office there and moved it to the new Braswell Building and sold the original real estate office building in May 1926 to G. B. Rickerson, formerly of the Orange Café in New Smyrna. Rickerson opened a modern and up-to-date restaurant in Braswell's former office later that same month.

Braswell Building

The Braswell Building, like its owner, had a meteoric rise and fall. The construction of the Braswell Building in June 1925 received a big play in the *Vero Press.* The new owners of the hotel property were planning to erect a modern, two-story structure on site. The Sebastian Hotel was purchased from Jack Salmela by S. A. Braswell of Sebastian, and Adolf Pesat and William Hildebrand of Antioch, Illinois. They moved the old hotel building to the lot next to it to make room for the new structure. A two-story hollow tile and stucco structure was contemplated.

The ground floor had four rooms for commercial use, three to face north on Main Street and one east on South Central Avenue. S. A. Braswell moved his real estate office in one of the ground floor rooms. A drug store occupied the ground floor corner room and Arthur Kroegel opened a grocery store in one of the other rooms. The second floor held the Braswells' living quarters, offices, and apartments. The new building adjoined the handsome brick store building that was in the process of being built for Vickers Bros. "With this entire block covered with an up-to-date building Sebastian will take on a decidedly citified appearance," the *Vero Press* announced.

A considerable loss occurred in January 1927 when the Hotel Bridges and Braswell Building both burned to the ground with nearly all contents lost, but everyone evacuated safely. The fire started on the third floor of the hotel, and was reported by the driver of the *Miami Herald* truck at 3:45 A.M. An alarm was sounded and several hundred citizens hurried to the scene. Some furniture was carried from the hotel, but flames spread too rapidly. Flames jumped to the adjoining Braswell Building, and it was quickly consumed. The Braswells escaped with nothing but a few articles of clothing. A bucket brigade of volunteers kept the post office building soaked with water, saving it. A stiff wind from the northwest carried the flames away from the Vickers' Bros. building west of the hotel, keeping it from damage. Sebastian had no firefighting equipment. A call was sent to the Vero Beach Fire Department but they arrived too late.

Rea Brothers and Raburn Letchworth

Another store was added to downtown Sebastian. Rea Bros. Store was on the northwest corner of Main Street and Dixie Highway, started circa 1920. It sold groceries and fresh meat, and was run by brother Delbert Rea. The Rea's garage was just to the north of brother Delbert's store. The Sebastian Garage was built by Vickers Brothers in 1918. By 1920, it was owned by Rea Brothers Delbert and Norman, run by Norman. It transferred around 1927 to Raburn Letchworth, who had formerly been a mechanic there. The Rea family lived just behind the garage in the middle of town. Advertisements ran for Rea Motor Sales Co. selling new Chevrolet sedans for $795. Raburn Letchworth had a new garage built circa 1930 by Mr. Amos on US Hwy 1. This building was later used by the Sebastian Volunteer Fire Department, and currently houses Mel Fisher's Treasure Museum. The Letchworths were another Lowndes, County, Georgia, family, and Raburn Letchworth arrived in Sebastian sometime around 1922 with other family members, including his parents Allen and Mary and his sister Maizie, who settled in Sebastian, as well. Raburn worked in the Rea Bros. garage before taking it over. He married Viola, related to the Lawson family, around 1925. That year he built a home on Palmetto Avenue, a one-story wood frame house. It earned inclusion on the National Register of Historic Places January 6, 2004, as part of Old Town Sebastian Historic District West. Raburn died in 1950, and Viola remarried.

Changes

This was an era when many individuals came and went. There were small businesses that were equally fleeting, among them boarding houses such as Henderson's that was taken over by L. P. Doss and his daughter, who then left it to farm. Little groceries sprang up, such as the one later taken over by Charlie Taylor's barber shop. Mrs. Meta Chesser opened the busy Coffee Shop on Dixie Highway at the entrance to the city. On May 19, 1926, the Dixie Café was taken over by Martin, formerly of the Sebastian Barber Shop. The Dixie Café on Main Street opened under the management of Mr. and Mrs. George Kimball in October 1926. Basil Lawson was an assistant at the Braddocks' Service Station. J. C. Rogers was employed at the Sebastian Cash Store in August 1929. The new Sebastian Garage opened for business around January 15th, 1928.

Roseland

In the 1920s, Roseland was a thriving community. Its village consisted of the train depot, a Methodist church, the Community Center, a large apartment house, a gas station, grocery stores, a post office, a school, and hotels. It also had an excellent harbor, a large nursery, a fish house, a few poultry farms, a park, and a city dock.

Roseland had 26 registered voters in 1920. In 1922, women were added to the voting register; Roseland had 42 total voters, including 19 new and 12 women. There were 47 registered voters in 1926. In Roseland, voting inspectors in 1921 were L. Ashburner, J. F. Morrison, and Thomas Garring, and E. S. Fear as clerk. Augustus Ruffner of Roseland was appointed Sheriff of St. Lucie County by Governor Hardee in April 1921. In June 1928, the voter registration book for Roseland was in H. E. Ashburner's electrical shop for the June 5 election on the canal bond issue. The inspectors for that election were R. W. Holtzclaw, Mrs. G. D. Gibson, Jan. F. Morrison, and Edna l. Holtzclaw as clerk. Voter registration took place in Holtzclaw's store in the November election in 1928 and the next year voter registration was moved to the community hall.

The opening of the Sebastian Inlet in 1923 galvanized Roseland the way no other amount of progress had. Roselandites felt that the opening would bring rapid expansion to the Roseland area and that it would be the headquarters for business caused by the opening of the inlet. The *Vero Press* of March 6, 1924, contained a Notice of Intent to organize a municipal government for Roseland. Roseland would be the fourth to incorporate after Fort Pierce, Vero, and Fellsmere. Unfortunately, the inlet soon closed again, open only sporadically, and this idea died.

Modern inventions and conveniences were coming to Roseland, as reported in the *Vero Beach Press Journal*. Southern Bell Telephone Company was putting up telephone poles and lines on Gibson Street in October 1925. It installed a pay telephone at the post office and Union Bridge & Construction Company working on the bridge had a telephone installed in March 1926. In September 1926, R. D. Hill, district sales manager for the Florida Power and Light Company from West Palm Beach, was in Roseland discussing the light proposition with citizens. The main line of the company went through the central part of town. Another discussion was held in the Community Building regarding electricity for the town in March 1927. In October 1926, Florida Power and Light Company utilized the services of the Union Bridge and Construction Company's barges and crew of three men to set poles in the Sebastian Bay. Florida Power and Light Company had a large crew at work on the poles and were finished soon thereafter in the Roseland section. Union Bridge & Construction Company also fixed the road crossing over the tracks at Sebastian Avenue, which had been in a dangerous state of disrepair. The county engineer was instructed in October 1920 to proceed with Roseland Road. R. G. Hardee was employed to supervise the roadwork. In October 1927, hard surfacing of the road from Roseland to the highway was accomplished. An airport signal beacon was erected in Roseland in November 1929.

When fire threatened homes and groves, Roselandites took care of the problem themselves; volunteers turned out with axes, shovels, and buckets, having no fire department. In late March 1927, a strong wind carried a raging fire through Roseland, damaging some homes and groves. Two weeks later, another fire swept through, burning up to the edge of town.

Roseland Methodist Church

Services were held every fourth Sunday at the Methodist Church. Contributions and volunteers kept the church in repair. In 1923, a communion set of silver plate was donated by former Campfire Girls in memory of their guardian Alma D. Holtzclaw (Mrs. W. S. Frantz), who died in 1921. The second quarterly conference of the Methodist church was held in Roseland in 1925. G. F. Blackburn of Miami officiated. The children of the Sunday School presented Christmas Eve programs of singing, recitations, and gifts for the community. In spring of 1927, many Roselandites attended a Revival Meeting in Sebastian Methodist Church by Rev. Boyd. J. D. Yongue built a new garage at the parsonage and the parsonage was re-roofed by James Morrison with materials furnished by the Ladies' Aid Society, and asphalt provided by Mr. Yongue in October 1927. Ralph Holtzclaw wired the church for electric lights in 1928. It was many years before the Roseland church was rebuilt; in July 1957, a building permit was issued for the construction of the Roseland Gardens Community Church. A dedication ceremony February 2, 1958, officially opened the new church. Rev. Denny R. Hendry was the new pastor.

School

For the 1920-1921 school year, Miss. Charlotte Ashburner was appointed teacher for the Roseland School. In 1922, repairs were made to the wooden, one-room Roseland school built on Dale Street, three blocks south of Roseland Road. There was one school teacher that year, and she lived at Hammon's hotel. The school children presented Christmas programs at the school with singing of carols, readings, recitations, and dialogs. Edson Beard of Hamilton, Indiana, taught at the school from 1925-1929. Nearly every summer, he and his family returned to Indiana until the next term started. As of June 1927, Roseland had fifteen students; there were seventeen students in 1928. Consolidating the Roseland school with Sebastian was discussed by the Board of Public Instruction due to financial problems in April 1929, but it decided to keep it open for the next school year. Mrs. Clark taught for the 1929-1930 school year. It did close later, however, and in 1936, the schools were consolidated; Roseland students were sent to Sebastian.

Post Office

In 1920, a two-story wooden building was built on Berry Avenue to house the post office next to the Holtzclaw store. Mrs. Anna B. Morgan was postmistress. The post office was in the Albert Haag family home in 1936, and Nell F. Haag became postmistress.

Holtzclaw Store

Another sign of the growth of Roseland was thieves. Holtzclaw's store at Roseland was burglarized in March 1923. More changes occurred. W. W. Holtzclaw ran a large advertisement in the *Vero Beach Press* May 10, 1926: "For sale entire stock of general merchandise at wholesale terms to reliable parties. Will sell building outright or will give lease. W. W. Holtzclaw, Roseland, Florida." He sold it to a woman who ran it for a time, then sold it back to Ralph Holtzclaw. Ralph and Joie Holtzclaw took over operation of the Holtzclaw Store with a smaller inventory in 1926. They made renovations to the store in March 1928. The Holtzclaw store remained a gathering spot in the town. A wienie roast next to the store ushered in 1929, followed by games and stories. Lester Hanshaw played taps for the dying year at midnight. That spot was the site of many other wienie roasts and get-togethers.

In 1932, when the original two-story store burned, it was rebuilt with parts of the unburned old store and new materials, but only one story high. They continued selling even while the store was being rebuilt. When Ralph became ill, he and Joie moved to Vero. Their niece Mrs. Dale Campbell and friends began operating it then, but it finally closed in November 1967.

Holtzclaw Family

The W. W. Holtzclaw house on Berry Avenue was wired for electricity by son Ralph Holtzclaw in 1926. The Holtzclaw family contributed greatly to Roseland life; they were all very active in Roseland civic and social affairs. William Holtzclaw was a justice of the peace and a voting trustee for Roseland and was the motivating force in promoting and the building of the Roseland United Methodist Church, donating his enthusiasm, labor, and funds. He became superintendent of the Sunday school and taught bible class. Boy Scouting was brought to the county with his efforts. Mollie Holtzclaw helped found the Roseland Woman's Club and was a member of the Roseland Ladies' Aid Society. William died after a long illness in 1932. He and Mollie were buried in Sebastian Cemetery.

Ralph Holtzclaw and Joie Gibson married in 1924. Joie, daughter of Quinn Gibson, became a local historian as well as operating the store. She also wrote a column in the *Vero Beach Press Journal,* "Roseland News." Ralph was the local electrician, wiring homes. They both carried the mail. The 1920s Roselandites were aware of their very early history of settlement. On June 25, 1925, the *Vero Beach Press* printed a lengthy article by historian Joie Holtzclaw outlining Roseland's early history, entitled "Northern Gateway to a New County Formed Part of a Famous Spanish Grant." On September 29, 1925, a second installment of her history was printed: "Roseland: Gateway to Indian River County has History Interwoven with Many Potent Romances." Ralph and Joie purchased a lot on Berry Avenue in March 1926 in order to build a home. The Holtzclaws fostered Girl Scouting, as well. A Girl Scout troop was organized in 1929 with Miss Hazel Holtzclaw as captain. A box supper was given by Sebastian-Roseland Girl Scouts in 1929. Hazel Holtzclaw won a scholarship to Florida State College for Women in August 1927 for her senior year there. She graduated in June 1928 with a BA degree. Nellie Holtzclaw married Dale Campbell from San Francisco in 1926.

Ercildoune

The Ercildoune on the bluff no longer operated as a hotel in the 1920s; it had been supplanted by the more modern Bayview and Bay Crest hotels, in spite of its excellent location. The building was still in good condition in the 1920s and the furniture was sold. It again changed hands and the former Ercildoune Inn was used as a barracks for the construction crew of the San Sebastian development in 1926. The old citrus grove and packing house were still on grounds in the 1920s. After that, it all fell into disrepair, and began being taken over by squatters and moonshiners. During the depression years, local people tore down the hotel bit by bit to use the lumber for building their own houses.

Bay Crest Hotel

The popular Bay Crest Hotel on the west side of the Sebastian River provided its seasonal guests with every amenity, including rental cars, steam-heated rooms, running water, electric lights, and private baths in each room. Dockage for their yachts was available. At the height of the boom, George and Mazeppa Tucker and family left the hotel business and moved to Blytheville, Arkansas, where they had farming and ginning interests. Mazeppa Tucker opened a store and restaurant there. They returned to live in Micco briefly in the 1920s. During the depression, the Bay Crest did not do well, and the Tuckers took it back again for back taxes. It prospered briefly, but in the 1930s it was largely outmoded and became primarily a one-night stop for tourists on their way elsewhere. George Tucker went to farm in Mississippi with son Rheutie. Mazeppa, daughter Mary, and Mary's daughters, Mary and Virginia, returned to the Bay Crest around WWII. By that time, the Bay Crest was no longer operating as a hotel. Later during the war, the Tuckers sold the hotel and the family returned to Mississippi. At the end of the war, Mazeppa Tucker bought a small cottage in Roseland where she, her daughter Mary, and her granddaughter Virginia lived for a few years before moving to Vero Beach. The Bay Crest was torn down when the highway was widened in 1957.

Bayview Hotel

By 1920, Ohioans Eugene and Elizabeth Hammon, for many years seasonal visitors, had moved permanently to Roseland and became hotel managers. In February of that year, they opened the Bayview Hotel for business on Bay Street on the Sebastian River next to the park. For a while Mrs. Hammon ran the hotel on her own and her husband ran the Roseland Hotel. Lizzie Hammon was also a real estate agent in Roseland. The Hammons often closed for the summers and returned to Ohio. Their son, Norman, had a successful well-drilling business. The Bayview Hotel was known for its meals with fresh vegetables from their own garden. Guests fished from the pier in the Sebastian River, or they could rent boats for fishing. Mrs. Hammon had a large pet alligator that ate from her hand, as did large leatherback turtles. The Bayview was painted and refurbished in October 1926. Many guests came back yearly and stayed for the winter season. The Bayview had guests at least through 1928. Eugene Hammon had a heart attack in April 1929. Eventually, the Hammons closed the hotel, but they remained living in Roseland. The Hammons died in the mid-1930s and are buried in Sebastian cemetery. After the Bayview closed, it became a fish house and was later condemned and torn down. The land eventually became part of the community park.

Union Bridge Dining Room

The bridge contractors created their own headquarters and dining for the use of their men on the north side of the railroad bridge. In August 1926, Mr. and Mrs. J. M. Goza moved to the north side of the Sebastian Bay, where Mrs. Goza ran the dining room until the old bridge was torn down. The Union Bridge & Construction Company closed down the operation when only a few men were left, giving Mrs. Goza full charge.

Other Businesses

Over time, other small businesses started and ended in Roseland. In 1925, J. D. Rea of Sebastian planned on opening a branch store in Roseland in the E. B. Potts Building on Berry Avenue, but was prevented by illness. It was opened a little later that year. In 1926, Rea was at his store in Roseland three days a week to take orders for meat and deliver. Charles P. Anderson and Agnes had a Roseland grocery in 1926-27. The Mays had a grocery store. C. E. Taylor had a barber shop in the store on Bay Street for many years. There was a hotel on Bay Street east of the railroad tracks. A gas station was on Berry Avenue and a hotel on was also on Berry Avenue, near the Holtzclaw store.

Roseland Civic League/Roseland Woman's Club

The Woman's Club was in existence from 1921 to 1934. It was founded November 14, 1921, as the Roseland Civic League, for the improvement of Roseland. Mrs. Budlong was president, Mrs. Morgan vice president, Mrs. Holtzclaw secretary, and Mrs. Fear treasurer. By December of that year, several more had joined, including the Mrss. Fisher, Dills, Hunt, Perrine, Liefner, Bigson, and Creary, and Leslie Morrison. They implemented their improvements through fundraising projects which included box suppers. The membership fee was used to clean streets, starting at the depot and going west; a pie sale was another fundraiser. Mr. Fisher was hired to do the work on the streets. The League petitioned the road commissioners to have the road rolled and asphalted. At some meetings, talks were given about the League of Women Voters. In 1922, they gave a Valentine party and supper to raise money to have lights and telephones installed in the post office. On March 1, 1923, the name was changed to the Roseland Woman's Club. They hosted a bazaar and street dance in the park in December 1925. Proceeds were used for street cleaning and other improvements. Roseland planned a Cleanup Week to improve the look of the yards and areas around town in 1925. Plans were discussed for a "Roseland" sign to be placed at the entrance to the Roseland Road on the Dixie Highway, along with plans for a cleanup. The "Roseland" signs at the highway and at the entrance to Roseland road were paid for by individual contributions from local residents in 1925. The Roseland Civic League discussed building a city hall in January 1926. Their chicken dinners continued, as well as barbeque and oyster dinners.

The Community Building

The Roseland Woman's Club moved to a new building originally called the Club House, the Community Building that was completed in 1929, on the Sebastian River on Bay Street next to the park. It was financed by giving chicken or oyster suppers, card parties, Valentine parties, dances, and other social events. Andrew Ross provided the underpinning for the building which came from the old wooden bridge. Other materials were donated as well. They were given permission to build on Roseland Park land on the Sebastian River, on Bay Street. In 1927, lumber and supplies were purchased. In March, an American flag was donated by Mrs. Helen Kretchner and Mrs. Hazel G. Arthur of Chicago. The Civic League continued to have suppers to pay the rest of the bills for the construction. In September 1927, the Civic League added a kitchen to the Community Building, and Mrs. William Hildebrand of Illinois, a winter Roseland resident, donated two barrels of dishes for the kitchen. The Florida State Board of Health presented a show and lecture there in 1927. On February 10, 1928, a Frolic was held, and a chicken supper the next night. Local residents volunteered time and furnishing for the building, and it was completed in 1929.

Roseland Ladies' Aid group

The Roseland Ladies' Aid Group did not meet May 19, 1925, according to the *Vero Press*, as everyone's time was taken up working against the proposed fill to be placed for the new railroad bridge across the bay for double-track rails. This group contributed to the repair and upkeep of the parsonage at Sebastian, raised money for conference claimants, and helped keep Roseland church in repair. Funds came from donations, bake sales, and chicken dinners. The menu of one such dinner consisted of stewed chickens with gravy, biscuits, honey, beets, mashed potatoes, rice, coleslaw, butter, coffee, and pies. Basket dinners were held on the lawn. Some of the contributors for various projects were Mr. Yongue, a bridge foreman; Mr. Abernathy, who was a construction worker; Mr. Frantz, an odd-jobs man; and Mr. Holtzclaw, a merchant. They raked and cleaned the churchyard in October 1925. W. W. Holtzclaw put new screening on the church windows. In 1927, some of the projects included repair of the minister's car and construction of a parsonage garage, and in 1928, electrical wiring in the church.

Roseland Dramatic Club

A Roseland Dramatic Club was begun in 1925. A city dock was built with proceeds from their performances.

Quinn O. Gibson

Quinn O. Gibson was one of the Roseland pioneers. He arrived with his parents, the David P. Gibsons, in the 1870s. He and his wife Christine were an integral part of the Roseland society, and they remained there in Roseland their whole lives. Quinn was remarkably responsible with his work for the Florida East Coast Railway, that of bridge tender and water pump manager. He and his wife Christine died in the 1940s in their 70s, and are buried together in Sebastian cemetery. Their daughter Joie married Ralph Holtzclaw.

The Ruffners

Henry and Joanna Ruffner continued to be gracious hosts, entertaining at their home on Indian River Drive. Henry died in July 25, 1925, at age 91 after an illness, and was buried in Spring Hill Cemetery in Charleston, West Virginia.

On January 27, 1928, one of Roseland's alligators made headlines in the *Vero Beach Press Journal*. The Ruffner's "King Bulger", their pet alligator, was given a new home at the Vero Del Mar hotel. According to the article, he was provided with a home on a conspicuous spot on the front lawn, and 300 steel Dixie Highway signs from St. Augustine to Miami advertised the largest alligator in captivity at the Vero Del Mar. He was considered to be the most perfect specimen in captivity. He was 12 feet long and his weight was estimated at a ton in 1928. Col. Jack Yates, a noted alligator hunter, and the Pitt brothers from Ringling Brothers circus, were engaged to assist with the transfer to his new home. The Del Mar provided him with a cement sand bath and cement freshwater pool, enclosed in a 7 foot high fence around a 16 by 16-foot enclosure. He was captured by Col. Ruffner in 1898 in Wabasso and was approximately eight inches long at the time. He lived with the Ruffners for 30 years. Mrs. Ruffner stated that he enjoyed play and attention. In March 1928, King Bulger was transferred to his new home, drawing a huge crowd. When he was in the process of being removed from the Ruffner's home, he went to Mrs. Ruffner and "laid his head at her feet and gazed at her with a pleading look in his eyes," as reported by the *Vero Beach Press Journal*. His first night in his new home was a restless one.

Joanna was noted for her active life in Roseland, even in 1955 at age 87. She received Civil War pension monies in 1959; however, she fell seriously ill that year, and eventually returned to West Virginia, where she died in 1962 at age 94. She was buried with her husband.

Herbert Elliot Ashburner

Herbert Ashburner was one of the long-time residents not engaged in the traditional pursuits of fishing, farming, or citrus, but maintained a respectable standing in the community. In 1928, Herbert Elliot Ashburner married Edna, taking over the H. E. Deal home, and in 1930, he, Edna and their daughter Edna were living in a rental home in Roseland, near the Gibson and Holtzclaw families. Herbert was employed as an electrician, doing such jobs as wiring a service station in Micco. He donated his services in wiring the Woman's Club in May 1928. He sustained an injury while working as an electrician at the local Power House of Florida Power and Light Company in 1929. As well as being an electrician, he held several other posts. He was chosen as a constable in 1928, and in 1929, according to the *Vero Beach Press Journal,* he was assaulted and disarmed by thief Eugene Beugnot, who was later arrested. Herbert was also a School Board trustee in 1929, and a County Commissioner. Herbert and Edna remained living in the area. Herbert died in 1973 and Edna died in 1989, and they are buried together in Sebastian Cemetery.

20

Travel, Social Life, and Commerce in the Age of the Automobile: 1920s

Undeniably, ease of travel revolutionized life in Sebastian and Roseland. Improved access brought growth. The older forms of transportation, the riverways and the railroad, still commanded the attention and funds to improve and maintain them. Their infrastructures were improved and polished. However, the most attention-getting form of travel was the roads. This was the decade of the automobile. The roads were a constant source of complaint and needed a great deal of improvement and expansion in the 1920s.

Sebastian Inlet

The very useful Sebastian Inlet was an ongoing project, one that was done, and re-done, time and time again. All agreed that it was very necessary to have an inlet connecting the Indian River to the Atlantic Ocean near the mouth of the Sebastian River. An inlet in the north part of the county would bring in saltwater fish, cleanse the river, and allow ocean access. There was no other inlet to the ocean in Indian River County. Continuing successful commercial and sport fishing depended on it.

A channel was dredged in 1921, but it quickly filled with sand again. In April 1923, bids were being accepted on the inlet bonds. "At last we are about the have an inlet," was the *Vero Press* editorial comment. And in 1923, a successful inlet was opened at the Gibson Cut site. It remained open sporadically. In 1924, jetties were completed and a "northeaster" opened the inlet. In 1941, the inlet closed from lack of maintenance and remained closed during World War II, reopening again in 1948 when the Sebastian Inlet Tax District opened and maintained it. The inlet commission placed huge blocks of granite and extended the jetties 250 feet during the 1950s. An unintended side effect during Prohibition was that an open inlet was a boon to rumrunners bringing in contraband from Cuba and the West Indies, providing easy access from the ocean to the dealers on the mainland.

Intracoastal Waterway

In 1927, the Florida Inland Navigation District was created by the Florida Legislature, and eleven counties voted a bond issue to buy the old canal and additional right-of-way land. It came to a vote in June 1928, and went into effect in 1929. Since that date, the U.S. government worked to create a 100-foot-wide canal with 8-foot depth. By 1935, the Intracoastal Waterway extended from Cumberland Sound to Miami, the work of the Florida Inland Navigation District and U.S. Engineer Department.

Railroad Bridge

On May 20, 1925, the citizens of Roseland were opposed to the railroad's plan for rebuilding the railroad bridge across the Sebastian River. It involved putting fill from the west bank of the river 838 feet, more than halfway across the river, which would effectively act as a dam, hindering its navigation and flow, and causing flooding of property along the river. After the hearing on this matter, the U.S. War Department stated that the railroad would not be allowed to hinder navigation.

The June 25, 1925 *Vero Beach Press* included a photograph of the completed bridge and on July 15, 1926, it reported that the new railroad bridge had been completed at Roseland; the first trains crossed over July 14. The construction of the new bridge took seven months. Some locals were hired to work on the construction. Once completed, the old bridge was torn down. The new bridge was 1,625 feet long and contained 1,635 tons of steel, constructed by the Union Bridge & Construction Company of Kansas City, Missouri. It was created with 84 concrete piers and two abutments. The steel spans were placed by the Virginia Bridge & Iron Company of Roanoke, Virginia. It was built 4 feet higher than the old one, and needed double tracking to conform to the double tracking of the Florida East Coast main line.

Railroad

The Florida East Coast Railway finished double tracking its rails in Indian River County in September 1926. Unfortunately, an increase in railroad traffic brought more tragedies. In September 1920, Jimmie Grant of Roseland was killed by a freight train when he ran onto the tracks at the Roseland station to retrieve a ball from a baseball game. The ball had fallen into the tracks in front of a train standing at the station. He was killed when the train started up. On April 22, 1926, Roseland received a scare; a passenger train and a freight train collided at the north end of the Sebastian River bridge. *Vero Beach Press* reported, however, damage to the engines was slight, and only one box car of cement turned over. The railroad did basic maintenance on the Roseland water tower in 1926, painting the tower and overhauling the pump.

Fellsmere Railroad

The Fellsmere Railroad underwent a change during the 1920s. It was taken over by a chemical company and became the Trans Florida Central Railroad, running both freight and passengers between Fellsmere and Sebastian. Best remembered and best loved was the "Dinky Train," a modified Ford Model T automobile that pulled a small passenger or freight car and ran six days a week. This railroad was officially abandoned on November 30, 1952, having become obsolete.

Sebastian River Bridge

The original Sebastian River highway bridge was constructed entirely of wood in 1911 and was insufficiently sturdy to meet the demands of 1920s traffic and vehicles. Plans were undertaken to replace it in the 1920s. The original wooden bridge is still best remembered for the fact that it was the site of an ambush to wipe out the Ashley Gang, a group of killers and thieves terrorizing the central part of the state in 1924, prior to the bridge's replacement. The *Vero Press* reported June 15, 1922, that the war department would hold a hearing June 16 on the application by the State Road Department for approval of plans for reconstruction of the Sebastian River Bridge between St. Lucie and Brevard counties. The hearing considered the sufficiency of the provisions for navigation made by the plans submitted.

"Sebastian River Bridge Longest on the East Coast" was the headline in the *Melbourne Times* November 21, 1923. The Sebastian River Bridge was located on State Road No. 4 between Brevard and St. Lucie Counties to the east of the wooden bridge it would replace, and was being built with state, county, and federal aid funds by contractors A. Bentley and Sons of Jacksonville. At the time, it would be the longest bridge on the East Coast, 1,200 feet long, with 900 feet of reinforced concrete and 300 feet of earth embankment. It consisted of 20 40-foot deck girder spans, with a clear roadway of 20 feet. It was waterproofed to prevent corrosion. The traffic census indicated a monthly average of 16,954.2 automobiles passed over State Road No. 4 in the first eight months of 1923. In January, there were cars from every state in the union except Idaho, Nevada, and Wyoming. The new bridge shortened the road about three-quarters of a mile. At the writing of the article, it was expected to be completed within eight or nine months, and was completed prior to January 1925.

Roads

The road-making decisions of 1919 began to be acted upon. With an influx of state and federal matching money, roads everywhere were being created and improved, and more people were traveling them. By the mid-1920s, Florida had almost 900 miles of hard-surfaced highways, including the Dixie Highway in 1915, and the Tamiami Trail in 1928. With better roads and automobiles, there was a considerable increase of trips to other nearby towns for business trips, shopping, services, or entertainment. Trips to Fellsmere and Vero Beach were commonplace. Bonds were voted for hard surfacing the road at Roseland from the railroad west in 1919. R. G. Hardee was employed as the road foreman to supervise the construction of Roseland Road under the direction of Miller Hallowes, an engineer, in October 1920. In 1921, bids were being accepted for completion of the Sebastian-Fellsmere Road. Ralph C. Holtzclaw made the trip from Roseland to Jacksonville in a Model T in sixteen hours, covering 212 miles, a little over thirteen miles an hour in 1925. A back road was opened from Sebastian to Fort Pierce in 1925. Newspapers were reporting the numbers of traffic deaths and accidents.

The main north-south route through Indian River County being refurbished this decade was a combination of the Dixie Highway, State Route 4, and U.S. Highway 1. This was due to money from Dixie Highway funding, state funding, and the National Highway Bill. The three routes did not always overlap and neither did funding. However, January 6, 1920, another resolution came to a vote for a $550,000 bond for the road and matching $240,000 from the state, and this one passed. Several alternative routes were proposed for the section paid by bond. The road from Vero north was to be built in two sections. From Vero to Wabasso, one alternative was followed. From Wabasso to the Sebastian River another was followed, to give the best road that could be secured under the conditions. Widening of the road was an early project. The hard surfacing of the Dixie Highway south of the Sebastian River Bridge began in June 1925. The New Dixie Highway, during one of its renovations, straightened its path through Sebastian, taking out the Central Avenue zigzag at Main Street.

The state-funded portion of the road was completed in 1927. In Vero Beach, there was a celebration and a formal opening of State Road 4 from Vero Beach to Stuart in November 1927. It included 5.5 miles of concrete surfacing 18 feet wide, completed by contractors Fowler and Banko, and done in less than 30 days. It had to cure for 21 days before it could be used.

The federal highway, US Hwy 1, became effective in 1926. In Sebastian, US Hwy 1 primarily follows the New Dixie Highway route, not the Old Dixie Highway, and not Central Avenue. In its entirety, US Hwy 1 runs from Maine to Key West.

Leisure and Social Activities

Adding to the long list of social and civic clubs popular at the time were new and old forms of social life and amusement, as varied as the population. Travel played a part in these activities; automobiles made outings at a distance easier.

Faster transportation brought the latest films. The era of silent films ran from 1895 to 1929, but effectively ended in 1927 with the moving picture "Jazz Singer," the first talkie.

Soon theatres were advertising "all-talking" motion pictures. Going to the movies in Vero Beach or the races in Fellsmere were popular outings. "Ben Hur" played in the Vero Beach Theatre in April 1928, drawing a large crowd from north county. In 1926, aquaplaning was becoming popular, standing on a small raft pulled behind a power boat. Beach parties never went out of style. Busy Bee Sewing Circle met to make articles for the bazaar in June 1926. Thimble bees were held. Ladies' Missionary Society met to hold a dollar tea at Mrs. Henderson's home. Auction bridge parties were held in individual's homes, with refreshments served for an evening's fun. Rival teams of other towns played baseball; boats raced. The newly organized Sebastian Dramatic Club put on a play called "Son John" in June 1920. Mrs. E. Hartman was the leader of the club. The Walter L. Main Circus with its two great herds of finely trained elephants appeared in Vero Beach November 28, 1927. The tented area for this troupe covered five acres and there was also a parade, menagerie, and band concert to draw in Sebastian and Roseland residents. They attended the Armistice Day celebrations in Vero Beach in 1927.

On December 10, 1926, a picnic was held by the pioneers of three counties: Okeechobee, St. Lucie, and Indian River. More than 100 residents attended the picnic at the Beachland Casino in Vero Beach, where it was decided to make the event an annual affair. "Pioneers of Three Counties have Picnic on Beach Today" was the *Vero Beach Press Journal* headline. This evolved into the Old Timers' Picnic in future years.

The Early Settlers Association created a monument honoring the settlers of the Indian River Colony who remained instead of fleeing in 1849, and placed it on the Burnham property in 1926. Over 400 individuals attended the ceremony. William I. Fee was Secretary of the association, and George A. Braddock was the vice president for Sebastian.

Sebastian Woman's Club

The Town Hall stage was papered by the Woman's Club in April 1923. "This was a much needed improvement which our wide-awake Woman's Club did not let slip by," was the *Vero Press* comment. In December 1925, the Woman's Club met in the Sebastian Town Hall. Mrs. B. F. Chesser entertained the Woman's Club in her home with a silver tea, with funds going to the club house fund, in June 1926. Mrs. S. A. Park was on the Christmas Tree celebration committee. On December 10, 1926, the Woman's Club and Chamber of Commerce held a joint meeting in the Town Hall in order to form a cemetery association, attended by 45 charter members. Elected were president P. Kroegel, vice president Mrs. T. B. Hicks, secretary Mrs. Myrtle Arnold, and treasurer Bascom Ryall. Mrs. Fear of Roseland, Mrs. E. A. Park, and Mrs. Bruce Ryall were directors and officers.

Sebastian Woman's Club Building 1928

The erection of the Woman's Club building reflected the difficulties faced locally due to the depression. Many projects were undertaken to raise funds for a proposed club building, but those funds were lost due to bank closures. In 1927, through bargain prices on the part of the East Coast Lumber Company, credit, many donations, and volunteer workers, work was begun on building the Woman's Club. Much of the work was done by Parris Lawson and Abraham Foster. William Martin donated the lot. This new club was named the Sarah Wentworth Rose Memorial Woman's Club when it opened May 21, 1928, in honor of their deceased founding president. It still exists on US Hwy 1 in downtown Sebastian.

Commerce

During the decade of the 1920s, while the area was undergoing upheavals of economy, for the most part commerce in north Indian River County was quietly flourishing. True, the two hurricanes and fruit fly epidemic damaged industry. Of course, there were individual tragedies, but fishing, farming, and fruit growing continued in good condition.

Citrus

Indian River was known to grow citrus of spectacular quality, and it commanded higher prices in the north. The best of the Indian River citrus grew on the barrier islands, because of its unique properties. The high water table, flat land, shell-mixed soil, ample rainfall, and ocean salt air were conditions preferred by citrus. Indian River oranges were sweet and thin skinned, with more juice. Citrus throughout the Indian River area was renowned, and there were many prosperous citrus growers in the Sebastian and Roseland areas who had been in the business for years, such as the Fosters, Braddocks, Kroegels, Lawsons, Vickers, Futchs, Groves, Martins, Rountrees, Ryalls, and more.

Unfortunately, there were continuing problems in protecting the Indian River designation. Local growers banded together in various groups to take steps to prevent this fraud. Vero-Indian River Producers Association formed in 1921 and met annually; Indian River Citrus filed as a corporation on April 9, 1928. The Indian River Citrus League, formed to protect the name, filed as a corporation March 1, 1931. The Indian River District area ran from Daytona to Palm Beach along the Indian River, and St. John's Marsh to the west.

The Florida citrus production for the 1927-1928 season was 14,000,000 boxes, according to the Florida Citrus Exchange official report, and 20,000,000 for the 1928-1929 season. In February 1927, a cold storage plant for citrus was under discussion for Indian River County by the Board of Directors of the Vero Beach Chamber of Commerce, as there were only 18 such plants in the entire state at that time. In 1930, the Indian River sub-district of the Florida Citrus Exchange got the highest prices ever for district fruit. Six packing houses in the sub-exchange, in Cocoa, Mims, Oak Hill, Wabasso, Vero Beach, and Fort Pierce shipped 400,000 boxes. Each house packed under an individual brand. Indian River Producers Association in Vero Beach packed under the "Checkers" brand to Chicago. The Sebastian Blue Duck Packing Company was one of the Sebastian packing houses shipping citrus.

Guy Hartwell Fields

One of the growers left behind a significant residence when he left Sebastian. Guy Hartwell Fields and his wife Julia Etta Fields, originally from Georgia, moved to Sebastian from Clearwater around 1908. He was a fruit grower in Sebastian for many years. They lived for a while in a house on Louisiana Avenue that burned. In 1921, they built a one-story, wood-frame house on Palmetto Avenue. It is one of the properties listed in Old Town Sebastian Historic District West, placed on the National Register of Historic Places January 6, 2004. Sometime around 1926-27, they divorced. Julia remained in Sebastian and is buried in the Sebastian Cemetery. G. H. Fields moved to Quay (Winter Beach), where he again was a fruit grower and remarried to Jessie B. Fields. In 1930, they had a one-year-old daughter and lived west of Dixie Highway. He died there in 1936 and is buried in the Winter Beach Cemetery.

Fishing

With the opening of the Sebastian Inlet in 1923 and the port channel in Fort Pierce, many saltwater fish began coming into the Indian River, greatly enhancing the fishing. The Indian River County area became widely advertised as an ideal sport fishing and commercial fishing area. The *Vero Beach Press Journal* of August 16, 1929, proclaimed: "Waters of County Abound with Fish." Indian River County was known to be a haven for fisherman. These openings brought in saltwater species of fish such as snook and tarpon and other species desired by sport fishermen. The bridges were lined with anglers; deep sea fishing and fresh water fishing were also available. Further articles discussed the fact that the inlets resulted in an increased flow of tide, bringing in more fish and better catches for commercial fishing. There was a steady increase in demand in northern markets for fish from the Indian River area, and at profitable prices. However, sharks also came in, some as large as 8 feet in length. Sawfish as long as 14 feet were also found.

The Indian River became known in the market for its availability of saltwater fish, and a commercial fisherman could send north as many as 100 barrels of fish a week, such was the demand for trout and mullet. Many individuals made a living at commercial fishing, for although labor intensive, it could be undertaken for relatively little expense, in comparison to working the land. There was no expense of raising fish, and little cost in catching and packing, in comparison with raising fruit and vegetables.

Archie Smith Fish House

The Archie Smith Wholesale Fish Company of Sebastian was one of the prosperous, long-lasting fisheries in the area. Archie Smith was an individual who, instead of failing, began a thriving business at the height of the Depression and prospered. Archie Smith was cutting railroad ties in South Port, Florida, when his friend George W. Knight convinced him to come to Sebastian in 1924. Believing that he could make a better living at fishing, he came by automobile with his wife Elizabeth and daughter Viola to Sebastian. He began freelance fishing, selling his catch to the Sembler Fish House. In 1925, the Smiths rented the apartment over the Braswell Building. He purchased land from G. W. Thomas and Fred W. Lewis in 1927 on the Indian River that had a one-story, two-room wooden building with a tar-paper roof on the property, originally erected by them as a gas station. The Smith family moved into this building, and Archie continued freelance fishing. Over the next ten years, he added to the premises, enlarging by adding rooms and outbuildings, including a kitchen, dining room, a roofed porch, a bedroom, and offices. The roof was changed to galvanized metal. The premises served as both fish house and living quarters. The dock reached 239.5 feet in length.

By 1932, Smith stopped freelancing, and successfully began his own business, the Smith Wholesale Fish Company. He added the equipment for weighing fish and made a fish box to ice the fish for shipping. He purchased his barrels locally and 300-pound blocks of ice were brought from the Sebastian Ice plant to pack the fish. He added wooden trolley tracks to his dock, later changed to metal ones. He used the services of freelance fishermen to bring in fish. The packed barrels of fish were pushed on a trolley to trucks that took the fish barrels to the train. In 1940, he expanded his business. A war-time spotters' tower was added and manned in 1942, demolished at the end of the war. Archie died at age 91, and the Fish house continued to be run by his daughter Viola Judah and her son Joe Warren. The Archie Smith Fish House still exists on Indian River Drive and was placed on The National Register of Historic Places October 28, 1994, one of the last remaining fish houses of this type in Florida.

Judah & Sons

The Judah's were relatives of Archie Smith, and at his urging, moved in 1926 from their home in the Florida Panhandle in Holmes County. Bascomb Judah had been farming as a sharecropper there. Bascomb, wife Bessie, and four children, Coolidge, Clarence,

Katherine, and Paul, came to Sebastian, where Bascomb became a fisherman with Archie Smith. Bascomb preferred farming and returned to the Panhandle a year later to farm again. The Judah family returned to Sebastian in 1940, and in 1950 began the Judah & Sons Fish business. They became one of the well-known and established families in Sebastian.

Indian River Fisheries

Indian River Fisheries filed for corporate status with the State of Florida May 24, 1926, and the entire plant was completed by December 1930. It was designed to be a complete resource for commercial processing of fresh-caught fish, and merited extensive coverage in the *Vero Beach Press Journal*. The plant was of modern design with the most modern methods of preserving, freezing, and refrigerating fish and shrimp for shipment. The site was selected by fishing industry promoters Henry H. Guerin and Charles O. Westin, its General Manager. The location was on the west bank of the Indian River, directly opposite the Sebastian Inlet. Land was purchased between the Old Dixie Highway and the new SR 4, with a 400-foot frontage on SR 4, including a small strip of land between the Indian River and SR 4 where the packing plant was located.

The plant was a one and two-story structure of reinforced concrete, steel, and tile, 48 x 90 feet and painted throughout. It contained eight rooms, with workrooms, cold storage rooms, and freezers on the first floor, and offices on the second floor. A dock was extended out into the river, so that fishing boats could bring their catch directly to the fishery. All of the processing of the fish and shrimp was done at the plant. Fish were completely cleaned, dressed, quick-frozen, and wrapped for shipping, and stored until orders for purchase were received.

Charles Weston was a refrigeration manager in Melbourne in 1930, and he and his wife Ethel relocated to Sebastian in order to manage the new plant. The Gibson house was purchased and moved to the plant site facing the highway and remodeled with a stucco exterior by Weston as a home for himself and Ethel. West of his home, a bungalow was erected for assistant manager Charles W. Sembler and his family. Six two-room cottages were erected on the site as employee residences.

Like so many other grand plans of the 1920s, this important facility was another victim of Florida's bust. The business folded, and the corporation was dissolved by proclamation September 16, 1936. In 1940, the Westons were still living in their home there. The Indian River Fisheries plant was used by Coast Guard as a Commissary around 1942.

Farming

There were a large variety of items successfully grown in the Indian River area other than citrus. The industry supported all types of businesses, from large companies, to small individual farmers, to those who worked in the industry for wages.

According to the *Vero Beach Press* in September 1927, there was a change that season in how truck growing was being conducted in the county from former seasons. There were more independent growers planting smaller acreages on their own account than ever before in the history of the county. Previously, growers were financed by larger conglomerates on a percentage or crop sharing plan. However, in 1927, there were fewer growers willing to advance credit to smaller growers, leaving the market to those small growers able to finance their own production. Those small growers were granted credit with fertilizer houses, however. The larger operators hired help for crop tending. Some of the large growers were in Oslo, Fellsmere, and Winter Beach; however, the Sebastian Land Company had extensive fields and good crops, as did George Braddock with his peppers and eggplant. That season, principal crops were beans, sweet peppers, eggplant, cucumbers, and tomatoes. The success of Indian River vegetables attracted the attention of seed houses, and their representatives were in the area canvassing. The Sebastian Land Company was also setting out 200 acres in citrus trees west of Wabasso that year. Sebastian Farms Company shipped eggplants and peppers. Gibson shipped palms.

W. C. Braddock was one of the successful tomato growers on 40 acres west of Sebastian. He built a new packing house on South Central Avenue where a whole carload of tomatoes was prepared for shipping in 1926. W. C. Braddock & Sons put in 60 acres of beans and egg plants, and 13 acres of peppers and tomatoes, squash, and paradise melons in 1927. George Braddock & Sons had acreage of peppers and eggplant that year. In 1928, W. C. Braddock & Sons began shipping produce successfully under their new name "Braddock Brand." They shipped 12,000 crates of peppers and fifteen carloads of tomatoes and watermelons. Beans were shipped by Vickers Brothers, W. F. Baughman & Son, G. A. Braddock, and W. C. Braddock & Sons. In April of 1929, Braddock & Sons Packing House had 50 employees readying shipments of vegetables from Braddock and Vickers fields. It added a new section to the packing house in 1928, doubling the floor space. In 1929, they experimented with growing and shipping squash. The Sebastian Groves Company had 12 acres planted in strawberries, along with tomatoes and peppers in 1928. Roy Braddock was also a vegetable grower.

Another 1927 newspaper article suggested something that at that time was a new possibility, that fruits and vegetables shipped green could be ripened at point of sale by gas. Ethylene, used as an anesthetic, could be applied to fruits and vegetables to increase their respiratory rate and to induce a natural ripening process. At that time, it was a recent development described in the *Scientific American*, and reported in the *Vero Beach Press Journal*. The idea took hold.

The film industry was finding itself useful in fields other than entertainment, and Sebastian tomatoes had a starring role. Sebastian's truck farming success was used to show the world how it was done profitably. In 1929, the Eastman Teaching Films Corporation of Rochester, New York, took 200 feet of motion picture views of tomato harvesting at the Sebastian Land Company grown by Indian River Fruit Growers, Inc.

This footage, along with more footage of processing tomatoes for shipment, was a teaching aid used in schools and colleges.

Bruce and Robert Ryall

Some Ryalls were farmers. Two of the other sons of Charles Wesley Ryall, Bruce C. and Robert B. (who came with the family to Sebastian from Hahira, Georgia, in 1908), began farming, and they continued farming into the 1920s. They were half-brothers; Robert, born in 1883, was the son of Ruth Alderman Ryall, and Bruce, born in 1887, was the son of Mary Alderman Ryall, her sister. Charles divorced Ruth and married Ruth's sister Mary some time before 1887. Sometime before 1918, Bruce married Annette Ganoe, who had come to Sebastian to care for the Hicks children and to attend school in Sebastian. Bruce and Annette were farming, and owned their own home on Old Dixie Highway in 1920, where they were living with their two children and Pauline Ganoe, Annette's younger sister. Robert married Ruby Lawson, the daughter of Ivey and Cassie Lawson, family friends from Georgia, sometime before 1912. In 1920, they were living with their four children near the other Ryall families, farming and renting.

Cattle

For cattlemen in Florida, there was one problem that kept recurring. With a growing population, trains running and motor vehicles everywhere, cattle running loose were a hazard and nuisance. However, fencing of cattle range was an extremely expensive proposition, one opposed by ranchers. In 1923, another procedure was enacted by Governor Catts that cattlemen fought, that of dipping cattle in insecticide to eradicate ticks. It was opposed due to the degree of difficulty of rounding them up. Killing deer to eradicate the ticks met with violent opposition. Both problems were solved in 1949, when legislation was passed to have cattle fenced in, and the free-range cattle industry ended. It was possible then to control and improve the herds. In 1927, the Sebastian Land Company had about 300 fenced acres of pasturage for fattening cattle for market. They were in better condition, with a high grade of meat at much less cost than western cattle. They kept a supply on hand for their local customers.

Leon Owen Baughman

Leon Owen Baughman, son of Walter and Belle Baughman, was a successful businessman who took over some of his father's business interests and became prominent in Sebastian's civic history. Leon had cattle interests and was in the citrus business. He also continued to operate the Baughman dairy. He was a city clerk, member of the city council for twelve years, and was president of the council when he was selected to fill the unexpired term of George T. Badger, long-time Sebastian mayor who died in office January 5, 1940. He served out the term until the December election of 1941, and then was re-elected mayor, leaving office in 1942. He was a veteran of WWII, serving in the Army. He died in 1971 while in a nursing home in Vero Beach, and was brought back to Sebastian for burial with the rest of the Baughmans.

Poultry

Like so many other enterprises, poultry raising was forming organizations. The Indian River County Poultry Association assisted in the organization of a branch group, the Roseland Poultrymen Association. The first regular meeting was held Saturday, June 16, 1927, at the Ashburner home. L. Ashburner won prizes for his White Minorcas, Rhode Island Reds, Pit Games, and Bantams at the February 1928 fair. Lester Hanshaw raised White Leghorns.

21

The Boom and Bust: 1920s

Booming Real Estate

Following the trend overtaking the whole state, Sebastian succumbed to the land frenzy of buying and selling. The *Vero Press* of April 2, 1925, headlines read "Important Deals in Real Estate. Sebastian property changes hands and extensive improvements are said to be in prospect." The article stated that frequent visitor E. M. Suddard of Chicago purchased two building lots from W. A. Martin on the Dixie Highway. J. H. S. Woodrolle of Melbourne took options on several important pieces of property in Sebastian; the Rea Motor Sales Company property and the Vickers Store building were pending sales. Woodrolle intended to erect in the next month a 50-foot, double-entrance store of stucco where the present Vickers Bros. store stood. E. W. Vickers remained in charge of the store and the store continued to be run under the same management. The four acres of land in the north part of Sebastian on the corner where the old Dixie Highway joined the new, at one time called the Gibson property, was sold by Dr. David Rose to H. J. Platten, who invested in extensive property in the area. The William B. Worstall grove in South Sebastian sold through George T. Badger to Walter Duncan of Vero. It was a 20-acre tract with bearing fruit trees and about three acres of nursery.

Booming Subdivisions

Florida was awash in real estate schemes, some genuine, some not. Sebastianites, as well as outside realtors and promoters, wanted to make their fortunes in the relatively pristine area of Sebastian, drawing buyers in and selling them land. Thus, there were many sorts of land sales going on in Sebastian, and subdivisions were popular.

San Sebastian

San Sebastian was one of the most ambitious and elaborate communities ever planned. The *Vero Beach Press* newspaper provided continuing extensive coverage for the new development being created along St. Sebastian Bay. The "New City of San Sebastian Rising on the Shores of the Indian River" piece from May 20, 1926, was one such article. The old Ercildoune Inn was on the property of the proposed San Sebastian, and was used as a barracks for the construction crew of San Sebastian. San Sebastian Development holdings included several hundred acres on the peninsula along the St. Sebastian River and from the Indian River to the beach, and north one mile from St. Sebastian Inlet. A causeway was planned to connect the beach area of their holdings to the mainland property. On the south side of San Sebastian Bay, from the Dixie Highway to the railroad, was a 300-acre tract crossed by Roseland Road in the south part. The land included 2,300 acres of high, rolling, heavily-timbered land, and small citrus groves. On the north side of San Sebastian Bay the town of San Sebastian was planned, with residential, business, and industrial sections. Also planned were golf courses, parks, hotels, a civic center, school, university, modern hospital, and sanitarium. Ten thousand acres to the west was planned for future agricultural use. Bird and game sanctuaries, hunting lodges, and club house were contemplated along the branches of the St. Sebastian back in the wilderness.

San Sebastian was the dream of R. H. Hemphill of South Carolina, and platting was started in 1888, but no backers were found and the idea died. In early 1925, five businessmen from New York City began plans and began acquiring 13,000 acres for San Sebastian. On October 16, 1925, San Sebastian Development Corporation was formed as a Florida corporation, with President Edgar H. Stapper of West Palm Beach, Vice President and Treasurer B. J. Cumber of New York City, Vice President H. B. MacAlpine of New York City, and General Counsel John B. Penneton of New York City, with corporate offices in New York City. Charles W. Leavitt of New York was chosen for city planning and engineering services. Laurence Swann of New York City was Publicity director, and the architectural firm of D. W. Baum and Company was selected. Famous sketch artist Levon Fairchild West was engaged to go to Spain to prepare etchings and paintings of Spanish and Moorish architectural designs to be incorporated into San Sebastian's look, with the cooperation of King Alphonso of Spain and U.S. Ambassador Moore.

Advertisements offering lots for sale began in the *Vero Beach Press* in 1926, and reservations for residences began coming in. In May 1926, extensive clearing, grading of streets, installation of sewers, and ornamental plantings were being accomplished by a crew of 150 men and 50 mules. San Sebastian Boulevard was 100 feet wide and ran from Dixie Highway to the north end of the bridge and along the contour of the bayshore. At the entrance stood a large sign: "This is San Sebastian the Sunporch of America Picture Your Home on the Magnificent Bay Front Ahead."

In June 1926, the first of the fleet of tourist coaches arrived. The golf course was nearly complete in September 1926. Mr. and Mrs. William Bayliss, Mr. and Mrs. Jarvis, and Mr. and Mrs. Davis were all residents of San Sebastian in 1927. San Sebastian Inn was a popular dining spot. On July 6, 1928, the Woman's Club hosted a thimble bee at the San Sebastian Inn. Georgia Tech athletes summered at San Sebastian doing construction work. However, San Sebastian failed to qualify for the Central East Coast Baseball League.

All of this planning, work, and promotion was not sufficient to keep San Sebastian afloat. Not enough lots were sold. San Sebastian owned 2,600 acres in Indian River and Brevard Counties to be subdivided in 1926, and another 10,000 acres optioned. The company mortgaged the land with five notes of $252,225 each, due 1926-1930, with one note payment due each of the five years. San Sebastian defaulted on the mortgage in 1928, and a foreclosure suit was filed against the corporation by H. F. Welles. The Sheriff was unable to serve the subpoena because San Sebastian at that time had no officers in Florida. The corporation dissolved by proclamation December 7, 1936.

Ocean Breeze Heights

Ocean Breeze Heights was another of the more ambitious subdivisions planned for Sebastian. It was the vision of promoter and realtor O. K. (Okey, Okie) Bland of Clarksburg, Virginia. He and his wife began coming to Sebastian in 1925, purchasing properties. A plat map of Ocean Breeze Heights was created September 18, 1925, by surveyors Lloyd, LaBruce & Watts. On September 24, 1925, a special meeting was convened by the city commissioners to inspect the plat of Ocean Breeze Heights as submitted by Okey Bland. As designed, the subdivision was bounded on the east by Central Avenue and on the west by Palm Avenue and the Florida East Coast Railway. Park Avenue ran north-south through the center of the subdivision with an oval park and playground areas in the center of the subdivision.

The *Vero Beach Press* printed an extensive description of the subdivision September 29, 1925, with a photograph of Mr. Bland. "Ocean Breeze Subdivision to be Nice Residential Section" was the headline. "Mr. Bland is one of the most enthusiastic developers to arrive in Sebastian, and with such competent supervision, Ocean Breeze Heights is bound to be the fulfillment of Sebastian's most cherished dreams." The Ocean Breeze Heights subdivision was situated in the northern part of town on Central Avenue, planned as a modern residential district. Engineers were working surveying streets and lots; laborers were clearing the land and preparing for the buildings that would be constructed. Artesian wells were being drilled around the land to give a plentiful water supply. A variety of homes, all fire-proof and modern in every detail, were planned in Moorish, Spanish or English styles, in wide ranges of size and cost. In November 1926, Okey Bland completed construction of an apartment building. Unfortunately, the times caught up with the subdivision, and it was never completely finished. Only a few lots sold, and only a few homes were built. Only one is known to exist currently.

Jackson Street House

One of the Okey Bland houses currently stands on Jackson Street in Sebastian. It is a beautiful example of the Spanish-style homes created by him, fully restored. According to Jeanne Shaw Kendler, in her October 21, 1998, program at North County Library for Sebastian Area Historical Society, entitled "Sebastian Revisited," Boyton Edwin Shaw and his family came to Sebastian from Cutler, Perry County, Illinois, with four children. They lived in an "Okey Bland" house at the top of the hill, south of the cemetery. In 1998, it was in ruins. Mrs. Shaw taught in Roseland in a one-room school. Jeanne Shaw Kendler was one of B. E. Shaw's daughters.

Madison Street House

Frank and Estelle Vickers purchased a lot and home from Okey and Lucy D. Bland April 4, 1936, on Madison Street. This was another of the Spanish-style "Okey Bland" houses, stucco over wood. This house was small, with no heat and no air conditioning. It faced north and the front door opened into the living room. In the living room, there was a fireplace. There was an arch in one wall leading out to a porch, and the kitchen was located in that area. Two bedrooms were on the east side. There was a goldfish pond on the east side and an artesian well. A garage stood behind it, on the southwest side. It had a circular drive paved with cement on the west side, leading to the garage. In 2013, the lot was cleared of brush and the home was found to be in complete disrepair and riddled with termites. It was destroyed.

Ocean Breeze Heights Service Station

For many years, the Ocean Breeze Heights Service Station was in use on Indian River Drive, north of Sembler & Sembler. It was operated by Art Smith, Bill Fisher, and Joe Cassell. The station was a gathering place for fishermen, had a small store with drinks and snacks, and sold gasoline. It no longer exists.

Edgewater Park

Edgewater Park, platted in September 1925, was the quintessential real estate development of the boom era. It involved prime land south of Main Street on the Indian River, stretching west with New Dixie Highway running through it, over to the East Coast Lumber & Supply land next to the railway. It was formed by a consortium of local and non-local realtors and businessmen, most of whom owned lots individually in the park. Familiar names were involved, Braddock, Hardee, Beugnot, Roberts, and Martin, to name a few. J. R. Odom of Macon, Georgia, one of the group, sent his son S. V. Odom to Sebastian to take control of his business interests there. The son had his own business, Odom Station, in Edgewater Park. Indicated on the plat was the site for the Sebastian Inn in Edgewater Park, another of Odom's enterprises. S. V. Odom and his new bride Joyce Weldon lived in apartments in the Sebastian Hotel. Unfortunately, even in 1925 and 1926, there were many delinquent tax notices for Edgewater Park. J. R. Odom was involved in more real estate ventures in Sebastian, and was having land cleared in the northern part of town for a new subdivision in June 1926.

New Sebastian Hotel/Sebastian Inn

Originally called the New Sebastian Hotel, the Sebastian Inn on the shore of the Indian River in Edgewater Park was a combination hotel, bar, and cocktail lounge. The inn's two boats, the *Jungle Bell* and *Leading Lady*, offered scenic cruises. It became a popular local gathering spot. However, the hotel changed hands numerous times. The New Sebastian Hotel was built by J. R. Odom with Spanish architecture, a two-story stucco building, and was owned and operated by Hylton Brothers at the time of its construction. It was located in Edgewater Park between the Dixie Highway and the Indian River. It opened February 18, 1926, with a dining room and dancing. In June, it was leased to Charles Haynes of San Sebastian.

In September of 1926, it was taken over by the new owners, Odom & Montgomery, who made some improvements before opening it again for business. In October, improvements continued, and a dining room was opened around November 1, with Mr. and Mrs. J. White of Miami in charge of the dining room. Owners and managers Messrs. Odom and Montgomery predicted a good season. There was a lunchroom connected with the hotel. In June of the following year, owner and City Alderman Joe Montgomery made improvements, as reported in the *Vero Beach Press Journal* of June 14, 1927. New electric signs were placed on the top if the building. The 40 rooms were equipped with thoroughly modern conveniences. The grounds were landscaped down to the river. Three fountains with large concrete basins that contained five varieties of fish were in the hotel yard that was enclosed by an ornamental fence and landscaped with plants and flowers. A tennis court, croquet grounds, and horseshoe court were planned. The hotel company purchased a motor boat for use by guests, and a dock out into the river was planned for larger boats to moor.

The New Sebastian Inn was sold again by J. R. Odom to Mrs. N. L. Baker of Jacksonville. J. S. Reed, also of Jacksonville, was manager by August of 1927. In May 1928, Mrs. Baker publicized that the hotel would be run on the European Plan while she was gone for the summer that year. In May 1928, Ralph Wolfe operated the New Sebastian Hotel; however, in June, it was being operated by Ferris Bougnot as a lodge. W. E. Garrett of Jacksonville leased it as the Hotel Sevilla for a term of three years beginning January 12, 1929. He and his wife were experienced hoteliers, having successfully operated the Hotel DeSoto in Jacksonville for seven years. The dining room was operated a la carte, specializing in shore dinners. The filling station was under the same management. During WWII, U.S. marines who operated a "secret" radar station at US Hwy 1 and Main Street were quartered there. The building was condemned and demolished in 1968.

Vickers Cemetery

Vickers Cemetery was platted November 22, 1926, situated west of the Park Cemetery and north of Ocean Breeze Heights. Most of the plots had names on them when the plat was drawn and so were either optioned or already sold.

Knight and French Tract

Knight and French, realtors of Vero, purchased approximately 50 acres of land south of Sebastian in January 1925, the tract lying between the New Dixie Highway and Indian River. The land purchased was three adjoining tracts from three property owners, a five-acre grove formerly owned by B. C. Ryall, 37 acres of grove and pine land owned by A. Kroegel, and eight acres of pine land owned by Paul Kroegel, reported the *Eau Gallie Record.*

More subdivisions and land deals were occurring, with varying degrees of success. Hardee Subdivision No. B. in 1924, the Esther Mae Subdivision in 1925, and the Orange Ridge Subdivision in 1926, were some of the others.

E. B. Potts Roseland Boom

E. B. Potts brought the spirit of the Florida real estate boom to Roseland. He and Mrs. Potts came to Roseland in early 1925, purchasing the E. B. Potts Building on Berry Avenue, where he set up as an agent for a wide variety of merchandise. Part of the building was rented out. He advertised extensively with catchy ads, as an agent for land, homes, a hotel, stores, a store manager, seven-passenger Cadillacs, and more. He advertised building Peter Pan doubles and double Baby Grand apartments (with no explanation as to what they were, unfortunately). He purchased waterfront property from H. G. Higly, built a new dock, and cleared the waterfront. He erected a tile double Baby Grand apartment house on the corner of Sebastian Avenue and Gibson Street. By July of that year, he and Mrs. Potts had relocated to Vero Beach, where their married daughter lived. He began advertising from his office at 18th and Deleon Streets that he was willing to build six to twelve apartment buildings in Vero Beach when suitable locations were found.

Prohibition

During the 1920s, there was also a boom in rumrunning and the smuggling of aliens and narcotics due to the beginning of national prohibition in January 1920. Florida's geography was ideal for smuggling, with its long coastline with many inlets and nearness to Cuba and the West Indies. Florida was one of the strongholds of smuggling in the U.S. Lax local enforcement and too few federal agents made it easier. There was some moonshine produced, but most liquor was smuggled in from Cuba and the West Indies in small boats. When it opened in 1923, Sebastian Inlet was a major entryway for small boat smuggling. It was possible at times to have a spontaneous beach party with cases of liquor that washed ashore from being tossed overboard by panicky smugglers.

Robert G. McCain

In the mid-1920s, Robert G. McCain bought a small auto repair shop on US Hwy 1 that he used to hold his autos and trucks. It backed on the river with a small dock. Due to its proximity to the Indian River, it was an ideal center for receiving and distributing smuggled liquor. McCain's autos and trucks were used for distribution. His home with Bessie and his children was on the west side of US Hwy 1, across from the shop, and had a small basement where smuggled goods were stored. Eventually he was caught and convicted. Bob's brother-in-law, Doc Sloan, was a bootlegger and grove owner, living in the former Tompkins Store near the McCains.

Some other Sebastianites were likewise convicted; Gene Beugnot was caught and charged with operating a still. In 1928, Arthur Kroegel was arrested and charged with possession of liquor and Mrs. Kroegel was charged with the sale of intoxicating liquor.

A raid was reported in the *Vero Beach Press* July 1, 1926, that was carried out by the Sheriff's office. A still and bottled goods were found in an old shed a few miles west of Roseland. The deputies arrived at the courthouse in the Seminole Building with a Ford touring car loaded down with the results of the raid, a complete moonshine-making outfit, 448 pint bottles of home brew, and a barrel of ingredients. The plant had been abandoned a short time before the raid. Such news was common until Prohibition ended in 1933, making the sale of alcohol legal again.

The Bust

While Sebastian and Roseland were enjoying a spurt of growth and prosperity, there were signs of the coming depression all around the state in 1926. Florida was feeling the effects of negative press on its tourism industry and real estate. Real estate fraud brought about a resultant decline in real estate purchases. Bank deposits began to fall off, and there were heavy withdrawals. There were concerns about additional taxes, and there were heavy stock selloffs. Real estate buyers were failing to make property payments. The hurricane that year was a final blow.

September 17-18, 1926 Miami Hurricane (or Great Miami Hurricane)

On September 17-18, 1926, Miami was hit by a Category 4 hurricane that devastated the area. It crossed the state at Moore Haven. The Okeechobee dike was damaged, and the storm damaged Sanibel Island, the Florida Panhandle, and Alabama. Although the worst damage was to Miami and the West Coast areas, the end result ruinously affected the whole state. The enormous destruction to infrastructure had a lasting effect on commerce and tourism and was one of the causes of ending the Florida land boom and ushering Florida into the Great Depression earlier than the rest of the country. Refugees from the Miami devastation came as far north as Indian River County. The governor organized relief for hurricane-stricken areas; the final figure was 392 dead, mainly at Moore Haven.

Sebastian itself suffered light damage, mainly beach erosion, and the road along the beach was nearly destroyed. Damage to buildings was slight. Wind drove water into the Indian River, raising the water level by several feet, overflowing banks, and causing damage to houses and roads along the riverfront. Fruit was blown off trees. Part of the roof of S. A. Braswell's building was removed. Fish houses, docks, nets, and fishing boats washed away. Two Sebastian fish houses were demolished by the wind, one belonging to T. B. Hicks and the other to Captain R. G. Hardee. The area received eight inches of rain, and storm debris and trash were strewn everywhere. Vero Beach received 6.72 inches of rain.

As it happened to so many, Thomas Hick's fortunes plummeted in the late 20s. The 1928 hurricane destroyed Hicks' dock and boats, and he was dealt another blow from financial losses he suffered from the great depression. The Hicks remained in Sebastian in 1930, but by 1935, they had moved in with their daughter Mattie and her husband in Vero Beach. In 1943, Thomas and Mabel had relocated to Jacksonville, where he was first a watchman, and in 1944, a railroad inspector. He died in 1945, at about age 73. It is said his health was destroyed by his losses in the 1920s, and he never completely recovered. Mabel died July 18, 1968.

August 7, 1928 Hurricane

A scant two years later, another hit. The 1928 Okeechobee hurricane was a deadly Category 5 storm. At least 2,500 were killed in South Florida from the flooding caused when storm surge breached the dike and Lake Okeechobee overflowed, flooding hundreds of square miles.

The *Vero Beach Press* August 10, 1928, local headline was "No Deaths or Injuries from Storm." Locally, there was heavy crop damage, several large buildings were blown down, and electricity went out, but no deaths. The worst of the storm was centered around the Fort Pierce area. It cut a 200-mile-wide swath from Melbourne to Jupiter. The municipal power plant at Sebastian was damaged, a number of buildings were unroofed, and windows were blown out. Trains were delayed by many poles and trees blown down across the tracks.

In the Sebastian column of the *Vero Beach Press* the following week, it was reported that the roof of the Braswell house was blown off where Mrs. Julian Fields' family was staying. Fields' garage was destroyed by the storm, a number of poles and lines were blown down, and power went out. The roof of a power plant was blown off, garages were demolished, and porches were torn off. One house was blown off of its blocks, but no houses were destroyed. Sembler & Sembler fish house was completely destroyed, and others were blown into the river. Some nets and boats were destroyed. The arches at the entrance to Fellsmere Boulevard and Ocean Breeze Heights were destroyed. Citrus growers suffered heavy losses, with 50-75% of fruit crops lost, leaves blown off of trees, and some trees uprooted. In Roseland, as much as two-thirds of the fruit crop was lost. The roof was blown off the porch of the Holtzclaw house, Mrs. Keifer's house was blown down, Tellier lost a number of hens when the chicken house was wrecked, trees were broken, and many other homes received damage. There was considerable damage to the Lester Hanshaw house, Camp Barbaric. In the spring following the storm, the grove trees put out new growth, but not many blossoms.

April 19, 1929 to October 15, 1929: Mediterranean Fruit Fly

Another tragedy struck Florida the following year. From April 19, 1929, to October 15, 1929, the Florida agricultural community was rocked by a terrifying seven months when another disaster struck. On April 19, 1929, the *Vero Beach Press Journal* reported that the Mediterranean fruit fly had been found in Orlando groves and in surrounding counties, the first in the United States. Every newspaper was full of updates, reports, bulletins, information, and speculation during this period. This tropical pest was regarded as the most destructive of all insects, the most dreaded in the whole world, affecting 72 known varieties of fruits and vegetables. No country had been able to eradicate it once it was established. In its maggot form, it eats the fruit and causes it to drop.

Florida immediately quarantined the area, and requested funds to start eradication of the pest. Many efforts were undertaken immediately to keep the pest out of the Indian River County, including inspections and improved packing and disposal methods. Cars entering the county from the north were inspected and sprayed with a disinfectant. A Clearing House Association was formed.

Unfortunately, this was not enough. The U.S. government placed the entire state of Florida under quarantine as of May 1, 1929. On May 26, 1929, a new rule prohibited the movement of fruits and vegetables to 17 states from all counties. The next phase, reported in July 1929, consisted of removing and destroying all cherry and guava fruit, fortunately not the extensive citrus fruit, before it ripened, in all Florida counties. In Indian River County, Sebastian, Roseland, Wabasso, and Fellsmere were quick to respond, but Vero Beach lagged. The following phase, reported in August, consisted of continuing the eradication by removal and destruction of the trees. Crews were dispatched to cut down and destroy all custard apple, guava, cherry, fig, and date palm trees, but not the vast citrus groves. Cars leaving the state were searched. In July, 6,000 men were engaged in the quarantine work throughout the state.

On August 2, 1929, it was anticipated by Governor Carlton that growers would be able to ship their produce by the fall season and that eradication would be complete. Selling juice and canned fruit was also contemplated by grove owners. By August 27, restrictions were being lifted in non-infected counties, allowing shipment to any except western and southern states and Puerto Rico. Indian River County was never infected. "Florida now commercially free of fly" was the September 10, 1929, headline. Previously infected areas were released from quarantine October 15, 1929. However, shipment was still prohibited to southern and western states and Puerto Rico. One unhappy aftereffect was that although they had not been required to destroy their fruit or trees, there were complaints that the subsequent fruit quality in remaining groves had been damaged by overzealous spraying of trees. Some growers considered abandoning their groves as a result.

These events were coupled with the decline in real estate values, the failure of some banks, and a decrease in tourism; Florida was losing its allure. Some individuals never recovered from the devastating losses they suffered during these years. These events helped Florida slide into depression in advance of the rest of the country. The stock market crash October 29, 1929, officially ushered in the Great Depression in the United States. Individuals were pulling back, spending less, and investing less. Banks failed, as did the stock market. By the advance of WWII, however, the economy began to revive.

Samuel A. Braswell

Samuel Asa Braswell's history closely mirrors the times of the 1920s. He came from a large, prosperous Georgia family. He and his brothers, Leon and C. C. Braswell, came to the Florida east coast in the mid-1910s and began investing in real estate. C. C. Braswell was involved in the Beachland Development Company in Vero and then formed his own company, Braswell Realty Company, and became heavily invested in the development of Winter Beach. Leon was a store clerk and fisherman.

S. A. Braswell came to Sebastian with his wife Esther, brother Leon, and niece and nephew Minnie and Clyde Wynn in the mid-1910s. He purchased the Carlile House around the time they arrived. Sam and Esther lived there until they rented the Carlile House in 1919 to the Park family, and after the Parks moved, the Braswell household lived there again. In 1920, he owned a farm. He set up a real estate office on Main Street, and over time, acquired the Sebastian Hotel and constructed the Braswell Building next to it. Braswell was a candidate for Sebastian mayor in 1924. The Braswells moved into the top floor of the Braswell Building in 1925.

This comfortable existence began deteriorating around 1927; just as the rest of Florida began slipping toward the crash, so did his life. Around 1927, he sold the Carlile house to Guy and Sadie Glasgow. Guy was the agent for Standard Oil Company. In January 1927, the Owens family took over the Braswell's former home. Around then, Sam and Esther apparently separated. Esther Braswell began living in a separate residence from that of her husband, on North Central Avenue, entertaining at home and traveling with friends and family alone, not with her husband. In the 1930 U.S. Census, Samuel Braswell is reported as married, but with no other household members. At age 51, he was still a self-employed realtor and owned his home on North Central Avenue next to his brother Leon's. Esther Braswell was head of her own household on Central Avenue that she owned that census year. The census reports her as age 62 and still married, but living with Minnie L. Braswell, who she named as her daughter, and two boarders, a married couple named Agnew and Louise Rogers. Her residence was next to that of the Glasgows. In some of the records, she is named Queen Esther Braswell. Ten years later, Sam was still living alone in a rental on the west side of Old Dixie. Sam Braswell died in 1947, as did his brother Leon. Sam and Leon are buried together in the Sebastian Cemetery.

John B. Carlton on Sebastian River, South Prong

John B. Carlton was another casualty of the crash. He started with ambitious plans for his land on the Sebastian River. He was an experienced realtor, part of the Florida Realty Corporation, according to the announcement in the *Vero Beach Press Journal* of January 29, 1925. He intended to create a 100-acre subdivision adjoining Sebastian on the west side of the Sebastian River on Sheepshead Bluff, south of the current Wimbrow Park area. The property was part of the 1,200-acre tract purchased by Carlton some time ago, according to the article. It would have had four miles of hard-surfaced streets, and clearing and plowing was already underway at the time of the article. The lots would be 75 x 260 feet. Carlton intended to have a hotel as part of the subdivision. However, this dream was never realized. The planned subdivision failed, and funding failed. His real estate bubble burst, along with so many others.

Around 1925, Carlton, his wife Elizabeth, son Chester, and Elizabeth's daughter Ruth moved from New York to Roseland, staying at the Bay View Inn while they awaited completion of their home. Actual construction was undertaken by Dave Dugger of North Carolina. All materials had to be boated down river and pulled up on the high bank.

Carlton was plagued by money woes as the Florida depression started to deepen. He brought a quiet title suit to clear the land title against Charles Downing, etc., and Indian River Land Improvement Co. in 1926. He was sued by Service Lumber & Supply Co. for payment of lumber for the house/hotel that same year. The Carltons spent the summer of 1927 in New York, returning to their new home in October. When completed, it was a lovely southern-style mansion with four columns in front, paneling inside, a chandelier, and a grand piano. Elizabeth joined the Ladies' Aid Society in Roseland. The home may have been intended to be the Carlton Hotel. However, funds dried up and the rest of the plan never materialized. T. W. Radinsky successfully sued Carlton for damages in 1928. There were later allegations of fraud.

In August of 1928, Carlton left on a business trip. Elizabeth and son Chester found it too difficult and lonely there on their own and moved to Roseland. Elizabeth and Chester were in Roseland in July 1929, traveling to the races with friends. However, by the time of the 1930 U.S. Census, John, age 60, Elizabeth, age 65, and son John (Chester), age 15, were all living together in Sebastian in their own home, next to the Bruce Ryall and Devore families.

Maurice M. Braddock

Maurice Braddock also was one of the individuals affected by the great depression that swept the country, in a life of many successes and reversals. He was born July 12, 1901, in Sebastian, the son of William Braddock Jr. and Kate Lawson Braddock. He was a member of the first high school graduating class, held in the town hall in 1918.

Maurice Braddock was a man of varied interests and abilities. An early job was for Graves Brothers in the Wabasso office. He then worked for Florida Citrus Exchange as a seller. By 1920, he began his career in merchandizing clerking in the family general store, and operated a general store, a dry goods store, and a drug store at Main Street and US Hwy 1. Maurice had musical talents, as well. When the Vero Band was organized December 13, 1924, Maurice joined. He was one of the judges at a Charleston contest at the town hall in March 1926.

Maurice Braddock's home on Washington Street was built in 1920, a one-story wood building with a broad front porch. It was later moved from Washington Street to Main Street, where he ran it as a drug store. It was later moved back to Washington Street. This was one of the buildings included on the National Register of Historic Places: Old Town Sebastian Historic District East on August 4, 2003, and it still remains on Washington Street.

Around 1925, his father had extensive farming holdings in Marietta, Georgia, and Maurice accompanied his parents on trips there for several summer months at a time. In 1925, he was the Sebastian City Clerk. Minnie Lewis of Vero Beach and Maurice were married in Palm Beach on June 15, 1926. Minnie wore a sports suit of white Canton crepe, with a matching hat and veil. A bridal dinner was given for them. On July 22, 1926, the newlyweds were in Atlanta, and Minnie's sister Marion Lewis visited them there. The couple honeymooned in New York for a couple of weeks, and then spent two months abroad. They returned to Sebastian to live in Maurice's home. According to the 1927-28 city directory, he worked for W. C. Braddock & Sons, his parents' company. He and his brother Roy were prominent realtors, and were members of the Fellsmere Masons. In 1929, Maurice was a part of the Vero Beach Follies musical production.

Maurice Braddock opened a department store in Sebastian in December 1927, reported to be doing well. In June 1928, the voter registration book for Sebastian was in the Maurice Braddock dry goods store. Unfortunately, this venture was not a success. Maurice Braddock made a petition in bankruptcy on September 14, 1929, and stock and fixtures of the store were sold. Braddocks Department Store reopened for business later in the month, but the Braddocks left town.

The Braddock home on Washington Avenue was rented at the end of October 1929 to Mr. Addington, the new superintendent of Sebastian Groves Company, and the Braddocks relocated to Miami. Minnie was hospitalized in Miami, and their daughter Mildred was brought back to Sebastian by Maurice's mother in November 1929, for the duration of her mother's illness. By the time of the 1930 census, three-year-old Mildred was back with her parents, Maurice, age 29, and Minnie H., age 23. They were living in a rental apartment in Miami and Maurice was employed as a dry goods salesman. Maurice became a member of the Mahi Temple of Miami and the Ancient and Accepted Order of the Nobles of the Mystic Shrine of Miami.

By 1945, his marriage to Minnie had ended and he had married Frances M. Braddock. He had relocated to the Nakomis section of Sarasota, where he remained at least until 1947. They lived in an apartment and he was a traveling salesman there. His final move was to Tampa, where he had a laundry and dry cleaning business. He died in Tampa May 3, 1991, at age 89. At the time of his death, his wife Francis Braddock and his daughter Mildred were still living. Theirs was a common tale of the reversals of the Great Depression.

In the 1930s

In 1930, Indian River County had a population 6,724; Sebastian population was 464, and that of Roseland was 82. Sebastian achieved the status of a city in this decade. On May 14, 1933, the Town of Sebastian was dissolved and the City of Sebastian was created with a charter created by Vocelle & Nisle. Its pioneering days were ended. The following decade of the 1930s would be a difficult era for Sebastian and Roseland.

Bibliography

Abstract of Brevard County Will Book No. 1 1886-1905 at Titusville, Florida (Cocoa, FL: Brevard Genealogical Society, 1980)

Alachua County Library District Heritage Collection. http://heritage.acld.lib.fl.us.

Anderson, Edward C. and William Stanley Hoole, *Florida Territory in 1844: The Diary of Master Edward C. Anderson, United States Navy* (Tuscaloosa, AL: University of Alabama Press, 1977)

Andrews, Allen H., *A Yank Pioneer in Florida* (Jacksonville, FL: Douglas Printing, 1950)

Armstrong Douglas R., *French Castaways at Old Cape Canaveral* (Palm Bay, FL: 1996)

Austin, Elizabeth S., *Frank M. Chapman in Florida* (Gainesville, FL: University of Florida Press, 1967)

Baisden, Katherine, *A History of Roseland and Vicinity* (Unpublished, 1956)

Ball, Jim, Roz Foster, Douglas Hendriksen and Vera Zimmerman, *History of Brevard County, Vol. 3* (Stuart, FL: Brevard County Historical Commission, 1995)

Barrow, Mark V., Jr., *A Passion for Birds: American Ornithology after Audubon* (Princeton, NJ: Princeton University Press, 2000)

Bass, Bob, *When Steamboats Reigned in Florida* (Gainesville, FL: University Press of Florida, 2008)

Bechtel, Stefan, *Mr. Hornaday's War* (Boston, MA: Beacon Press, 2012)

"Boston Literary Notes." *New York Times* (New York, NY), December 3, 1910.

Brooks County Genealogical Society, *Brooks County Echoes of Its People* (Madison, FL: Jimbob printing, 1993)

Burnsed, Kathy, 1935 State Census, Indian River County, Florida.

Burnsed, Kathy, 1945 State Census, Indian River County, Florida.

BYU Harold B. Lee Library. http://lib.byu.edu/digital/jackson.

Canning, Charlotte, "Traveling Culture: Circuit Chautauqua in the Twentieth Century," *The University of Iowa Libraries*, 2004. The University of Iowa. http://www.lib.uiowa.edu/sc/tc/.

Canova, Andrew P., *Life and Adventures in South Florida* (Tampa, FL: Tribune Printing 1885, 1906)

Chapman, Frank M., *Bird Studies with a Camera* (New York, NY: D. Appleton & Co., 1900)

Chapman, Frank M., *Camps and Cruises of an Ornithologist* (New York, NY: D. Appleton & Co., 1908)

"Chronology of the National Audubon Society: 100 Years of Conservation 1899 to 1999." High Lauter Levin Associates. http://hughlevin.com/reference/audu-chron.html.

Cleveland, Weona, *Crossroad Towns Remembered* (Melbourne, FL: Florida Today, 1994)

Cleveland, Weona, *Mosquito Soup* (Cocoa, FL: Florida Historical Society Press, 2013)

Clifton, Geraldine McLeod, *Lowndes County Georgia Marriages 1870-1920* (Thomasville, GA: Craig Miles & Associates, 1998)

Commercial Atlas of the World, New 1930 Census Ed. (Chicago, IL: Geographical Publishing Co., c. 1931)

Commissioners of the Florida Inland Navigation District, *Florida Intracoastal Waterway from the St. Johns River to Miami* (Jacksonville, FL: Associated Advertising Agency, 1937)

Culberson, James E., *Images Through the Doors of Time* (Melbourne, FL: Sea Bird Pub, 1995)

Dau, Frederick W., *Florida Old and New* (New York: G. P. Putman's Sons, 1934)

Daughters of the American Revolution General James Jackson Chapter, *History of Lowndes County: Georgia 1825-1941* (Valdosta, GA: General James Jackson Chapter, D.A.R., 1942; reprint, Spartansburg, SC: Reprint Company Publishers, 1978)

Daughters of the American Revolution, *Pioneer Churches of Florida* (Chuluota, FL: Mickler House Publishing, 1976)

Daughters of the American Revolution, www.dar.org.

Dickinson, Jonathan, *Jonathan Dickinson's Journal, or, God's Protecting Providence, being the Narrative of a Journey from Port Royal in Jamaica to Philadelphia between August 23, 1696 and April 1, 1697* (Port Salerno, FL: Florida Classics Library, 1985)

Digital copies, plat maps. Archive Center, Indian River County Main Library, Vero Beach, FL.

Dumas, Tim. "Paradise Regained, Sort of." *Vero Beach Magazine* (Vero Beach, FL), March-April 2000.

Eau Gallie Record (Eau Gallie, FL), 1924.

Encyclopedia of Florida Sheriffs (Clanton, AL: Heritage Publishing Consultants, 2008)

Erikson, John M., *Brevard County: A History* (Tampa, FL: The Florida Historical Society Press, 1994)

Fellsmere Tribune. (Fellsmere, FL),1913-1921.

Ferry, Richard J., *Soldiers of Florida in the Indian, Civil and Spanish American Wars* (MacClenny, FL: Board of State Institutions, 1983)

Florida Department of Military Affairs, *Florida Veterans of the First World War, All Services, 1917-1919, Brevard, Indian River, St. Lucie, Martin, Palm Beach, Broward, Dade* (St. Augustine, FL: Florida Department of Military Affairs)

Florida Historical Quarterly (Tallahassee, FL: Florida Historical Quarterly, 1937)

Florida Star (Titusville, FL), 1880-1915.

Florida State Census Records, 1885.

Florida State Division of Corporations. www.sunbiz.org.

Florida State Gazetteer and Business Directory 1886-1887 (New York: South Publishing Co.)

Ft. Pierce News (Ft. Pierce, FL), 1902-1920.

Gore, Tommy, The *Rainbow Chasers In The Great Florida Treasure Hunt* (Alma, GA: T. Gore, 2010)

Green, Linda L., *Florida 1860 Agricultural Census, Brevard County* (Westminster, MD: Heritage Books, 2005)

Guide to Historic Sebastian and Roseland (Sebastian, FL: Sebastian Area Historical Society, Inc., 1996-2006)

Hales, Peter, *William Henry Jackson and the Transformation of the American Landscape* (Philadelphia: Temple University Press, 1988)

Hanna, Alfred Jackson and Kathryn Abbey Hanna, *Florida's Golden Sands* (New York, NY: Bobbs-Merrill Co., 1950)

Hartman, David, *Biographical Rosters of Florida's Confederate and Union Soldiers, 1861-1865* (Wilmington, NC: Broadfoot Publishing, 1995)

Hawks, J. M., *Florida Gazetteer* (New Orleans, LA: J. M. Hawks, 1871)

Hawworth, Esther Bernice Howell, *Jottings and Echoes Related to Newnansville: One of Florida's Earliest Settlements of Alachua and Columbia Counties* (Storter Printing, 1975)

Hellier, Walter R., *Indian River, Florida's Treasure Coast* (Coconut Grove, FL: Hurricane House, 1965)

Henshall, Dr. James Alexander, *Camping and Cruising in Florida* (Cincinnati, OH: Robert Clarke & Co, 1884; reprint, Florida Classics Library, 1991)

History Clarinda Chamber. http://Clarinda.org/history.

"Historical Markers." Florida Department of State Division of Historical Resources. http://dos.dos.myflorida.com/historical/preservation/historical-markers/.

Hopwood, Fred A., *Grant, Florida: The First 100 Years* (Grant, FL: Grant Historical Society, 1990)

Hopwood, Fred A., *Steamboating on the Indian River* (Cocoa, FL: Florida Historical Press, 1998, reprint)

Indian River Advocate (Titusville, FL), 1891-1896.

Indian River Genealogical Society, *Cemeteries of Indian River County, Florida* (Vero Beach, FL: Indian River Genealogical Society, 1987)

Jackson, William Henry, *Time Exposure, the Autobiography of William Henry Jackson* (New York: Van Rees Press, 1940; reprint, Albuquerque, NM: University of New Mexico Press, 1986)

Johnston, Sidney P., *A History of Indian River County, 2nd Ed.* (Vero Beach, FL: Indian River County Historical Society, 2002)

Kersey, Harry A., Jr., *Pelts, Plumes, and Hides, White Traders Among the Seminole Indians, 1870-1930* (Gainesville, FL: University Press of Florida, 1975)

Keyes, George, unpublished research materials. Sebastian Area Historical Society Archives, Sebastian, FL.

Kjerulff, Georgiana, *Tales of Old Brevard* (Melbourne FL: Kellersberger Fund, 1972)

Korker, Clarence F. and Richard B. Votapka. *A Photographic History of Fellsmere* (Clarence F. Korker and Richard B. Votapka, 2011)

Kroegel, Rodney. *Photographs of Pathfinder Hydroplane*. 1923. Central Brevard Library, Cocoa, Florida.

Lanier, Sidney, *Florida: Its Scenery, Climate and History (Bicentennial Floridiana Facsimile Series)* (Gainesville, FL: University of Florida Press, 1973)

LeBuff, Charles, *J.N. "Ding" Darling National Wildlife Refuge* (Charleston, SC: Arcadia Publishing, 2011)

Littler, Mark M., *Waterways & byways of the Indian River Lagoon: field guide for boaters, anglers & naturalists* (Washington, D.C.: Offshore Graphics, Inc., 2003)

Lockwood, Charlotte Daniels, *Florida's Historic Indian River County Bicentennial Edition* (Vero Beach, FL: Media Tronics, 1975)

Maltby, Barbara, *Little Hollywood* (Micco, FL: Little Hollywood Improvement Association, 1992)

Marion Ball interviews, 1987-1998. Archive Center, Indian River County Main Library, Vero Beach, FL.

Melbourne Times (Melbourne, FL), 1894-1927.

Miami Herald (Miami, FL), 1910.

Miley, Charles S., *Miley's Memos* (Vero Beach, FL: Indian River County Main Library, 1994)

National Register of Historic Places, United States Department of the Interior, *Archie Smith Fish House*. Florida Master Site File #81R00083. Washington, DC: 1994.

National Register of Historic Places, United States Department of the Interior, *Bamma Vickers Lawson House*. Florida Master Site File #8IR00149. Washington, DC: 1990.

National Register of Historic Places, United States Department of the Interior, *Old Town Sebastian Historic District East*. Florida Master Site File #81R00148b, Washington, DC: 2003.

National Register of Historic Places, United States Department of the Interior, *Old Town Sebastian Historic District West*. Florida Master Site File #81R00148a, Washington, DC: 2004.

National Register of Historic Places, United States Department of the Interior, *Sebastian Grammar and Junior High School*. Florida Master Site File #81R00142. Washington, DC: 2001.

Newman, Anna Pearl. "Stories of Early Life Along the Beautiful Indian River." *Stuart Daily News* (Stuart, FL), 1953

Outland, Robert B., *Tapping the Pines: The Naval Stores Industry in the American South* (Baton Rouge, LA: Louisiana State University Press, 2004)

Owens-Voyles, Judy, *History of Education in Indian River County* (Vero Beach, FL: Florida Retired Educators Association, 1998)

Packard, Winthrop, *Florida Trails as seen from Jacksonville to Key West and from November to April inclusive* (Boston, MA: Small, Maynard and Co., 1910; reprint, Englewood, FL: Pineapple Press, 1983)

Park Collection. Sebastian Area Historical Society Archives, Sebastian, FL.

Peters, Virginia Bergman, *The Florida Wars* (Ann Arbor, MI: Archon Books, 1979)

Phillips, Kevin, *1775: A Good Year for Revolution* (New York, NY: Penguin Press, 2012)

Pierce, Charles, *Pioneer Life in Southeast Florida* (Coral Gables, FL: University of Miami Press, 1970)

Pierce, Charles. *On the Wings of the Wind,* unpublished manuscript in Tim Robinson, *A Tropical Paradise: Pioneers and Settlers of Southeast Florida, 1800-1890* (Port Salerno, FL: Port Sun Publishing, 2005)

Prints & Photographs Catalog, Detroit Publishing Company, Library of Congress. http://www.loc.gov/pictures/collection/det/.

R.L. Polk & Company's Florida Gazetteer & Business Directory 1907-1908 (Jacksonville, FL: R. L. Polk & Company)

R.L. Polk & Company's Florida Gazetteer & Business Directory 1911-1912 (Jacksonville, FL: R. L. Polk & Company)

R.L. Polk & Company's Florida Gazetteer & Business Directory 1916-1917 (Jacksonville, FL: R. L. Polk & Company)

Richards, J. Noble, *Florida's Hibiscus City, Vero Beach* (Melbourne, FL: Brevard Graphics, 1968)

Rights, Lucille Rieley, *A Portrait of St. Lucie County, Florida* (Virginia Beach, VA: Donning Co Publishing, 1994; expanded 2nd Ed., 2006)

Rinhart, Floyd and Marion, *Victorian Florida, America's Last Frontier* (Atlanta, GA: Peachtree Publishing, 1986)

Robinson, Tim, *A Tropical Frontier: pioneers and settlers of southeast Florida 1800-1890* (Port Salerno, FL: Port Sun Publishing, 2005)

Schene, Michael G., *Hopes, Dreams and Promises. A History of Volusia County* (Daytona Beach, FL: News-Journal Corp., 1976)

Sears Archives. http://www.searsarchives.com/catalogs/homes/history.

Sebastian Area Historical Society Archives, Sebastian, FL.

Sebastian River Area Historical Society, *More Tales of Sebastian* (Sebastian, FL: Sebastian River Area Historical Society, 1992)

Shofner, Jerrell H., *History of Brevard County* (Stuart, FL: Brevard County Historical Commission, 1995)

"Soldiers of the Seminole Indian War 1835-1843 and The Mexican War." Genealogy Trails. http://genealogytrails.com/fla/Warspg2.htm.

St. Lucie County Tribune (Ft. Pierce, FL), 1905-1920.

Star Advocate (Indian River Advocate) (Titusville, FL), Aug. 15, 1890-Dec. 29, 1925.

Tales of Sebastian (Sebastian, FL: Sebastian River Area Historical Society, 1990)

Tapia, John E., *Circuit Chautauqua, from rural education to popular entertainment in early twentieth century America* (Jefferson, NC: McFarland & Co., 1997)

Tebeau, Charlton W. and William Marina, *A History of Florida, 3rd Ed.* (Coral Gables, FL: University of Miami Press, 1999)

Tebeau, Dr. Charlton W. and Ruby Leach Carson, *Florida from Indian Trail to Space Age, A History, Vol. 1-3* (Delray Beach, FL: Southern Publishing Company, 1965)

Thompson, William C., *Pioneer Chit Chat* Vol. 1 and 2 (Sebastian, FL: Sebastian Area County Library, 1987-2004)

Thurlow, Sandra Henderson, and Deanna Wintercorn Thurlow, *Gilbert's Bar House of Refuge* (Stuart, FL: Sewall's Print Company, 2008)

Thurlow, Sandra Henderson, *Stuart on the St. Lucie: A Pictorial History* (Stuart, FL: Southeast Printing Company, 2001)

Turner, Gregg M., *A Journey into Florida Railroad History* (Gainesville, FL: University of Florida Press, 2008)

Turner, Gregg M., *A Short History of Florida Railroads* (Charleston, SC: Arcadia Publishing, 2003)

U.S. Bureau of the Interior, Bureau Land Management. http://www.glorecords.blm.gov/default.aspx.

U.S. Census Records.

U.S. Enlistment Records, WWI.

Van Landingham, Kyle S., *Pictorial History of Saint Lucie County, 1565-1910* (Florida: Kyle S. Van Landingham, 1988)

Vero Beach Press Journal (Vero Beach, FL), 1919-1991.

Vero Beach Press Newspaper (Vero Beach, FL), 1925-1927.

Vero Press (Vero Beach, FL), 1919-1925.

Vertical files and collections. Archive Center, Indian River County Main Library, Vero Beach, FL.

Wagner, Kip, *Pieces of Eight* (Port Salerno, FL: Florida Classics Library, 1998)

Warner, Ruth, *Brief History of the Sebastian Methodist Church* (Vero Beach, FL: Treasure Coast Chapter N.S.D.A.R., 1989)

Webb's History Industrial and Biographical, Florida Pt. 1 (New York: W. S. Webb & Company, 1885)

"World War I Service Cards." Florida Memory. www.floridamemory.com/Collections/WWI.

WWI draft registrations army and navy for Indian River County (Vero Beach, FL: Indian River County Main Library Genealogy Department)

WWI Draft Registrations, Army and Navy, Indian River County.

Wynne, Nick, *Tin Can Tourists in Florida 1900-1970* (Charleston, SC: Arcadia Publishing, 1999)

Ziemba, Caroline Pomeroy, *Martin County, Our Heritage: a Historiography* (Stuart, FL: Stuart Heritage, Inc., 1977)

Index

The Author Ellen Stanley

Originally from New York, Florida has been Ellen Stanley's home since the 1960s. She has lived in Miami, DeLand, Naples, Tampa, and now in Sebastian, Florida. She has earned BA, MEd, and MLS degrees, and has had a varied career. Since retiring, she has been a volunteer at the Sebastian Area Historical Museum, and is an officer on the Board of Directors for the Sebastian Area Historical Society, Inc.

Ellen has been researching and writing, both technical writing and for pleasure, for most of her adult life. She has had several articles and books published. Arcadia published *Indian River County,* a photograph book, in 2010, and she chaired the publication of a postcard book, *Indian River County*, in 2007, also by Arcadia. Genealogy and more history works are planned.

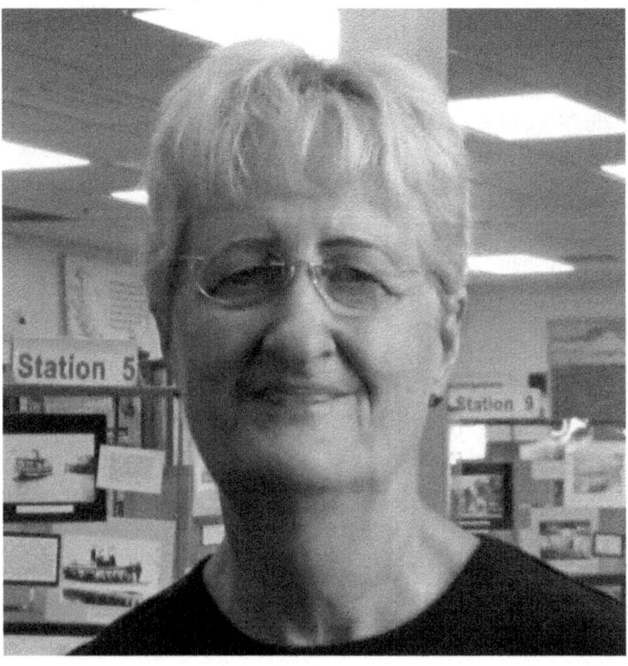